Antiracism in Cuba

Envisioning Cuba

Louis A. Pérez Jr., editor

Envisioning Cuba publishes outstanding, innovative works in Cuban studies, drawn from diverse subjects and disciplines in the humanities and social sciences, from the colonial period through the post–Cold War era. Featuring innovative scholarship engaged with theoretical approaches and interpretive frameworks informed by social, cultural, and intellectual perspectives, the series highlights the exploration of historical and cultural circumstances and conditions related to the development of Cuban self-definition and national identity.

Antiracism in Cuba

The Unfinished Revolution

Devyn Spence Benson

The University of North Carolina Press
Chapel Hill

Publication of this book was assisted by a grant from the history department of
Louisiana State University.

The paper in this book meets the guidelines for permanence and durability
of the Committee on Production Guidelines for Book Longevity of the
Council on Library Resources.

The University of North Carolina Press has been a member of the
Green Press Initiative since 2003.

Cover image: A political cartoon showing a KKK member being strangled by
Fidel Castro's beard, and a black, childlike figure playing with the leader's beard,
epitomizes the contradictions of the revolution's attitude toward antiracism and
blackness. From *Lunes de Revolución*, 3 October 1960, 16.

Library of Congress Cataloging-in-Publication Data
Benson, Devyn Spence, author.
Antiracism in Cuba : the unfinished revolution / Devyn Spence Benson.
    pages cm. — (Envisioning Cuba)
Includes bibliographical references and index.
ISBN 978-1-4696-2672-7 (pbk. : alk. paper) — ISBN 978-1-4696-2673-4 (ebook)
1. Racism—Cuba. 2. Cuba—Race relations—History—20th century. 3. Blacks—Cuba—
Social conditions—20th century. 4. Equality—Cuba—History—20th century.
5. Cuba—Politics and government—1959–1990. I. Title. II. Series: Envisioning Cuba.
F1789.A1B46 2016
305.80097291—dc23
2015031948

Portions of this work appeared earlier in somewhat different form in Devyn Spence
Benson, "Cuba Calls: African American Tourism, Race, and the Cuban Revolution, 1959–
1961," *Hispanic Historical Review* 93, no. 2 (May 2013); and "Owning the Revolution: Race,
Revolution, and Politics in Havana and Miami, 1959–1963," *Journal of Transnational American
Studies* 4, no. 2 (Fall 2012), and are reprinted here by permission of the publishers.

For Mommy, Daddy,
Dionne, and Tracey

Contents

Figures

Acknowledgments

Many people/organizations are to thank for their financial and emotional support of this project. Awards from the Foreign Language and Area Studies program and the Doris G. Quinn Fellowship housed at the University of North Carolina (UNC) at Chapel Hill were essential to funding my early research in Cuba as well as in the United States. Without the monetary support and leave for writing provided by the Gaius Charles Bolin Fellowship, the Hellman Family Foundation, and the Oakley Center for the Humanities and Social Sciences at Williams College, I would not have completed this project in such a timely manner. Additionally, residencies at both the Schomburg Center for Research in Black Culture in Harlem and the W. E. B. Dubois Research Institute at the Hutchins Center for African and African American Research at Harvard University were invaluable during my final revision process. I am also grateful to Louisiana State University (LSU) for the Office of Research and Economic Development's Council on Research Summer Stipend award, complementary funding supporting a full year of leave, and the History Department's and College of Humanities and Social Sciences' assistance with costly image reproductions.

While in Cuba, I benefited from the friendship and collaboration of a supportive scholarly community at the University of Havana, Instituto de Literatura y Linguistica (ILL), Instituto de Historia, the Archivo Nacional, Fundación de Fernando Ortiz, and the Instituto Juan Marinello. In particular, I would like to express my sincere appreciation to Milagros Martínez Reinosa, Carmita Castillo Herrera, Lourdes Serrano, Lourdes Pérez, Jorge Macle, Gloria Leon, and Tomás Fernandez Robaina for facilitating and assisting my research in Havana. To the black women of the Afrocubanas organization—especially Daisy Ruberia Castillo, Georgina Herrera, Irene Ester Ruiz Narváez, and Inés María Martiatu Terry (Lalita, you left us too early, my friend)—without your support, faith in my project, and willingness to talk to me for hours about blackness in Cuba, I would never have gotten this far. Your scholarship and community organizing are an inspiration and model of what an intersected revolution should look like. To the many librarians at the Biblioteca Nacional, ILL,

Instituto de Historia, and Biblioteca Provincial de Oriente Elvira Cape in Santiago, thank you for locating my sources, suggesting places to eat, and guiding me through the research process. Likewise, I am grateful to the undergraduate students who composed the UNC-Chapel Hill Study Abroad cohort of 2007, Williams College group of 2012, and my new LSU travel partners (both 2014 and 2015 student groups); you all opened my eyes to another Havana. I would also like to thank Marguerite Jiménez, my fellow resident director in Havana, for her friendship, support, and humor during that long spring 2007 in Vedado. Lastly, my Cuba experiences would have been incomplete without the welcome I received from Marta, Llanes, Lisi, and Nerea Pis. Thank you for opening your home and your hearts to both me and my students. Hopefully, one day we can return the favor.

Of course, there are many folks in the United States, especially from my Ph.D. program at UNC-Chapel Hill, whom I owe for their help in this process. To my esteemed advisor, Louis A. Pérez Jr., thank you for always being tough on me and pushing me to think critically, check my footnotes obsessively, and not accept mediocrity. It was and continues to be an honor to work with you and to call you not only a mentor but a friend as well. I would also like to extend my sincere appreciation to Kathryn Burns, Jerma Jackson, John Chasteen, and John French. Each of you contributed to this project in your own way, without which it could not have reached its full potential. Outside readers, recommenders, colleagues, and mentor-friends have been an invaluable part of the revision process of this book. To that end, I owe Alejandro de la Fuente, Frank Guridy, Lillian Guerra, and Melina Pappademos for their constructive feedback on various conference papers, articles, and now this book—even when we did not agree, I was appreciative for your thoughtful engagement with my work. We have all gone our separate ways now, but I will never forget those long history seminars with my graduate school cohort from Chapel Hill (especially writing partner Mike Huner), where we all spent countless hours reading and learning from each other's work. I am also grateful for the intellectual community I found at the 2005 Interrogating the African Diaspora Summer Seminar at Florida International University, sponsored by the Ford Foundation. Some of you have become lifelong friends and I want to thank Reena Goldtree, Andrea Queeley, and Chantalle Verna for your comments on my writing, support on being a black woman in the academy, housing in Miami, and overall warm companionship. Similarly, I also had the pleasure and honor to be a part of the Tepoztlán Institute for the Transnational History of the Americas Conference and Collective team where brilliant scholar-friends like David Sartorius, Lessie Jo Frazier, Micol Seigel, Elliot Young, María Elena Martinez, Ben Cowan, Alexandra Puerto, Laura Gutiérrez, and Nicole Guidotti-Hernandez gave me the space to develop my own voice in a Latin American historiography context. To the Cubanists I met at UNC-Chapel Hill and beyond (including Lisi Martínez Lotz, Lupe García, Rachel Hynson, David Sartorious, Enver Casimir, Toby Nathan, Josh Nadel, Bill Van Norman, Dave Carlson, Jennifer Lambe, Michael Bustamante, and Rainer Schultz), it has been a true pleasure to take classes, attend conferences, and explore Havana (and Miami) with each of you. Lastly, the directors and archivists at the Cuban Heritage Collection, at the University of Miami, including Maria R. Estorino, Gladys Gómez-Rossié, Annie Sansone Martinez, and Meiyolet Méndez have been an invaluable resource for locating materials about Cubans in exile. Thank you.

Transitioning into the world of assistant professorship would have been a much more daunting task without my amazing colleagues in the History Department and Africana and Latina Studies programs at Williams College. In Africana Studies, Travis Gosa, Neil Roberts, Stéphane Robolin, and Kenda Muntongi each have my eternal gratitude for their support, laughter, and endless teamwork that went into building a fabulous Black Studies program at Williams. Those early years together, when we would walk around campus as a posse and it seemed like anything was possible, are cemented in my memory forever (along with all the cookouts, football games, and wing nights). I learned something from each and every one of the talented historians I was so fortunate to call a colleague at Williams College. Roger Kittleson, Sara Dubow, Eiko Siniawer, Leslie Brown, Jessica Chapman, Patrick Spero, and staff members Linda Saharczewski and Megan Konieczny—you all inspire me as teachers, scholars, and friends. Finally, I would never have flourished at Williams, or anywhere else for that matter, without the support of the Williams Latin@ Studies faculty. "Thank you" is not enough for Carmen Whalen, Mérida M. Rúa, Ondine Chavoya, and Jacqueline Hidalgo—you not only read countless drafts of each and every chapter, but you also comforted me when I thought I could not go on, advised me through the publication process, and always had my back in the messy world that was college politics. Jax, it has been such an honor to call you a friend and colleague—I will never forget our apartment/sometimes kitchen adventures in Washington Heights, pupusa/Starbucks runs to Pittsfield, or the Winter Study course in Miami (where you let me drive that huge

Expedition). Additionally, I am lucky to have taught, worked with, and been assisted by a special group of undergraduates during my five years at Williams. Whether they took a class with me, served as a research assistant through the Williams Class of 1957 Summer Research Program in the Humanities and Social Sciences, or traveled with me for study abroad programs, I cannot imagine my Williams experience without Melinda Salaman, Adriana Mendoza Leigh, Amanda Reid, Dayana de la Torre, DJ Polite, Anyela Perez Garcia, Eilin Perez, Jaliz Albanese, Fernando Lora, and Jillian Schwiep. Thank you again to the whole Williams College community for your support during my first years in the academy.

To my new colleagues at LSU, while I have not known you as long, I cannot say enough about how much I appreciate your warm welcome to Baton Rouge. Who would have thought that I would feel so at home in southern Louisiana, but people like Gaines Foster, Victor Stater, Maribel Diaz, Paul Hoffman, Joyce Jackson, and Darlene Albritton (who all initially invited me to join LSU) have made it so. I would also like to thank Stephen Andes, Kodi Roberts, Aaron Sheehan-Dean, and Christine Kooi (plus all your families) for being my support system during my first year in Baton Rouge. I was in a long-distance relationship, but I never felt alone because you opened your homes to me. And, to my new Cubanist friends at LSU—Solimar Otero, Eric Mayer-García, and Andrea Morris—thank you so much for your endless hospitality and willingness to read and comment on drafts of my work. I look forward to getting to know you all more in the years to come and building on Louisiana's long-standing connection with Cuba to reformat the campus Caribbean Studies program we keep dreaming about.

As this project was coming to an end, I was fortunate to benefit from the support of two very special institutions—the Schomburg Center and the W. E. B. Dubois Research Institute. I cannot even begin to describe the amazing intellectual climate that I found in each place. To all of my fellow fellows, directors, and staff at each institution, thank you for your pressing questions, revision ideas, and incredible upbeatedness while I struggled to complete this book. All of those smiles and words of confidence went a long way when it seemed like the book would never be finished. In the same vein, I want to thank the staff and series editors at UNC Press (Elaine Maisner, Lou Pérez, Alison Shay, Dino Battista, and many others) and the selected anonymous reviewers for their insightful feedback and encouragement in bringing this project to fruition. Thank you for your patience with all of my first-time author questions and your enthusiasm for work on race in Cuba. In the end, despite the collective debt I owe to everyone listed above (and many other unnamed contributors) and their efforts to make this a better book, any errors or mistakes are all my own.

Ultimately, I dedicate this book and my career to a larger extent to my family: Mommy, Daddy, and Dionne. Each of you helped shape who I am as a person, daughter, sister, teacher, and scholar. Without your prayers, hugs, and long-distance phone calls, I would not have been able to complete this project. Thank you for giving me the courage to tackle such an arduous task and the faith to believe that I could achieve anything. To my dearest husband, Tracey, this book is as much yours as it is mine. You traveled to Cuba, sat in the archives, edited every page, and put up with all of my moments of success and self-doubt. Similarly, I want to thank my extended Spence, Benson, Dawkins, Walker, Keodouangsy-Corrales, and Mount Carmel Baptist Church families and my lovely, smart, and funny stepson Camoren for your support and understanding, especially when research trips and writing deadlines kept me away from home longer than I intended. Both of my grandmothers passed while I was completing this book. And while they are not here to see its final version, I hope that both Mrs. Bernice Spence (Grandmafoxx) and Mrs. Henrietta Dawkins (Grammie) know that they will never be forgotten. I try every day to model my life and work on the fortitude, kindness, and empathy they both embodied as southern black women. It takes a whole family to write any book, but it takes a strong black family to take a stand against racism (in Cuba, the United States, and everywhere)—I believe in a better future because each of you make me want to. Mommy, Daddy, Dionne, and Tracey, thank you now and forever for your patience and love.

Abbreviations

ACF	Associación Cultural Femenina (Women's Cultural Association)
AJR	Asociación de Jóvenes Rebeldes (Association of Young Rebels)
CHC	Cuban Heritage Collection
CNA	Comisión Nacional de Alfabetización (National Literacy Commission)
CNC	Consejo Nacional de Cultura (Nation Culture Council)
CTC	Confederación de Trabajadores Cubanos (National Confederation of Cuban Workers)
DR	Directorio Revolucionario (Revolutionary Directorate)
FEU	Federación Estudiantil Universitaria (University Students Federation)
FGTO	Federación General de Trabajadores de Oriente (General Federation of Oriente Workers)
FMC	Federación de Mujeres Cubanas (Federation of Cuban Women)
FNOA	Federación Nacional Obrera Azucarera (National Federation of Sugar Workers)
FPCC	Fair Play for Cuba Committee
ICAIC	Instituto Cubano de Arte e Industria Cinematográficos (National Cuban Film Institute)
INIT	Instituto Nacional de Industria Turística (National Institute of Tourism)
INRA	Instituto Nacional de Reforma Agraria (National Agrarian Reform Institute)

M 26-7   26th of July Movement

NAACP   National Association for the Advancement of Colored People

OAS   Organization of American States

ONRE   Organización Nacional de Rehabilitación Económica
(National Organization for Economic Rehabilitation)

PCC   Partido Comunista de Cuba (Communist Party of Cuba)

PIC   Partido Independiente de Color (Independent Party of
Color)

PRC   Partido Revolucionario Cubano (Cuban Revolutionary Party)

PSP   Partido Socialista Popular (Popular Socialist Party,
Cuba's Communist Party from 1944 to 1961)

UN   United Nations

UR   Unidad Revolucionario (Revolutionary Unity)

Antiracism in Cuba

Introduction

Race and Revolution in Cuba

"The black race has always been very oppressed and now is the time for them to give us justice, now is the time for them to give us equal opportunities to live," Cristobalina Sardinas asserted only three weeks after Fidel Castro's 26th of July Movement (M 26-7) forces ousted U.S.-backed Cuban president Fulgencio Batista. The new government's young leaders were about to embark on a set of social reforms and policy changes that would make the Caribbean's most populous nation beloved and admired by some and hated and maligned by others for decades to come. But when Sardinas was interviewed for an issue of *Revolución* (M 26-7's official newspaper) in January 1959, Cuba's future was uncertain and it seemed like everyone had an opinion about what the new government should do first. Sardinas and the eight other Afro-Cubans (five men and four women) interviewed lived in Las Yaguas, one of Havana's poorest and most disreputable slums; and they clearly had their own plans for the new Cuban leadership—they expected Castro to put an end to the racial discrimination they faced daily. Each recounted similar life experiences before 1959. Their narratives involved extreme poverty, limited access to resources, and endless searches for affordable housing. In particular, the women noted the awful situation faced by "the black race" in Cuba and described how discrimination had kept their families from acquiring jobs and renting apartments regardless of what political party was in power. Sardinas specifically expressed some optimism that this time a new Cuban regime might fulfill its promises. "When a person goes to rent a house and they see that the person is from the colored race, they don't want to rent to them. This is an injustice and we hope that the Revolution will put an end to it," she said. A few days later, *Revolución* printed excerpts from the Las Yaguas interviews, along with large photographs of the community's residents, under the title, "¡Negros No . . . Ciudadanos!" ("Not Blacks, but Citizens)."[1]

I was struck when I first encountered this full-page article in *Revolución*. Hand-sized photographs of each interviewee sat above the small excerpts from their conversations with the newspaper's journalist, José

Hernández, and almost dared the reader to recognize the humanity of the Las Yaguas residents as well as the membership of poor and black Cubans in the nation. Other than the interviewees' comments, the only editorial text in the article was the journalist's description of getting access to the *solar* (tenement house) and his surprise at their eagerness to speak with him. Rather it was the piece's title, written in bold letters on the center of the page, which framed the interviews and conveyed a wide range of competing images about race in Cuba. Despite many attempts to find an opening anecdote that better represents the multifaceted story about race and revolution, especially the conflict between Afro-Cuban expectations and state rhetoric, that I tell in this book, I kept coming back to this article. Because even though it misleadingly portrays a simplistic dichotomy between blackness and Cubanness that does not exist for many of the island's residents, in other ways it epitomizes the 1959 Cuban Revolution's ambitious antiracist stance and contradictory relationship to blackness.

The new government passed over 1,500 pieces of legislation during its first thirty months in power, including laws delivering land redistribution, free health care, and educational scholarship programs.[2] Added to these reforms, in March 1959 Castro announced a public antidiscrimination campaign that promised to fulfill late nineteenth-century aspirations to build a raceless and unified Cuba. National headlines, like the one titling this Las Yaguas article, outlined plans for integrating previously white-only spaces, especially private schools, beaches, and recreational facilities, and providing employment and educational opportunities to Cuba's most marginalized citizens. These changes created unprecedented social opportunities for blacks and *mulatos* (mixed race Cubans) in the ensuing decades and had lasting effects on Afro-Cuban lives. By the 1980s, black and *mulato* Cubans had virtually the same life expectancy, high school education rates, and percentage of professional positions as white Cubans—in sharp contrast to the United States and Brazil where significant disparities existed between whites and blacks in each of these markers of equality.[3] Today, large numbers of Afro-Cuban professors, doctors, and other professionals (working in racially integrated public spaces) attest to the ways revolutionary actions brought about change and opened doors for Cuba's citizens of African descent.

Yet, Cuba's 1959 campaign against discrimination was a program full of contradictions, consisting both of real social change and national myth-making about a government's, even a revolutionary government's, ability to eliminate racism from above in three short years. Although M 26-7's antiracist program provided many tangible social reforms that Afro-Cubans like Sardinas had expected, as the title of the January 1959 article, "Not Blacks, but Citizens" foreshadowed, the new Cuban government's attitude toward blackness was ambivalent and unstable and left little space for Afro-Cubans to be both black *and* a citizen. Building on nineteenth-century discourses that imagined Cuba as a raceless space of "not blacks, not whites, only Cubans," the article's title suggested that residents of neighborhoods like Las Yaguas had to discard their poverty and their blackness to join the revolution. This was and remains a false dichotomy for many Cubans of color. In January 1959, Sardinas expressed her frustrations with previous administrations and expectations for the new government as a *black* person, a *Cuban*, and a *woman*. She felt entitled to certain rights, like other citizens, and was aware and proud of her blackness. As we will see, some Cubans of color agreed with the revolution's raceless sentiments. Others used the state rhetoric to demand additional reforms. And a third group found the image of revolutionary nationalism without blackness unsettling and paternalistic, and looked for ways to lead organizations that recognized both their blackness and Cubanness. In the end, just like the irony of titling an article about black demands, "Not Blacks, but Citizens," 1959 revolutionary promises of equality and national integration programs sat alongside inconsistent state rhetoric that allowed racism to continue and infiltrate Cuban ideologies in subtle, but lasting, ways.

How do ideas about racial difference, racist stereotypes, and racially discriminatory practices persist, survive, and reproduce themselves despite significant state efforts to generate social and racial equality? In what ways can racism and equality exist together? How does a state's antiracism campaign become compromised? And, how have people of African descent challenged, participated in, and negotiated such processes? These are the central questions of this book and the paradoxes facing revolutionary Cuba and other postcolonial and former slave societies in the Americas. In the twenty-first century, when few people recognize the perseverance of racial violence, and many more would argue that national campaigns against discrimination (whether referring to the U.S. 1960s civil rights movement, Cuba's 1959 antidiscrimination campaign, and/ or various twentieth-century decolonial projects in the Caribbean) have successfully removed historic barriers imposed by skin color, it seems fitting to revisit these questions. In each of these cases, state actions have yielded uneven results. In the United States, more blacks and Latinos are incarcerated than were enslaved in the eighteenth century.[4] Economic difficulties in Cuba and around the globe have revealed how national antiracist discourses frequently hid racial prejudices instead of wiping them out. And while anticolonial projects might have garnered political independence in Jamaica, Trinidad and Tobago, Guyana, and Barbados in the 1960s, they rarely led to equality.[5]

To answer the question of *how* racism continued and grew along state claims of antiracism, this book engages with and builds on previous scholarship that has established the persistence of racism despite revolutionary reforms, especially after the "Special Period"[6] economic crisis of the 1990s revealed sharp inequalities in contemporary Cuba. First, it finds that state-led, predominantly white, antiracist campaigns were often packaged or built on racist ideologies and stereotypes—sometimes on purpose, but mostly unconsciously. In the case of Cuba, early 1960s revolutionary programs (like integration plans and education and health care reforms that have been and should continue to be celebrated) frequently negated their own antiracist efforts by reproducing traditional racist images and idioms, especially in public representations of blacks in revolutionary propaganda, cartoons, and educational materials. Many of these contradictions have their roots in how Cuban leaders, and residents in the Americas more broadly, have failed to challenge ideologies of black savageness and inferiority even in the highest moments of revolutionary struggle. Secondly, Cuban conversations and policies about race in the early 1960s were intensely transnational and profoundly ambiguous. For example, relationships between Cuban officials and African Americans allowed Afro-Cubans to demand equality by mobilizing the same politically charged language employed by the state to draw U.S. black tourists to the island. I also emphasize the often overlooked participation of black and *mulato* exiles in transnational exchanges and examine how the predominantly white exile community in south Florida tried to silence Afro-Cuban exiles in the same way that the revolutionary government censored some black activists on the island. Lastly, the experiences and stories of Cubans of African descent, like the Las Yaguas community, illustrate how blacks and *mulatos* were not passive recipients of revolutionary reforms. In fact, Afro-Cuban men and women, intellectuals and workers, social club members and volunteer teachers built, negotiated, and challenged official rhetoric about race (in diverse and sometimes competing ways) during the first decade after 1959. Using newly released sources and the voices of Afro-Cubans whose lived experiences highlight the nuances of negotiating life as both black and Cuban during the revolution, *Antiracism in Cuba* works to reconcile post-1959 stories of black censorship with narratives of revolutionary opportunity. In doing so, it exposes the limits of state action—even a revolutionary state's actions—to eliminate racism.

The legacies of the 1959 Cuban Revolution's dreams and racial contradictions continue to reverberate in the present. In 2006, shortly after Fidel Castro fell ill with a health crisis that caused him to pass control of the government to his younger brother Raúl, Yusimí Rodríguez López, a young black woman, participated in a troubling conversation at work. It began when one of her colleagues criticized his Afro-Cuban neighbors for hosting a loud and boisterous party following the announcement of Castro's failing health. The coworker was a high-ranking white official in the Cuban Communist Party (Partido Comunista de Cuba, PCC) and while he admitted he was not clear whether the festivities had been planned before the revelation by Fidel (as many Cubans call him) or were in response to it, the man felt that the celebration was in bad taste and should have been postponed out of fidelity to the aging leader. Describing the many things he had willingly given up for the revolution, the unnamed official implied that his Afro-Cuban neighbors were unappreciative of the state reforms they had received. According to Rodríguez, he said that "if he, the white child of rich parents, was able to sacrifice, then blacks should have done the same, because *the Revolution made blacks into people*."[7] A shocked and angry Rodríguez fought against this comment in two significant ways. First, she immediately disputed his position, calling him "racist" and arguing with him in front of other coworkers until he returned to his office. Later, Rodríguez published an analysis of the incident in the 2011 edited collection, *Afrocubanas: Historia, pensamiento, y prácticas culturales* (*Afro-Cuban Women: History, Thought, and Cultural Practices*). In her essay, she pushed against her coworker's claim that blacks, who were positioned as a homogenous working-class group, should be grateful to revolutionary leaders. Rodríguez argued that his attitude denied Afro-Cubans' agency to contribute to or resist the revolution as equals. "Is he saying that people of color only received dignity thanks to the triumph of the revolution? . . . Or that whites are able to choose to oppose the government, [that whites] are able to decide to sacrifice or not to sacrifice, but that blacks cannot because the revolution made them people?" she asked. Rodríguez noted that this type of thinking, which she described as prevalent among some white Cubans, impeded the country's ability to solve racial inequalities and to develop a revolutionary agenda because it devalued and denied citizenship to a large sector of the population. At the same time, she lamented how, despite her direct rebuttal of her coworker's claims, two other Cubans of color who were listening to the same conversation refused to speak up with her, although they remarked afterward, "You are right, of course, but it is better that you remain quiet. It is not good to announce it [his racism]."[8]

As the Rodríguez episode reveals, Afro-Cuban responses to the revolution's contradictory racial program range from direct confrontation to public silence and many other reactions in between. This diversity of Afro-Cuban opinion complicates how all Cubans respond to issues of race in Cuba's new globally integrated future. Since the collapse of the Soviet Union in 1989, the transition to a global economy has provided Cubans with unprecedented opportunities for public debates about the legacy and the future of the revolutionary process. Afro-Cubans have begun to publish, speak, and blog about their expectations and experiences in the post-1959 period. New work, including recently published memoirs, oral history collections, and books like *Afrocubanas*, continue the debates begun by black and *mulato* intellectuals in the 1960s by forging a space within the revolution for an appreciation of blackness and the development of a revolutionary national culture that respects and includes the history of people of African descent, especially black and *mulata* women. In doing so, black Cubans are breaking the silence on the coexistence of racism and antiracism by demanding that revolutionary leaders live up to national goals and promises. But before moving forward, let's take a glance back.

"Not White, Not Black, only Cuban": Earlier Revolutions and Racial Discourses

In 1959, revolutionaries addressed the question of racial discrimination in ways that converged and diverged from national discourses generated during the abolition of slavery, wars of independence, and Cuban republic. This book builds on this robust existing literature by examining how the 1959 revolution was both a break from and a continuation of Cuba's racial past. In particular, the story of Cuba's first revolution, fought to obtain independence from Spain—called the Ten Years' War and lasting from 1868 to 1878—set up a series of national myths and approaches to raceless nationalism that later solidified with the 1959 revolution. As later chapters will show, this question of how to build an inclusive national project frequently set Afro-Cubans at odds with Cuban authorities.

In 1868, increasing tensions between white creoles and Spanish immigrants over jobs and governing positions led to Cuba's first push for independence. Discussions about race and blackness factored prominently into organizing the 1868 revolution because many white Cubans feared that the island's large population of enslaved African and African-descended laborers would lead an antislavery revolt like the massive uprising in Haiti in 1791.[9] In fact, Africans and their descendants were a majority of the island's population between 1846 and 1862 because Cuban planters continued to import slaves from Africa even as the cross-Atlantic trade diminished elsewhere (forcing nearly one hundred thousand Africans to Cuba between 1858 and 1861 alone). Major slave rebellions, including the 1812 Aponte Rebellions and the 1843–44 La Escalera Rebellions, also demonstrated that Cuban slaves had a hunger for and political understanding of freedom long before creole insurgents began promising to abolish slavery if blacks fought against Spain.[10] The most immediate consequence of nineteenth-century Cuban slave rebellions was the implementation of harsher regulations restricting and monitoring slaves' activities. But the rebellions also created lasting anxieties about black-led politics that reappeared throughout the early republic and post-1959 anytime Afro-Cubans pressed too strongly for racial equality.[11]

Despite anxieties about arming enslaved Africans to fight for independence, on 10 October 1868, Carlos Manuel de Céspedes and other dissatisfied creoles declared war against Spain and urged slaves to join in the battle. Officially, Céspedes avoided the question of abolition in his war declaration other than a brief statement about the "gradual emancipation of slavery with indemnification."[12] This silence was strategic and stemmed from a desire not to alienate western plantation owners or slaves from the independence movement. Creating a pattern that would be repeated throughout the twentieth century among opposing political parties in the republic, creole insurgents in the 1860s fought among themselves and with the Spanish Crown for the loyalty of enslaved Africans and free blacks. Independence propaganda went as far as portraying the war as a fight between Spaniards who wanted to keep blacks enslaved and creole Cubans who envisioned everyone as equal. Finally, in 1869, creole insurgents announced a new constitution that proclaimed all inhabitants of Cuba free men and women and called on the newly freed citizens to enlist in the Liberation Army. In reaction to this constitution, Spain issued its own gradual abolition legislation in July 1870. Titled the "Law of the Free Wombs," it freed children born to enslaved mothers after 1868, slaves over the age of sixty, and all slaves who were fighting or had fought for the Crown during the rebellion.[13]

Numerous people of African descent took advantage of these promises of freedom in exchange for their participation in the Ten Years' War. Pedro Díaz Molina, the son of a slave woman from Yaguajay, a small town in central Cuba, joined the revolutionary forces in 1868.[14] Although he was only seventeen when he began to support the insurgency, he was promoted to colonel and later general for his abilities.[15] Other African slaves also joined the war effort to secure their freedom. Esteban Montejo described in *Biography of a Runaway Slave* how in Las Villas, a province also in central Cuba, the Lucumís built a reputation around their fighting skills in the independence war.[16] James O'Kelly, a journalist from the United States who visited Cuba during the war and took note of the composition of the rebel forces, estimated that "about one-third of the fighting men are white, and the majority of the other two-thirds are of color other than black, all shades of brown predominating."[17] Some slaves and freed blacks also fought against creole insurgents on the Spanish side of the battlefield as they tried to position themselves to survive the war with as much independence and social mobility as possible.[18]

In the end, creole and Spanish debates about abolition foreshadowed the unevenness of black freedom in the coming decades. After the Ten Years' War ended in 1878, life on the island changed dramatically, even though Cuba failed to win its independence. In the Pact of Zanjón, Spain gave creoles more influence in the political and economic leadership of the island and offered a general amnesty for all political crimes, and, most importantly, the Crown freed all enslaved Africans and people of African descent who had fought in the war.[19] Two years later, in 1880, Spain passed another abolition law, but it did not grant immediate freedom to remaining slaves. Rather, like the process of gradual emancipation proposed by Céspedes and applied previously in the British Caribbean colonies, this legislation implemented an eight-year apprenticeship period in which slaves could not leave the plantation, but instead received a small wage for their labor. Slavery continued to exist in this way under a new name, the *patronato*, and African-descended peoples remained on the plantation not as slaves but as *patrocinados*.[20] The *patronato* ended two years early, and by 1886 all Cuban slaves were legally free. With the issue of abolition no longer dividing Cuban creoles, the island turned its attention to a final push for independence. Tales of integrated forces composed of former slaves and former slave masters fighting together in the Ten Years' War became a significant means of gaining support for the 1895 revolution and quieting persistent fears of black rebellion.

José Martí, Cuban Nationalism, and "Raceless" Independence

In 1891, Cuban intellectual and nationalist José Martí called on his countrymen and women to "unite Cubans, in this another faith: with all and for all: the inevitable war . . . for the recognition and the frank practice of genuine liberty."[21] Martí, the son of Spanish parents, was born in Cuba in 1853 and grew up amidst the Ten Years' War. After anti-Spanish statements forced him into exile in the United States, he quickly rose through the ranks of the Cuban exile community and founded the Cuban Revolutionary Party (Partido Revolucionario Cubano, PRC) in 1892 to streamline the political and fundraising efforts needed for Cuba's final push for independence in 1895. Historian Louis A. Pérez concluded that "like a master weaver, Martí pulled together all the separate threads of Cuban discontent—social, economic, political, racial, historical, and wove them into a radical movement of enormous force."[22] Martí injected the 1895 war with the unifying rhetoric of "racelessness"—the idea that the country was not composed of whites or blacks, only Cubans—that would become one of the tenets of Cuban government platforms in the republic and into the 1959 revolution.

José Martí's new framing of race and nation brought the diverse insurgent populations together under the PRC in 1892 by simultaneously pacifying white fears about black rebellion and promising blacks equality in the new republic. Beginning with his first visit to Tampa, Florida, in 1891 where he announced the need for a Cuba "with all and for all," Martí used his skills as an orator, poet, and intellectual to sell the idea of a unified Cuba, free of racial and class differences, as the force needed to defeat Spain. In a speech before a packed audience, he examined each of the previous dividing forces in the struggle for independence and warned against allowing those forces to undermine the cause once again. He specifically advised his listeners to accept in solidarity the Spaniard "who loves liberty as much as we love it, and who seeks with us a just country." In addition, he raised the question of whether Cubans should fear their black compatriots: "Should we fear the Negro, the generous Negro, the black brother, who because of the Cubans who died for him has forgiven forever all others who have mistreated him? Well I know that the hands of the Negro are more full of virtue than some white ones I know. . . . Others fear him; I love him: and to him who would speak badly of him . . . I say with a full mouth: 'He lies!' "[23] Martí repackaged the Ten Years' War and the soldiers who died in it as reparation for the institution of slavery. He claimed that the joint bloodshed of black and white Cubans in the 1870s conflict had erased the sins of slave owners and any resentment held by enslaved laborers. In doing so, he calmed the fears of white Cubans who questioned why former slaves would fight for an independent Cuba, often called "Cuba Libre" (Free Cuba), in light of the island's history of slave rebellions and conspiracies.

Previous scholarship has shown that Martí was not alone in his efforts at building an integrated and unified fighting force through a strategic retelling of the history of the Ten Years' War; if anything, without the support and influence of key Afro-Cubans his project would have been futile. Leading Afro-Cuban patriots including General Antonio Maceo and intellectual Juan Gualberto Gómez contributed to building this vision of a raceless Cuba between the independence wars because they hoped doing so would eliminate inequality in the future republic. Maceo, in particular, participated in constructing Cuba's raceless nationalist project in his political writings and private letters. Together black and white writers prepared for the final war of 1895 by constructing the archetype of the "loyal black insurgent" to counter existing ideas about savage slave rebels or revengeful Haitians. As Ada Ferrer notes in *Insurgent Cuba*, "in their interpretations of the Ten Years' War—and of the slave's and master's roles in that struggle—white and nonwhite writer-activists constructed a black rebel who recognized the sacrifice of the white master and who repaid that sacrifice with the dedication of his person and his country." But while many black and white insurgents shared general attitudes about the transcendence of race and saw the Ten Years' War as erasing each other's sins and resentment, the intellectuals leading this movement had different reasons for supporting Cuba Libre and different interpretations of what that support meant. One of their major arguments, and one that would reemerge between some Afro-Cubans and the revolutionary state after 1959, centered on how grateful blacks and *mulatos* should be to former slave owners. Because while Maceo and many other Afro-Cuban insurgents fought and died for Cuban independence, they also challenged white creole leaders' refusal to promote black generals and were aware of the persistent discrimination in military camps. In the end, Cuba's success in forging a multiracial coalition against Spain was due to both goodwill and practical needs—but the legacy of the loyal black insurgent and the willingness of Afro-Cuban activists to strategically use military service as a claim to national inclusion continued into the new republic.[24]

The narratives constructed to build a multiracial fighting force quickly dissolved after the war. But these occurrences cannot be blamed solely on the U.S. intervention in 1898; nor were they unique to Cuba. When racially integrated Cuban forces were on the verge of victory against Spain, the United States intervened in the war under the pretense of supporting Cuba Libre but actually in pursuit of its own interests. U.S. officials had long been attracted to the island for its potential to host naval bases and provide new economic markets, and for its strategic location in the Caribbean. After the fighting was over, Spain agreed to hand Cuba, the Philippines, Puerto Rico, and Guam over to the United States but refused to negotiate with Cuban rebels. Cuban insurgent forces were prevented from entering into the peace negotiations or claiming victory after their nearly thirty-year struggle for independence.[25] For former slaves and other Cubans of African descent who had participated in the wars as a vehicle for freedom from slavery, the new authorities from the United States posed an even greater threat because of the racist assumptions that they brought with them about blacks and mixed-raced Cubans. White Cubans, many of whom had had their own reservations about incorporating freed blacks into the new nation, honed in on U.S. racist practices as an excuse to further exclude veterans of color from leading the republic. Esteban Montejo, a runaway slave, described the shift from recruiting black soldiers to fight and die for Cuban independence to later dismissing their participation: "When the war ended, the talk started about whether the blacks fought or not. I know that 95 percent of the blacks fought in the war. Then the Americans began to say it was only 75 percent. Well, no one criticized those statements. The blacks ended up out in the streets as a result."[26] But, even though independence-era visions of racelessness proved inadequate for challenging white privilege and building racial equality, they did change the way race was talked about in Cuba by linking antiracist rhetoric to revolutionary nationalism.

Since the wars of independence, different Cuban leaders (and later 1959 revolutionaries) have mobilized both Martí's and Maceo's legacies as founders of a Cuban national identity that was both colorblind and raceless in diverse and often repressive ways. While Cubans from various racial groups and economic classes fought side by side from 1895 until 1898, the idea of raceless nationalism oversimplifies the changes that occurred on the island in that period. Despite allowing Cubans to come together to defeat Spain, the ideological challenge to racial privilege constructed during the Ten Years' War—and later repurposed by republican and revolutionary leaders alike—remained incomplete. For one, its portrayal of white creoles' benevolent efforts to abolish slavery failed to acknowledge that many white Cubans had fought against full emancipation and that the end of forced black labor was more of an unintended consequence of war than an act of social justice. Moreover, the narrative of the loyal black soldier, epitomized by the iconization of General Maceo, constructed false images of grateful and passive Afro-Cuban men willing to sacrifice everything for Cuba Libre that limited what white Cubans imagined to be acceptable black citizenship well past 1959. Maceo's significance to Cuban nationalism only grew following his death in 1896. Future Cuban politicians and leaders repackaged Maceo's legacy to celebrate the black soldier who readily died for the nation, promoted raceless nationalism, and silently stood by while others made political decisions—hence the frequent comparison between the intellect of Martí versus the brawn of Maceo. All of this occurred despite the fact that the *mulato* general had challenged acts of racial discrimination throughout his life and vocally criticized white creoles who signed a peace treaty with Spain at the end of the Ten Years' War.[27] As historian Lillian Guerra has shown, the ambiguity of Martí's statements allowed Cuban governments throughout the republic and post-1959 to "create several Martís." This idea applied to Maceo as well because nearly every political party in Cuba (and in exile) appropriated both nineteenth-century figures and their antiracist rhetoric for their own purposes throughout the twentieth century.[28] Lastly, after the fighting ended in 1898 it became clear that while concepts of racelessness might have been useful in creating a unified fighting force, they failed to lay out a clear plan for a multiracial postwar democracy. If anything, the language of "not black, not white, only Cuban" that became popular during the war silenced competing narratives valuing blackness and represented Cuba's first efforts to obscure African influences on the island in favor of a *Cubanidad* (Cubanness) often coded as white.

The United States stole Cuban independence from revolutionary forces in 1898, occupied the island until 1902, and left Cuba with the Platt Amendment guaranteeing the United States' right to intervene to protect the life, liberty, and property of North Americans on the island. Each of these actions limited Cuban sovereignty in the early twentieth century, but Cuba's own racial negative stereotypes linking blackness to either savage rebels or loyal soldiers originated in the plantation system and solidified during white creole debates over the abolition of slavery—long before U.S. influence arrived on the island.[29] This is not to say that Cuban and other Latin American ideas of racial democracy and raceless nationalism were not progressive in the nineteenth century—they certainly were, especially for their time period—and Afro-Cubans helped to develop these concepts and hoped that participating in revolutionary struggles would lead to equality. However, these national ideologies failed to transform the island's negative relationship to blackness or positive link to whiteness and ultimately silenced other potential discourses. When Castro and other M 26-7 leaders mobilized these same ideologies in 1959 they faced similar limitations, if not more, because it had been nearly 60 years since Cuban insurgents had first called for a Cuba that was "more than white, black, or *mulato*" and Afro-Cubans had yet to be fully incorporated into the nation as equals.

The Limits of Racelessness in the Cuban Republic: Universal Suffrage, Informal Segregation, and Transnational Ties

Cuban ideologies of raceless nationalism and promises of equality for all in the new republic handcuffed national debates about race in the early twentieth century by limiting how Afro-Cubans could challenge persistent discrimination. But these failings were not simply rhetorical. Cuban officials created racial categories, built segregated communities, and limited black veterans' full political participation immediately following independence. Nevertheless, within this space, freed slaves and their descendants found ways to challenge racial discrimination. For one, universal male suffrage meant that emerging political parties had to take seriously (at least in public) Afro-Cuban concerns. Afro-Cuban mutual aid and recreational societies, in particular, mobilized members to vote for local politicians in exchange for resources.[30] These societies also formed transnational relationships as a means of accessing resources from black Americans.[31] In many ways, both the challenges and the successes of Afro-Cuban struggles for equality in the republic influenced how blacks and *mulatos* encountered the 1959 revolution.

Cuba implemented universal male suffrage in 1901 against the objections of U.S. military occupation officials and in doing so provided Cubans of African descent with one of their most enduring tools to influence society. Political parties in Cuba reached out to Afro-Cubans during election season because blacks and *mulatos* compromised at least one-third of the island's population in 1899. As historian Alejandro de la Fuente notes, "No party could dare to utterly affront one-third of the electorate without risking electoral defeat" in the republican period.[32] Afro-Cuban leaders recognized this situation and used it to their advantage by holding political parties accountable for campaign promises about racial inclusion. Afro-Cuban societies will be explored in chapter 2, but it is important to note that leaders from social clubs like the Club Atenas in Havana and Club Aponte in Santiago acted as go-betweens, or what historian Melina Pappademos calls "black brokers," connecting Afro-Cuban communities to local and national politics from the beginning of the republic. Universal suffrage combined with patronage networks holding over from the colony meant that Afro-Cuban electoral influence in the republic was not something to be taken lightly.[33]

Still, even with these political resources at their disposal, many Afro-Cubans faced continued discrimination, informal segregation, and racial violence in the first half of the twentieth century, especially in areas of housing and employment. And while Cuba never implemented formal segregation laws like those in the Jim Crow South, informal practices of locating black neighborhoods on the edges of town, racially and class-exclusive private schools, and accepted norms such as white Cubans walking on one side of the park and blacks on the other in rural provinces meant that most Cubans lived racially separate lives during the republic.[34] As we will see, after 1959 revolutionary leaders publicly targeted these informal segregation practices and encouraged national integration in public schools, beaches, and parks. These actions helped to construct Cuba's reputation in the 1960s as an island that had eliminated racism, especially to foreign visitors, but addressing discriminatory actions without interrogating stereotypes linking black politics to savageness and/or loyalty allowed racism to continue.

A pattern emerged during the republic of publicly including people of African descent in the performance of the nation through election campaign propaganda without changing private attitudes toward former slaves and their descendants. In addition to informal segregation, many black veterans struggled to find employment after the wars of independence. The 1907 census revealed that Afro-Cubans held mostly service and agricultural jobs—not a single black or *mulato* banker or broker was listed—and when they did find government jobs it was usually a position at the lower end of the pay scale, such as porters or messengers.[35] The barriers keeping Afro-Cubans out of the labor market paralleled those barring black Caribbean immigration to the island. In the first decade of the republic, Cuban officials encouraged white immigration from Spain (even as they discouraged Haitians and Jamaicans from entering the country) as a means of whitening the population and creating what they imagined to be an appropriate labor pool. Such whitening policies devalued and denied black and *mulato* contributions to the nation by making whiteness, not blackness, "an intrinsic part of Cubanness."[36]

The lack of employment opportunities especially frustrated black veterans who had risked life and limb for Cuban independence. By 1908 a group of black activists disillusioned with existing electoral options formed a political party focused on progressive social reforms called the Independent Party of Color (Partido Independiente de Color, PIC). Many Cubans (white and black) interpreted the PIC as a racist threat to national unity despite its general platform demands, which included an eight-hour work day and employment for all. In the eyes of these critics, organizing a political group based on race was anti-Cuban and violated the tenets of Martí's raceless ideologies. As a result, the army massacred over two thousand members and supporters of the PIC in what has become known as the "race war" of 1912.[37] Rather than being a race war, this event was a government-sponsored massacre of black PIC members and some nonaffiliated Afro-Cubans that revealed the limits of racial equality and white tolerance for black-led politics in the new republic. Moreover, by using the language of Martí to discredit the PIC—critics labeled the party racist due to its all-black administration and refusal to accept white leaders—the 1912 event warned Afro-Cubans against autonomous political organizing. One Afro-Cuban contemporary noted that the PIC's destruction was a result of both Cuban leaders' racism and blacks' failure to challenge raceless ideologies in the late nineteenth century. He said Afro-Cubans "had forgotten their 'black identity' during the wars of independence when they were forced to fuse their own future (slave freedom and racial equality) with the future of the nation (independence)."[38] Ironically, the famed Antonio Maceo monument that stands in Havana was unveiled in May 1916 and its inauguration coincided with the four-year anniversary of the government's massacre of the PIC in 1912. In a speech inaugurating the statue, independence leader José Miró highlighted Maceo's patriotism and loyalty to the Cuban nation without ever mentioning the PIC massacre. In doing so, he reinforced Maceo as an acceptable and valuable black leader, while disavowing alternative black political approaches even though it was PIC members who had initially demanded that the government build a statue to recognize the Afro-Cuban general in the first place.[39]

After the PIC, black and *mulato* Cubans continued to push for equality through mainstream political parties and local networks and by "forging diaspora" with people of African descent throughout the Americas.[40] Afro-Cubans pursued educational opportunities at Tuskegee Institute, joined Marcus Garvey's Universal Negro Improvement Association, and built artistic and cultural relationships that merged the Harlem Renaissance that spanned the 1920s with the Afrocubanismo movement of the 1920s and 1930s. As historians Frank Guridy, Lisa Brock, and Digna Castañeda have shown, exchanges between Afro-Cubans and African Americans became a way of accessing resources and building community during the republican period. Chapter 4 examines how these historical relationships continued after the 1959 revolution, albeit in new and distinct ways.[41] During the Afrocubanismo movement, intellectuals and artists highlighted African contributions to Cuban culture and national identity. Cubans, white and black, reclaimed rhythms, dances, and religions from Africa to shift images of what it meant to be Cuban away from Spain and counter the United States' growing political, economic, and cultural influence on the island.[42] While this movement inserted a type of Africanity into Cuban identity, it did not confront racial stereotypes about blackness—this story of how Cuban intellectuals deracialized African culture in order to fit it into a raceless national identity is one that continued after 1959 as well.

Yet, even as blacks and *mulatos* used a variety of strategies to build a better life, participate in national politics, recognize Afro-Cuban culture, and fight racial oppression, narratives about the dangers of black politics persisted from the colonial period through the early twentieth century and past 1959. In 1933, after a multiracial coalition of opposing political parties forced the collapse of President Gerardo Machado's dictatorship (1925–33), rumors emerged that, rather than fighting Machado, blacks had supported him. One politician stated, "The black race has been indifferent to the hardships suffered by our unfortunate republic during the struggle against the Machado tyranny."[43] White opponents of the incoming president, Grau San Martin, invoked rumors and myths about black aggression—including propaganda that drew on long-standing stereotypes and fears about black savageness, black conspiracies to take over the island, and black immigrants stealing jobs from white laborers—to alienate Afro-Cubans from laying claim to the new government.[44] Some revolutionaries later used these same tropes after 1959 to link Afro-Cubans to the Batista regime and deny that their political demands were a part of the revolution.

Debates during the Constitution Convention of 1940 highlight another moment in the republic when Afro-Cubans were selectively incorporated in some arenas and silenced in others. Black and *mulato* communists and social club leaders participated heavily in the 1940 convention, especially in relation to the existing (and largely ineffective) general antidiscrimination clause (Article 20). Some Afro-Cuban leaders wanted legislation that was more specific and that would not only outlaw racial discrimination directly, but also sanction offenders. After much debate, government officials rejected the 1940 proposal because most Cuban politicians felt that dedicating an amendment only to eliminating racial discrimination was unnecessary and anti-Cuban. This same conversation was repeated when the leading Afro-Cuban communist Lázaro Peña called on Castro in 1959 to enact a law against discrimination and implement legislation moving blacks to the top of the employment lists used for hiring. Both before and after 1959, Afro-Cuban demands for laws punishing discrimination clashed with raceless nationalist claims that Cubans and later revolutionaries could not be racist.[45]

Cuban society entered the 1950s and the war against Batista with multiple existing ideologies about what it meant to be Cuban and how people of African descent fit into the nation. Revolutionary rhetoric decrying racism was not new in 1959—the island had been struggling since the abolition of slavery to achieve the equality promised during the wars for independence. Afro-Cubans had made strides in employment, voting, and political representation at different moments in the republic. But many of the stereotypes and fears about blackness that had been used to justify slavery and economic inequality persisted throughout the republic and past 1959. For example, as we will see in chapter 1, political cartoons in the 1950s perpetuated colonial ideas linking blackness to savagery by depicting African-descended Cubans as dark and thick-lipped in exaggerated caricatures (similar to the *bembón* or *negrito bembón* figures used in the early republican period).[46] It is within this context that we can begin to imagine the 1959 campaign against racial discrimination as another chapter in the history of Afro-Cuban inclusion and exclusion, rather than a complete break with the republican past. Doing so allows for a better understanding of how racism and antiracism coexisted and developed alongside each other in revolutionary Cuba.

Writing Race in Cuban Politics and Historiography

Antiracism in Cuba carries these narratives about the meanings of blackness, racelessness, and revolution in Cuba into the post-1959 period and contributes to three ongoing conversations in Cuban historiography. First, this book is a part of a long-standing tradition of Cuban Studies that is informed by contemporary grassroots organizing. However, unlike 1960s commentators who frequently framed their analysis about racism in Cuba based on their support for or against the new government, I do not examine blackness within a Cold War mentality where extremes like "revolutionary" or "counterrevolutionary" or "racist" and "antiracist" closed more conversations than they opened. For example, in the 1960s and 1970s, a debate arose, mostly between social commentators in the United States, over whether the Cuban revolutionary government had achieved its 1959 pledge of eliminating racial discrimination. For many Cubans and North Americans the answer to this question was predetermined by their support of, or disagreement with, Cuba's socialist revolution, and thus not actually focused on investigating the experiences of Afro-Cubans. On one side were those who believed that the Cuban Revolution had solved the race problem in Cuba.[47] In opposition, another group, including some exiled Afro-Cubans, saw the new government as fraudulent and maintained that racism had increased in postrevolutionary Cuba.[48] Contemporaries and historians often place the work of Afro-Cuban Carlos Moore into this category of scholarship because he has lived in exile since the late 1960s and was a frequent and outspoken critic of the Cuban Revolution's racial politics.[49] In his 1988 book, *Castro, the Blacks, and Africa*, Moore argued that middle-class black intellectuals quickly became frustrated with the new government's failure to promote blacks and *mulatos* to leadership positions, while working-class Afro-Cubans were duped into supporting a racist revolution. Ultimately, he characterizes the new government's public rhetoric about improving the situation of people of color as a hoax. Because Moore's account relies heavily on personal recollection and interviews with exiled Cubans it offers one perspective on the continuance of racism after the revolution; however, it fails to provide a concrete explanation for why so many Cubans (of all colors) accepted and believed in the narrative of an antiracist Cuba, and how that dream was able to coexist with persistent discrimination. Moore's research has been discounted as counterrevolutionary in Cuba where they accuse him of being funded by the Central Intelligence Agency and rejected in Miami where they dislike his emphasis on blackness and critique of race relations before the revolution. Moore's alienation from both sides of the United States and Cuban political spectrum epitomizes the lingering Cold War ideologies that have long influenced scholarship about the 1959 revolution that this book and other new research are working to dismantle.[50]

Providing a fresh and more nuanced perspective on race and revolution in Cuba, scholarship produced since the 1989 collapse of its former chief trading partner, the Soviet Union, has documented the persistence of racism in Cuba. Typically called the Special Period, the decade of the 1990s began with a dramatic economic disruption on the island when financial transactions came to a near standstill, the national currency collapsed, and the United States tightened the trade embargo instead of offering desperately needed aid. Revolutionary leaders worked to implement new economic policies, including a restructuring of the health care, educational, and agricultural systems in an attempt to stabilize the economy. The entire population felt the impact of these developments in the form of food shortages, long queues to buy basic essentials, and the chronic instability that comes from not knowing what would happen next. Black and *mulato* Cubans suffered these hardships more than their white counterparts because of limited access to remittances from family members in the United States. Afro-Cubans also encountered an increase in instances of racial discrimination in the spheres of employment and recreation as the requirement for *buena presencia* (good appearance) frequently meant that you needed to have fair or white skin to qualify for lucrative hotel positions in the growing tourist sector. As a result, there was an explosion in public discussions about the persistence of racism in Cuba, as residents, public intellectuals, and scholars began to question what numerous scholars and contemporaries have called the "return of racism."[51]

Cuban scholars, who had avoided writing about contemporary racial inequalities since the revolution declared the successful elimination of discrimination in 1961, began to theorize about why Afro-Cubans faced such different life chances after the Special Period than whites.[52] Afro-Cuban political scientist Esteban Morales authored one of the most notable studies on this issue. Morales argues that racial inequalities continued to exist in Cuba in the late 1990s despite early efforts by the revolutionary government to combat these problems because of the ineffectiveness of 1960s attempts to assist Afro-Cubans by increasing the general standard of living. These colorblind policies, he finds, did not solve racial inequities because the populations that were the lowest on the socioeconomic spectrum, namely Afro-Cubans, started from an unequal position.[53] Using the analogy of running a race, this thesis, popular among Cuban scholars, argues that black and *mulato* Cubans "took off" from a lower social position than white Cubans and were thus unable to achieve, even with the benefits of revolutionary programs, sufficient stability to cushion them from the crisis of the 1990s.[54]

In *A Nation for All: Race, Inequality, and Politics in Twentieth-Century Cuba* (2001), Alejandro de la Fuente offers a provocative overarching analysis of race in Cuba throughout the twentieth century. As one of the first historians to deal directly with racial politics during the initial years of the revolution, he agrees with the "return of racism" thesis and argues that the 1959 government was mostly successful in eliminating discrimination until the economic challenges of the 1990s undermined the legitimacy of the socialist regime and hindered its ability to financially maintain racial equality.[55] Recognizing the continuation of racial prejudices in private spaces, de la Fuente offers preliminary answers to the Cuban paradox of the coexistence of racism and antiracism. He suggests that the gradual nonconfrontational approach advocated by revolutionary leaders did not tackle underlying racist culture and fears. Instead, it focused on ending certain visible markers of inequality while leaving areas like housing discrimination and black criminalization nearly untouched.[56]

Antiracism in Cuba: The Unfinished Revolution troubles the very notion of the "return of racism." Implicitly, the claim that racism has returned to Cuba rests on the belief that revolutionary leaders successfully eliminated discrimination between 1959 and 1961. Not only do contemporary situations demonstrate this claim to be false, but a close reading of the sources from the revolution's earliest years reveals how racism and antiracism coexisted and infiltrated every part of Cuba's dramatic social reform program. This narrative of return also silences the multiple ways Afro-Cubans participated in, built, supported, and sometimes challenged revolutionary integration and antidiscrimination policies, pushing them to go further than the state intended throughout the 1960s. And while useful explanatory theories about racism's return to Cuba exist, most of these ideas only focus on external factors—such as the 1990s economic crash or the U.S. trade embargo. In the end, these arguments remain incomplete without an internal examination of the ways negative stereotypes about blackness and long-standing racial inequalities from Cuba's colonial past invaded its present in 1959.

My choice to focus on the first three years after 1959 parallels other new histories about the Cuban Revolution by emphasizing how between 1959 and 1961 the course of the revolution was up for grabs.[57] It was not clear then that the new government would become communist, that Fidel Castro would remain its leader for nearly five decades, or that Cuban dreams of building a colorblind and equal society would stall and ultimately fail. In this dynamic moment, Cubans weighed and argued over what path the revolution would take and debates over racial politics became a crucial metaphor for thinking about the nation. Revolutionary officials implemented far-reaching antiracist social reforms while simultaneously perpetuating racist narratives and images that devalued blackness and silenced Afro-Cuban radical voices. Additionally, zooming in on the earliest years of the revolution allows for a closer inspection of ruptures and continuities in Cuban racial politics across the often overemphasized 1959 divide. But Cuban domestic racial policies did not exist in a bubble. As Lara Putnam finds in the early twentieth-century Caribbean, "the denunciation of certain elements of scientific racism and the erection of new forms of state racism routinely went hand in hand" via migration and state responses to black migrants.[58] To that end, I also examine how transnational exchanges with African Americans and Cuban exiles opened and closed doors for debates about race in revolutionary Cuba. It is my hope that by examining the structures, choices, and images that allowed for racism to continue in the face of the 1960s revolutionary upheavals, Afro-Cuban challenges, and transnational antiracist movements, this book will contribute to understanding the central paradox of the twenty-first century—the persistence of racism in a postracial world.

Outline of the Book

To examine these processes, *Antiracism in Cuba* draws upon oral histories that I have collected in the past seven years, cultural history methodologies, and a transnational perspective to illustrate how fractures leading to the present-day "return of racism" were visible in the early 1960s Cuba. The political conflicts between Cuba and the United States have created an environment where access to archival material by North

Americans is extremely limited. Consequently, most of my analysis, like other new work on the revolution in the 1960s, is based on the Cuban press, published books, films, and oral histories. Using cultural history techniques similar to the ones employed by Louis A. Pérez Jr. in *Cuba in the American Imagination: Metaphor and the Imperial Ethos* (2008), I analyze revolutionary press and visual materials such as political cartoons and posters to uncover how stereotypical representations of Afro-Cubans in need of aid, in overly aggressive stances, or as comic relief sat side by side with 1959 declarations of racial equality. I conducted nearly twenty open-ended oral histories (frequently doing multiple interviews with the same person) and used materials from over twenty-five published interviews and testimonies for this project.[59] Oral histories of elderly Cubans, especially blacks and *mulatos* who participated and experienced the dramatic change of the 1960s, supplement gaps in the Cuban archival record where material about the early revolutionary period is either non-existent or classified and unavailable to foreign researchers at the time of writing. Oral histories also reveal the perspectives of some Afro-Cuban women, whose written and artistic work becomes more visible by the late 1960s, but whose contributions remain largely absent from the available archive in the early period under study. This late 1960s and early 1970s increase in black and *mulata* women's work raises important and hereto-fore unanswered questions about the gendered and racialized nature of revolutionary activism.[60]

Disjunctures between national goals and Afro-Cuban expectations have existed since the wars of independence and followed Cubans into the diaspora in the United States. The following chapters trace these two intersecting themes by examining key revolutionary moments and their impacts on Afro-Cuban lives. Chapters 1, 2, and 5 focus on the first theme and analyze conflicts between state rhetoric and Afro-Cuban experiences *in Cuba* during the first three years of the revolution. Chapters 3 and 4 illustrate the second, more transnational, theme by exploring how Afro-Cubans used interactions with African Americans and Cuban exiles to challenge racial inequality locally.

Chapters 1 and 2 use government speeches, articles, and editorials in Cuban newspapers and writings by black and *mulato* intellectuals to illustrate the major steps and missteps in the state-sponsored campaign to eliminate racial discrimination and create a postracial society where Afro-Cubans would just be Cubans. Chapter 1 finds that the revolution's choice to speak to the unequal situation facing Cubans of color was somewhat surprising given M 26-7's silence about race during the 1950s war against Batista. However, the need to unify the nation against U.S. opposition and respond to pressure from Afro-Cuban leaders led the post-1959 government to break the silence on racial discrimination that had been in place throughout much of the republic. In doing so, Castro built what would become the revolution's legacy as an antiracist government. Unfortunately, the revolution fell into the same trap that plagued nineteenth-century patriots—the desire to resolve racial inequalities by moving beyond race to a colorblind society. Chapter 2, in particular, deals with the multiple ideologies about race, blackness, and combating discrimination that Afro-Cubans brought into the post-1959 period and how those ideas fit (or did not) with the official rhetoric coming from above.

In the 1960s Cubans moved back and forth between Cuba and the United States, but even when they did not, the flow of ideas, histories, and debates about race shaped how Cubans, Cuban Americans, and African Americans understood race and revolution. Chapter 3 explores three parallel forces that defined the role race played in the Cuban diaspora: 1) the influences the campaign to eliminate racial discrimination had on Cuban decisions to go to the United States; 2) the movement of racial rhetoric between Cuba and southern Florida; and 3) the similar but divergent ways that Afro-Cubans experienced exile. Importantly, this chapter uses oral histories to examine how Afro-Cuban exiles struggled to create a safe space for their families in Cuba or southern Florida—a situation that led many of them to relocate to northern U.S. cities instead of Miami.

Chapter 4 emphasizes how Cubans and African Americans exploited temporary transnational alliances in the 1960s to fight local battles against racism. Comparing the United States' "colorstruck democracy" to the supposed racial paradise in Cuba, African American newspapers pointed out the dangers of labeling the Cuban Revolution an oppressive dictatorship while U.S. blacks remained second-class citizens at home. Similarly, Afro-Cubans invoked the promises revolutionary leaders made to entice U.S. blacks to visit the island and demand domestic social reforms for themselves. Ironically, the images each group used to describe the other were often inaccurate and illustrate more about local struggles than transnational solidarity. The temporary nature of black alliances with the revolution is a major theme of chapter 4. It speaks to the need to rethink assumptions that political change can achieve racial equality and that momentary collaboration between peoples of African descent necessarily means solidarity.

In chapter 5, I return to domestic struggles and explore the iconization of Conrado Benítez, a murdered volunteer teacher, to reveal how the Cuban state mobilized images of black martyrs to celebrate the resolution of the fight against racial discrimination. Cuban newspapers, literacy campaign publicity, and oral histories from this period demonstrate a shift in revolutionary discourses on race. Revolutionary leaders closed official conversations about racism in 1961 when they proclaimed that the new government had eliminated discrimination and linked continued racism to counterrevolution. The story of Benítez and the way he was used as the figurehead for the literacy campaign epitomizes these shifts. Revolutionary leaders constructed a narrative about Benítez's life that celebrated the incorporation of black soldiers into the nation while simultaneously limiting black citizenship to loyal and grateful clients of the state. This move shut the metaphorical "door" on debates about racism out of a fear that the issue would be divisive and threaten the national unity needed to defeat threats against the new government like the April 1961 Bay of Pigs invasion by U.S.-supported Miami exiles.

The official conclusion to the campaign to eliminate discrimination made it nearly impossible for Afro-Cubans to criticize leading figures who maintained prejudicial ideas or practices because of the accepted belief that good revolutionaries could not be racists. The epilogue traces how despite these challenges some Afro-Cuban intellectuals, especially black and *mulata* women, found subtle ways to fight continued discrimination and reclaim and revalue blackness as a part of revolutionary culture in the late 1960s. Using the work of 1960s filmmaker Sara Gómez and twenty-first-century Afrocubana activists, the final section of the book highlights how Afro-Cuban struggles for equality continue today using both old and new strategies.

A variety of historical processes constructed how race and revolution became linked in Cuba's public imagination of the nation in the post–1959 period. The following attempt to explore those forces by focusing on the experiences of Afro-Cubans and how they benefited from and challenged the Castro government's campaign to eliminate racial discrimination is a story of contradictions. In showing how the revolution was able to construct an internationally recognized antiracist narrative and provide unprecedented opportunities to Cubans of color *while* also building a cultural framework that paved the way for the "return of racism" in the 1990s, *Antiracism in Cuba* hopes to shift conversations about race. Only by ending the long silence about the limits of revolutionary programs to eliminate racism can scholars, contemporary Afro-Cuban activists, and modern-day revolutionaries hope to prevent repeating the mistakes made by advocates of nineteenth-century colorblind policies.

Translating Race in Cuba: A Note on Terms

In January 2007, I stood in line in Havana to give an immigration official my name, passport number, age, height, and, of course, race as a part of the process to apply for my *carnet de identidad* (residency identification card). A brown-skinned Cuban woman in her thirties took down my information and when she asked my race, I immediately said, "*negra*" (black). She made a confused face and said, "No, you are not, you are *mestiza* or at least *mulata*." *Mulata*, like the English mulatto, signals mixed white and black ancestry in Cuba and can be modified as *mulato claro* (clear mulatto) for fairer-skinned Cubans who have obvious "black" features (thicker hair, or fuller nose and lips). *Mestizo* in other Latin American countries often refers to a mix of Spanish and indigenous heritage, but because Spanish disease and violence decimated nearly all of the resident Taino population living in Cuba when Christopher Columbus arrived in 1492, in Cuban racial paradigms *mestizo* represents a lighter-skinned mixed-race person who is not obviously of fully Spanish or African parentage. On the other end of the color spectrum, Cubans use *negro* (black) or *prieto* (dark-colored) to describe someone who is more obviously of African descent and darker-skinned. I have even heard *trigueno* (wheat-colored) used to characterize someone who has straight black hair, finer features, but light-brown skin or *chino* for a Cuban with Asiatic features.

Cuba's history of racial mixing and corresponding racial terminology set up the conflict that transpired between me and the Cuban official over my identification card. We went back and forth for a while over whether I was *negra*, *mulata*, or *mestiza*. I argued that my parents were black and I self-identify as black and that I wanted my card to represent that identity. I even tried to participate in the Cuban naming process by saying that I was willing to consider *mulata* since that is what I am frequently called on the streets of Havana, but that *mestiza* was taking things too far. The official listened, laughed uncomfortably, and finally said, "Fine. 'Negra' is ok." I relaxed, helped the students in my group with weaker Spanish skills fill out their applications and waited to pick up the final products. As you can imagine, I was surprised and angry when I got my card back a few weeks later and it had "Mestiza" in the box for race (figure I.1). Cuba's

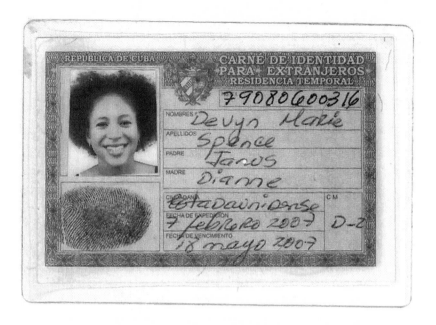

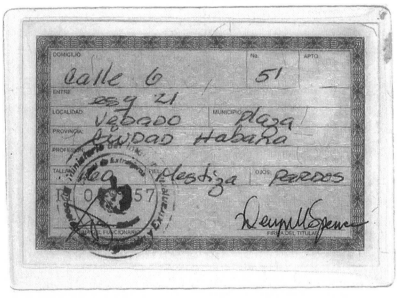

Figure I.1 Cuban temporary resident identification card from 2007. Author's collection.

racial system had translated not only the way I looked, but my class status, or at least my position as a PhD candidate, as well. Others later explained to me that it was likely that the official had upgraded me from *mulata* to *mestiza* because I was the leader of the student group, educated, and on my way to being a professor.

Since my first trip to Cuba in 2003, when I spent thirty deathly hot July summer days in Yaguajay (a small town in the north central province of Santa Clara), until the time of writing, I have made over twenty trips to the island, the longest being a six-month stretch during which I directed a semester study abroad program for eager undergraduate students in Havana. Cuba has changed a lot in the ten years that I have been traveling there, a decade that has coincided almost exactly with the rebuilding process following the Special Period. Every day, there are more foreign tourists in and out of major hotels owned jointly by Cuban and European or Canadian entrepreneurs. Cubans have opened small businesses selling products ranging from apples and CDs to home nail salons and accounting operations. Public debates about the legacy and the future of the country abound as the revolutionary leadership ages and transfers authority to a new, younger, but equally anti-imperialist and socialist, generation of revolutionaries. One thing has remained the same over my many research trips to Havana, Trinidad, Santiago, and Yaguajay. I am always asked, "Are you Cuban?" When I respond "no," usually with a chuckle, the inevitable guessing game begins: "Well your parents are Cuban, right?" "Are you of Latino descent?" Each time, I reply that I am an African American from North Carolina, whose parents and grandparents, and great-grandparents are from the United States, the descendants of slaves. "Ah, well you look very Cuban," the questioner always replies and we move on with the conversation. The first few times that this occurred I was surprised by the energy expended in trying to locate my citizenship somewhere other than the United States and even more so by the discomfort Cubans seemed to have trying to place me only in the category of African American or simply "black." I am a light-skinned woman, with brown eyes, and I usually wear my hair in a natural, slightly curly Afro. I am not any more or less mixed than any other African American from the southern part of the United States, meaning that I cannot point to a particular white ancestor in my lineage, just a collection of other "black" people who range in skin tone from super fair or "high yellow," as some family members say, to very dark. For me, seeing people with a variety of skin tones in one Cuban family was not shocking and I did not balk at the prevalence of "interracial" couples on the island or the many textures of Cuban women's hair. These characteristics seemed fairly normal; in fact, I was initially confident that other than the palest Cubans, with blue eyes and blonde hair whom I encountered in the less racially integrated provinces of rural Cuba, all these curly haired, some-shade-of-brown-skinned Cubans were "black" just like my family. I could not have been more wrong—or more right.

In the end, I accepted my "Mestiza"-labeled identification card in 2007 and have since adjusted to the various ways that Cubans read me and I read them; but these experiences taught me more than any book I had read about race as a social construction. Not only are racial markers socially constructed, but that process changes, shifts, and evolves based on national, regional, and local racial systems. In the United States, I am "black" or African American on any application I am required to complete. But at home in Charlotte, North Carolina, I am just as frequently called "high yellow," "light-skinned," or "red-boned" to indicate my skin color inside the black community. And, in Cuba I can be *mulata* or *mestiza* depending on whether an onlooker knows my education or employment status. In writing this book, I had to decide how to translate race across time and space for my English-reading audience. I chose to use the terms "African-descended," "people of color," "Afro-Cuban," *mulato*, and "black" interchangeably to discuss the descendants of Africans living in Cuba. This choice parallels the terms employed in the historical primary documents, where the words and phrases *negro*, *mulato*, *raza de color*, and *gente de color* are seen most frequently. I also decided to italicize *mulato* because I am using the Spanish word (all other Spanish words are in italics as well). I'm doing so to distinguish the Spanish *mulato* from the English "mulatto," which carries a lot of baggage (at least for African Americans) because it is tied to derogatory images of violent racial mixing and mules. My default terms when I am talking about groups of African descent on the island are Afro-Cuban or black and *mulato*. I am very aware of the diversity of Cuban experiences based on locality, social class, and skin color that get collapsed into general terms like Afro-Cuban or black. However, to understand the legacies of race and revolution in Cuba is to interrogate the "ongoing struggle over resources, wealth, and power" that is linked to racial categories, especially skin color, in the Americas.[61]

Today, black and *mulato* activists in Cuba are themselves using and reclaiming terms like *afrodescendiente* (Afro-descended) and "Afrocubano," or simply *negro* to demand racial equality in the twenty-first century.[62]

My terms try to reflect these contemporary changes. Racial mixing may have led to a diverse list of words to describe a person's closeness to or distance from blackness, but it never meant that people did not talk about or allude to race. When someone wants to indicate black group identity in Cuba, they are often more likely to brush their forearm in a silent gesture toward the skin color of Afro-Cubans—a subtle visual cue indicating blackness—than they are to say anything. Sometimes gestures or images articulate more than words. In the end, Cubans of African descent experienced the revolution individually and collectively and this book tries to unpack those experiences using the terms that were and are available while eschewing any universal ideas about blackness. And where my best efforts at language and translation fail, I have included quotations from oral histories (in English and Spanish), photographs, and political cartoons so that readers can see for themselves the multiple ways Cubans express race.

1

Not Blacks, but Citizens

Racial Rhetoric and the 1959 Revolution

During a heated televised interview on 25 March 1959, just three days after his first speech announcing the revolution's campaign to eliminate racial discrimination, Cuban leader Fidel Castro had to defend his intentions against naysayers who disapproved of the new government's integration plans. Castro recounted what he saw as a troubling event. He described a recent rally where audiences cheered wildly when he discussed lowering telephone taxes, reducing rents, and opening private beaches; yet the same crowd fell silent, or "made ugly faces" when he talked about "helping the negro." After asking what the difference was between one injustice and the other, the young leader of the 26th of July Movement (M 26-7) concluded that the discrepancy resulted from "people who call themselves Christian and who are racist . . . people who call themselves revolutionaries but are racist . . . [and] people who call themselves good but are racist."[1] By openly critiquing Cubans for their hypocrisy and silence on racial inequality and publicly addressing the problems of people of color, Castro distinguished himself and other revolutionary leaders from past regimes.

Cuba's state-sponsored campaign to eliminate racial discrimination began officially in March 1959, in response to pressure from Afro-Cuban groups demanding that racial justice be included in emerging revolutionary policies.[2] "We have heard that Fidel Castro is thinking about this injustice . . . we hope that now we can begin to erase the discriminatory practices used by many people in business and industry," wrote the presidents of the San Miguel de Padrón Social Union in February 1959.[3] The following month, Castro made his first official announcement about the "hated injustice" of racial inequality. In front of thousands of Cubans, he outlined plans for blacks and whites to work and attend school together.[4] Newspapers across the island reprinted Castro's March speech and opened a brief three-year public dialogue about how to eliminate racial discrimination and ease racial tensions on the island. The official publication of M 26-7, *Revolución*, printed speeches from the rally under the headline, "A Million Workers: More United than Ever!" *Revolución*'s coverage of the event also included a small text box noting that the "Four Great Battles for the Well-being of the Cuban People" were to "1. Reduce unemployment; 2. Lower the cost of living; 3. Raise salaries of workers who earn the least; and 4. End racial discrimination in the work place."[5] Similarly, *Noticias de Hoy*, newspaper of the Cuban Communist Party (also known as the Partido Socialista Popular, or PSP, after 1944), published the 22 March speech under the headline, "In our country, of [Antonio] Maceo and [José] Martí, Oppression will not return."[6] Together, these headlines reveal key components of the young revolution's racial rhetoric, specifically an emphasis on ending public discrimination in work centers and schools and the importance of mobilizing the legacies of nineteenth-century independence heroes to legitimize the new government and unify the population.

The revolution's choice to speak to the unequal situation facing Cubans of color was somewhat surprising given M 26-7's vagueness about race during the 1950s war against Fulgencio Batista. The guerillas' platform and Castro's speeches called for a return to the Constitution of 1940 and general social welfare reforms, but did not reference racial tensions in any substantive way. However, the need to unify the nation against U.S. opposition and respond to pressure from Afro-Cuban leaders led the post-1959 government to incorporate plans to eliminate discrimination into its public platform within months of taking power from Batista. In doing so, Castro built what would become the revolution's legacy as an antiracist government and paved the way for Afro-Cuban defense of and defiance against the new government.

1950s Understandings of Race:
M 26-7's Platform vs. the Popular Press

Like political movements before them, M 26-7 was vague about its future plans to govern the island in the 1950s, especially in relation to racial politics. Castro, a member of the Orthodox Party, stepped into the spotlight of the anti-Batista coalition when he and a small group of rebels attacked the Moncada military barracks on 26 July 1953. The attack was a colossal failure, many died and even more were arrested, but as word spread about the uprising, Cubans rallied around the young men and women standing trial for treason against the state. In what would become one of his most famous speeches, "History Will Absolve Me," Castro defended his actions to a full courtroom and defined his plans for building a new Cuba.

"The problem of the land, the problem of industrialization, the problem of housing, the problem of unemployment, the problem of education, and the problem of people's health: these are the six problems we would take immediate steps to solve along with restoration of civil liberties and political democracy."[7] Castro invoked statistics to paint a portrait of the hundreds of thousands of farmers without land, underpaid teachers, and rural laborers living in substandard housing who would benefit from his movement. However, despite the myriad of detail in the 189-page speech, the young rebel remained silent on the issue of racial discrimination—a topic he later promoted as strongly as he advocated for the more well-known Agrarian Reform. As historian Hugh Thomas notes, "To read 'History Will Absolve Me' would suggest that Castro was addressing a racially homogenous nation."[8]

The absence of a specific program directed toward Afro-Cubans was especially glaring in comparison to the detailed ideological and political plans outlined in M 26-7's *Program Manifesto* (1957). Listing the ten focal points of the revolution, including a desire for national sovereignty, an independent economy, and a strong education and employment sector, the *Manifesto* employed quotations from Martí to introduce each bullet point of the group's platform. M 26-7 foreshadowed the type of post-racial program Castro would later promote by using Martí's words as a launching point for their policies. Because while the nineteenth-century Cuban patriot had emphasized the need to build a raceless Cuba after independence, a nation "without whites, without blacks, just Cubans," Martí's writings included few specifics about how to construct the idealized "nation for all." In a similar manner, point number four of M 26-7's *Manifesto* offered only a dim assessment of the island's social inequalities and plans to tackle them. "From Martí, M 26-7 takes the position in respect to social problems. . . . In agreement with this concept, no group, class, race, or religion should put its interests over the common good, nor consider itself indifferent to the larger social order."[9] Like other pre-1959 references to discrimination, this statement placed racial prejudice among a long list of other intolerances. Only in the final pages of the *Manifesto* did the group mention plans to include an "educational plan for understanding others and racial integration."[10] As one of the more direct statements made by Castro and M 26-7 about race before overthrowing Batista, this declaration fit with their general ideological foundation mirroring that of nineteenth-century patriots. The young rebels repeatedly announced that they were completing the unfinished revolutions of 1868 and 1895;

therefore their speeches and correspondence before 1959 rarely mentioned race outside of vague references to Martí's language of "not rich or poor, not white or black."[11]

And while M 26-7 did not directly address race or the situation of Afro-Cubans in public speeches or private correspondence, popular Cuban magazines, newspapers, and other political movements engaged with blackness and whiteness on a daily basis.[12] Articles, advertisements, and political cartoons depicted blacks and *mulatos* "negatively" as either ignorant and poor, or "positively" for their physical strength and creative abilities using familiar colonial tropes. Cuba's oldest general-interest magazine, *Bohemia*, was founded in 1908 and provided a weekly mix of contemporary political commentary, historical analysis, and up-to-date fashion advice. Despite having its editorial office in Havana, *Bohemia*'s circulation throughout the island meant that the magazine both reflected and influenced popular opinions nationwide. *Bohemia* reinforced notions of Afro-Cuban poverty and helplessness by printing images of homeless and poverty-stricken black communities or *barrios humildes*. The magazine frequently ran articles about unemployment and the plight of the urban and rural poor to highlight the economic challenges facing Cuba in the 1950s. Photographs of blacks and *mulatos* almost always accompanied these articles.[13] Drawing attention to the poverty existing in some black neighborhoods was an important part of the magazine's political commentary and social justice project; however, the lack of positive portrayals of Afro-Cubans to balance the pervasive visuals of black slums reaffirmed popular notions of blacks and *mulatos* as social pariahs.

Cuban advertisers linked blackness to service positions in the 1950s using familiar race and class norms. Advertisements published in *Bohemia* built on consumer aspirations for a middle-class lifestyle and the very real economic hierarchies on the island where an overwhelming percentage of the domestic servants in white homes were Afro-Cuban.[14] In a full-page color advertisement for Kresto, a sweet flavoring used to enhance the taste of milk, the company introduced the character of Esmérida, a brown-skinned Afro-Cuban maid, to promote their product (figure 1.1).[15] The six-panel advertisement is structured like a comic strip and titled "Domestic Problem." It paints a heteronormative lunch scene in a white family's home where a business suit-clad father, a mother in a black gown, a blonde daughter, and an athletic son sit in the dining room while Esmérida, dressed in a recognizable white apron and maid's hat, cooks and serves lunch. According to the advertisement, everything was

Figure 1.1 "Domestic Problem." Kresto milk flavoring advertisement. From *Bohemia* (4 January 1953). Courtesy of the Cuban Heritage Collection, University of Miami.

going well until the meal ended and the whole family began to argue because the children did not want to drink their milk: "The Senora cried . . . the gentleman yelled, and the children fussed. (This happens in even the best families)." Esmérida assesses the scene and quickly intervenes by waving a white flag and offering a solution: "In other houses where I have worked, this [commotion] never happens because they drink their milk with Kresto, which gives it a delicious flavor." The family agrees to try Kresto and in the final panels everyone (with the exception of Esmérida) happily consumes their beverages, while the text explains that for her "brilliant" idea the family promoted Esmérida and gave her the keys to the house. She becomes the "Ama de Llaves" (head domestic worker with access to the house's keys).

A number of themes about race in 1950s Cuba arise from this advertisement. Not only does the advertiser locate Esmérida as a lifelong servant who has held other domestic positions, the company also uses visual cues such as the expensive attire worn by the white family to contrast white economic success with black servitude. The advertisement invites readers to identify with upper-class leisure lifestyles by implying that it is advantageous to have a black maid not only for her cooking prowess, but also for her ability to solve domestic problems. And while the piece concludes by celebrating Esmérida and giving her new responsibilities in the home, her success is based on preparing, not participating in, the family meal. In her new position she continues to be cast as a grateful but accommodating subordinate as she is shown kissing the bottle of Kresto and beaming when she is given the keys to the house.

Other marketing campaigns also situated blackness and whiteness at opposite ends of the beauty and economic spectrum. Advertisers linked dark skin to domestic service and ugliness (via exaggerated black features) while setting fair skin and straight hair as the standard of Cuban beauty and financial success. To market the Tu-py brand of coffee, promoters introduced an Afro-Cuban waiter with dark skin and excessively full lips frozen in a wide smile (figure 1.2).[16] The advertisers give the waiter the same name as the brand—the coffee and the black character that serves it are both identified as "Tu-py." In doing so, they made it impossible for readers to distinguish the black male body from the product being promoted or the service he/it provides. Tu-py became even more of an unreal or invisible caricature in subsequent advertisements as the producers of the campaign alternated between representing him as a sketch (like a political cartoon) and using a photograph of a black minstrel doll. In

Figure 1.2 "The best flavor of Tu-py: The preferred coffee everywhere."
From *Bohemia* (9 November 1952). Courtesy of the Cuban Heritage Collection,
University of Miami.

each Tu-py ad, marketers reinforced the idea of Afro-Cubans, at worst, as nonhuman caricatures and, at best, as happy and contented servants by drawing blacks with oversized lips set in compliant grins.

In contrast, advertisers for Allyn's hair-straightening cream sold their product, a chemical relaxer, using photographs of a white woman with long, shiny, dark hair (figure 1.3). This advertisement did not use a dark-skinned face or curly hair like the ones in the Kresto and Tu-py advertisements, despite claiming that the cream was created "especially for persons of color—men, women, and children." Instead, Allyn's cream relied on Cuban norms of Spanish fair-skinned and straight-haired beauty to encourage readers to strive for straighter tresses.[17]

Not all representations of Afro-Cubans in 1950s magazines followed these stereotypes of poverty, servitude, and unattractiveness. A few articles, especially those published each year in December commemorating the death of *mulato* general Antonio Maceo, recognized Afro-Cuban participation in the wars of independence and Cuba's victory against Spain.[18] One journalist highlighted how "the Habanero [Martí] and the spirited Oriental [Maceo] joined together as brothers and baptized the opposite poles of the country with their spilt blood" to reinforce the often repeated claim that the sacrifice of both Martí and Maceo erased the shame of slavery from the island and united the races in brotherly fraternity.[19] Another article titled "The Past That Still Lives Today: The Death of Acea" described the valor and bravery of Colonel Isidro Acea, an Afro-Cuban soldier from Cienfuegos, who fought alongside Maceo in the famed Tiradores de Maceo (Maceo Shooters) brigade.[20] These representations of Afro-Cubans recognized their roles in fighting for Cuban independence and tried to highlight their continuing relevance to the nation. But despite flowery language commemorating the joint history of black and white revolutionary soldiers, the Cuban popular press mirrored M 26-7's platform and said little about how many black soldiers died in poverty after the war, frequently struggling to find employment after 1898.[21]

Features about Afro-Cuban athletes and performers were the main exception to articles and advertisements portraying blacks as either ignorant servants or martyred long-gone rebels in the 1950s. Journalists writing the sports pages of Cuban media outlets repeatedly announced the achievements of black and *mulato* boxing and baseball champions.[22] Similarly, articles about Afro-Cuban musicians, including famous mambo performer Arsenio Rodríguez, expressed pride in black culture.[23] The

Figure 1.3 "Allyn's marvelous cream!" "Especially created for people of color: Men, women, and children. Straighten your hair with Allyn's cream." From *Bohemia* (2 November 1952). Courtesy of the Cuban Heritage Collection, University of Miami.

men whose photographs graced these pages were shown as strong, muscular, and smiling representatives of black masculinity. However, even as Cuban readers applauded the success of these athletes and artists, this attention reinforced certain colonial tropes about the Afro-Cuban male body. Photographs depicted black male performers as physically fit and sexual, with nonthreatening smiling faces, even when tackling difficult work or sports conditions. And while these "positive" representations of blackness provided certain opportunities for social mobility, via sports and arts, that were unavailable to domestic workers like the fictional Esmérida or Tu-py, they also illustrated how most Cubans in the 1950s encountered and imagined blacks and *mulatos* as less than equal contributors to the nation.

It should come as no surprise given the political turmoil of the ensuing civil war that even as M 26-7 remained silent about confronting racism and popular media sources represented Afro-Cubans in socially prescribed roles of servants and/or entertainers, the threat of black political activity continued to smolder in the public sphere. In fact, some members of the anti-Batista coalition routinely portrayed Afro-Cubans as supporters of the besieged dictator and used racist epithets like "black monkey" and *el mulato malo* (the bad mulatto) to attack Batista.[24] Political cartoonists, like *Bohemia*'s regular contributor Silvio, highlighted the president's black heritage by sketching Batista with features that had long been used to signal Afro-Cubanness (thick lips and curly hair). Batista, who was usually considered *mulato* in Cuba's racial hierarchy despite his unwillingness to identify directly with Afro-Cubans, had a very public link to black social clubs by the late 1950s. The Cuban president used lottery money to fund black societies and worked strategically to make alliances with upper-class "black brokers"—Afro-Cuban professionals, intellectuals, and social club leaders who traded votes with local political parties for resources from national politicians.[25] As a result, cartoonists like Silvio, the author of "El Reyecito Criollo" ("The Creole King")—a cartoon that ridiculed Batista's policies—drew the president with exaggerated black features to highlight his Afro-Cuban heritage *and* to link Afro-Cuban leaders to the president's unpopular regime.[26]

This perception of Afro-Cubans as Batista supporters was widely held at the time and persists in contemporary debates. The Afro-Cuban M 26-7 commander and future high-ranking member of Castro's revolutionary government, Juan Almeida, remembered how Cuban soldiers attacked his fellow rebel Armando Mestre after the assault on the Moncada barracks in 1953 for being dark-skinned. "Comrade Mestre, who has died since, got the worst of the manhandling. They [Batista soldiers] kept telling him, 'Come over here. *You* a revolutionary? Don't you know Negroes can't be revolutionaries? Negroes are either thieves or Batista's supporters, but never revolutionaries!'"[27] In 1971, historian Hugh Thomas reinforced this point: "Batista's army and police were full of Negroes and mulattoes. Yanes Pelletier, the officer who arrested Castro in 1953 after Moncada, was black." He contrasts this assertion with the numerous white radicals who fought against Batista and argues that only about 12 percent of the soldiers with Castro at Moncada were black or *mulato*.[28] And while the exact compositions of Batista's and Castro's armies are unknown, it was widely accepted in 1959 that M 26-7 and its leadership were not of color. Today, among exiles, the debate over whether blacks and *mulatos* supported Batista in the 1950s lives on. Lydia Mesa-Martí Betancourt Sharpe, the widow of Afro-Cuban activist Juan René Betancourt, has lived in the United States since 1960 and gave an interview in 2011 about her family's life in Cuba and decision to leave the island.[29] As she recounted how her husband, who swiftly distanced himself from Castro in 1959, was solidly anti-Batista, the interviewer interjected and said that "he remembered blacks who were for and who identified with Batista as one of their own." Mesa-Martí Betancourt Sharpe quickly interrupted him, saying, "Batista was *medio-mulato*, but he didn't think of himself as black." More than fifty years later, over 1,500 miles between Havana and New York and conflicting political attitudes about Castro separated Afro-Cubans Commander Almeida and Mesa-Martí Betancourt Sharpe; yet, both encountered situations where white Cubans claimed that they or other blacks and *mulatos* had supported Batista. The idea of blacks as followers of besieged presidents and dictators was not new in 1959 or 2011. Official discourses in the republic frequently painted Afro-Cubans as unpatriotic supporters of ousted regimes to dismiss black and *mulato* citizenship claims after political openings.[30] The persistence of these accusations and repeated denials reveals the ways that race was and continues to be invoked to define legitimate revolutionaries. The normalization of stereotypes about blacks moved beyond simply seeing Afro-Cubans as second-class citizens in the 1950s and became a method of spreading long-standing fears of a black political takeover via Batista or other unpopular political parties.

Another *Bohemia* cartoon, this time featuring a group of scantily clad black figures in a supposed tribal meeting, associated Afro-Cubans with a different 1950s political threat—communism. In the cartoon, the leader of the group asks a potential recruit, "Before admitting you to our council, Toibal, you have to answer only one question: Are you or have you ever been a member of the Party?"[31] Even as this cartoon reinforced notions of blacks as savages, it hinted at common perceptions and fears linking Afro-Cubans to the Communist Party. In the 1940s, the PSP had been one of the only political parties with an explicit antiracist platform, which garnered it much Afro-Cuban support as we will see in the next chapter. However, the closeness between blacks and *mulatos* and PSP leaders was potentially threatening in a Cold War setting. Most historians agree that Castro and M 26-7 were not communists prior to announcing their commitment to Marxist Leninism in April 1961 during the U.S.-backed Bay of Pigs invasion.[32] Therefore a reluctance to associate with the maligned party (which also had links to Batista in the 1940s) might have led M 26-7 to remain silent about race in the 1950s. Ultimately, it was easier and less divisive for the predominantly middle-class and white leadership of M 26-7 to maintain a vague, Martían platform about race as they navigated the ever-changing social milieu of the anti-Batista struggle. However, in doing so, Castro and other members of M 26-7 made Afro-Cubans politically invisible at a time when blacks and *mulatos* were hypervisible in the pages of the popular press and on the sports field, and were the subject of everyday talk against Batista. This choice was strategic and influenced by the particular circumstances of the 1950s, and had little to do with M 26-7's later turn to socialism in 1961. Rather, it fit with late nineteenth-century discourses constructing the island as a raceless nation. And while M 26-7's silence made sense in the scope of Cuban national ideologies, it left the rebel movement open to criticism from Afro-Cuban leaders, foreshadowed what would become Castro's simultaneous public and indirect attack against racism, and revealed the limits of revolutionary thought.

Race Meets Revolution: "Now Is the Time to End Racial Discrimination"

On 1 January 1959, as the bearded rebels of M 26-7 celebrated Batista's hasty departure to the Dominican Republic and the triumph of their revolution, few Cubans or international onlookers knew what would happen next. Nothing was for sure during those early morning festivities on New Year's Day; it was not obvious that the revolution would center on Fidel Castro, that relations would break with the United States, or that the new government would turn to communism. And it certainly seemed unlikely that Cuba would undertake a now globally recognized campaign to eliminate racial discrimination within three months of Batista's flight. At the start of 1959, M 26-7's platform was overly idealistic and lacking in concrete plans and it looked doubtful that the hodgepodge of political allies who had come together to defeat Batista could resolve their remaining differences to collectively govern the island. Castro, however, was certain of two points: 1) that the history would not repeat itself in regard to a U.S. intervention; and 2) that the 1959 revolution was connected to, and the fulfillment of, the 1895 independence struggle. In a speech given on 2 January in Santiago de Cuba and broadcast on national radio, the young leader proclaimed: "This time the revolution will not be thwarted. ... This time, fortunately for Cuba, the revolution will be consummated. It will not be like the war of 1895, when the Americans arrived and made themselves masters of the country; they intervened at the last minute and did not even allow Calixto Garcia, who had been fighting for thirty years to enter Santiago de Cuba. ... This time will be different."[33] By invoking the unfulfilled promise of Cuba's first revolution for independence, Castro tapped into long-standing and in some ways universal Cuban ideologies that iconicized the beliefs of the late nineteenth-century rebels. As historian Louis A. Pérez Jr. notes, the leaders of M 26-7 saw themselves as "the generation of *centenario* (century-old)."[34] They attacked Moncada in 1953, one hundred years after Martí's birth in 1853, and they marketed their struggle and victory as the resolution of a fight that had spanned a century. During the new government's first three years, M 26-7 worked to stabilize its position by recruiting allies from the popular classes. Social reforms in the shape of land redistribution, rent reduction, and the nationalization of foreign business benefited most working-class Cubans and generated excitement for the new government. Parroting the unifying ideals of Martí and implementing general social reform could not guarantee M 26-7's ability to lead the country in 1959. But doing so and responding to pressure from Afro-Cuban intellectuals for an anti-discrimination campaign pointed the new government in the direction of attacking racism. In fact, it was the unexpected national campaign to eliminate racial discrimination, beginning in March 1959, that drew many working-class blacks and *mulatos* to the revolution, even as it distanced other sectors of the Cuban population.

One of Castro's earliest comments about race came in response to a question posed by a U.S. reporter during a press conference at the Hotel

Riviera in January 1959. The journalist asked, "How do you feel about the ways that Cubans of color are treated when they go to the United States and do you think people of color are treated the same way in Cuba?" In a roundabout response, Castro hinted that the new government would tackle the issue of racial discrimination, but failed to relay a clear plan of action: "In Cuba, the same problem that occurs in the southern part of the United States does not exist. Racial discrimination exists here, but to a much lesser extent. Our revolution will help to eliminate the latent prejudices and injustices that remain.... In this sense our thoughts are those of Martí and we would not be revolutionaries or democrats if we did not dispose of all forms of discrimination."[35] Consistent with pre-1959 comments about race and the revolution, Castro's answer distanced Cuban racism from U.S. racism, reinforced the legacy of colorblindness built in 1895, and downplayed the gravity of the island's racial conflicts. Most importantly, by claiming that racial discrimination only existed in Cuba on a small scale—he called it "latent"—Castro failed to acknowledge the daily acts of discrimination faced by blacks and *mulatos*.

Afro-Cubans, of course, disagreed and insisted that Cuba's racial conflicts were more severe than Castro alleged.[36] Take the case of Lorenzo Fernández Aguílera, a young black man from Havana who put his education on hold to enlist in the revolutionary army. "I joined the rebels to fight for justice for all Cubans, to give everyone the opportunity to succeed without exclusions or privileges," he stated in an interview titled "From Student to a Soldier for Liberty." Fernández became the assistant editor of *Adelante*, a newly minted youth newspaper in Havana, after M 26-7's victory. Under his direction, the editorial staff of the newspaper invoked the memories of the same national heroes Castro used to reinforce racelessness to describe the limits of Cuba's equality and propose a path for change.[37] In a report called "In Cuba Discrimination Should Not Exist," one journalist exposed the contradictions in how Cubans, and even some revolutionaries, practiced "the thoughts of Martí." The author described an episode on 28 January where two social clubs, one white and one black, hosted racially separate parties to honor the birth of Martí. In accordance with procedures that had been practiced since the slave era and continued after the revolution, the white club planned to celebrate in the Liceo and the black club would meet next door in the Bella Union. At the last minute, the revolutionary governor of Santa Clara, Calixto Sanchez (whom the author identified as white), intervened and said, "It is impossible that blacks and whites should be divided in the ceremony honoring our venerated independence leader." Sanchez forced the two groups together, "to the thrill of some, the stupor of others, and the repulsion of many." That racially segregated celebrations had occurred in these clubs for over fifty years is not that surprising given the distance between how Cubans preached and how they lived the raceless words of Martí. However, the hostile reactions of both clubs' members to forced integration shows the difficult realities Castro and other M 26-7 members had tried to avoid by remaining silent about discrimination in the 1950s. Maybe most telling about this case was the conclusion of the *Adelante* article: "The revolution that bravely fought against tyranny in the Sierra [Maestra], now has to fight with the same force against the discriminators and prejudices of old."[38] The author of the piece used an example of successful revolutionary integration, and one that occurred on Martí's birthday no less, as a way of insisting that Castro and the leaders of M 26-7 fulfill their promises to attain equality for all Cubans. Governor Sanchez had taken the first step by integrating the 28 January festivities, but Afro-Cuban intellectuals wanted a more comprehensive antiracism plan.

Adelante continued its push for a campaign against racial discrimination, no doubt with Fernandez's support, by exposing spaces and facilities where Afro-Cubans were denied access. Under the headline "It Is Necessary to Destroy the Discrimination in UAAC," a journalist argued that "this is the moment to rectify" the discriminatory practices in the Cuban Amateur Athletic Union. "Although the color barrier has been broken completely in baseball and boxing, the same thing must be achieved in basketball, swimming, tennis, and all the other Olympic sports."[39] Additionally, writers for the newspaper issued calls to open private beaches and admit blacks and *mulatos* into workers' unions.[40] In "The Black Worker and Big Industry," a former union member demanded that David Salvador, the general secretary of the Cuban Workers' Confederation (Confederación de Trabajadores de Cuba, CTC), investigate the systematic discrimination facing black employees, especially in the culinary industry and its unions. "If the revolution aspires to equal citizenship for all, if it is going to be a liberating force that will allow all Cubans to enjoy their constitutional and legal rights, then it must—we repeat—work on this issue . . . so that the black apprentice, the *mestiza* girl, the secretary of color, etc. will be admitted to the unions of these big industries." Given M 26-7's language of equality for all, young journalists at *Adelante* insisted that antiracism be a part of the revolution's platform and pushed for the new government to take action. They went so far as to single out the secretary general of the CTC, saying, "Today, a message for David Salvador. We are not demanding a rapid solution, but we want a preliminary study that will move toward the eradication [of racial discrimination]."[41] Afro-Cubans recognized that ending racism would be a process, but they also believed that early 1959, when the course of the revolution was still undecided, was an ideal moment to make their demands heard. For Fernández, joining the rebel movement had been a physical way to fight injustice, but after M 26-7's victory he used his education and position as the assistant editor of *Adelante* to draw Castro and other revolutionary leaders' attention to the battle for Afro-Cuban rights.

Other blacks and *mulatos* pressured the new government to use the momentum of the revolutionary victory to eliminate racial injustices by publicizing specific cases of discrimination and insisting on a response from the young leaders. The presidents of the San Miguel de Padrón Social Union, an Afro-Cuban society, wrote to both President Manuel Urrutia Lleó and Fidel Castro in February 1959, saying, "We hope that now we can begin to erase the discriminatory methods used by many people in business and industry."[42] *Noticias de Hoy* published excerpts from San Miguel de Padrón's letter under the headline, "They Ask for Punishment for Racial Discrimination in Cuba: In Defense of the Black Family." The article's title highlighted the illegality of employment discrimination under the Constitution of 1940, but the heading also suggested that employees had a moral obligation to distribute jobs fairly so that all Cuban families could succeed. A few weeks later, in an episode that showed the irony of blacks being able to work, but not socialize, in certain spaces, Afro-Cubans rallied around four rebel soldiers who were denied entrance to the Casino Deportivo, a white social club. Black employees from the club condemned the facility for refusing to allow the men inside, despite their contributions to the "national liberation" of Cuba, simply for the "sin of being black." To support the case, another black social club, the Juan Gualberto Gómez Society, named after the early twentieth-century *mulato* intellectual and politician, penned an open letter to the new Federation of Cuban Societies demanding that the government investigate Casino Deportivo and take a stance on racial discrimination in social clubs.[43] In these cases, black and *mulato* Cubans emphasized contributions to the revolution as a means of justifying equal rights and pressured the new government to live up to its promises of equality for all.

While the PSP newspaper and smaller publications with Afro-Cuban editorial staff members pushed for a comprehensive, state-led attack on discrimination, M 26-7's *Revolución* appeared to watch this debate from the sidelines in the first months of 1959. Only one four-part article and photojournalism series by José Hernández Artigas established the rebel movement's initial position on race and showed it to be more circuitous than what Afro-Cubans demanded. As described in the introduction, during the first three months of the revolution Hernández and two photographers visited one of Havana's worst slums, the barrio of Las Yaguas, and interviewed the community's predominantly Afro-Cuban residents. Las Yaguas was located alongside an abandoned quarry in East Havana and was home to about 3,500 residents in 1959. The majority of these inhabitants were people of color who had migrated to Havana from various rural towns in hopes of finding employment in the capital. Given its reputation as a neighborhood of thieves, prostitutes, and hoodlums, Las Yaguas appeared an ideal place for a government reform project (in fact, previous administrations had tried to rehabilitate the area as well).[44] Headlines in *Revolución* from as early as February 1959 demonstrate that "Transforming Las Yaguas" quickly became a priority in the new government's plans to reconstruct Cuba by reforming black and *mulato* families.[45] M 26-7 journalists wrote full-page articles complete with images from the neighborhood, and used coded language about "transform[ing]" the community and "reintegrat[ing] its families" that cast Las Yaguas as a broken space in need of salvation.[46] The press built the campaign to transform Las Yaguas on the neighborhood's reputation as an uncivilized community of "delinquents" with few "decent people."[47] These types of portrayals characterized early revolutionary efforts to focus on Afro-Cuban social and economic problems.

In the first three months of 1959, *Revolución*'s team published articles about their visits to black communities that included a few paragraphs of text and numerous black and white photographs depicting residents' everyday lives and struggles with poverty. In the first piece, "Not Blacks, but Citizens," published just three weeks after M 26-7's victory, Hernández interviewed eight Afro-Cubans, including seventy-three-year-old widow Carmen Torres. Torres told him that blacks faced a resource problem characterized by a lack of work opportunities: "Above all, we want more jobs and to be treated better." Hernández was interested in what he called "poor neighborhoods," and the title of his article epitomized M 26-7's and *Revolución*'s platform about race—namely that it was the revolution's responsibility to provide a fair playing field for all Cuban citizens. The question remained, however: What made someone a revolutionary citizen?[48] Hernández attempted to answer this question in three further articles, "The Revolution Transforms Las Yaguas," "2,000 Children Live in Las Yaguas," and "A Poor Barrio in Santiago de Cuba," where he identified poverty as a "grave social problem" and argued that the revolution needed to quickly build houses and provide jobs for parents in Las Yaguas if it wanted to "save the children from becoming criminals."[49] By emphasizing that the situation in Las Yaguas was a "social problem," Hernández called on the new revolutionary government to take specific actions for blacks and *mulatos* (particularly resource reallocation), but he did so without referring to race. Because while the Afro-Cuban residents repeatedly used racial labels like "black," "race of color," and "people of color" to identify themselves and their neighbors, *Revolución*'s journalists characterized Las Yaguas and residents of other poor neighborhoods by their social position, using labels like "a sick child" or "a father without work" to illustrate the reforms they needed to undergo to become citizens. According to Hernández, residents living in slums were "decent people" who were disposed to the revolution. In Santiago, slum dwellers even sang the "Hymn of Liberation" as the reporters left the barrio. Now, the article argued, it was the new government's task to "integrate these families into citizenship."[50] The emphasis on Las Yaguas residents and other Afro-Cubans as a people in need of aid and on the path to citizenship was underscored by the large photographs of unclothed black children, thin female prostitutes, dilapidated housing, and malnourished men looking for employment that accompanied each article.

Blacks in Las Yaguas, however, understood the actions of the revolutionary government in ways that fit with their historical experience and that interpretation routinely differed from the perspective of the new leadership. Despite their difficult economic situation, residents of the neighborhood sustained the routines of daily life and were proud of the community they had built. Cubans in Las Yaguas recognized the leadership of a popularly supported mayor, shopped at one of the eight grocery stores in the community, and engaged in various neighborly activities. Nearly every home in the neighborhood exhibited a mix of religious traditions, including Catholicism and Santeria, and many maintained an altar to both the family's preferred Afro-Cuban deity and Catholic saint.[51] One Afro-Cuban resident recounted how the move from a tenement building in Havana to a house in Las Yaguas affected his wife. "Eloisa was satisfied. For one thing, she had my attention, and for another, she loved to feel that she was, so to speak, the owner of a house. She felt real proud of that."[52] For this couple, the move to Las Yaguas symbolized upward mobility and better opportunities rather than a slide into delinquency. And while hunger and inaccessibility to resources clearly marked the everyday lives of inhabitants of Las Yaguas, first-person accounts from before 1959 demonstrate that despite its poverty, members of the community participated in the rituals of civilized society that remained invisible to revolutionary leaders.

The Las Yaguas community was historically the target of government initiatives to eliminate slum housing in Havana.[53] A 1944 incident, in which inhabitants took up arms to defend their homes from destruction, left many residents with suspicious, if not hostile, attitudes toward government intervention in community affairs.[54] According to anthropologist Douglas Butterworth, who interviewed residents of the community in 1962, "The reaction of many Las Yaguans [to the revolution] . . . was at first ambivalent. For many, harassed by outsiders for decades, the thought of joining national political groups seemed absurd. Some were barely aware of the political upheaval that culminated in Batista's flight from Cuba."[55] Similarly, a black resident from the community remembered that the "people's feelings were mixed when Fidel entered Havana."[56] Such attitudes suggest that while the Cuban leadership may have considered Las Yaguas an ideal neighborhood to civilize, its inhabitants were less receptive to government interference than the published articles indicate.[57]

Newspaper accounts also differed from oral histories when describing an incident between revolutionary police and the residents of Las Yaguas. Lázaro Benedí, a longtime Afro-Cuban inhabitant of the community, remembers being awakened on the night of 10 February 1959 by revolutionary police and accused of plotting against the government. He told U.S. anthropologists that "even though we supported the Revolution, the people of Las Yaguas were under suspicion immediately . . . we were herded into trucks and taken to police station 13."[58] While at the police station, the black residents were questioned about their involvement in an antirevolutionary plot and charged with marijuana possession. At the end of Benedí's story the situation was resolved and everyone went back to sleep, mostly as a result of his superior leadership skills. However, despite the self-lauding tendencies of the informant, his narrative of unfair incarceration differs from the account printed in the national press.

Revolución called the episode a "public disturbance" in which the police entered the neighborhood in pursuit of certain "delinquents." There was an exchange of blows and four people were injured before the intervention of a revolutionary officer prevented the altercation from escalating.[59] According to one article the conflict ended peacefully with all involved appreciative that the "revolution would soon be able to integrate these families into the [Cuban] citizenry."[60] Yet, when *Revolución* claimed that Afro-Cubans needed to be "integrated" into the nation, it overlooked the fact that blacks and *mulatos* were already citizens! And while Benedí later became an ardent supporter of the new government and grew to appreciate its intervention in Las Yaguas, this initial exchange reveals that the two groups did not always have the same perspective on events. Many Afro-Cubans from the community resisted government proposals to level the slums and refused to believe that the revolutionary leadership planned to build the promised new low-income housing.[61] Previous negative experiences with national governments shaped the hesitation of some Las Yaguas residents as most poor Afro-Cubans distrusted and tried to distance themselves from projects sponsored by white leaders.

In the end, journalists for M 26-7's *Revolución* reinforced ideas of black poverty and constructed, from the onset, a paternalistic relationship between Afro-Cubans and the revolution by highlighting familiar images of blacks and *mulatos* as social discards rather than publishing articles from black social club leaders and intellectuals denouncing racial discrimination in the early months of 1959. The tension between black leaders pushing for access to public spaces in other newspapers and *Revolución*'s editors seeking to reform poor Afro-Cuban neighborhoods was not necessarily an irresolvable conflict. Both goals were essential to achieving equality and constructing a revolutionary society. However, the main distinction lay in how each group imagined Afro-Cubans and their potential for contributing to the nation. M 26-7's earliest gestures positioned blacks and *mulatos* as unfit Cubans, who needed to move beyond blackness and/or poverty ("Not Blacks . . .") to become citizens, whereas Afro-Cuban leaders, fully aware of their citizenship, saw whites and the spaces they controlled as the objects that needed reforming, not themselves.

In the same way that Hernández engaged in an island-wide investigation into poverty and citizenship, Cubans living in Santiago (and reading Havana newspapers like *Revolución* and *Noticias de Hoy*) contributed to debates in the first three months of 1959 about the course of the revolution.

However, the rhetoric surrounding race and revolution in Santiago sometimes departed from the norms of Havana due to the larger population
of Afro-Cubans living in Oriente (the eastern part of the island). The
attitudes published in the local press revealed a substantial divide between
groups that wanted a direct plan of action against racism and those who
would have preferred not to talk about race. *Revolución's* editors recognized the uniqueness of race relations in Oriente explicitly when they
printed a piece by a local intellectual titled "A Social Problem in Santiago
de Cuba." A short editorial note accompanied the article: "Warning: We
know that these problems are not exclusive to Santiago, or Oriente, but
we are using this example because in these places it is super important."
The author, Alcibíades Poveda, argued that blacks and *mulatos* faced a
"racial-social" problem but not one of Cuba's own making. Instead, the
Santiaguero writer introduced an idea that Castro later used frequently
to justify the campaign against discrimination. He argued that the U.S.
intervention in 1898 had frustrated the first revolutionaries' abilities to
overthrow the unjust existing social, economic, and political structures of
the colonial period and left blacks as slaves in the new republic. Therefore,
for him white Cubans were not to blame for lingering racism on the island. Rather, "blacks were victims of a social injustice" that no U.S.-backed
government had been willing to tackle. Poveda concluded by encouraging
the revolutionary government to pay "special attention" to this issue "not
out of generosity . . . but out of an inescapable duty to act."[62]

It is likely that Poveda's editorial found its way to the Havana-based
Revolución because it combined the integration plan that Afro-Cuban
intellectuals and club leaders had demanded when they published articles condemning cases of racial discrimination in early 1959 with more
vague platforms that imagined the revolution's work as a "unifying,"
raceless project. One of the strongest supporters of a revolutionary agenda
that stressed national unity over racially specific programming was the
National Integration Front (Frente de Integración Nacional) in Santiago.
Organized by Andrés Collazo Duany and Efrain Vinent R., this committee promoted national cohesion and reconciliation among the diverse
members of the anti-Batista coalition. Without mention of race, despite
using the word "integration" in their title, the group claimed that "national
integration has the flavor of Cuban sugarcane, the smell of Cuban tobacco . . . and the blue color of our Cuban sky."[63] Santiagueros must have
misinterpreted the mission of the group and mistakenly imagined it as
a campaign for *racial* integration because after the publication of the

initial article introducing the group and inviting others to join its cause, the committee made several public statements clarifying that "national integration is not ethnic integration."[64] Their most direct announcement ran under the polemical headline, "Racial Integration, No; National Integration, Yes." In defense of their position, Collazo and Vinent accused black social clubs of being racist and suggested that *sociedades de color* (societies of color) were unconstitutional and counterrevolutionary. The committee also argued that the "problem of prejudices and its immediate consequence racial discrimination is a product of ignorance and poverty . . . and if we get rid of poverty and ignorance once and for all, these problems will cease to be. . . . The Agrarian Reform will strengthen internal markets and eliminate unemployment . . . the Literacy Campaign will eliminate ignorance. These are the works inspired by the Revolution. These are the works that are in favor of truly new Cuba, one that is happier. Racial or ethnic discrimination is not in the same vein . . . only National Integration!"[65] For this group, there was little room for racial integration campaigns in what they saw as the larger work of unifying the island and pressing forward with the revolution's agenda. Opinions against racial integration were rarely expressed so clearly in the Cuban press in the early months of 1959 as they were in Collazo and Vinent's article; however, various sectors of the population considered racism to be a social problem (linked to poverty) that could be quickly eliminated with revolutionary programs rather than special legislation for Afro-Cubans. Many members of M 26-7 aligned with this position. Moreover, the group's denial of any reason why black societies, which had fought for both racial and social justice since the colonial period, should exist in Cuba and its claim that the color of Cuba was the blue of the sky revealed a desire to disappear blackness under the guise of national unity. Akin, to the gesture suggested by Hernández in the headline "Not Blacks, but Citizens," Santiago's National Integration Front imagined a raceless Cuba where Afro-Cuban demands found little traction.

The leaders of M 26-7 were aware of these debates and likely weighed the pros and cons of each proposal as they negotiated the rapidly changing political environment of early 1959. Added to these deliberations was the prevailing notion that some blacks and *mulatos* supported Batista and rumors that Castro was antiblack.[66] In March 1959, Castro finally addressed Afro-Cuban concerns directly and launched a national campaign aimed at eliminating racial discrimination, especially in relation to employment and education. Revolutionary leaders broke their prior silence on issues of race to broaden their appeal to the *clases populares* (who were predominantly of African descent) and respond to pressures from black and *mulato* intellectuals because their commitment to the late nineteenth-century ideologies of racelessness required them to do so.[67] Yet, the challenges of the 1950s and M 26-7's earlier reluctance to define their racial program limited the state's ability to respond to racial discrimination throughout the two and half years of open dialogue.

March 1959: Steps and Missteps in the Campaign to Eliminate Racial Discrimination

Castro announced the revolution's antidiscrimination campaign during a public rally on Palm Sunday, 22 March 1959. In front of thousands of Cubans, with many more watching on television, he outlined plans for black and white Cubans to work and go to school together. Castro argued that there were two types of discrimination: "One is the type in recreational or cultural centers, and the other, which is much worse and the one we have to fight, is racial discrimination in work centers (applause). And, while the first type limits access to certain clubs, the other is a million times crueler because it limits a person's ability to satisfy their basic needs." The topic of discrimination was not the only theme covered in the nearly six-hour speech, but that day, 22 March, was the first time that Castro directly and publicly answered Afro-Cuban questions about the revolution's stance on race. Castro offered humanitarian reasons for announcing the campaign with a line that later became a headline in *Noticias de Hoy*: "In the colonial period, they killed blacks with work and beatings, now we kill our black brothers with hunger."[68] In doing so, he framed racial discrimination as a problem of access, not attitudes. In fact, according to Castro, the revolution did not need to implement laws or legislative policies against discrimination because by providing jobs to all Cubans the new government would solve the problems raised by black and *mulato* intellectuals. Castro's appeal was both revolutionary and moderate at the same time. It was a departure from M 26-7's previous silence and, given the outcry that followed the announcement, it was clear that many Cubans were stunned, excited, and/or appalled by Castro's statements. But, the 22 March speech also left unanswered questions about the parameters for the revolution's antidiscrimination campaign.

Newspapers across the island spread the news of the state's antidiscrimination policies by reprinting either the entire text or excerpts from

Castro's Sunday speech the next Monday.[69] *Revolución*'s coverage, in particular, highlighted the moments when the crowd cheered at the young leader's words: "The Revolution will end racial discrimination in the workplace and whites and blacks will be able to agree and we will all join to place an end to the hated racial discrimination (applause)."[70] Reproducing the speech in national newspapers meant that even Cubans who did not attend the rally could learn about the new campaign, but by adding the "applause" parentheses throughout the text *Revolución*'s editors simultaneously represented and constructed the rally as a movement with mass support. While Fidel made his announcement in public, his brother, Raúl Castro, proclaimed the same plan in a private meeting at the Afro-Cuban Club Atenas. He declared to a group of blacks and *mulatos* that the revolution would make "social integration a reality." But Raúl admitted that the revolution did not have all the answers and asked members of the club to provide the new government with a "model" for how to eliminate discrimination. In response, the president of Atenas offered the young commander a bill outlining "all of the aspirations of the race," which Raúl promised to pass on to other revolutionary leaders. The actual text of the document is unknown, but it is likely that the elite group of Afro-Cubans were interested in job creation, equal education opportunities, and the ability to join in any ruling coalition. Moreover, the fact that *Surco*, a newspaper in Santiago, reported on this event emphasized the national reach of the antidiscrimination campaign and the watchful eye that Afro-Cuban clubs across the island were paying to the new government's initial attempts to answer black demands.[71]

Cubans responded in a variety of ways to Castro's 22 March speech. Those who imagined the campaign to eliminate racial discrimination as a central component of the revolution's project celebrated Castro's announcement as a bold and just move.[72] Take the editors of the Havana monthly *Nuevos Rumbos*, for example. They described the young leader's words as "touching the hearts of the Cuban people" because "no one before had discussed so genuinely and profoundly this question." According to the newspaper, Cubans who heard the speech were inspired to ask themselves and their neighbors (repeating Castro's words), "Whites, for what? Blacks, for what? All Cubans with equal rights!"[73] During the first half of the twentieth century, Cuban politicians had included pledges to end discrimination in their electoral platforms, but the emerging consensus in circles supporting the new campaign was that Castro's antidiscrimination speech not only broke M 26-7's and prior leaders' silence about racism, but that it also epitomized the hopes and dreams of what a new Cuba could be.[74] Other Cubans feared that the new leadership was encouraging racial mixing in the most intimate areas of life. Opponents asked, "What does Fidel want, that the white girls from the Yacht Club go dancing with the blacks and the *mulatos* from the Club Atenas?"[75] And, Haitian author René Depestre, who was in exile in Havana during the early part of 1959, noted: "I remember that the speech was very well received by the majority of white revolutionaries . . . but all of the bourgeois whites, most of the white petite bourgeoisie (and the comfortable *mulatos*) . . . panicked as if an atomic bomb were coming."[76]

In response to rumors spreading across the island that Castro intended black men to invade elite social clubs and dance with white women, revolutionary leaders and their supporters couched antidiscrimination policies in the language of social class and social justice.[77] They insisted on labor opportunities for Afro-Cubans, a less threatening form of integration for critics worried about social spheres. In a widely broadcast roundtable discussion a few days after his initial speech, Castro soothed critics by emphasizing labor, leaving the social question aside: "And I ask what difference is there between one injustice and another injustice, what difference is there between the *campesino* [farmer] without land, and the *negro* who is not given the opportunity to work; don't they both die equally of hunger, the *negro* who can't work and the *campesino* without land? And why does the revolution have the obligation to resolve other injustices and not the obligation to resolve this one?"[78] Castro also vehemently denied that he was trying to force blacks and whites to dance with each other. He claimed that his speech the previous Sunday sought only to address "the most grievous discrimination of them all, the discrimination keeping blacks from getting a job."[79] Both in this initial response and later in other speeches and rallies, revolutionary leaders established the campaign against racial discrimination as a fight for economic justice. In doing so, they diffused the emotions that racial mixing raised for many Cubans. By subsuming racial tensions into a matter of class, Cuban intellectuals and politicians tried to make whites more sympathetic to Afro-Cubans' plight while allowing blacks to feel that their concerns were a key aspect of revolutionary doctrine.

The national press both respected and challenged state attempts to focus on economic disparities. One reporter for *Revolución* recounted a time when he entered a bank in Santiago to obtain information for a newspaper article. The reporter had asked the bank's administrator if there was any type of racial discrimination occurring at his establishment. The banker had replied, "No, here there is not any racial discrimination. Look, the doorman is of color!" And while the absurdity of having only one black employee in the position of doorman did not seem to bother the banker, the journalist recognized the need to increase the number and types of positions available to people of color. In a subsequent article, he summarized his experiences and reinforced official revolutionary rhetoric by arguing that the racial problem in Cuba was actually a "social issue" because it hindered blacks from obtaining regular employment, buying houses, or saving sufficient money to fund the education of their children.[80] Similarly, Dr. Manuel Rey Araque penned an editorial for *Nuevos Rumbos* titled "Discrimination versus Development," arguing that Cubans who were not persuaded by Castro's humanitarian or social justice rationales for ending racial discrimination should consider the positive impact Afro-Cuban workers and consumers would have on the developing Cuban economy.[81]

As revolutionary leaders framed racial inequality along the parameters of unemployment and inaccessibility to resources, however, racism became a situation the government could resolve, in principle. This gesture appeased critical fears that the new campaign encouraged racial mixing and minimized government intervention in private spaces. Unfortunately, it also allowed individual racial prejudices to continue and foreshadowed the lingering presence of racism in Cuba throughout the twentieth century. As we will see in the next chapter, some Afro-Cubans were aware (and accepted) that the government's choice to focus on employment-based discrimination was strategic; others were less sympathetic.

During the 25 March 1959 televised interview in which Castro cast racism as a social problem, he also asked intellectuals and journalists to educate the Cuban population about the legacy of slavery and the situation of blacks and *mulatos* on the island. He specifically challenged social scientists and newspaper editors to create a public forum where Cubans could discuss the roots of racial discrimination and the best solutions for combating it.[82] Consequently, throughout 1959 the national press published a variety of articles and editorials answering this call. Unlike revolutionary leaders who focused mostly on eliminating discrimination in employment and recreational facilities, academics attempted to tackle the cultural or attitudinal components of racism. Dr. Diego González Martín, a specialist in mental health, published a three-part series in *Noticias de Hoy* titled

"Conditional Responses and Racial Discrimination." González delineated the deep roots of racial prejudice and traced the ways racism became normalized in culture, particularly in the case of Cuba where people were unaware of the negative characteristics they associated with blackness. He concluded that the revolution could eliminate conditional racist responses but only with a comprehensive early education program that would teach white children not to fear darker skin.[83] Another intellectual, Dr. Luis Conte Agüero, concurred with González in a public lecture for a workshop series on the "Roots of Ethnic Prejudices in Cuba." Combining the expertise of sociologist Dr. Elías Entralgo, television reporter Dr. Alfredo Nunez Pascual, Castro friend and later anticommunist foe Conte Agüero, and other intellectuals, the National Library–hosted forum presented historical perspectives and future solutions to racial discrimination in Cuba. Like González, Conte Agüero argued that racism was due to a lack of education and suggested that the revolution use all of the "propaganda at its disposal" to reeducate the population.

The emphasis these scholars placed on the psychological causes and impacts of racism became a significant component of Cuba's racial rhetoric in the 1960s. But the idea of a national education movement as the primary solution to racism did not go unchallenged and other Cubans argued over whether a new antidiscrimination law was needed more urgently than education. One participant in the forum, Dr. R. P. Pastor González, disagreed with Conte Agüero over whether the new government should pass laws against discrimination. Conte Agüero claimed that additional legislation would only divide the population, while Pastor González supported Afro-Cuban intellectuals like Juan René Betancourt who wanted the government to cement its antiracist policies into laws similar to the Urban Reform or the Agrarian Reform decrees.[84] In the end, the new government did not pass a law against racial discrimination, instead choosing to push an antiracist agenda through far-reaching social reforms that provided all Cubans with more access to resources and integrated employment, educational, and recreational facilities. This national movement infiltrated the cultural framework of the revolution as Cubans participated in and responded to the new leader's call to eliminate discrimination. The campaign against racial discrimination invoked the successes and failures of nineteenth-century raceless ideologies and showed Afro-Cubans as active, and thus worthy, contributors to the nation, but it also reinforced certain 1950s stereotypes about blackness.

Cuban history and interpretations of the past played a significant role in this discourse as revolutionary leaders, intellectuals, and citizens struggled to define post-Batista Cuba. The new government mobilized the legacies of Martí and Maceo to construct the revolution as the fulfillment of an interrupted historical legacy, to press for integration, and to demonstrate Afro-Cuban abilities. For example, PSP leader and future director of the National Institute of Agrarian Reform Carlos Rafael Rodríguez argued that the revolution should follow the teachings of the "Apostle" Martí and "go forward with blacks or not go at all."[85] This strategy reveals the continued salience, in 1959, of the two independence heroes as fathers of the nation—so much so that Castro and other revolutionaries sought to portray themselves as the legitimate heirs of these icons. General Maceo, in particular, was a cultural signifier demonstrating the potential for Afro-Cuban inclusion in the nation because his legacy invoked a specific positive memory among Cubans, as we will see below.

The PSP newspaper *Noticias de Hoy* reinforced connections between the wars of independence and the revolution by publishing vivid sketches of black and white cooperation both in 1895 and 1959. Political cartoonist Adigio Benítez (pen name Adigio) had been a member of the Union of Socialist Youth and a longtime contributor to the Communist Party's local and national newspapers before the revolution. After 1959, he continued drawing cartoons that he described in his own words as working to "divulge ideas, principles, slogans, and actions of the Revolution . . . I saw it as a necessity of the revolutionary artist to use this medium of communication and expression to take ideas to the *pueblo*."[86] Adigio's cartoons merged the PSP's long history of advocating for Afro-Cuban rights, especially equal employment and union opportunities for blacks and *mulatos*, into the state's 1959 campaign to eliminate racial discrimination. The series of drawings that he completed to accompany Castro's March announcement visually linked the 1959 fight against discrimination to nineteenth-century ideologies and the successful battle against Batista.

In his first cartoon, published two days after Castro's speech, Adigio drew two men hugging under Martí's often repeated quote that "Cuban is more than white, more than black" (figure 1.4).[87] Two later cartoons applied this century-old raceless rhetoric to the present by showcasing the rewards of black and white soldiers jointly fighting for the nation and against racism. In the first, two men defeat the "snake of racial discrimination" with their combined machetes. Adigio leaves these two figures

Figure 1.4 "Cuban is more than white, more than black." From *Noticias de Hoy* (24 March 1959).

nameless, thereby inviting any willing Cuban to see themselves in and join the struggle against racism (figure 1.5).[88] In the second, Adigio specifically identifies the patriots fighting for "national unity" as the "black hero and the white hero," namely M 26-7 commanders Juan Almeida and Fidel Castro (figure 1.6).[89]

These representations paralleled headlines in *Noticias de Hoy* claiming that "The Unity of Whites and Blacks Is Essential for the Revolution."[90] Unlike the visual representations of Afro-Cubans found in other newspapers described below, Adigio's cartoons portrayed white and black workers as equal partners in building the new nation. Such sensitivity was likely a result of the high numbers of black and *mulato* organizers in the PSP's leadership and, as we will see in the next chapter, fit with pre-1959 Communist Party propaganda. The images in Adigio's cartoons highlight how the PSP used Martí's late nineteenth-century ideology to push

Figure 1.5 "Racial Discrimination." From *Noticias de Hoy* (31 March 1959).

La unidad nacional: el héroe negro y el héroe blanco

Figure 1.6 "The Battle of Uvero." "National unity: The black hero and the white hero." From *Noticias de Hoy* (27 March 1959).

Castro's government toward a 1959 version of raceless nationalism. These sketches invoked Martían language and linked images of present-day black and white collaboration with the multiracial nineteenth-century fighting forces that nearly defeated Spain. In doing so, the cartoons fit with the revolution's emphasis on reclaiming the legacy of the wars of independence and its interrupted raceless national project.

Perhaps one of the most fascinating national discourses about race was a version that blamed the 1898 U.S. intervention for the failure of racial equality in the republic. In "Racial Discrimination," an article printed on the front page of *Revolución*, Carlos Franqui, the newspaper's chief editor and the former director of M 26-7's radio station during the war against Batista, concluded that "the Republic that was born from the intervention was not the Cuba that the mambises fought for." This tactic—telling a "new" version of the Cuban past—had been popular in Communist Party circles before the revolution. But only after 1959 did it gain national prominence as it worked to erase the historical role white Cubans played in limiting black and *mulato* social mobility throughout the twentieth century by blaming racist U.S. statesmen for interfering in Cuban affairs fifty years earlier.[91] To appease critical readers who might object to integration campaigns, the Cuban press frequently introduced potential solutions for resolving racial tensions in a manner that highlighted past success while downplaying previous abuses. The idea that the revolutionary government invoked history to buttress its legitimacy is not new. However, it is significant that the narrative told by Cuban leaders frequently involved a less than accurate rewriting of the past to blame the United States for the existence of racial inequality on the island, not Cubans themselves.

Other journalists also implied that the young revolutionary leaders were the modern-day heirs of Martí and Maceo, sometimes going so far as to say that they were their reincarnations. *Verde Olivo*, the official newspaper of the armed forces celebrated Maceo's birthday by linking the nineteenth-century *mulato* general to Fidel Castro. A piece titled "The Bronze Titan Lives in the Work of the Revolution" connected Maceo's stance against discrimination and push for Cuban unity through integration to the plans announced by M 26-7 leaders.[92] As far away as Santiago, national discourses claimed that Castro was completing Martí's unfinished work by building the dreamt-of nation "without whites or blacks," only Cubans.[93] Castro himself utilized the memory of the nineteenth-century leaders to offset criticism about his new policies: "Here, everyone feels pride in the history of Cuba. . . . Here everyone is honored that Maceo has been considered one of the best generals of all time. And Maceo was black."[94] This 1959 description of Maceo as "black" conflicted with the usual portrayals of the general as *mulato* or the "bronze Titan." In effect, Castro tried to create a new and simplified black constituency by collapsing familiar color divisions like black, *mulato*, or *trigueño* (wheat-colored) into one group, *negro* (black). Moreover, he used the image of a "black" Maceo, similar to Adigio's naming of Commander Almeida as a "black hero," to prove the capabilities of

Afro-Cubans and to prod whites to accept new revolutionary policies based on the legacy of the wars of independence.

Repeated references to late nineteenth-century moments when racial democracy was more of a popular (although still contested) ideology reveal how controversial revolutionary proposals to end discrimination were in 1959. Instead of a campaign directly addressing the ways white Cubans had fought over, and less than enthusiastically supported, the abolition of slavery in the 1860s and 1870s, or how they had feared and felt threatened by Afro-Cuban national participation in the 1910s and 1920s, or the continued discrimination in the 1950s, invoking the legacies of Martí and Maceo transferred revolutionary racial policies into the realm of national pride. Revolutionary leaders and Cuban authors recognized that a large proportion of their audience needed to be persuaded of the value of programs aimed at ending racial discrimination. Consequently, they strategically linked the post-1959 inclusion campaign to more established ideas of Cuban nationalism and well-known Cuban patriots. In a sense, the ideas of Martí and Maceo were more popular in 1959 than they had been in the 1890s because fifty years had given many Cubans the opportunity to construct ambivalent images of what they stood for. Justifying the 1959 antiracist campaign with late nineteenth-century ideologies highlights continuities between pre- and postrevolutionary Cuba. The M 26-7 leaders could only break with certain parts of the island's past. These discourses worked to (re)construct antiracism as a part of Cuba's national—and now revolutionary—identity; however, they also limited the potential for change. Because while the unifying strategies mobilized to create a rhetorical nation for all might have seemed appropriate to fight against Spain in the 1890s, they did not provide all the tools needed to attack deep-seated racism in the twentieth and later twenty-first centuries.

Across the island, Cubans of all sorts supported the campaign to eliminate racial discrimination and participated in debates over new ways of thinking about blackness, whiteness, and *Cubanidad* (Cubanness). Members of the University Students Federation gathered at the University of Havana for an event endorsing the social component of the movement and demanded "equal opportunities for all Cubans in work centers," while the newly formed National Movement for National Orientation and Integration held its first meeting in the capital on 4 April to "begin the work of the revolution" by implementing the antidiscrimination portion of Article 20 of the 1940 Constitution.[95] Other revolutionary officials answered Castro's call to start a national conversation with speeches and appearances of their own. Local television stations featured interviews with PSP leader Salvador García Agüero on one day and the minister of labor, Augusto Martinez Sanchez, the next. Both encouraged audiences to support the campaign and promised that the revolution would eliminate discrimination.[96] In Oriente province, student members of United Civic Youth held a meeting in the central park and announced that for the first time in Santiago's history, the youth were prepared to "defend the revolution and fight against racial discrimination."[97] In each of these cases, Cubans linked antiracism to the 1959 revolution and imagined the new Cuba as both an antiracist and a raceless space. As Jorge Risquet, a representative of the revolutionary army who attended the Santiago event, recorded, "The revolution does not have a color. Rather it is the olive green of the revolutionary army, the pure white of valor, and a combination of all colors because it is a revolution of the people."[98] Artists, filmmakers, and musicians spread ideas about race in the cultural sphere. Well-known Afro-Cuban music groups like the Benítez Sisters popularized songs such as "Angelitos Negros" ("Black Angels"). In the lyrics, the sisters questioned why artists never included black figures in religious murals: "You always paint churches / you paint beautiful angels / but you never remember to / paint a black angel."[99] The influence of the song was such that not only can Cubans still sing its words fifty years later, but *Verde Olivo* printed a cartoon in May 1959 that showed a white workman happily painting one of the two angels on a fountain black.[100] The support that the campaign received from M 26-7 and PSP leaders, student and civic groups, and cultural workers shows how casting racism as an issue of access to resources and as a move toward the raceless dreams of the previous century when Cubans had hoped to eliminate not only racism, but race altogether, was not simply a top-down endeavor. A combination of state and local actors constructed the parameters of antiracism in revolutionary Cuba.

A 2 April 1959 full-page "advertisement" featuring a photograph of a young dark-skinned boy fits into this pattern of including Afro-Cubans while redirecting debates about blackness toward racelessness. The speech line coming from the boy's mouth reads, "I am a child too," and is accompanied by a poem describing his aspirations. The author of the piece expressed how the boy wanted to eat fine sweets, study in a good school, and grow up to be a "useful man." In addition, the writer emphasized how as an adult the child hoped to raise his own children in a place where people seeing his son would remark, "There goes a child," rather than "There goes a *negrito* (little black child)." The poem ends with the question, "Isn't it true that I am asking for little?," indirectly comparing the position of the poor child with the opportunities afforded to white Cubans.[101] By implying that certain obstacles had prevented the child from achieving his dreams before the revolution, the author criticized the injustices facing many blacks in Cuba. Showing the boy's arms raised in supplication, the photograph of the young black child suggested that revolutionary leaders imagined that Afro-Cubans required salvation—and that what they needed to be saved from was their blackness. The piece, which resembles an advertisement due to its size and lack of title or byline, stressed the boy's desire for Cuban society to see him only as a child and not a little *black* child. This distinction was a critical aspect of the emerging racialized discourses in Cuba. Like headlines claiming to turn "Blacks into Citizens" or editorials describing how young black delinquents could be transformed into useful contributors to the revolution, revolutionary racial rhetoric routinely validated Afro-Cubans by emphasizing their need to undergo reform before becoming raceless Cuban citizens.[102]

Cubans reading national newspapers in spring 1959 encountered numerous images celebrating black participation in the anti-Batista struggle and advancing the campaign to eliminate racial discrimination. One of the reasons these visuals were so powerful is because they constructed complex and often contradictory notions of revolutionary blackness. Images of fallen war heroes certainly commemorated black contributions to the revolution, but they also encouraged black loyalty and military sacrifice in a fashion that did not always fit with how Afro-Cuban intellectuals wanted to participate in the new nation. Nearly every edition of *Noticias de Hoy* consisted of a column titled "Victims of Tyranny" featuring stories about Cubans who had suffered during Batista's dictatorship.[103] The section printed a photograph and a brief summary of the experiences of various individuals, the majority of whom had darker complexions to emphasize how black men like Captain René Wilson and Oscar Fernández Padilla were brutally beaten and tortured by Batista's soldiers.[104] In each of these cases, editors highlighted how, despite harsh treatment and tough conditions, soldiers survived and remained dedicated to Castro's vision of a new Cuba.

Similarly, the story of Afro-Cuban martyr Armando Mestre provides a clear example of the discourse built in early 1959 stressing black loyalty and sacrifice to the revolution. Mestre died fighting against Batista's forces in 1958. A year later, *Revolución* announced a fundraiser to build a day care center in the young man's honor. Journalists reported that the facility was near completion and emphasized how Mestre's revolutionary legacy of bravery and valor would live on through the children who attended the center.[105] On 19 April, popular Afro-Cuban commander Juan Almeida, who had also fought with Castro in the Sierra Maestra, laid the first brick of the building's foundation.[106] Both the center itself and the widespread coverage of Almeida's participation in its construction celebrated the role Afro-Cuban soldiers played in overthrowing Batista. Revolutionary leaders highlighted the successes of these prominent blacks and *mulatos* as a means of showing the abilities of people of color to contribute to the nation. Castro invoked similar imagery in a televised response to critics of the campaign to end racial discrimination. He asked Cubans to "remember Mestre, hero of Moncada, and the exceptional behavior of Juan Almeida, one of the best captains . . . in the Battle of Uvero. Thanks to their heroism we had a decisive victory; decisive because if we had lost either of these battles it would have cost us the Revolution."[107] These discourses combated widely accepted ideas that M 26-7 and its supporters were primarily white and middle-class and justified the antidiscrimination campaign based on Afro-Cuban revolutionary sacrifices. Almeida was a frequent subject of, but not a participant in, this rhetoric. While he was often featured in the press, both in photographs and references to his bravery and work for the revolution, newspapers rarely carried articles where he spoke about racism or antiracism. Together these articles, antidiscrimination speeches, and images celebrating late nineteenth-century and 1950s multiracial unity on the battlefield built an antiracist campaign in early 1959 that honored black martyrs and expected black loyalty, while prescribing a certain role for black revolutionaries.

Some political cartoons published shortly after Castro's March 1959 speech, however, were especially contradictory. The drawings discussed below highlight the new government's embrace of Afro-Cubans while simultaneously using familiar colonial tropes to distinguish black caricatures from white ones. From the beginning of the revolution, cartoonists working at *Revolución* utilized political sketches to represent its ideals. The competing positive and negative messages about blackness found in these cartoons foreshadowed the future coexistence of racism and antiracism despite revolutionary reform efforts. Cartoons were, and continue to be, powerful indicators of revolutionary political culture because they reveal the symbols that have meaning in Cuban society. Regardless of their level of literacy, residents on the island who perused the newspapers in 1959 were able to understand the meaning behind political cartoons because cartoonists invoked familiar cultural imagery.

JULITO 26　　　　　　　　　　　　　　　　　　por Chago Armas

Figure 1.7 Julito 26: "A hug, compadre!" From *Revolución* (28 March 1959).

Santiago Armada (pen name Chago Armas) was one of the most prolific revolutionary cartoonists after 1959. Armas had fought with anti-Batista forces in the Sierra Maestra and had published cartoons in Ernesto "Che" Guevara's rebel newspaper *El Cubano Libre* since 1957. As the artistic editor for M 26-7's *Revolución*, he was most well known for creating the character of "Julito 26," a small bearded figure that represented the insurgent army and Fidel Castro. There was a *Julito 26* cartoon in nearly every edition of *Revolución*, visually representing the newspaper's headlines and other important changes happening at the time.[108] On 28 March 1959, just days after Castro's speech, Armas drew *Revolución's* first cartoon about the antidiscrimination campaign (figure 1.7). It featured Julito 26 running to offer a hug to his *compadre* (friend); but instead of embracing the closest person in the cartoon, a white man, he seizes the dark-skinned Afro-Cuban figure to the right.[109]

This imagery visually welcomed Afro-Cubans into the national fold and provided a powerful package for revolutionary leaders' ideas. The cartoon makes clear that revolutionary solidarity embraced black laborers, not the soon-to-be estranged middle class. Armas imagined and drew a new national community that explicitly excluded the white Cubans who had attended segregated private schools and beaches in favor of Afro-Cuban workers. The confused expression on the face of the white man in the cartoon as he stands alone acknowledged the surprise, and potential criticism, some white middle- and upper-class Cubans felt toward the new government and its policies.

Armas attempted to confront and respond to this possibility of white estrangement by drawing black characters standing in large, enthusiastic, and multiracial groups. In one cartoon, three men proclaim in unison, "Everybody knows that when we all come together and unify something

COOPERANDO
—¡No, no!... ¡Ya me estás quitando ese cartel!...

Figure 1.8 "Shoot the White [Bull's-Eye]"; "No, no . . . I'm taking down that sign!" From *Revolución* (31 March 1959).

good always happens."[110] These cartoons imagined a multiracial and unified revolution and argued that rather than causing chaos or disorder, allowing blacks and whites to work side by side would result in celebrations and good fortune. The depictions addressed racial concerns in ways that included Afro-Cubans politically while not offending or scaring whites who might have imagined that their positions would be threatened by accepting blacks as equals. Another *Revolución* cartoonist, Arsenio Bidopia, also engaged with the theme of white estrangement and fears about black retaliation in a cartoon titled "Shoot the White [Bull's-Eye]" (figure 1.8). In this sketch, a black caricature angrily bangs on a counter at a popgun stand and yells his refusal to follow the game's directions: "No, no," he exclaims, "I'm taking down that sign!" By ridiculing the very idea that shooting at a white bull's-eye implied violence against whites, Bidopia illuminated and attempted to diffuse brewing racial tensions over the campaign to eliminate discrimination.[111] Unfortunately, in its efforts to legitimize its policies for reaching out to blacks on the island, the new government reinforced paternalistic attitudes held by many whites toward Afro-Cubans.

The cartoonist Miko further advanced the potential of racial integration in a *Revolución* cartoon titled "Carnival" that begins with two men, one black and one white, running into a costume store (figure 1.9).[112] In the cartoon's second panel, the customers leave the store after exchanging outfits. The black man is now in "white face" and wearing the clothes of his companion, while the white man is in "black face," in the other's outfit. The pleasant expressions on the faces of the two characters (like the smiles worn by the angels in the earlier cartoon) suggest that switching colors (and racial identities) is not only possible but desirable. This sits in stark contrast to a 1953 *Bohemia* cartoon where two men appear uncomfortable, even angry, with the idea that a white baby and a black baby have been mistakenly swapped in a hospital: "Don't you think there's been a mistake?" one asks the other.[113] The new semi-acceptance of racial mixing in 1959 shows the progress between the revolutionary government's racial attitudes and those of previous decades. However, Miko's decision to connect the racial swap to Carnival undermines this message and hints that the celebrated racial unity is not completely "real." Readers who might have found this image appalling due to its implication of racial mixing could interpret the cartoon as a Carnival joke. Readers hoping for a new Cuba, without racial divisions, could imagine the cartoon as a statement against racial discrimination.

Cubans coming across these cartoons most likely felt the excitement and radical reenvisioning of their nation that each one depicted. However, planted within these hopeful images of new, racially inclusive Cuba were seeds of the old, republican past. No doubt revolutionary leaders were aware that ending racial discrimination was an issue that needed to be handled carefully and cartoonists used comedy and humor to try to alleviate doubts about racial integration. But the ways in which cartoonists sketched Afro-Cubans also point to the continued existence of pre-1959 stereotypes about people of color. Because cartoonists had to draw characters in political cartoons in ways that were consistent and familiar to audiences, they frequently sketched black characters with curly hair, ex-

Figure 1.9 "Carnival": "Costume Shop." From *Revolución* (20 April 1959).

cessively dark skin, and thick lips. In contrast, cartoonists illustrated white characters as tall with slim noses and straight hair. Besides the obvious exaggerated and opposite poles seen in these physical characteristics, cartoonists also marked Afro-Cubans as infantile, comical, and animal-like because audiences equated these representations with blackness both before and after 1959. In "Carnival," for example, the white caricature seems particularly manly and mature in comparison to his shorter and

Not Blacks, but Citizens   69

stouter black comrade. Similarly, in both the above "Julito 26" sketches, Armas drew the black caricature in worker's overalls and with exaggerated black skin and features. Doing so allowed the artist to identify the figure as Afro-Cuban but also contributed to existing ideas that blacks were savage and buffoon-like. Ironically, *Revolución* published many of these cartoons on the same page as speeches claiming that Afro-Cubans were worthy citizens who should receive employment and educational opportunities as an important part of the new nation. The distance between antiracist proclamations and cartoons laden with pre-1959 racist imagery is one of the ways that revolutionary racial rhetoric fell short of its goal.

Despite potentially benevolent intentions, the campaign to end racial discrimination reinforced certain negative stereotypes about blackness. But these messages were not delivered all at once and they often contradicted one another. For example, images of Afro-Cuban poverty in urban slums or political cartoons showing black caricatures with infantile and animal-like features perpetuated long-standing beliefs that most blacks possessed undeveloped intellectual capabilities and limited economic resources, and were in need of salvation.[114] But Adigio's PSP advertisements calling black workers to rallies to support the revolution often represented Cuban workers as members of an integrated labor force. It was the very messiness and inconsistent nature of the images created by and presented to Cuban audiences that allowed racism and antiracism to coexist in the early years of the revolution.

Conclusions

Race and discussions about racial discrimination became a central part of revolutionary politics in spring 1959. Public debates about how to improve the situation of Afro-Cubans and educate whites about the injustice of racial prejudice filled the headlines and front pages of national newspapers. Within these conversations the revolutionary government struggled to address the doubts of all Cubans. Using the legacy of the wars of independence, examples of both worthy and needy Afro-Cuban citizens, and humorous cartoons to accomplish its goals, the new government found strategic ways to talk about a historically taboo subject. For the white revolutionary leadership, blacks were valuable citizens when they were workers and revolutionary soldiers who vocally supported the revolution. These Afro-Cubans, often used in revolutionary promotional materials, could then cease to be black and become citizens. Other Afro-Cubans required reform and assimilation before they could be granted citizenship: the small child in the "I am a child too" advertisement distances himself from the diminutive *negrito* in order to become like other children. The new leadership imagined the post-1959 nation as one devoid of racial labels. Yet, in doing so, they also devalued blackness by presenting flawed descriptions of Afro-Cuban communities and requiring assimilation and reform in exchange for full citizenship.

Prominent themes found throughout the new government's revolutionary discourse reveal the important role "raceless" ideologies and memories of the wars of independence played in 1959. Even if the young leadership had wanted to fight against racial prejudice and discrimination directly, they were limited by the responses of their audiences. Bringing Afro-Cubans into the national fold and eliminating centuries of racism were not simple projects that could be resolved with public announcements. Castro and his team were forced to confront a variety of doubts both within the Afro-Cuban community and among white critics. Moreover, they had to fight against attitudes within themselves. Their belief in the same nineteenth-century colorblind ideologies that had been used in 1912 to eliminate the Independent Party of Color, combined with post-1959 anxieties that talking about racism was divisive and therefore had to be done carefully, laid the foundation for an incomplete antiracism campaign. Because while Cuba's newest leaders might have achieved a form of racial integration, lingering attitudes about the appropriate place for Afro-Cubans (as revolutionary soldiers, grateful clients, or marching workers) limited their ability to see blacks and *mulatos* as equal partners in the nation.

2

The Black Citizen of the Future

Afro-Cuban Activists and the 1959 Revolution

On 26 April 1959, one month after Fidel Castro announced the revolution's campaign to eliminate racial discrimination, Afro-Cuban Juan René Betancourt gave a speech exposing the limits of the new government's racial politics. Betancourt explained in a talk titled "The Black: Citizen of the Future" that "the black has to liberate himself . . . a friendly government can help . . . but no government from above, by way of laws or decrees can eliminate something that has its roots in the history and the economy [of a country]." In doing so, he touched on two delicate issues about race in Cuba. First, Betancourt encouraged Afro-Cubans to organize politically (and economically) on their own—an idea considered anti-Cuban since independence and especially dangerous after Cuban forces massacred the all-black Independent Party of Color (Partido Independiente de Color, PIC) in the misnamed "Race War" of 1912. Equally threatening to revolutionary narratives about national integration, however, were Betancourt's doubts that the revolution (or any government) could eradicate racism from above. Betancourt argued that it was impossible for the new—predominantly white—leadership to distance itself from the legacy of Cuba's racism because "no matter how good its intentions," a national government cannot abolish prejudice since it is "impotent in regard to the practices outside of it . . . [and] even within the government's breast . . . the hateful customs will have a space." Betancourt's claim that racism continued in "the [revolutionary] government's breast" was based on the fact that there were fewer blacks in the public administrative and state offices than ever before. Consequently, he called for blacks to lead their own liberation struggles and rejected multiracial organizing, which he claimed Afro-Cubans had tried unsuccessfully in the past.[1]

Betancourt's plan for creating the new black citizen of the future in 1959 was a response to his understanding of earlier Afro-Cuban struggles for equality. His lack of faith in white revolutionary leaders was likely based on his experiences with white officials in previous decades who policed racial boundaries in his hometown of Camaguey, forcing black and white Cubans to walk on separate sides of the central park even as they claimed to support Martí's raceless nationalism. Moreover, by mid-1959 Betancourt was also beginning to distance himself from Castro and the 26th of July Movement (M 26-7) whom he had initially defended in January as not having prejudices against blacks. Betancourt also distanced himself from rival black leaders, including black Liberal, Conservative, and Communist Party members, whom he accused of subsuming antiracism into national politics for their own interests and to the detriment of equality. Other Afro-Cuban leaders disagreed with Betancourt and labeled him racist for his autonomous organizing ideas. Historians Alejandro de la Fuente, Aline Helg, Frank Guridy, Alejandra Bronfman, Melina Pappademos, and Karen Morrison have shown the heterogeneity of black political activism in the Cuban republic.[2] The Afro-Cuban intellectuals working and living in Cuba when the revolution began in 1959, analyzed in this chapter, are no different. Black and *mulato* activists brought a variety of strategies with them into 1959. To understand what happened to these Afro-Cubans during the early years of the revolution, we need to look back at the diverse ways blacks and *mulatos* challenged racism before Castro came to power. Black political activity did not take a time-out in 1959; rather, Afro-Cubans adapted strategies they had used in the Cuban republic (1902–58) to gain access to local resources and combat discrimination in a new revolutionary setting. At times, Afro-Cuban goals and approaches to fighting racism intersected with the 1959 revolution's official antidiscrimination campaign, but other times they did not. The ideas (and people) that revolutionary leaders willingly accepted and those they rejected show the limits of Castro and M 26-7's imagination when it came to fighting racism.

Both before and after 1959, Afro-Cuban activists were the most ardent defenders of racial equality. Sometimes Afro-Cubans collaborated to find the most practical tactics and other times they diverged down class, geographical, or ideological lines. Black and *mulato* leaders often worked toward similar goals, including equal access to state jobs, political representation, leisure spaces, and quality education, because they had faced common experiences of racial exclusion. Pappademos uses the terms "black elites" and "black brokers" to describe Afro-Cuban intellectuals, professionals, politicians, and social club members who traded votes for local political parties for resources during the republic. These Afro-Cubans were elite because of their local leadership status rather than simply due to high-income levels. Therefore, the politics of sugarcane cutters turned labor leaders and those used by established middle-class social club presidents are both significant here because despite their different occupations each acted as a "broker" or liaison between popular constituencies and national politicians.[3] But while these black elites shared certain goals and collaborated in response to major events before 1959, condemning racial violence and lobbying for antidiscrimination amendments at constitutional conventions, Afro-Cuban leaders also diverged over the best strategy for achieving racial equality. Geography, class status, and relationships with various ruling coalitions distinguished black leaders from each other. The debates between Afro-Cubans over how to achieve black social mobility and fight the racial violence and inequality that occurred in the republic foreshadowed the divergent politics of the post-1959 black leaders—and their different levels of inclusion into the revolutionary project. Consequently, the first part of this chapter will examine briefly the major goals and strategies of black activists in republican Cuba before investigating how Afro-Cuban intellectuals adapted and reworked those ideas to fit the 1960s.

By the time 1959 arrived, Afro-Cuban activists interacted with the new government from three primary (physical and/or other ideological) spaces. For one, black elites had been fighting for equality and access to jobs, education, and national appointments from inside Afro-Cuban social clubs throughout the twentieth century. Club presidents across the island collaborated with a variety of different republican administrations before 1959—Batista in particular was a central supporter of these recreational societies and he often provided funds for new buildings and entertainment in exchange for Afro-Cuban support of his politics. The exchanges between black and *mulato* social club leaders and the new revolutionary government reveal one of the areas of dispute between Afro-Cuban activists and M 26-7. As the revolution pushed national integration, it faced the question of what to do with these historic Afro-Cuban social clubs. In the end, despite similar class status and commitments to Martí's raceless ideology, Afro-Cuban societies were too "black" to coexist with the revolution. Revolutionary leaders closed most clubs by 1961 (with the support of some Afro-Cuban club leaders and the opposition of others) because they argued that the societies were no longer needed in a racially integrated Cuba.

Black Cubans also worked within national political parties, using the 1902 universal male suffrage legislation to their advantage by trading votes for resources throughout the first half of the twentieth century. In the 1940s, the Communist Party (known as the Partido Socialista Popular, PSP, after 1944) was one of the foremost leaders in antiracist ideology and popular black and *mulato* labor organizers made sure eliminating employment-based racial discrimination was a key tenet of the party's platform. The PSP newspaper, *Noticias de Hoy*, was one of the few places where Cubans repeatedly encountered positive images of black Cubans and articles attacking racial discrimination both before and after 1959. In some ways, Afro-Cuban communists had more success integrating their programs into the 1959 revolution than black social clubs because black labor leaders and PSP members agreed with the new government that eliminating employment discrimination was the most important aspect of tackling racism on the island. Black communists had another advantage over other black activists—they had an existing national propaganda program that revolutionary leaders quickly appropriated to publicize the new campaign to eliminate discrimination. After 1959, Cuban leaders promoted a number of prominent black PSP members and subsumed their ideas into the revolutionary fold—Nicolás Guillén, Lázaro Peña, and Blas Roca among them.

Lastly, this chapter will examine the politics of Betancourt and other black and *mulato* leaders who advocated for an approach to confronting racism in the 1960s that was not based on ideologies of racelessness. These Afro-Cuban intellectuals built on the history of black activism in Cuba and tried to outline new strategies where they felt old ones had failed. In particular, they opposed a simplistic iconization of Martí and raceless nationalism, inserted forgotten black leaders into the pantheon of Cuban heroes, and promoted *negrismo* (a Cuban version of black consciousness that was popular in the Caribbean in the 1950s and 1960s) as a viable philosophy.[4] Intellectuals like Betancourt, Walterio Carbonell, and Carlos Moore offered a frontal challenge to colonial-era common sense about the inferiority of blackness and superiority of whiteness. Revolutionary leaders had little interest in this type of black radicalism and the new government banned many of the writings about the topic in the early years of the revolution. As a result, some black activists went into exile rather than face continued censorship and/or mandatory labor camp sentences for so-called counterrevolutionary beliefs.

Each of the men and women who participated in the emerging conversation about how to eliminate racial discrimination at the start of 1959 built on an existing continuum of strategies for fighting racial discrimination in the republic. A close look at what happened to black activists after 1959 provides an understanding of why revolutionary leaders incorporated some Afro-Cubans (and their ideas) into the "official" revolutionary fold while others, like Betancourt, were labeled counterrevolutionary and forced into exile. This story of black inclusion and exclusion from revolutionary power demonstrates how interactions between Afro-Cuban leaders and the new government allowed for the coexistence of racism and antiracism in the 1960s Cuba. Unsurprisingly, the black intellectuals who left a written record about racial politics were mostly male and composed only a small percentage of the Afro-Cuban communities who encountered Castro in the early 1960s. Oral histories and interviews with black women, workers, prostitutes, and rural residents show a much more ambivalent attitude toward the new government's racial rhetoric. Later chapters will explore how some of these groups, especially black female filmmakers and artists, adapted and negotiated with M 26-7 to make lasting contributions to the revolutionary movement. Tracing the development of Afro-Cuban activists here and how their approaches diverged and converged with debates occurring in national speeches and newspapers in the 1960s highlights the central role that conversations about race, especially the value of blackness and integration, played in defining Cuba's twentieth-century revolution.

Early Republican Activism: Afro-Cuban Debates over Raceless Nationalism

Afro-Cuban activists in the early republic used a number of strategies to overcome the legacies of slavery and colonialism in Cuba. For one, the recent abolition of slavery in 1886 and the growing field of eugenics that preached the inherently inferior status of people of African descent meant that most black intellectuals writing at the turn of the twentieth century had to engage with what many characterized as the "stain" of slavery. To counteract these portrayals, Afro-Cuban intellectuals called on narratives of General Antonio Maceo fighting for freedom, Juan Gualberto Gómez's organizing the anticolonial movement, and the unifying and raceless dreams of José Martí to remind white Cubans of their contributions to independence and justify their place in the nation. Black and *mulato* activists in the early republic applied a citizen-centric approach that highlighted racial uplift through "regeneration" and encouraged blacks to join Martí's nation "without blacks, or whites, just Cubans." In essence, early intellectuals preached that Cuba's "racial problem" could be solved through assimilation into Cuban culture (coded as white). Additionally, the passage of universal male suffrage in 1902 meant that local and national politicians could not ignore black voters in the early republic. Afro-Cubans used the influence of the black electorate as a way of obtaining resources and showing that people of African descent were worthy of Cuban citizenship.

Independence leader Juan Gualberto Gómez was one of the most prominent Afro-Cubans in the early republic. He was well known across the island for his work organizing black tradesmen in the anticolonial movement despite being in exile from 1880 to 1890.[5] After independence and the passage of universal male suffrage, Gómez joined the Liberal Party and held a variety of public offices. Gómez used these positions to create reciprocal networks between regional black liberals and the capital, assist local black leaders in bids for elected office, and help black clubs get access to national funding. In one case, José Vantour, another *mulato* liberal, wrote to Gómez to request state assistance halting police raids against the Luz de Oriente, a black social club in Santiago. Vantour reached out to the Havana-based Gómez because of his reputation for shortening the gap between specific local organizations and national parties.[6] As an early black activist, however, working within the confines of and contributing to building Cuba's ideology of raceless nationalism, Gómez often structured claims for equality using universal rather than racially specific language.[7]

Gómez also used his influence and connections with elite African Americans to support Afro-Cuban education. Many black activists believed that education was the key to "racial uplift" and the best way to fight the "stain" of slavery. By the early 1900s, the widespread circulation of Booker T. Washington's *Up from Slavery* (translated into Spanish as *De Esclavo á Catedrático* [*From Slave to Professor*]) and recruitment efforts by school leaders inspired Afro-Cubans to send their children to the former slave's Tuskegee Institute in Alabama. Hundreds of Cubans wrote letters admiring Washington's journey and hoped that they too might be able to climb the social ladder and become a professor as the Cuban title of his autobiography encouraged. Tuskegee appealed to the island's black elite who struggled to provide their children with education opportunities since public schools were virtually nonexistent in the early republic and private schools frequently refused admission to blacks. This emphasis on education as a tool of social mobility claimed that Afro-Cubans needed to improve to become better Cuban citizens. The repeated use of words like *mejorar* (improve), *adelantar* (advance), or *regeneración* (regeneration) in the writings of some black elites demonstrated an implicit acceptance of white racial superiority as well as a disdain for the black masses.[8]

Early Afro-Cuban activists emphasized European civilization and culture over African traditions. To them, Africa represented savagery and African-derived religions were an impediment to racial advancement. Even before independence, in 1888, Gómez characterized *cabildo*-sponsored celebrations for Three Kings Day as "raw savagery" and repeatedly tried to discourage membership in African-based ethnic organizations.[9] Later, Afro-Cuban intellectual Ramón Vasconcelos penned a column in *La Prensa* that he directed toward "blacks without primitive behaviors, *mestizos* without shame, and whites with enough common sense [to accept them all]."[10] Encouraging Afro-Cubans to shed so-called primitive characteristics, Vasconcelos concurred with other black elites like Gómez and Conservative Party senator Martín Morúa Delgado who pushed blacks to identify as Cuban rather than with African ethnicities like Congo or Lucumí. Afro-Cuban leaders used this rhetoric of national over racial or ethnic identification strategically, especially when trying to escape the legacy of slavery and appease white fears of black political participation that came with universal suffrage. But early black activists' rejection of all things African (*lo Africano*) and their emphasis on uplift through assimilation into a raceless *Cubanidad* also made them complicit in building a racist national identity that left little room for future possibilities of autonomous black politics or appreciation of black culture.

Although many early republican black thinkers embraced an "uplift" framework, there have always been dissenting (and more radical) visions for how to achieve racial equality. Rafael Serra, a black intellectual from Oriente, published an edited collection, *Para blancos y negros: Ensayos políticos, sociales, y económicos* (*For Whites and Blacks: Political, Social, and Economic Essays*), in 1907. The anthology included essays written both by Serra and other authors on a range of topics such as "Education and Money"—which encouraged Afro-Cubans to improve their situation through individual efforts—and pieces celebrating Booker T. Washington's Tuskegee Institute.[11] Serra's belief in education as a path to social mobility fit with other early activists' approaches to equality. However, he also recognized and lamented the fact that education was not readily available to black Cubans. Unlike white North Americans, whom he praised publicly for their benevolent philanthropy, white Cubans had not provided schools or other resources for Afro-Cuban education after independence.[12] Serra's direct critique of white Cubans and his acceptance that blacks needed to organize on their own to achieve racial equality marked his departure from politics as usual in the early republic and distinguished him as a precursor to an alternative type of black politics.

Para blancos y negros shows the evolution of Serra's thinking from a belief in raceless nationalism to achieve equality to a disillusionment with existing political parties by 1907 and a desire for different approach—namely separate black political movements. Serra attacked white Cubans for relinquishing the ideals of Martí so quickly after independence in 1898. He did not accept the often repeated national narrative that U.S. intervention had frustrated Cuba's plans for racial equality; instead, he criticized white Cubans who either tried to deny the existence of or persuade blacks to be patient about lingering racism in the republic. "The war ended. Spaniards and Cubans hugged . . . and left the blacks almost in the same position as when Spain ruled. But, still they tell us: Suffer just a little now, because what is happening here is the Yankees' fault . . . work for these lynching Yankees [for just a little while], and they will leave, and we will stay."[13] Serra's argument that blacks received little for their efforts in the wars of independence became a central tenet for other black activists in later decades. To be clear, during the late nineteenth and early twentieth centuries Serra self-identified as a Martíano and supported many of Martí's ideas. However, Serra serves as an example of a black thinker who was a precursor to Betancourt's 1950s *negrista* politics because he critiqued white Cubans who abandoned Martí's vision, advocated a more expansive interpretation of the meaning of black inclusion in the republic, and recognized that when multiracial alliances failed blacks needed to organize on their own. As historian Aline Helg has shown, Serra was a forerunner of one of Cuba's most infamous attempts at autonomous black organizing, the PIC.[14]

A year after the publication of *Para blancos y negros*, another group of Afro-Cuban leaders demonstrated their disillusionment with raceless nationalism ideologies and the political status quo in Cuba. Generals Pedro Ivonnet and Evaristo Estenoz formed the PIC to protest black exclusion from national office, demand the rights promised to veterans after the wars of independence, and offer a more progressive agenda for Cuban politics. The PIC enjoyed popular support from Cubans of African descent across the island, especially black veterans who lamented their continued inability to find stable employment or enter certain public spaces despite their contributions to Cuban independence.[15] However, because the PIC's success threatened existing political parties, both black and white Cubans participated in its persecution. Afro-Cuban Conservative Martin Morúa

Delgado introduced a law in Congress in 1910 outlawing race-based political parties and targeting the PIC that was quickly passed. After President José Miguel Gómez banned the PIC and refused to allow the party to participate in the upcoming elections, Ivonnet and Estenoz led a nonviolent (albeit armed) protest against the Morúa Amendment. In response, the Cuban army attacked the PIC (and unaffiliated bystanders), massacring over two thousand Afro-Cubans, many of whom were guilty only of being black. Blacks and *mulatos* from leading Afro-Cuban societies, including Santiago's Club Aponte and Luz de Oriente, wrote President Gómez denouncing the PIC's actions as a threat to "national unity," while other influential Afro-Cuban activists demanded arms to help defeat their unruly black compatriots. These responses to the PIC in 1912 reveal how despite their often repeated claims to be advocates for the entire race, some early Afro-Cuban leaders worked actively to maintain a social order that preserved their individual privileges—black Liberal and Conservative Party members did not want the PIC taking votes away from their party any more than whites did.[16]

The repression of the PIC highlights the ways that radical politics in Cuba have often been conflated with colonial fears about black political takeover. The party's platform actually said little about racism. Instead, it demanded a better and more transparent government, improved working conditions for all Cubans, an eight-hour work day, and free university education. The mission statement stressed the need to eliminate racial prejudice in public office and appointed positions such as the armed forces, diplomatic corps, and civil government. In many ways, the PIC's goals were in line with those of black leaders in the Liberal and Conservative Parties who mobilized a raceless nationalist approach to Cuban politics; however, the PIC's decision to insert and keep "of color" in its name impacted (to its detriment) how other Cubans and national officials saw the organization.[17] As Afro-Cuban communist Serafin Portuondo Linares explained in 1950, by refusing to delete "of color" from their name and banning whites from holding leadership positions (they could join the party, but not lead it), the PIC sealed its fate.[18] Even though the PIC did not have a racist or even an excessively radical political platform, many Cubans found the very idea of blacks organizing for themselves unacceptable and labeled the PIC's actions as racist in the early Cuban republic. Such attitudes continued after 1959 as well.

After 1912, most black and *mulato* activists continued accessing resources through patronage networks with existing political parties while also promoting a particular set of ideas about racial uplift through cultural progress. In 1917, a select group of Afro-Cuban politicians, lawyers, doctors, and other professionals founded the elite Club Atenas in Havana. Nearly all of the club's first members belonged to national political parties and currently held or had held elected offices. As Portuondo Linares has noted, the club was a "collection of black movers and shakers bound across [political] party lines . . . [who] emphasized their refined culture, bourgeois-liberal respectability, and commitment to intellectual pursuits."[19] The founding members of Atenas and other clubs formed around this time opened their own social and recreational societies because they could not join the elite, whites-only Havana Yacht Club or Colony Espanola.[20] These clubs, however, were often as exclusive as white clubs—they had dues and literacy requirements that limited membership by class and distinguished club members from the black masses. Both men's and women's clubs encouraged racial uplift and "improvement" (*mejoramiento*) through education, as seen in the bylaws of the Women's Cultural Association (Associación Cultural Femenina, ACF): "We will tend to the civic and cultural improvement of women." But even as black club leaders created new leisure spaces for Afro-Cubans and used those spaces to collaborate with other black "movers and shakers," they did so in a way that often refused to speak directly about race (the ACF did not mention race or blackness anywhere in their mission statement).[21]

But Afro-Cuban club activists were not silent when racial violence rose up and threatened their hard-earned privilege. A 1930s incident in Trinidad shows some of the ways black and *mulato* social club members challenged racism while working through national legal and political systems. In 1933, young black club members protested the accepted practice of whites walking on one side and blacks on the other of a Trinidadian park. After a *mulato* couple walked on the "white side" of the Parque Cespedes, local elites belonging to white supremacist groups looted black businesses, destroyed homes, and murdered the son of one of the town's leading Afro-Cuban families. As historian Frank Guridy demonstrates, the two white supremacist groups, the ABC Revolutionary Society and the Ku Klux Klan Kubano, were responding to not only the young couple's encroachment on white public space but also black political and social mobility in Trinidad. In this case, Afro-Cuban political activism in the early republic had been so successful that whites felt threatened by the town's upwardly mobile black and *mulato* population. At the time, Afro-Cubans composed 49.1 percent of Trinidad and presented an electoral challenge to the status quo as well. After the overthrow of the Gerardo

Machado's dictatorship in 1933, whites in Trinidad worried that Afro-Cubans would use the new political opening and their voting bloc to gain control of local politics. The park episode stimulated this fear and led the town to erupt in violence. After the incident, Trinidad's black club leaders teamed up with Cuban leftists, including Juan Marinello, and Afro-Cuban communists to form a multiracial antidiscrimination organization, the Committee for the Rights of the Negro, that raised funds to bring a lawsuit against the perpetrators and get reparations for Afro-Cuban property lost in the riots. Committee members wrote letters to national newspapers and pressed the new president into forcing the mayor to resign. Local courts dismissed the case and the rioters were left unpunished. Still, this incident represents an example of the ways Afro-Cuban club leaders actively used local and national patronage networks to fight against racial violence in the republic.[22]

Black activists in the early republic were limited by and contributed to building Cuba's ideology of raceless nationalism. Pappademos sums up the general attitude of Afro-Cubans working within the national party system in the first two decades of the twentieth century by saying, "Given the general climate against black political mobilization, it is unsurprising that when faced with an ultimatum—of either principled death or partnership with the capricious game of patronage—black activists turned to the devil they knew."[23] In many ways, these strategies were successful in that black politicians and social club leaders were able to channel resources including limited jobs, political appointments, and infrastructure into Afro-Cuban hands. However, the focus on cultural progress and education was too often only available to the middle class and frequently relied on denouncing popular Afro-Cuban religions. Lastly, by wedding their progress to national parties, black and *mulato* activists in the early republic remained vulnerable to the political winds of change, as was the case when the Conservative Party, including some of its Afro-Cuban candidates, lost the support of black voters after it helped support the suppression of the PIC in 1912.

1930s–1940s: Afro-Cuban Labor Activism and the Creation of the "New Cuba"

Black activists in the third and fourth decades of the twentieth century participated in national efforts to build a new Cuba. Many of the larger changes facing the island opened doors for Afro-Cubans to continue to fight discrimination and demand resources using new strategies. The Afrocubanismo movement of the 1930s made a space for cultural challenges to Eurocentrism. And, the growth of Cuba's Communist Party (initially founded in 1925 as the Partido Comunista de Cuba, PCC, and later reorganized as the Partido Socialista Popular, PSP) combined labor activism with antiracism for the first time. Many of these ideas influenced the 1959 campaign to eliminate discrimination and set the stage for the interaction between revolutionary leaders and Afro-Cuban intellectuals in the 1960s.

Few Afro-Cuban leaders encouraged autonomous black political organizing in the decades following the PIC massacre. Still, some writers critiqued how the government only applied the Morúa Amendment to censor black political parties. For example, in 1937 journalist Gustavo Urrutia called for a revision to the 1910 Morúa Amendment so that instead of being "a trap for the Afro-Cuban" the legislation would punish predominantly white parties that excluded blacks from their candidate rosters.[24] Urrutia is most well known for his popular column "Ideals of a Race" ("Ideales de una raza") published in *Diario de la Marina* from 1928 to 1931. In the column he promoted black pride and combated racist stereotypes about Cubans of African descent. Urrutia frequently collaborated with *mulato* communist Nicolás Guillén in writing the column. Guillén was one of the key poetic voices in the 1930s Afrocubanismo movement. Realizing the dangers of politically organizing around blackness, Afro-Cuban musicians, artists, and writers like Urrutia and Guillén worked to validate black contributions to Cuba's national culture.[25]

Urrutia defined Cuba's "New Negro" as the "Afro-Cuban . . . who is liberated from the inferiority complex that the slave system put on him" in a 1937 speech titled "Points of View of the New Negro." Urrutia's decision to reclaim the term *afrocubano* which Cubans used in pejorative ways in the early republic to link black culture with savageness and ignorance highlights the decolonizing agenda of some black authors in the 1930s and 1940s.[26] The "New Negro," according to Urrutia, was proud of his African past and saw himself as equal to the white. In contrast to some black elites, who believed that Afro-Cubans, especially working-class blacks, needed "regeneration" and "improvement" before they could be acceptable citizens, Urrutia argued that the black masses were the ones who had won Cuban independence.[27] Urrutia also opposed his compatriots' desire to whiten the country through immigration and claimed that ideologies promoting *mestizaje* (race mixing) only hid white racism. "The

Anglo-American considers his Negrophobia as a natural and legitimate sentiment, and he gives expression to it frankly. For the Spanish Cubans, it is a shameful sentiment which they will not on any account confess to the Negroes. They try to dissolve the black race in a torrent of Aryan blood, and aim at their extinction in every possible indirect way."[28] Urrutia exposed the intentional work ideologies of racelessness did to disappear blackness, even as they claimed to want equality. By encouraging Afro-Cubans to decolonize their minds and reassert their value to the nation, Urrutia and other Afrocubanismo thinkers in the 1930s and 1940s pushed beyond previous black activists who had promoted raceless nationalism in the early republic.

The Communist Party quickly developed a public stance against racial discrimination and became a home for Afro-Cuban leaders fighting for black workers' rights following its founding in 1925. Both under its first name, PCC, and its later one, the PSP, black union leaders combined ideologies about proletariat-based organizing with antiracism to defeat racial, sex, and class-based discrimination. The sheer number of blacks and *mulatos* in the party—by 1934 one communist leader said that one-third of its members were black and by 1944 this estimation was as high as 75 percent—led competing liberal and conservative politicians to nickname the PCC the "Negro Party."[29] These proportions applied not only to the at-large membership but in leadership positions as well. Afro-Cubans such as Lázaro Peña, Jesús Menéndez, Teresa García, Salvador García Agüero, Nicolás Guillén, Severo Aguirre, Serafin Portuondo Linares, Blas Roca Calderio, Elvira Rodriguez, Esperanza Sanchez Mastrapa, and Juan Taquechel led key workers' unions, published communist newspapers, and ran for and held national offices. In the party's first decade, Communist leaders suggested a "separate, but equal" platform where there would be equality among workers but also a separate state in Oriente province for Afro-Cubans. This radical proposition met with strong opposition among the black editors of *Adelante*, who published an article titled "Black Nation? No!" to attack the very anti-Martían idea of an independent black state.[30] The party admitted their mistake, denounced the policy in 1935, and from then on advocated what Alejandro de la Fuente calls "pan-racial/national movement based on class."[31] In doing so, black communists promoted ideologies that combined previous raceless nationalist themes (for example using Martí to push for national unity without races) with labor organizing.

Black communists offered a class-based analysis of racism that divided Cubans not into blacks or whites but into exploiters and exploited. In a 1940 speech, Severo Aguirre affirmed that his party would fight "against all manifestations of imperialist, reactionary, and bourgeoisie discrimination." He continued, "For us men aren't divided into whites and blacks, but imperialists and exploiters on one side and on the other the young worker . . . who is oppressed and exploited. In the workers' *filas* [lines], blacks and whites are brothers, we have the same interests, the same enemies. The same red blood, the same sweat."[32] In tying the fate of Afro-Cubans to labor, black communists argued that Afro-Cubans were discriminated against as blacks *and* as workers. Consequently, in nearly every one of *mulato* Lázaro Peña's speeches as the secretary general of the Cuban Workers' Confederation (Confederación de Trabajadores de Cuba, CTC) he highlighted blacks' exclusion from the job market and pushed for equality in pay, promotion, and training opportunities for all workers.[33] Black labor organizers were largely successful in the early 1940s in obtaining tangible benefits for their constituencies. Jesús Menéndez, leader of the National Federation of Sugar Workers (Federación Nacional Obrera Azucarera, FNOA) in Oriente, collaborated with Peña and the Batista government to increase salaries for canecutters.[34] Similarly, Teresa García, the Afro-Cuban general secretary of the Tobacco Workers' Union Executive Committee, pushed delegates at a special meeting to vote for a 50 percent wage increase. After union members approved the demand, she met with Peña and Labor Minister Dr. Suárez Rivas to negotiate a 25 percent raise for all tobacco stemmers.[35] The successes these communists had in bringing more employment opportunities, higher pay, and more equitable work hours to Afro-Cuban workers facilitated black allegiance to the party and gave the PSP influence in national elections.

Like black Liberal and Conservative Party members, Afro-Cuban communists negotiated with national leaders to access resources for workers. One of the reasons that Peña, Menéndez, and García enjoyed so much success in the 1940s was because Batista had legalized the Communist Party in 1938, permitted it to continue publishing *Noticias de Hoy*, and promised its leaders control of the CTC in exchange for votes in national elections.[36] As a result, not only did Batista win with large working-class support in 1940, but so did the communists. Out of 162 congressional seats, the communists won ten and Afro-Cuban labor leaders were elected to four of those.[37] In 1942, Lázaro Peña, one of the newly elected representatives, and current head of the CTC, publicly thanked Batista for his government's contribution of 57 million pesos from the National Lottery fund (*sorteo*) to build a brand new CTC headquarters in Havana.[38]

Black communists' presence in national politics was especially visible at the convention that preceded the passing of the 1940 Constitution, and they used their large numbers to push for a clearly defined statement against racial discrimination. Arguing that the general nondiscrimination legislation (Article 20) proposed by other parties was ineffective because it failed to define discrimination clearly or enact consequences for violating the law, Afro-Cuban delegate Salvador García Agüero maintained that the new Constitution needed a statement against "any regulation or act that prevents any citizen from gaining access to services and public spaces, to employment and culture in all its aspects, and to the full use of his civic and political functions." Black communists wanted Cuban laws to move beyond vague statements saying that all citizens were equal and delineate the places where blacks and other groups should have access and the sanctions that would be imposed if public spaces failed to meet those requirements. In the end, the convention failed to pass the proposal supported by García Agüero, Roca, and Peña, but black communists succeeded in putting the call for a specific antidiscrimination law and demanding sanctions against its violators on the national agenda.[39] Because of their common belief about the need for a national antidiscrimination law, black communists received substantial support from black social club leaders in the constitutional debates over Article 20. Afro-Cuban labor leaders gave speeches and held events at black societies like the Club Atenas in Havana as both groups pressured Congress to implement the law. This alliance between black communists, social clubs, and Batista (who funded much of this work) was one of the ways that black activists overlapped in the republican period.[40]

Martían versions of raceless nationalism continued to influence Afro-Cuban communists in the 1940s. Black labor leaders argued that racism was a legacy of colonialism and U.S. intervention in Cuba. Blaming "Yankee imperialism" and the Cuban bourgeoisie for racial discrimination, Aguirre, Roca, and Peña frequently claimed that white workers had "always rejected prejudices" and when they had not it was because they had been "deceived" by white leaders.[41] In positioning white owners and bosses (both Cuban and North American) as the root of racism, black communists built the foundation for a national workers' movement that embraced racial equality. White workers were free of the stain of being racist because of their class status and similar experiences as "exploited" laborers. This particular classed version of Martí's "with all and for the good of all" ideology still invoked memories of the wars of independence but added labor leaders to the pantheon of Cuban heroes. For example, Aguirre encouraged communist youth organizations to publicize the ideas of their "teachers, Martí, Maceo, and Mella"—thereby inserting Julio Antonio Mella, a labor leader who died prematurely in the 1930s, to the familiar founding father list.[42]

Communist Party publications also showcased Martían ideologies of racial integration by including images of blacks and whites working together in party promotional materials. The aforementioned Jesús Menéndez, a dark-skinned Afro-Cuban, began his work as a labor organizer at a young age in Oriente. As a youth he had worked on a large plantation but by the early 1940s he had become the leader of one of Cuba's largest unions, the FNOA. Menéndez edited the organization's monthly publication *Azúcar* (*Sugar*) and illustrated the FNOA's (and the larger Communist Party's) complementary goals of national unity and racial integration through the magazine's colorful covers.[43] Nineteenth-century figures haunted Communist Party visuals both before and after 1959. The January 1943 cover explored the century's most significant conflict, World War II, using an image of José Martí. In the sketch, Martí gazes over the shoulder of a worker/soldier as he defeats fascism, symbolized by a Nazi soldier. Every month, the editorial ("Nuestra Portada" ["Our Cover"]) appeared on the inside of the cover; this issue's explained how the FNOA supported Martí's dream of "freedom for all" and encouraged Cubans to "follow in his footsteps and defeat Nazi Germany."[44]

Racial integration, however, had a particular meaning for sugar workers. In Cuba, there had traditionally been two separate sugar unions, one for canecutters, who were predominantly Afro-Cuban, and another for the technicians who processed raw materials in sugar refineries and were often white or lighter-skinned. Menéndez repeatedly argued against separating canecutters (*agrícolos*) from technicians (*industrías*): "The worker who cuts cane is just as much a worker as the one in the mill house . . . discrimination against *agrícolos* is unjust discrimination."[45] *Azúcar* tried to ease implicit racial hostilities between the two groups by portraying them as equals, especially by encouraging FNOA members to support national mobilizations like the 1943 May Day parade and the Fourth National Sugar Workers' Congress. The April 1943 cover of *Azúcar* showed two

Figure 2.1 "Uni-ty." From *Azúcar* (April 1943).

muscular male workers, one black and one white, shaking hands, with the words "May First" hovering over them. The cover artist lettered "Uni-" on the black man's arm and "-dad" on the white worker's arm to spell *unidad* (unity) and highlight how both races were essential to the organization's success. In the drawing, each man wears the uniform representing his position: the black canecutter is dressed in field clothes (long pants, short-sleeved shirt, wide-brimmed hat) and carries a machete, while the white technician is in overalls and holds a sledgehammer (figure 2.1).[46] The cover for the next issue featured the same two men standing arm in arm but this time the black character wears overalls and carries the sledgehammer and the white man has the sun hat and holds the machete.[47]

These *Azúcar* images promoted worker unity by redrawing (and in a sense undoing) the racial and work-related differences that had separated canecutters and technicians since the colonial period. Menéndez's magazine highlighted the constructedness of racial difference in order to dismantle the *agrícolo/industría* dichotomy. This was not easy work. However, Menéndez and other black communists believed it was necessary because racial discrimination both negatively impacted Afro-Cuban lives and impeded the unity that a successful labor movement demanded.[48] As Peña concluded his speech in front of the Ninth Congress of the CTC, "We go forward *companeros*, together as we have been so far, all the parties, all the races, all the industries, the whole Island, together as we have so far, United, United, United! More United than ever under the flag of our glorious CTC!!!!"[49] Peña's emphasis on worker unity and racial integration stemmed from the belief among many black communists that socialism would defeat racial discrimination. In a 1944 interview, Afro-Cuban communist leader Esperanza Sánchez Mastrapa explicitly highlighted this strategy while celebrating the absence of racial and sexual discrimination in the PSP.[50] In doing so, black communists foreshadowed M 26-7's attitude toward racism on the island, namely that discrimination was an employment issue that could be resolved though resource reallocation.

Not all black communists agreed with Martían versions of raceless labor organizing, however. Born in 1882 in Matanzas, Ángel César Pinto Albiol came of age during the final push for Cuban independence in 1895 and developed strong opinions about Cuba's first revolution and its often celebrated founding figure, José Martí. And while Pinto identified himself as a communist, his polemical exchange with two leading members of the Cuban Communist Party, Drs. Juan Marinello and Julio Le Riverend in the late 1940s—whom he called "Martí-Marxists" because of the way they celebrated the nineteenth-century figure—differentiates him from other black communists.[51] In contrast to *mulato* labor leader Blas Roca, who dedicated his 1943 *Los Fundamentos de Socialismo en Cuba* (*The Fundamentals of Socialism in Cuba*) to Marinello, Pinto's public battle with the leading white PSP member illustrates his departure from PSP politics as usual.[52] Pinto argued that instead of being the father of Cuba's "nation for all," Martí's middle-class status and bourgeois positionality limited his ability to be a change agent. According to Pinto, Martí failed to build a truly revolutionary movement in Cuba and/or attack racial privilege. In fact, Pinto claimed that Martí laid the groundwork that reinscribed racial and class categories in the republic. Pinto critiqued Cubans who put Martí on a pedestal as unwilling to see the contradictions in his philosophy, which he summed up with this quote: "Martí cries with the poor, but does not want to get rid of poverty; he loves until delirium his black brother, but doesn't go against the causes that maintain the black's inferior social standing; he wants a Republic 'with all and for all,' but he doesn't want to abolish social classes." For Pinto, Martí and other white revolutionaries fought a revolution that brought tangible benefits, in the form of independence, to members of their social class—middle-class white creoles—while leaving blacks with only vague promises of equality (figure 2.2).[53]

Figure 2.2 The caption for this image, "The black: In the zone of public values," highlights how little worth Cuba placed on black contributions to the nation. The flag-wielding Afro-Cuban in this sketch appears poor and downtrodden despite being a war veteran and committed patriot. The rhetoric of blacks being betrayed or left behind by white Cubans after the 1895 revolution was a popular component of black radical positions. From Ángel Cesar Pinto, *El Dr. Manach y el problema negro* (Havana: Editorial Nuevos Rumbos, 1949).

El negro: En la zona de los valores públicos.

—46—

Pinto's critique of Martí was based on a specifically racialized reading of Marx and foreshadowed similar attacks that some black activists, like Betancourt whom we met at the start of this chapter, would later launch at Fidel Castro, the self-named heir of Cuba's nineteenth-century ideology. Pinto highlighted drawbacks in the vague language of Martí's 1892 Cuban Revolutionary Party (Partido Revolucionario Cubano, PRC) that promised to create a republic where all Cubans could be equal. "We do not find at any point in the document, despite how much effort we put into looking for it, we do not find, I repeat, how or by what supernatural magic [the PRC] was going to change the economic, political, and social situation for blacks after the triumph of the [1895] revolution," he preached.[54] Calling attention to the lack of detail in Martí's plans and labeling the leaders of the PRC as "small bourgeoisie" was a radical position in the 1940s and Pinto's comments drew the ire of leading PSP figures. He claimed that one "revolutionary" magazine refused to publish an article he wrote about the differences between proletariat patriotism and bourgeoisie patriotism because they felt his critiques of Martí were steeped in "hate."[55] Dr. Julio Le Riverend responded at length to Pinto's arguments by encouraging the black radical to "reread Martí more carefully" and defending the nineteenth-century leader as "progressive in his time."[56] Debates like these within the Communist Party signal some of the ways that black activists like Pinto, who had aligned themselves with the PSP because of the liberal and conservative parties' failure to stand against racism and promote black leaders, continued to be frustrated with the terms of the debate about race in Cuba.

Afro-Cuban activists like Pinto were disillusioned with Cuba's contradictory rhetoric celebrating Martí's unrealized "nation for all" while simultaneously ignoring the work of black revolutionaries. If anything, instead of idealizing romantic notions of a unified Cuba built by and for middle-class whites, Pinto drew attention in the 1940s to black leaders who had fought for tangible black rights, like the PIC's leader Evaristo Estenoz, and encouraged Cubans to see them, not Martí, as the most useful examples for bringing change to the island.[57] Pinto died in 1952, never having the opportunity to see and challenge the ways that M 26-7 leaders revived Martí's words to placate racial tensions in the revolutionary period. But if Castro was the heir of Martí's PRC, and its ideology of "with all and for all," Juan René Betancourt, Walterio Carbonell, and Carlos Moore inherited and continued the work Pinto began in the 1940s.

Most black communists and labor leaders endorsed a proletariat-based antiracism in the decades leading up to the 1959 revolution that followed them into the revolutionary period. And while they advocated progressive ideas about reducing work hours, increasing salaries, and promoting racial unity in labor unions, they were also pragmatic. Afro-Cuban communists strategized with national governments and other black elites to bring tangible resources to their constituencies in the 1940s and 1950s. These skills aided them as they tried to regroup from a new round of repressive moves against the PSP in the 1950s. Following the height of the party's success in the early 1940s, the PSP lost control of the CTC to the Auténtico Party and its leading organizer Eusebio Mujal. Mujal did not agree with black labor leaders about the importance of using the union to fight racial discrimination. His determination to rid the CTC of communists and the island's increasing anticommunist stance in the midst of the Cold War meant that black members of the party faced added persecution. Peña was thrown out of the CTC leadership, Menéndez was assassinated in 1948, and other black labor leaders such as Santiago's Juan Taquechel fell out of favor with the national government, lost high-level union positions, and were relieved of their leadership roles in black societies as well. Even Batista, one of the PSP's strongest supporters, outlawed the party and its newspaper *Noticias de Hoy* in 1953 under pressure from the United States and arrested Peña for his supposed cooperation with Castro in attacking the Moncada barracks.[58] Thus, it became very clear to Afro-Cuban communists in the 1950s that many of the advances black workers (and all workers) had made in the early 1940s were defenseless without government support. The 1959 overthrow of Batista and M 26-7's efforts to consolidate the revolution provided the opening black PSP leaders had been waiting for to reclaim their position in national politics, while also eradicating employment-based racial discrimination.

Afro-Cuban Intellectuals in the Revolutionary Era: Social Clubs and National Integration

One of the most visible changes that occurred during the eighteen months after 1959 as a result of the campaign against racial discrimination was the desegregation of private and public spaces. However, as we will see, integration had its consequences—namely the closing of historical Afro-Cuban social clubs where blacks and *mulatos* had fought for decades against racial discrimination. Still, legislation to open private beaches, schools, and social clubs allowed Cubans of color access to recreational facilities that had previously been off limits. Journalists and Cubans writing letters to national newspapers promptly applauded these efforts. An article in the Havana student newspaper *Combate 13 de Marzo* titled "About the Progress in Las Villas" celebrated how revolutionary leaders had eliminated one of Cuba's oldest vices, the *paseos* (walkways).[59] Since colonial times, Cuban youth had engaged in courtship rituals where men and women walked and greeted each other in the park. In rural towns in central Cuba these walkways had always been segregated by race. A young Afro-Cuban interviewee explained how this changed after 1959: "The greatest conquest for the people of Santa Clara after the triumph of the revolution is the change that occurred in the everyday lives of the black race. In Santa Clara, the revolution is working intensely to achieve rapid integration. This began when they eliminated the bands of whites and blacks in the park." For this student and other black and *mulato* youth, the parks had been a tangible representation of racial inequality in the provinces. Their reconstruction served as a clear example of revolutionary progress toward eliminating racism. Nevertheless, the process of integrating the parks was not always simple, and in many cases local officials turned to renovation projects that tore down existing park paths and built new ones to circumvent resistance.[60]

Efforts at rebuilding an integrated Cuba also targeted private beaches. Before 1959, wealthy social clubs controlled the majority of the island's most pristine beaches. These clubs frequently excluded Cubans based on race and class status and therefore Afro-Cubans rarely had access to the sea. Even the most elite black and *mulato* societies seldom owned beach property, leading one candidate for the presidency of Santiago's Club Aponte to include acquiring land along the seashore as a priority in his election platform.[61] As a first step, Castro opened the doors of the exclusive Havana Biltmore beach club to local workers in early 1959 and renamed the facility Cubanacán. According to reports, he purposely erased the North American name of the building and replaced it with an indigenous one to symbolize that the new Workers' Social Club (Círculo Social Obrero) was for the people of Cuba.[62] Other private facilities quickly followed suit as Castro initiated a new government agency, the Office of Organization and Control of the Workers' Social Clubs, to oversee the changes. Revolutionary leaders rechristened the Havana's Officers' Club the Círculo Social de Fuerzas Armadas (Armed Forces Social Club) because "now that the revolution had arrived" black soldiers were accepted into the facility.[63] And, in Santiago, the Siboney Yacht Club, Oriente's version of the prestigious Havana Biltmore, was forced to suspend its membership fees and admit the general public (*los humildes*) to visit the beach in early March 1959. It did so with some reluctance. *Surco*, a Santiago newspaper directed toward *campesinos* (farmers), reported that the yacht club allowed all races and classes of Santiagüeros to swim outside in the "natural resources of the ocean"; however, the institution requested and was granted permission by local officials to turn non-members away from the private pool and bathrooms *inside* the building. Simply put, they refused to provide changing areas for swimmers. *Surco* characterized the decision to "preserve the exclusivity of the Casino Club and the pool . . . a flagrant" mistake.[64] Despite these setbacks, as the year progressed most formerly all-white, private spaces were made public, leading an editor for the Havana daily *La Calle* to author a satirical poem about the transition of Vivien House—a "white oasis" for "Yankees" and "good Cubans, that is white Cubans from good families"—into a social club for predominantly Afro-Cuban sugar workers on the Niquero Central plantation:

Here is Miguel Mariano
throwing out the settee
where before only sat
Miss Mabel and Mr. Fred.

Music, the smell of *guarapo* [sugar-cane liquor]
an organ, maraca, and the *tres* [Cuban instrument]
so that the people from the INRA
and the CTC can dance.

The house of the Magnates
the house of Bridge and tea
now hosts a party
with an organ, a maraca, and a *tres*.

Martí and Maceo's Cuba
rebellious Cuba of Hatuey
Cuba, the only star
on Fidel's shoulders.

What happened to the Company, Juanico?
everything has been turned upside down!

Hurry, bring me the Almanac
so that I can know for sure
if this is a nightmare or a dream
that my eyes see.[65]

The rapid renaming, state takeover, and racial integration of previously white social spaces marked one of the starkest distinctions between pre- and post-1959 Cuba. Revolutionary rhetoric frequently connected white privilege to the island's early twentieth-century past when U.S. owners like Miss Mabel and Mr. Fred regulated the Cuban economy, while constructing post-1959 Cuba as an integrated national space. In the new Cuba, membership in state-sponsored organizations like the National Agrarian Reform Institute (Instituto Nacional de Reforma Agraria, IRNA) or the CTC and attending social events at Workers' Social Clubs was meant to replace racially segregated leisure time. A 1962 *Mujeres* political cartoon epitomized this vision. A black child asks his mother, "What is racial discrimination?" while standing on the beach of a new Workers' Social Club that had been recently integrated by the revolution (figure 2.3).[66]

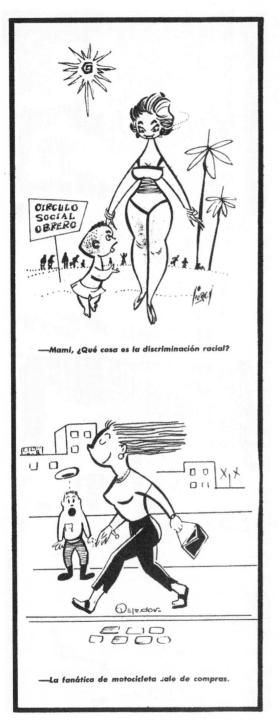

Figure 2.3 (*top cartoon*) Workers' Social Club; "Mommy, what is racial discrimination?" From *Mujeres* (15 October 1962). Courtesy of the Cuban Heritage Collection, University of Miami.

One of the goals of the revolution's integration campaign was to create a world where Afro-Cuban children, like the boy in the cartoon, were unaware of the meaning of discrimination because in the new Cuba they too could patronize previously exclusive beaches. In many ways, Cuba accomplished this goal through an expansive integration campaign in the public sector. However, even as revolutionary leaders opened private schools, beaches, and white social clubs to Afro-Cubans, their vision of a country without races or race-based awareness targeted blacks and the organizations they represented.

One area of discord involved the future of black and *mulato* social clubs. When the new government began to integrate and abolish elite white societies and recreational facilities, it faced the question of what to do with similar organizations for people of African descent. As we have seen, these mutual aid societies had existed since the early republic and served as spaces for middle- and upper-class Afro-Cubans not only to gather and network, but also to push for social and political change. After M 26-7's victory over Batista and the March announcement to eliminate discrimination, Afro-Cuban social club leaders immediately expressed their support for the revolution by writing letters endorsing the execution of Batista's henchmen, hosting fundraisers for the Agrarian Reform, and offering their facilities for revolutionary events.[67] Club presidents used the language of the moment to show their fidelity to the new government, proclaiming, "The Federation of Cuban Societies in Oriente supports completely the Revolutionary Laws, the Agrarian Reform, and the campaign against racial discrimination initiated by Dr. Fidel Castro." And they encouraged their members to send telegrams to Castro congratulating him on his work toward national integration and achieving the nation of "one Cuba, with all, and for the good of all" that Martí prophesized.[68] Black activists' outreach to revolutionary leaders showed their willingness to continue the patronage networks that had facilitated their survival throughout the republican period. In fact, such public declarations of support were reminiscent of black clubs' "homage" to Presidents Gerardo Machado, Carlos Prío, Grau San Martin, and Batista, all of whom were eventually ousted for their corruption and dictator-like rule.[69]

Revolutionary leaders, however, questioned the very public link between black and *mulato* elite societies and the Batista dictatorship. The former president had used lottery money to fund the building of black club meeting houses and beach property in the republic. Afro-Cuban activists had also traded votes to local political parties in exchange for resources and favors from national politicians, especially Batista.[70] Many black clubs, including Havana's Unión Fraternal and Santiago's Club Aponte, ousted old board members and elected new governing bodies after 1959 in an attempt to emphasize their revolutionary orientation to local M 26-7 leaders.[71] Despite these efforts and proclamations of support for Castro and the new government, in March 1959 police captain José A. Valdés Diago reported to the new Department of Associations his suspicion that board members of Havana's Club Atenas had "conspired" with the previous regime.[72] Similarly, members of the Unión Fraternal voted to send a representative to clarify their position on the revolution with the provincial governor and the appointed club "Intervener" after hearing rumors that the state planned to take over organizations such as the Buenavista Social Club, Unión Fraternal, Club Atenas, and Cubanaleco. When a Unión Fraternal member asked why the revolutionary government would be interested in "intervening" in these associations, the club president tellingly replied, "There have been rumors that the majority of the black community supported the old regime; this is a great error that we have the responsibility of rectifying."[73] Continued doubts about black clubs' loyalty to the new government fit with pre-1959 narratives of M 26-7 as mostly white and blacks as Batista supporters; however, the revolutionary leadership's dispute with Afro-Cuban leaders reached beyond concerns about the economic links some black associations had with Batista. Revolutionary officials also saw Afro-Cuban clubs as antithetical to the campaign to eliminate racial discrimination, which was quickly becoming a colorblind national integration movement that did not want to talk about race or blackness.

In 1960s Cuba, revolutionary leaders interpreted eliminating racial discrimination to mean that white clubs had to accept black members and that black clubs had to accept whites. In fact, Cuban newspapers celebrated the integration of black societies as much, if not more so, than white associations, especially in the case of Santiago's Club Aponte. In May 1959, Aponte held a three-day festival to raise money for the Agrarian Reform and elect a Queen of Agriculture. Captain Tony Pérez, a white Cuban representative of the local government, crowned the dark-skinned Ursula Massó Anaya with the honor and used the platform to applaud Aponte's integration efforts. Pérez congratulated the new board (Aponte was one of the societies to replace its pre-1959 administrative board with all new members) for "having the patriotic initiative to organize an event in support of the Revolution's maximum law [the Agrarian Reform] and to carry out the work against racial discrimination, because this society will not be exclusively black [in the future]; it will be Cuban, without distinction of color." He continued by characterizing discrimination as an "economic problem" that the Agrarian Reform would resolve by raising the standard of living for all Cubans. Two Aponte members echoed Pérez's comments. Narciso Morell Simonó described how he was in charge of recruiting new members for the society "without distinction of race" and Octavino Vidal Sánchez, a former M 26-7 combatant and longtime Aponte member, said that the society would continue to "march forward without discrimination." This celebration in the Club Aponte revealed more than Afro-Cuban solidarity with the Agrarian Reform. It also demonstrated black club leaders' attempts to transform previous strategies, such as making partnerships with national governments while fighting for additional opportunities for their own social class, in the post-1959 period. Unfortunately, by publicly performing racial integration to appease the new revolutionary government, some black elites unconsciously conceded that Afro-Cuban societies were as racist as white ones and foreshadowed their demise.[74]

A few months after the Agrarian Reform fundraiser, Aponte publicly enrolled a white member into the institution in another attempt to support the revolution's racial integration campaign. *Surco* published images of the white Captain Fernando Ruíz Bravo flanked by two Afro-Cuban board members as he signed the paperwork to become a *socio* (member) of the organization under the caption "Racial integration in Santiago."[75] Along with the picture, the editor, who reprinted the same photograph in two editions, explained the importance of the occasion: "In this simple ceremony of profound patriotic significance, the municipal commissioner of Santiago de Cuba, Captain Fernando Ruíz Bravo, signs the enrollment forms for the prestigious institution 'Club Aponte,' making real with his actions the principles of racial fraternity predicated by our Apostle José Martí and put into practice by the revolution under the guidance of Dr. Fidel Castro Ruz."[76] Ruíz Bravo's inscription into the Club Aponte linked revolutionary leaders, especially Castro, to nineteenth-century heroes while also framing the campaign against racial discrimination as one where both blacks and whites were at fault and had to evolve to be fully integrated into the new nation.

It is unclear how black club members specifically felt about white members joining their clubs, but Afro-Cuban leaders did disagree over whether race-based clubs remained salient after 1959. Publicly, Santiago's newspapers carried only statements of praise from the Aponte board about integration. As Migdonio Causse, the president of the association, stated, "We think that integration is necessary in our society because we understand that in the union of all Cubans lies the victory of the Revolution." But in addition to support for a raceless national unity, Causse also expressed concern about Aponte's empty treasury and described the organization's need for a loan to fund its daily expenses since the "subsidies particular institutions [had received before] constituted a privilege that have been exiled from our country." Causse's statements illuminate the tension between trying to support the new revolution and missing the funding that the Batista government had provided for routine club operations. Ultimately, leaders of Club Aponte recognized that they had to make certain concessions to ensure the continued existence of the club and its long-held missions of fighting for racial uplift and providing spaces for blacks and *mulatos* to socialize. In describing the ejection of particular club members, Causse explained that the "purification," as he labeled the process in an interview, was a requirement for "marching in rhythm with the honorable and decent programs that today preside over our country."[77]

In some ways, Aponte's very public racial integration program was as much a billboard for the revolution's antidiscrimination campaign as Castro's speeches or the political cartoons in *Revolución*, M 26-7's official newspaper. The debates about integrating white and black clubs revealed the various interpretations of the meaning of antiracism in Cuba. As we saw in the last chapter, Afro-Cubans pushed for a state response to racism at the beginning of 1959 and demanded that the revolution provide equal opportunities for education, employment, and entrance into racially segregated spaces. But it is doubtful that the black and *mulato* activists who published critiques against racism in the national press and pressured Castro to talk about race in the first months of 1959 expected the new government to use the language of antidiscrimination to shut down the very societies where they had formulated their initial demands.

Despite Club Aponte's and other Afro-Cuban societies' efforts to adapt and march forward with the revolution, few clubs survived into the mid-1960s. Government officials routinely sent final closure notices to small and large black and *mulato* clubs saying that they were "incompatible" with the revolution.[78] Ironically, given that it was named for the nineteenth-century patriot so often invoked to represent revolutionary blackness, the Antonio Maceo Society for Instruction and Recreation in Oriente was one of the clubs to receive a letter. So did Havana's illustrious Club Atenas: "The Club Atenas is no longer in compliance with the goals for which it was created . . . and it is now a serious obstacle to the achievement of the objectives of Cuban cordiality, revolutionary integration, and the work of the Revolutionary Government is trying to accomplish."[79] Other associations closed through a slower process of bureaucracy and revolutionary officials shut these clubs down because they did not submit the appropriate paperwork to the new government. Some black club members supported the organizations' dissolution, however. Afro-Cuban journalists Roger Fumero and Manuel Cuéllar Vizcaíno argued that given the revolution's plans to eliminate racial discrimination and create integrated facilities for all Cubans, there was no longer a need for black clubs.[80] Cuéllar Vizcaíno went so far as to call the Unión Fraternal a "racist society" in a speech titled "Racial Discrimination" at the University of Havana.[81] For these Afro-Cuban leaders, revolutionary reforms, especially national integrations programs and opportunities for education and health care, answered the grievances black advocates of raceless nationalism had fought for since the dawn of the republic. The revolution met and exceeded many of the items on these Afro-Cuban leaders' agenda, thereby leading some black and *mulato* leaders to not only accept but also advocate for the closing of the social clubs.

Other Afro-Cuban activists disagreed, insisting that black and *mulato* societies were ideal venues for assisting new government plans to create a racially inclusive Cuba.[82] Juan René Betancourt was the president of a leading Afro-Cuban social club in Camaguey before seizing the presidency of the National Federation of Black Societies (Federación Nacional de Sociedades Negras) in early 1959. The federation initially formed in 1936 to consolidate various black and *mulato* social clubs into a cohesive unit to fight discrimination and gain access to national resources. However, for nearly twenty years leading up to the revolution the institution had floundered, sometimes coalescing and other times dissolving.[83] As its new "revolutionary" president Betancourt hoped to mobilize the organization for a more radical agenda to unify blacks in an independent fight for equality. He also used the federation platform to weigh in on the new government's integration campaign. Betancourt criticized the closure of historically black clubs and the publicized integration of select white spaces as a ploy to deceive Afro-Cubans into believing that they had received advantages from the revolution. After going into exile in 1961, Betancourt argued that instead of taking pride in "being allowed to patronize previously 'all-white' places," black Cubans should ask why the leaders of the revolutionary government were mostly white.[84] As late as 2010, Berta, a middle-class black woman from a small town outside of Havana, still looked back with fondness at the pre-1959 societies and lamented their demise. Comparing photographs of the local black club her parents had attended before the revolution to images of that same club after its "destruction" in the 1960s, she remembered how dismantling the clubs had left a vacuum in her neighborhood.[85] Other Cubans described the integration of the white clubs as *congri*, a Cuban rice dish prepared with a small amount of black beans, to critique a partial integration that added only a few dots of black.[86]

Eventually, the new government eliminated black social clubs along with white ones. This decision failed to acknowledge that black and *mulato* clubs served different purposes than white ones traditionally and arose out of distinct historical experiences. Not dealing openly with the reasons Afro-Cuban clubs might still have been necessary was a missed opportunity for revolutionary leaders to listen to—rather than silence— the voices of black elites. Closing black social clubs alienated some black activists and fueled antigovernment sentiments among Afro-Cubans who disagreed with the condescending nature of the new state that acted as if it knew what was most appropriate for Cubans of color. The closure of the social clubs also robbed blacks and *mulatos* of their most enduring institutional seat of power and made it more difficult for them to participate in the revolutionary process *as blacks* and *mulatos* or access national resources the way they had in the past. Ultimately, it was an ironic twist of fate that despite having similar goals as the leaders of the new government (creating Martí's raceless society), black social clubs still did not fit into the revolution's national integration plan—their institutions were too black to coexist with newly emerging raceless revolutionary organizations. The eradication of black social clubs as a part of M 26-7's antidiscrimination campaign symbolized a major change in the post-1959 period, but one that was still linked to Cuba's racial history portraying autonomous black organizing as anti-Cuban. That black social club leaders had been able to collaborate with republican governments who were also leery of PIC-like organizations but tolerated and worked with Afro-Cuban society leaders because of their similar class and ideological background suggests that the revolutionary government was trying to accomplish a different type of national integration—a plan that fit more closely with the Cuban Communist Party than those of black social club leaders.

Black Communists Meet the Revolution:
May Day Parades and the Consolidation of the
National Racial Integration Campaign

In January 1959, the *mulato* communist and well-known poet Nicolás Guillén returned to Havana after seven years in exile due to Batista's 1950s anticommunist crackdown. His arrival coincided with the reopening of *Noticias de Hoy*. The PSP newspaper saluted the author for returning to fulfill "his responsibility as an artist and a militant in this grand moment that our land is living."[87] Like other Cubans, black communists were excited about the opportunity brought by the 1959 ouster of Batista and immediately expressed their willingness to cooperate with the new leadership. Afro-Cuban labor leaders especially imagined the revolution as an occasion for the antidiscrimination legislation they had advocated in prior decades to finally pass. When asked in a televised interview in May 1959 if the PSP believed that a law against racial discrimination should be added to the Constitution, Blas Roca quickly replied, "Yes . . . it is necessary." The *mulato* leader stressed how Castro's March speech had drawn national attention to racism and brought the "extraordinary prestige" of the revolution's top leader to the fight against inequality. Yet, Roca also acknowledged that the PSP had been working on this issue for years and therefore could support the new government in integrating the population into "one nationality: Cuban." Roca's focus on adding a complementary law to the Constitution instituting sanctions for discrimination, assisting black workers in finding employment, and celebrating a raceless national identity epitomized the positions with which black communists met the 1959 revolution. It is easy to see how these ideas would have fit with the revolutionary racial rhetoric espoused by Castro and other M 26-7 leaders (explored in the previous chapter). However, the tense relationship between M 26-7 and the PSP during the war against Batista meant that Afro-Cuban communists had to prove their loyalty and highlight their potential contributions to the new leadership. In some ways, the party's history of fighting racial inequality and its existing national advertising infrastructure made the PSP an attractive partner to the revolutionary leadership, who were predominantly white, and needed help bringing black workers into the revolutionary fold.[88]

The communists' collaboration with Batista in the late 1930s and early 1940s meant the PSP had little legitimacy in the eyes of many Cubans in the post-1959 era. Both the PSP (with its large numbers of black labor leaders) and the Mujal-led anticommunist CTC had made various pacts with the unpopular dictator that paled in comparison to the heroic acts M 26-7 members had accomplished fighting Batista's tyranny. In fact, the PSP only allied with M 26-7 in 1958. As a result, in early 1959 Communist Party and CTC leaders, including many black labor organizers, used the pages of *Noticias de Hoy* to express their support for the M 26-7-led revolution and carve out a position in the emerging governing coalition.[89] One of the ways that black communists joined the revolution was by building on their strengths as promoters of national integration via racial inclusion. As early as 7 January 1959 Roca demanded a "real and effective policy against racial discrimination" in a column titled "Declarations of the PSP: The Defeat of Tyranny and the Immediate Work [of the Revolution]."[90]

Similarly, after Castro's March speech against discrimination, Salvador García Agüero and Nicolás Guillén joined other intellectuals, some outside of the PSP, in forming the National Integration and Orientation Committee in Havana.[91] The group held conferences debating the causes and consequences of racism, including an event in April 1959 at the Electrical Workers' Union where M 26-7 commander Che Guevara was in attendance. García Agüero, one of the organization's vice presidents, spoke at the meeting and linked racial discrimination to class differences and counterrevolutionary ideas: "Discrimination and prejudice only increase the dominant and exploitative classes. . . . They are used by reactionaries (inside and outside of Cuba) to divide the working class."[92] It was only fitting given black communists' pre-1959 work that they (re)built spaces for conversations about race, but Guevara's appearance at the April meeting also pointed to an emerging collaboration between M 26-7 and black labor leaders. After the first Integration Committee meeting in Havana, Afro-Cuban labor leaders like María Arguelles played a substantial role in opening additional chapters of the new group.[93] Arguelles also penned an article titled "The Progress of the Revolution and the Fight against Racial Discrimination" in *Noticias de Hoy* in August 1959 that commended Castro for publicly condemning racism and providing more opportunities for blacks in the workplace.[94] Arguelles's comments and the overwhelming positive response of other black labor leaders to the revolution paralleled initial reactions by Afro-Cuban social clubs and the larger population in general. In the early months of 1959, Afro-Cuban communists rallied behind Castro and M 26-7 in hopes of obtaining legitimacy for their positions and watched to see what path the new government would take toward achieving racial and class equality.

Black labor leaders agreed with revolutionary officials that employment discrimination was the most significant impediment to racial equality; and from the start of 1959 Roca and Guillén accepted the new government's label that racism was a "social problem." As Guillén stated in *Noticias de Hoy*, ending racial discrimination in applicant selection "is important [work] because how many blacks or *mulatos* do you know who have access to bank offices, train stations, or even a nice shopping store? None."[95] But it was former CTC leader Lázaro Peña who offered the most radical and specific outline for employment reform. In a 29 March article titled "We Should Combat Racial Discrimination Practically from Cuba's Unions," Peña argued that labor unions were the ideal place to fight inequality because they would allow the revolution to reach the nearly half million unemployed Cubans, a large majority of whom were black. Peña planned to add Afro-Cubans to the top of eligible candidate rosters, above white Cubans, who he claimed had been privileged for decades. Recognizing that some might think his plan "created privileges based on color," Peña dismissed this critique, saying, "Putting them [blacks] on the list at the bottom is a fake attempt at justice, just like the gestures of previous regimes."[96] Peña based his plan on the historical role (and success) black labor leaders had in battling employment-based discrimination since the rise of the PSP and the CTC in the 1930s and 1940s. Additionally, in Peña's case, making this argument and encouraging cooperation between labor unions and M 26-7 put him on the path to recover his position as secretary general of the CTC, a post he had lost to Eusebio Mujal during the expulsion of communists from the national labor federation in the late 1940s. The year 1959 offered Peña and other black communists the opportunity to regain their dominance in leading both racial and class equality struggles, with the added benefit of holding national office. Nevertheless, the PSP's confidence that undoing class hierarchies and racial privilege in the workplace would resolve centuries of racial inequality was somewhat shortsighted. This approach still relied on Martían goals of achieving a raceless Cuba; only for PSP leaders the objective was to achieve a country where both blackness and class distinctions were unnecessary (figure 2.4).[97]

Statements praising racial integration continued to be both explicit and implicit in communists' discussions of national integration after 1959. Afro-Cuban communists pressured the revolutionary government to create a new education system where teachers would "reeducate" children about the island's history and struggles against imperialism. One of the

"Un triunfo arrollador y pleno del Ejército Rebelde ha sido el paso decisivo para dar una nueva vigencia a los ideales mambises"

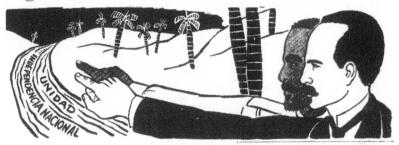

Figure 2.4 *Noticias de Hoy* published this image of José Martí and Antonio Maceo pointing the way toward national independence and unity on the anniversary of the start of the 1895 war. "The Rebel Army's overwhelming and complete victory has been the decisive step giving new life to the mambises' ideals." Linking M 26-7 to nineteenth-century independence heroes, this PSP sketch legitimizes the new government and its rising communist allies as the uncontested heirs of Martí and Maceo. From *Noticias de Hoy* (24 February 1959).

main tenets of this new education formula included instilling in Cubans the ways black and white cultures had evolved together. As Guillén noted in March 1959, "Without the black, Cuba would not exist the way it is today. Cuba with her character, would not exist without the white, it is both the black and the white that makes our people . . . together, combined, joined." The poet continued by identifying Cuba as a *"mestizo* nation" where the "white is *mestizo*, the black is *mestizo*, and the *mestizo* is *mestizo*."[98] Such statements celebrated biological racial mixture as the solution to racism and mirrored the ideologies of other black labor leaders. In a televised interview, Roca claimed that the island only had "one nationality: Cuban," and he questioned some residents' fears that Castro was encouraging racial integration in intimate spaces. "As if whites and blacks had not married each other for years, white men and black women and black men and white women! Where do they think all of the *mulatos* in Cuba today come from? (applause and smiles)" (figure 2.5).[99]

Figure 2.5 This sketch corresponds with Blas Roca's argument that Cuba is already racially integrated: "Where do they think all of the *mulatos* in Cuba today come from?" Roca asked. The image is reminiscent of nineteenth-century *casta* paintings which attempted to catalog the outcome of racial mixture in Latin America. From *Noticias de Hoy* (8 May 1959).

Theories of *mestizaje*, like the ones expressed by Guillén and Roca, were popular in Latin America in the early twentieth century both as a counter to U.S. critiques that former Spanish colonies were unprepared for self-government and as a way to unify diverse populations into a cohesive nation.[100] Their resurgence in Cuba in 1959, however, as an answer to racism left little room for conversations attacking white privilege, movements to revalue blackness as something more than an ingredient in the mixed nation, or recognition that *mestizaje* had frequently occurred through violent sexual conquests as often as consensual unions.

By 1 May 1959, the revolution's racial rhetoric had solidified around the core ideas of promoting unity, national integration, and black patriotism. PSP leaders integrated these ideas into promotions leading up to the first May Day parade in almost ten years (Batista had outlawed the PSP-sponsored event in 1952). Cartoons by Adigio Benítez (pen name Adigio) in *Noticias de Hoy* illustrated three men enthusiastically marching in the parade while carrying a hammer, a gun, and a book.[101] The three props fit with what was quickly becoming the new revolutionary holy trinity of "work, fight, and education."[102] The composition of the drawing, with the black man in the middle holding a rifle, reinforced the important role PSP leaders imagined for the black soldier. Similarly, the entire back cover of *Verde Olivo*'s 27 April edition, the last magazine before the parade, depicted the upcoming rally as the culmination of the revolution's integration campaign by featuring a half-black, half-white male figure with curly dark hair and dark skin on his left side and straight blond hair and fair skin on his right. In the foreground, the artist inserted a small image of a bearded rebel, most likely a representation of Fidel Castro, holding a Cuban flag.[103] Implied in this image was the idea that Cuba's new leaders were mobilizing *mestizo* nationalism and antiracism to neutralize the potentially divisive racial components on the island.

Black labor leaders in Santiago, many resuming posts they had lost in the communist crackdown, used the May Day parade to link their commitment to racial equality to the new government. Afro-Cuban Juan Taquechel returned to his position as leader of the General Federation of Oriente Workers (Federación General de Trabajadores de Oriente, FGTO) in 1959 and his organization led the way in publicizing the May Day parade in Oriente newspapers and posters. National unity was the most frequently discussed goal of the event as "We March United!," the slogan repeated in numerous advertisements, indicated.[104] Other advertisements for the mass mobilization billed the rally as a moment to celebrate the revolution's most popular reforms: announcements promoted workers' injury compensation, an increase in the standard of living, and higher salaries.[105] Still, the influence of Afro-Cuban labor leaders in the eastern city meant race was never absent from discussions about workers' rights. Black members of Santiago's FGTO Pro 1 May Committee, like Taquechel, sponsored promotions that featured Afro-Cuban faces and campaigned against discrimination: "Against Racial Discrimination, Social Justice for All Cubans. That Nobody Misses the Big May 1st Parade"[106] (figure 2.6). This image mobilized all of the themes we have discussed. The Cuban flag flying above the words "Against Racial Discrimination" equated antiracism to Cuban, and now revolutionary, nationalism. The sketches of the two present-day Cuban workers, identifiable

Figure 2.6 "Against Racial Discrimination / Social Justice for All / Cubans / That Nobody Misses the Big May 1st Parade." From *Oriente* (20 April 1959).

by their blue-collar clothing, symbolized the two parts of the island that labor leaders planned to help the revolution unite—the black and the white sectors. And the lower panel featuring Martí and Maceo connected the contemporary movement to late nineteenth-century leaders.

Santiago's May Day celebration fused leading black communists to the new government.[107] The visuals and rhetoric that emerged around the parade highlight the push-pull pattern of talking about race in revolutionary Cuba and the ways some black labor leaders willingly transferred the influence they had with Afro-Cuban workers to the new leadership in exchange for the opportunity to reenter national politics. *Surco* interviewed FGTO's May Day organizers a day prior to the event. Taquechel expressed his hope that workers would attend the event in large numbers because, after ten years of repression, it was time to show their "enthusiasm, and unity, not just for the working class, but for the nation and the rebel forces." Sergio Valiente, a black member of the dockworkers' union, spoke in the same interview and explained how this May Day represented a "Day of Liberation" for the working class after the brutal and bloody tactics of Mujal and Batista.[108]

In public speeches at the 1 May rally, Afro-Cuban communists continued this theme of thanking the new government for allowing them to organize. But, they also encouraged their followers to cooperate with Castro. *Mulata* labor leader Ana Elsa Angulo from the Electric, Gas, and Water Plants' Union told workers "to stay united, defend their liberty, and support all of the Revolutionary government's programs and laws." Likewise, dock organizer Valiente reminded audiences that "we have to maintain our revolution at all costs . . . like Comandante Raúl Castro said a few days ago . . . 'before we [*nuestro pueblo*] lose the Revolution, we would prefer to drown in the sea.'" Black communists allied themselves with revolutionary leaders during the 1 May rally in words and deeds. Of the nine speakers on the podium, including Che Guevara, at least four were Afro-Cubans who spoke in support of and showed enthusiasm for the new government.[109]

Cuba has sponsored many 1 May events since this first one in the post-1959 era; yet, the link between antiracism and workers' rights continues because black leaders in the national PSP and local organizations like the FGTO were among the most ardent advocates for racial equality both before *and* after 1959. A *Noticias de Hoy* 1960 May Day poem chanted, "In one hand grab your gun / and in the other your plow or your hammer / you, the guy with the white arm / and you the guy with the black arm / Workers, farmers, Unite!"[110] Reminiscent of the 1943 *Azúcar* cover that spelled "unity" with half of the word written on a black arm and half on a white, this short refrain highlights the ways black communists inserted their ideas into the new racial politics. Unfortunately, the trade-off for being able to participate was that revolutionary leaders took credit for eliminating discrimination and expected loyalty from Afro-Cuban labor leaders. M 26-7 commander Che Guevara gave the closing remarks for Santiago's 1 May rally: "There are those who say that the blacks are lazy, idle, alcoholics. But, you have to realize that in Cuba we did not finish with slavery until the first day of January. The triumph of the Revolution was when the people of Cuba were truly freed. In all of Cuba slavery is finally finished, I repeat, because this Revolution belongs to the '26th of July.'"[111] Ironically, even as he stood shoulder to shoulder with black labor leaders who had been waging the battle against racial discrimination since the 1930s and 1940s, Guevara claimed antiracism as M 26-7 territory rather than crediting the PSP for its previous antidiscrimination work. The limits of how M 26-7 leaders imagined blackness—as a patron-client relationship—signaled the compromise that black labor leaders would ultimately have to make to remain inside of the revolutionary fold.

By the mid-1960s, some black labor leaders had begun to distance themselves from the Afro-Cuban social clubs that they had collaborated with and worked within during key moments in the republican era (1933 and 1940, for example). Blas Roca updated the original version of his 1943 *Los Fundamentos de Socialismo en Cuba* in 1961 to fit with new revolutionary ideologies attacking Afro-Cuban social clubs. Roca chronicled the history of black clubs to demonstrate how Cubans of color had built separate clubs, thereby adopting the "same principles as the discriminators." Worse still, black clubs were, according to Roca, "the most modest and economically challenged" of all the organizations and by denying whites the opportunity to become members, black elites had "forced the white masses into the arms of the discriminators."[112] This indictment of black societies conflicted with the close working relationship between black club leaders and black communists in the 1940s. It is unclear if and for how long PSP leaders like Guillén, Peña, Roca, and García Agüero maintained private ties with members of Club Atenas or Unión Fraternal. Afro-Cuban communists publicly turned away from their previous allies and their race-based societies around the same time that black clubs came under attack from the revolutionary leadership. As black labor leaders forged new alliances and found common ground with Castro and communist-friendly M 26-7 leaders, their rhetoric shifted from calling for the eradication of discrimination to celebrating the revolution's achievements in this area by the mid-1960s.

Peña continued in his post as the secretary general of the CTC, although by 1965 it had been renamed the CTC-R, with the "R" standing for "Revolucionaria" (Revolutionary) and declaring the organization's new revolutionary credentials. From this position, Peña toned down his more radical calls for black affirmative action and maintained the organization's position that Castro was the embodiment of Martí's dream of raceless equality.[113] Roca also remained a high-ranking figure in the newly communist Cuba (Castro announced the Marxist-Leninist nature of the government in April 1961 after the Bay of Pigs invasion) and the Revolutionary Instructional School Division of the government published multiple editions of *Los Fundamentos de Socialismo en Cuba*. Chapter 7 of Roca's book, "Discrimination and the Blacks," told a celebratory narrative of how Castro eliminated U.S. influence from Cuba and in doing so struck a "terrific blow" to racial discrimination on the island.[114] Likewise, Castro awarded García Agüero a post as Cuba's minister to Guinea in

1961.[115] However, it was *mulato* poet Nicolás Guillén, who wrote articles about race in *Noticias de Hoy*, who most epitomized the accommodation that black labor leaders made with Castro in exchange for political participation in the first half of the 1960s. In "Racism and Revolution," Guillén lamented the existence of segregated public spaces, separate social clubs, and limited employment for Afro-Cubans in the pre-1959 era. "No; Cuba was not comfortable for blacks before the Revolution," he wrote. But, thanks to the revolution, according to Guillén, "blacks and whites march together, in equal conditions, and the next generation will speak of the races as an old and abolished fantasy."[116] Cuban historian and bibliographer Tomás Fernández Robaina has said that Guillén's position revealed his belief that the revolutionary government had taken sufficient steps to eliminate racial discrimination in the early 1960s and that with education and time prejudices would diminish. The poet's celebrations of racial integration and the move toward a raceless *mestizo* nation also fit with his pre-1959 positions.[117]

Black labor leaders wedded their fate to a class-based approach to fighting racism back in the 1930s when they began to join the Communist Party in mass. It was only fitting then that once M 26-7 began moving toward a similar type of revolutionary nationalism and made their alliance with the Soviet Union, black communist leaders would be on board. This collaboration was a mutually beneficial relationship whereby Afro-Cuban communists got to reinsert themselves into national politics and revolutionary leaders were able to diversify their governing coalition by integrating well-known black labor leaders into their ranks. For black leaders, working with Castro was ultimately a complicated compromise because while a few Afro-Cubans like Guillén, Peña, and Roca achieved national prominence in the 1960s through the 1980s (and practically more Cubans of color had jobs than before), only 9 percent of the Central Committee of the new PCC was black or *mulato* in 1965, 7 percent in 1975, and about 12 percent in 1980.[118] Nor did black labor leaders ever achieve the complementary law enacting specific sanctions against discrimination that they had fought for since the 1940 Constitution Convention. Castro disagreed with the idea that Cuba needed a law against discrimination, saying in his March 1959 speech that "we should not have to issue a law to establish a right that is earned by the mere fact of being a human being ... we should not have to have a law against an absurd prejudice."[119] Revolutionary officials maintained this position despite initial arguments from black social club and Afro-Cuban labor leaders. In this way, participation did not automatically result in leadership and influence for black communists, but their history of labor organizing did allow them to survive the 1959 upheaval and negotiate revolutionary politics in a manner that was not always available to other black activists.

Creole Integrationism versus *Negrismo*: Black Activist Challenges to the Revolution

By the early 1960s, some black activists had begun to call for a new type of politics—one that rejected Martí's vision of a raceless Cuba, critiqued white revolutionaries (both the 1895 variety and Castro's 1959 movement), and pursued a national identity that valued African history and culture. I call this 1960s ideology Cuban black consciousness or *negrismo*. While all black activists both before and after 1959 had an awareness of their blackness usually based on experiences of racial exclusion or violence, I am using *negrismo* here to indicate a strategy of fighting racism that was not afraid of naming blackness, that saw a value in recognizing African and black culture, and that was willing to use black-led autonomous political organizing when all else failed. Additional research is needed to see how Cuban black consciousness activists were influenced by and had an impact on other Caribbean notions of black consciousness (Negritude) and U.S. versions of black nationalism. Building on historian Lillian Guerra's examination of black *fidelismo* and revolution *con pachanga*, this section explores direct challenges to Castro and M 26-7's rhetoric of revolutionary raceless nationalism.[120] The two Afro-Cuban intellectuals who wrote the most about these ideas were Walterio Carbonell and Juan René Betancourt. Carbonell had supported Castro's rebellion against Batista since 1953 when M 26-7 attacked the Moncada barracks. A member of the PSP at the time, Carbonell praised the failed uprising, which resulted in him being expelled from the party. Like Pinto, Carbonell was in the process of developing a particular black Marxist ideology (he had read the works of Frantz Fanon, Aimé Césaire, and Richard Wright) that pushed the limits of the communist stance on race and likely contributed to his dismissal from the PSP as well. In 1959, Castro awarded Carbonell the position of ambassador to Tunisia for his support of M 26-7.[121] Similarly, Betancourt benefited from shifting power structures after the ouster of Batista. He gained a new post as president of the National Federation of Black Societies after "revolutionarily seizing" leadership of the organization and even defended Castro from attacks from other intellectuals who called the revolutionary leader prejudiced in January 1959.[122] Unfortunately, this collaboration between revolutionary leaders and Afro-Cuban activists encouraging a type of black consciousness politics was short-lived. As the months passed and Castro announced that the new government planned to tackle racial discrimination from mostly an employment perspective, Carbonell and Betancourt both worried that this choice and M 26-7's obsession with Martí would allow racist attitudes to persist even as the revolution opened beaches and hotels to black Cubans.

Betancourt's politics before 1959 almost guaranteed that he would disagree with the racial rhetoric announced by the revolution. In 1954, Betancourt founded the National Organization for Economic Rehabilitation (Organización Nacional de Rehabilitación Económica, ONRE). The Camagueyan native planned for the ONRE to build an autonomous economic force where blacks would fundraise and use the monies collected to create jobs by opening new businesses and hiring blacks in industries that excluded Afro-Cubans from employment. Nearly ten years before, Betancourt had done similar work in his hometown in a commercial cooperative (La Cooperativa Comercial de Camaguey) that served as a predecessor to the ONRE. Betancourt outlined his goals for an autonomous black economic system in his 1959 book *El Negro: Ciudadano del futuro* (*The Black: Citizen of the Future*) compiled from a series of weekly Sunday talks he had given over the years to the ONRE membership on his *Doctrina Negra* (Black Doctrine).[123] A short while later in 1961, after a car accident caused him to return from Tunisia, Carbonell collected his thoughts about how the revolution should approach race in *Crítica: Cómo surgió la cultura nacional* (*Critique: How to Build a National Culture*).[124] Together, these two texts represent black consciousness challenges to the revolution and offer a glimpse of the type of racial politics that were available but ultimately not incorporated into the revolution.

Interpretations of Cuban history, especially the relationships between slaves and masters, and Afro-Cuban contributions to the island's independence struggles played a large role in some black consciousness thinking after 1959. Like Pinto in the 1940s, Betancourt described Martí's vision of a raceless country as "romantic" and "vague" and agreed that blacks had not obtained any more resources from participating in the war than if they had sat on the sidelines. In *El Negro*, Betancourt argued that while most white Cubans believed that blacks gained emancipation from Cuban independence, this was a false claim because slavery was already on the decline throughout the Americas and Cuban slaves had already organized several nearly successful rebellions against the institution when the wars began. Betancourt also rejected white Cuban claims that the descendants of slaves should be grateful for their freedom by emphasizing that Afro-Cubans remained at the bottom of the social hierarchy in the Cuban republic even after dying "with all and for all."[125] In fact, black intellectuals like Betancourt frequently took the opposite position and argued that it was white Cubans who should be appreciative of blacks for initiating a revolutionary attitude in the loyal colony.

Black consciousness thinkers envisioned an important role for Afro-Cubans as makers of revolution—in both Cuba's past and future—that moved people of African descent from the margins to the center of the island's history. Carbonell argued that back when white Cubans wanted to stay with Spain, blacks wanted revolution: "In reality the 10th of October 1868, the 'beginning' of the anti-slavery revolution, was no more than the coronation of the anti-slavery movement [of slaves] for more than a century. The slave is the protagonist of the history."[126] By positing Afro-Cubans as the ideal revolutionaries and theorizing about the special understanding that slavery and resistance to slavery gave the descendants of Africans, Cuban black consciousness contested emerging ideologies of Che Guevara's *El Hombre Nuevo* (New Man) as the model Cuban citizen. This position also furthered a key tenet of black Marxism proposed in C. L. R. James's *Black Jacobins*, where the spark needed for Marx's revolution shifted from the urban masses, or even rural farmers, to slave plantations and black barrios. Carbonell also disagreed with Marx's position that religion was an "opiate for the masses." Instead, he argued that black Cubans used African religions to interpret the world in a progressive way and to formulate revolutionary concepts.[127] These ideas sat in stark contrast to M 26-7's and Castro efforts to portray blacks and *mulatos* as grateful and loyal soldiers and to position Afro-Cuban religion as folklore, a relic of the neocolonial past.

After 1959, Afro-Cubans mobilizing a black consciousness approach persisted in Pinto's reassessment of Martí's ideologies and warned Castro against following in the footsteps of administrations that had used the nineteenth-century leader's words to dismiss antidiscrimination struggles. Carbonell did not directly challenge Martí's vision for Cuba in his texts, but he denounced the ways that others had misused Martí. He critiqued the "invocation of a republic 'with all and for all'" as having historically only served the ends of the dominant bourgeoisie class. Carbonell disapproved of contemporary revolutionary literary critics who wanted to hold up nineteenth-century white proslavery authors as the epitome of Cuban culture, saying, "The Revolution cannot make national gods out of these men [proslavery authors], these same men who were elevated by the bourgeoisie to the category of national gods."[128] Carbonell would likely have self-identified as a Martíano in 1959, albeit a revisionist Martíano, because his version of Cuban nationalism was anything but raceless. Rather, as we will see, he pushed ahead of Martí and expanded nineteenth-century ideologies to incorporate Afro-Cuban history and culture.

Betancourt took a more direct approach to challenging Martí and M 26-7's invocation of him. Labeling the policies of Martí's PRC as "creole integration," Betancourt compared them to Castro's new "revolutionary integration programs." In *El Negro*, the author outlined four characteristics of these lackluster integration plans: "1) They do not mention the words black or white 2) They do not want blacks to ever organize [alone] 3) They condemn all attempts for blacks to organize 4) They want black societies to admit whites." Betancourt unpacked the problems with creole integration by emphasizing places where the logic of each of these points failed. He explained that blacks had tried to fight racial discrimination as blacks, as communists, as workers, as party members, but all of these efforts had failed, so now they had to try something different—organizing alone. Secondly, according to Betancourt, creole integrationists who refused to talk about black or white, and instead pushed a racially mixed identity—a utopia of sorts—bred inferiority in blacks. This plan, he claimed, would ultimately disappear black or African culture into Spanish or white culture. And lastly, in response to Castro and other revolutionary leaders' push to integrate black social clubs, Betancourt said, "Integrationists want to open the black clubs to whites and according to them this would be a revolutionary move and it would undermine racial prejudice." But, he asked, are "the black clubs the cause of racial prejudice? . . . The answer is no, they are a symptom, Racial Prejudice exited before them." Pointing out that you do not cure a disease by treating its consequences, Betancourt followed up by predicting that if whites were allowed into black social clubs they would quickly take them over because they have more money to fund dances and events, leaving blacks without influence to make choices in their own clubs. Betancourt concluded by labeling proponents of integrationism as cowards: it was clear why "white racists and black cowards like integrationism because it is something that says nothing and does nothing."[129] Black consciousness thinkers like Betancourt were suspicious of Castro's racial rhetoric because it made empty promises based on nineteenth-century ideologies that had already been tried in Cuba and failed. It is important to note that these Afro-Cuban activists were not antiwhite or anti-Cuban. Betancourt made just as harsh judgments of black leaders who whole-heartedly accepted nineteenth-century plans for resolving racism in Cuba as he did of white revolutionaries.

Black Caribbeans formulated black consciousness ideologies around specific recommendations about how to escape the legacy of racism, racial discrimination, and colonization in the region, namely through a revaluing of Africa as a key component in Caribbean nationalisms.[130] Afro-Cuban activists using this approach integrated some of these larger regional notions into their politics and made them specifically Cuban by applying them to local historical events. Carbonell insisted that as the revolution worked to construct a new national culture, it had to tackle the larger question of what national culture to revive. He claimed that he raised this very question at a meeting with Castro and President Osvaldo Dorticós Torrado at the National Library, but was dismissed.[131] For Carbonell and other black consciousness thinkers, it was essential to acknowledge Cuba's African past and insert African history into revolutionary culture: "So far, they have only studied Spain. . . . Without detailed knowledge of the African cultures that influenced us, it is not possible to understand the process which formed our national culture." Carbonell also pushed for the inclusion of modern Afro-Cubans into national history textbooks. For example, he said that black heroes like José Antonio Aponte, the leader of a nineteenth-century slave rebellion, had to be recovered as a part of Cuban history.[132] Similarly, Betancourt criticized Cuban scholars who silenced the "heroic" deeds of PIC leader Estenoz because his acts did not fit into a neat story of raceless progress. Describing Estenoz as a "leader of blacks, a hero, [and] a martyr," Betancourt maintained that he was a better representative of a Cuban revolutionary than Martí or other icons made famous by the "winners" of history.[133]

In addition to theorizing about how to revolutionize Cuban history, culture, and national ideologies, these Afro-Cuban activists also favored autonomous black organizing and black leadership of any movement to combat racism. Betancourt was the most vocal proponent of this idea. Yet, photographs of groups of well-dressed Afro-Cuban men and women attending his Sunday lectures suggest that his was not a lone position. One can only imagine how his audiences reacted to talks promoting an "economic revolution" for blacks or describing Fidel Castro as "well-intentioned" but misguided when it came to talking about race. In one of these public Sunday speeches, titled "The Black: Citizen of the Future," given only a month after Castro's announcement that M 26-7 would fight employment discrimination and desegregate educational centers and beaches, Betancourt offered his advice to Castro and Cuba: "If the government and more specifically Fidel Castro wants to do something for the black, he only has to do the following: First, do not permit discrimination in public administration. Second, create a bureau of propaganda dedicated to spreading the values and merits of the black race in Cuba. Third, do not try in any manner to impose your black friends as leaders of the masses."[134] Betancourt's plan highlighted two of the shared points between black activists before and after 1959: the desire for more Afro-Cubans in upper-level administrative positions and the importance of employment reform. Betancourt was also in accord with Carbonell in the 1960s about the need for a reinterpretation of 1930s Afrocubanismo that would construct a new curriculum to teach all Cubans, especially blacks and *mulatos*, about their history, contributions to the nation, and links to preexisting African civilizations. But Betancourt remained leery of false or incomplete integration, something he criticized in raceless nationalism, especially when revolutionary leaders promoted their "friends" (white and black) without considering if they held hidden negative thoughts about blackness or wanted to eliminate Africa from the national culture.

In another public speech, Betancourt directly announced that the ONRE was a *negrista* organization. Similar to Caribbean ideas of Negritude, Betancourt coined *negrista* to convey that Afro-Cubans "were proud of their race and not ashamed of their race, their traditions, their culture or their ancestors." He stated, "For those of us who want to make blacks into an economic, social, and political force, they [the integrationists] have scornfully called us *negristas*, but now we have reclaimed the name . . . [because] there is no political party, no religious sect, nor institution that is more important than the [*negrista*] Organization. *Compañeros*, to be *negrista* is the call of the day!"[135] This call to be a *negrista*, to organize as blacks and for blacks, was undoubtedly outside of Castro's and some Afro-Cuban activists' notion of "not white, not black, only Cuban." However, it is likely that just as black workers were familiar with Afro-Cuban communist leaders and trusted them to make good on promises about jobs and higher wages, Betancourt and Carbonell also developed a following of individuals who imagined 1959 as a revolutionary moment for race on the island where Cuban black consciousness politics could finally reclaim a space left void since the massacre of the PIC in 1912. This approach certainly resonated with a young Afro-Cuban named Carlos Moore, who arrived in Cuba in the early 1960s after living in exile in the United States during the war against Batista. Moore recounts feeling like he was "playing hide and seek with an invisible enemy" when it came to talking about race upon his return to the island. Only after he met Carbonell, who introduced him to the works of Betancourt, did Moore find language to talk about the limits of the systematic change that was occurring in Cuba.[136] Moore's experience with U.S. black nationalism in New York likely sparked his interest in Caribbean radical traditions and the Cuban manifestations of those ideas.

The 1960s were a moment when the transnational circulation of black consciousness and black nationalism held sway for many people of African descent frustrated with cross-racial alliances. Unfortunately, the philosophical home that Moore and surely some other Afro-Cubans found in the works of Carbonell, Betancourt, and other regional black consciousness thinkers was fleeting because revolutionary leaders moved quickly to dismantle this strand of black activism and its challenge to revolutionary raceless nationalism by labeling it anti-Cuban. M 26-7 leaders banned Betancourt's book *El Negro*, calling it racist. After it became clear that there was no place for autonomous *negrista* organizations like the ONRE in revolutionary Cuba, Betancourt moved his family into exile. However, like other black Cubans who left the island in the 1960s, he did not stay in Miami long. He and his wife quickly moved north in an attempt to escape the racism of both Americans and Cubans in south Florida. Betancourt continued his critique of the revolution's racial policies from exile, publishing in the National Association for the Advancement of Colored People's *Crisis* newspaper and writing another sociology book on racial prejudice that was published in Buenos Aires.[137] Carbonell's work was also banned—historian Lillian Guerra describes how his *Crítica* disappeared from stores and libraries shortly after its publication and was not reprinted until 2005.[138] Revolutionary leaders also placed Carbonell in a type of "internal exile" that included forced labor in Military Units to Aid Production (UMAP) camps and confinement in psychiatric hospitals until his death in 2008. As Carlos Moore wrote in 2009: "Walterio really passed through his own *via crucis*. They ripped him apart, they destroyed him systematically in those mental hospitals. They sent him there for precisely that purpose, of course, to destroy him . . . because Walterio Carbonell had a clear vision of the racial question *within* the Revolution. Walterio was never someone who viewed the black issue *outside* of the revolution. No, *inside* of the revolution. He wanted to reform the Revolution in order to channel it toward a sense of negritude—for whites and for blacks. Because Walterio saw that until whites could understand blackness, they would continue to be prisoners not only of racial prejudices but also of racism as a historical vision."[139]

Revolutionary leaders silenced this form of black activism in the early 1960s by claiming that it was racist and counterrevolutionary in much the same way that Cuban historians silenced the memory of the PIC. In 1959, Betancourt described how the "dominant classes" routinely celebrate the "meek or tame" black leaders by building memorials to them and celebrating their anniversaries in an effort to make other Afro-Cubans believe there is justice in society. In contrast, "For José Antonio Aponte and for Evaristo Estenoz there was no one-hundred-year celebration, no celebratory words, no beautiful epitaphs . . . for them there was first death and then excommunication. They committed the mortal sin of defending the rights of their people . . . of going against the interests and privileges of their exploiters, and for this we can't forgive them. We have to falsify history and misrepresent these 'monsters' to the generations that come so that they don't inspire them. . . . [But] we, the men of ONRE, aware of the history, are in our posts and doing our duty, as the best homage that we are able to give to those that died for us."[140] Afro-Cuban black consciousness thinkers intended to reclaim the revolutionary spirit of blackness and to combine that history with a form of black leadership in economics and culture that would dismantle the racist ideologies of *mestizaje* and raceless nationalism. To do so, they recovered the ghosts of the Cuban past, including the leaders of the Aponte slave rebellion and the PIC, but they also foreshadowed their own future. Because not only did the revolution reject their proposals, after Carbonell's time in Cuba's UMAP labor camps and Betancourt's exile, revolutionary leaders also "excommunicated" them from history. Very few works on the early years of the Cuban revolution or new scholarship about race written on the island or in the United States acknowledge Pinto, Betancourt, or Carbonell.[141]

The official silencing of black consciousness in Cuba in the early 1960s is only one side of the story of black radicalism on the island. Afro-Cuban activists who appropriated a black consciousness approach were not counterrevolutionary, no matter how many times the government tried to label them as such. If anything, their ideologies about the value of blackness and its potential to create a unique national identity in Cuba (and the larger Caribbean) planted the seeds for future Afro-Cuban activists who, unlike Betancourt and Moore, remained on the island and developed unique understandings of a revolution inside of the revolution.

Conclusions

At the start of 1959 more than one idea about how to eliminate racial discrimination existed among black intellectuals because Afro-Cuban activists had used multiple strategies to fight racism since the start of the republic. The ways that black activists supported, negotiated, and, at times, challenged the official racial rhetoric of both the 1895 and 1959 revolutions highlights the role conversations about race played in creating national narratives in Cuba. Not everyone bought into the raceless ideologies that Castro claimed to inherit from José Martí. If anything, it starts to become clear that one of the consequences of the 1959 revolution was to once again prioritize the Martían vision over other competing ones. As the 1960s progressed, Castro's idea of "Not Blacks, but Citizens"—as the *Revolución* headline characterized M 26-7's antidiscrimination campaign—pushed Betancourt's ideas in *El Negro: Ciudadano del Futuro* out of public conversations. These opposing philosophies each had their roots in Cuban history and the racial struggles that preceded them. The multiple sides of these debates did not necessarily divide evenly into whites versus blacks or vice versa. All of the approaches used by black activists influenced predominantly white revolutionary leaders. Even as they rejected the black consciousness position, Castro and other M 26-7 officials had to deal with its call for an attention to black culture—something they addressed by highlighting Afro-Cuban traditions as folklore.[142]

By 1961, the revolutionary government declared the successful elimination of racism and invited African Americans and other people of African descent to the island to see the new "racial paradise." Later chapters will explore that process and the ways that revolutionary leaders characterized racism as counterrevolutionary—both among whites and blacks. The early 1960s marked the beginning of a long silence about talking publicly about race or racism that did not end until the economic crisis of the 1990s brought critiques of racial inequality to the surface with new force. But exploring the continuities in black political thought before and after 1959 suggests the improbability of silencing such a long history of racial protest. Moreover, looking at the ways that other blacks and *mulatos*, especially

AfroCubana artists like filmmaker Sara Gómez, exposed continued racial (and gender) discrimination in the late 1960s after this official closure reminds us that government silences do not mean total silence. Afro-Cuban activists shifted strategies after 1961, but like before 1959, many of their goals remained the same.

3

From Miami to New York and Beyond

Race and Exile in the 1960s

Looking back on the first few years after the Cuban Revolution, Reynaldo Peñalver remembered the March 1959 speech in which Fidel Castro first promised to end racial discrimination on the island. The sixty-eight-year-old Afro-Cuban recalled Castro's announcement that Cubans could dance with whomever they wanted as long as they danced with the revolution. That, he remembered, "was the end of the honeymoon [period] and the true start of the exodus."[1] Peñalver was referring to the 215,000 Cubans who left the country before 1963, choosing to go into political exile in the United States rather than support the nationalist revolution of M 26-7 and its allies.[2] A *Miami Herald* headline from 27 August 1962, "African Savages Take Over Her School: A Cuban Girl Flees in Terror," supports Peñalver's opinion that fears about interracial intimacy had a potent impact on Cuban decisions over whether to stay on the island or leave for Miami, where the majority of the exiles fled. Cuba was still in the process of revolutionary change in the early 1960s when the first wave of exiles left the country. As we have seen, the new leadership announced a campaign to eliminate racial discrimination—especially in relation to employment and education—to broaden their appeal to Afro-Cubans and respond to pressures from black and *mulato* activists in March 1959. One part of this strategy involved Castro and M 26-7 leaders labeling anyone who disagreed with the new government and left the island as "counterrevolutionary." Revolutionary leaders frequently called dissenters "racist" as well—to discredit potential opposition movements and to bind Afro-Cubans to the new state. This strategy opened a brief dialogue about racism among Cubans both on the island and in exile that coincided with the radicalization of the revolution and led many Afro-Cubans, like Peñalver, to believe that exiled counterrevolutionaries were indeed racist.

Scholars explaining the multiple reasons Cubans went into exile often overlook the role of discourses about racial privilege.[3] Instead, they argue that the post-1959 government enacted a series of changes that fundamentally altered society to the point where many chose to leave even before the revolution's official commitment to a Marxist-Leninist ideology in

April 1961.[4] This scholarship highlights measures such as the Agrarian Reform and limits placed on rental prices, as well as early tensions with the United States, as factors distancing many middle- and upper-class Cubans from the new government. While each of these issues contributed to some Cubans' electing for exile, the explanation remains incomplete without an exploration of how anxieties over racial integration—especially fears about interracial intimacy—shaped the ways Cubans understood the 1959 revolution. Alejandro de la Fuente argues that some whites "found it hard to adjust" to increased integration in the workplace, but had few opportunities to protest because the "revolution had created the dominant 'ideal'" that "revolutionaries could not be racists."[5] Exploring how various actors established this ideal by connecting racism and counterrevolution, this chapter illuminates how and why Cubans interpreted and redeployed revolutionary racialized discourses both on the island and in exile. In so doing, it also uncovers the contradictions and consensuses that often disappear in the imposed "gulf" between Havana and the south Florida city of Miami, where over half of the island's dissenters fled.[6]

Popular conceptions of Cubans living in Havana and Miami in the 1960s often resort to extremes: groups were either "revolutionary" or "counterrevolutionary," "racist" or "antiracist." Yet these labels emerged from a particular historical moment and evolved from interactions among Cubans on the island and those in the diaspora, structured as well by each group's relationship with the United States. Looking transnationally at these processes reveals how Cuban communities in Havana and Miami developed in opposition to each other in the decade after 1959. I build on Jesse Hoffnung-Garskof's insight that postrevolutionary Cubans inhabited a "transnational social field" and explore how doing so influenced Cuban discussions about race, both on the island and in exile.[7] Cuban newspapers show that during the Cold War, just as U.S. officials had to manage race relations with an "international audience in mind," leaders in Cuba had to translate the social and political aspirations of the revolution for a transnational audience.[8] Revolutionary discourses focused on winning allies throughout the world and undermining critiques from exiles to offset the threat of armed intervention from the United States. Cuban politicians had invoked the term "racist" to discredit opposition groups long before 1959, especially during election years in the first half of the twentieth century.[9] However, these accusations rarely resulted in more than the loss of a particular voting bloc. When revolutionary leaders reappropriated this discourse as a component of post-1959 politics, they explicitly connected lingering racial prejudices to opposition groups to garner support from Afro-Cubans and prevent potential accusations that the new leadership, who were largely white, were themselves racists.

Meanwhile, exiles in Florida were influenced by civil rights and Cold War debates even as they carried particular memories of the island and its racial system with them. They disagreed with revolutionary leaders' identifications of them as counterrevolutionary or racist. Rather, exiles accused Castro of inventing racial tensions and claimed that their fight was not with blacks or *mulatos*, but with "reds" or communist Cubans. Across the ninety miles between Havana and Miami, these debates and memories shifted to fit a new racial and national landscape as exiles deployed the rhetoric of anticommunism in their discursive struggle for Cuba and against Castro. The use of anticommunist rhetoric to contain black civil rights claims was not new, having limited African American demands since just after World War II.[10] In many respects, being in Miami allowed exiles to create a new, heterotopic space—the Cuba they felt the revolution was destroying—in which certain privileged values could be reconstructed under the aegis of a government friendly to their cause.

Blacks and *mulatos* on the island were aware of the transnational power struggles occurring between island and exile leaderships and responded, though historians tend to neglect both that understanding and the reactions it generated. Most of the literature on this period fails to explain why so few people of color went into exile during the first years of the revolution. Historian María Cristina García briefly suggests that the new leadership explicitly called critics who chose to leave "racists" to prevent a similar migration on the part of Afro-Cubans.[11] Labeling counterrevolutionary and exile groups racist not only kept some blacks and *mulatos* from leaving the island, however; it also provided people of African descent with a language for attacking lingering prejudicial practices in Cuba. Furthermore, establishing the link between counterrevolution and inequality in the early 1960s helped to build the enduring international reputation of the Cuban revolutionary government as antiracist.

Miami Cubans, however, failed to acknowledge the persistence of racism in new exile communities in the same way that the Castro government failed to acknowledge the fact that some Cubans of color disagreed with the revolution and left the island as a part of the first wave of exiles. Familiar silences about racial tensions occurring among Cuban leaders in Miami and Havana demonstrate that popular narratives imaging the revolution as antiracist and the exile community as racist remain constructed and false. In fact, some Afro-Cubans did go into exile, but their reasons for leaving were less about disagreeing with the transformations occurring in Cuba and more about pursuing additional economic opportunities for their families or avoiding the ongoing civil war that continued as anti-Batista groups fought for power in the early part of 1960. Oral histories with Afro-Cuban exiles reveal that many of them struggled to avoid racism and create a safe space for their families in Cuba and south Florida—a situation that led some exiles of color to relocate to northern U.S. cities instead of Miami.[12] A closer look at these debates over race and racism in the Cuban diaspora uncovers the ways in which revolutionary politics were shaped by global historical processes, while simultaneously shaping the specific, local experiences of Cubans such as Reynaldo Peñalver.

Racial Anxieties and Resistance to Integration

After the revolutionary government announced plans to eliminate racial discrimination, a rumor spread across the island that the new leaders intended for black men to invade elite social clubs and dance with white women.[13] Previous chapters have discussed how revolutionary leaders responded to these critiques with a national campaign to clarify their intentions. Official state rhetoric sought to incorporate Afro-Cubans into the revolutionary project, while also offsetting fears of change by emphasizing plans to fulfill the legacy of José Martí and Antonio Maceo and provide Afro-Cubans with equal educational and employment opportunities. Despite the government's cautious language in the campaign against racial discrimination, some Cubans were threatened by the opening of private beaches, the integration of social clubs, and the nationalization of private schools. They criticized government integration projects vehemently. Political scientist Richard R. Fagen correctly emphasizes the importance of the perceived difference between the new and the old Cuba in the decision of some exiles to leave the island: "The rejection of this new way of life was profoundly affected by prior experiences and by allegiance to the old way of life. *Comparisons* as well as *deprivations* are at the core of exile perceptions and motivations."[14] Revolutionary policies promoting racial integration in schools and the workplace contributed to the view held by some middle- and upper-class Cubans that the emerging "new" Cuba was radically different from the "old," ultimately pushing some Cubans into exile.

Prior to 1959, most well-to-do Cubans sent their children to private institutions for schooling. These establishments educated predominantly white middle- and upper-middle-class students, with the exception of the occasional wealthy *mulato*. Opening educational centers to all Cubans was one of the radical social changes implemented by the new government and began in 1959. Marta, a white woman from the well-to-do neighborhood of Vedado, was then a seventh-grader at Ruston Academy, an elite institution for the children of North American and Cuban businessmen, diplomats, and government officials.[15] As she remembered, "I spent my whole life in this American school and there was not a single black or *mulato*." After the revolution, she recounted, children began to be absent from school, more and more every day. She quickly learned that this meant that their families had left for the United States in opposition to the revolution. The Ministry of Education nationalized Ruston in 1961, along with other private educational facilities, and began to require all Cuban children to go to public schools. Marta said that for her this was like leaving a "cocoon." "My old school was beautiful. I only had twenty-four students in my class. But, after, in my new school, there were seventy students in one class and lots of blacks and *mulatos*. Many people left Cuba because they did not want to mix with them." Despite rumors that Castro was communist and anti-Catholic, Marta's parents remained on the island because of their support of the revolution and their reluctance to begin a new life in the United States. She admits that it was difficult to interact with people from different racial and social backgrounds in her new school and in other revolutionary organizations.[16] Her story underscores the anxieties experienced by some Cubans during the early years of the revolution. Racial integration in the realm of education was problematic for Cubans such as Marta's peers. This discomfort led a number of Cubans to criticize the opportunities provided to people of African descent and ultimately leave the island.

Occasionally the rejection of antiracist revolutionary policies was framed in timeworn discourses of excessive black male sexuality versus white female chastity. These suggested that white women were helpless victims incapable of defending themselves, while marking black men as sexually aggressive opportunists, eager to exploit revolutionary plans to offer Afro-Cubans new employment and education opportunities. One example of this hysteria was reflected in concerns expressed by the opposition group Revolutionary Unity (Unidad Revolucionario, UR). According to UR, white women refused to be treated by black doctors because of their concerns that Afro-Cuban men would "use revolutionary doctrine as an excuse for becoming more and more familiar and bold."[17] The fears that Castro wanted black and white Cubans to dance together emphasized precisely these anxieties over white women coming into certain types of intimate social contact with black men.

As a result of these changes, some white middle- and upper-class Cubans accused Afro-Cubans of becoming *insoportable* (unbearable, intolerable). The repetition of expressions such as "You give them [blacks] a finger and they will take the hand, and the arm too!" highlights the common perception among critics that blacks and *mulatos* had become overtly disrespectful and demanding of equal rights since the announcement to eliminate racial discrimination.[18] These characterizations of people of color epitomize one set of adverse reactions to shifting social boundaries that previously had kept blacks and *mulatos* in subservient roles. In response to the excitement expressed by some working-class Afro-Cubans toward the revolution, some whites felt threatened and expressed the need to keep blacks and *mulatos* in their place. An account from an eight-year-old boy highlights this development. He describes being "tortured" by an insolent black maid, Caridad, shortly after the revolution: "She loved Fidel, and she listened to the radio in the kitchen all day long. . . . Caridad used to taunt me when my parents weren't around. 'Pretty soon you're going to lose all this.' 'Pretty soon you'll be sweeping my floor.' 'Pretty soon I'll be seeing you at your fancy beach club, and you'll be cleaning out the trash cans while I swim.' With menacing smirks, she threatened that if I ever told my parents about her taunts, she would put a curse on me."[19] His characterization of Caridad as insolent and labeling of her enthusiasm as torture reveal white and upper-class alarm and distaste for perceived changes in the social hierarchy.

Regardless of whether Cubans of African descent carried themselves with additional sentiments of entitlement, it is significant that others thought they did and reacted to these perceptions. A 1961 *Mujeres* cartoon poked fun at this situation and further linked Cubans who left the island to U.S. racist organizations like the Ku Klux Klan (KKK). The cartoon depicts a smiling Afro-Cuban woman eagerly waving goodbye to a wealthy white woman bound for Miami who has "KKK" printed on her dress, pearls, and a fancy hairdo. The cartoon's caption states: "Goodbye, Marquise! Cleaning floors is hard, but you will get used to it"[20] (figure 3.1). Often before quantifiable changes in the social hierarchy took place, middle- and upper-class Cubans interpreted the new regime's vocal

Figure 3.1 (*bottom cartoon*) "Goodbye, Marquise! Cleaning floors is hard, but you will get used to it." From *Mujeres* (15 December 1961). Courtesy of the Cuban Heritage Collection, University of Miami.

solicitation of Afro-Cuban support along with positive reactions by blacks and *mulatos* as indicators that the island was changing rapidly in ways that made them uncomfortable. It was distressing to certain Cubans to imagine working-class people of color moving into their neighborhoods or assuming positions of authority in the new government because that was an inversion of accepted social norms and an uncommon occurrence in the old Cuba.

Blacks and *mulatos* were aware of these characterizations and frequently linked them with counterrevolutionary attitudes. Afro-Cuban assistant secretary of labor José Causse described how "*señoras*, influenced by the counterrevolution," resisted the idea of paying a minimum wage to maids and other domestic workers, many of whom were of color.[21] Exiled Haitian intellectual René Depestre noted that many respectable women left Cuba because "after Castro's speech, the blacks had become disrespectful."[22] People of color like Causse and Depestre publicly attributed specific events such as being fired from a job or learning that an employer's family was headed to the United States to white women's—not white men's—fear of Afro-Cubans. By mirroring the oppositional rhetoric that gendered countergovernment fears to focus on white female experiences, these responses by some people of color perpetuated the pattern of pitting black men against white women.

Other Cubans disguised their discomfort with new racial policies with humor and sarcasm. Depestre arrived in Havana a few days before Castro's March 1959 antidiscrimination speech in flight from Haitian dictator François Duvalier's regime. After hearing Castro's passionate denouncement of racism, Depestre quickly became a visible supporter of the new Cuban government and published his observations about the island's social reforms and white reactions to those changes with the state-run Casa de las Américas press. Depestre described in "Letter to Cuba" (1966), and oral histories confirm, that it was common for an interracial couple walking through Havana to hear comments labeling them as a pair that *quema petróleo* (burned oil) in reference to the white partner's preference for the black or petroleum-colored skin of an Afro-Cuban. A white man who dated a black woman was referred to as an *administrador de ferretería* (owner of a hardware store) to suggest the low-class or unrefined nature of dating a person of color or as someone who *anda con alambres* (walks with wires) to highlight the curly or kinky texture of a black or *mulato* woman's hair.[23] Relationships between Cubans of different skin colors were not new; they had been common and controversial long before 1959. Yet, the continued prevalence of jokes insulting interracial pairs by linking blackness to poverty and pejorative stereotypes about skin color and hair type in the mid-1960s reveal lingering anxieties about race mixing that some feared would increase due to revolutionary programs eliminating barriers to formerly white-only spaces. Critics worried that the campaign to eliminate racial discrimination would infiltrate private realms such as dating and commonly said that a black Cuban could be a revolutionary "brother" but not a "brother-in-law," through interracial marriage.[24] More than before, some whites saw "disrespectful" black and *mulato* workers and mixed-race partnerships as tangible symbols of a new and revolutionary Cuba, an island that was quickly changing into a different and uncomfortable place.

The following account from Depestre relating to early 1960s Havana offers another example of concerns about black uplift. Depestre remembered how it was common to hear stories such as: "A white woman sees a black man walking perilously on the rooftop of a ten-story building and thinks to herself, that *negrito* [little black] is going to fall and kill himself, when the man plummets to the ground. But, to her amazement, before his feet can touch the street, he straightens up and continues walking as if he had just finished jumping over a short wall. The woman observing the scene exclaims 'the Virgin of Charity protects you extremely well!' The man replies, 'No, it is not that, it's just that after the triumph of the Revolution, Fidel gave us [blacks] wings.'"[25] The anecdote implies that Afro-Cuban social mobility was undeserved by first suggesting that black men had supernatural powers before equating black advances with Castro's patronage. And while humor was one way that critics called attention to the revolution's investment in blacks, other popular sayings were more direct. Afro-Cuban author Pedro Pérez Sarduy remembers that the slogan "Neither black nor red" was a familiar aspect of "white backlash against major redistributive measures in the early revolutionary years."[26] By calling for a "neither a black nor red" Cuba, critics linked blackness to communism and expressed fear of a new government led by members of either group. Ultimately, all of these types of opposition, both implicit and explicit, shaped the way revolutionary supporters, in particular Afro-Cubans, imagined dissenters and countergovernment groups.

During the early 1960s, most Cubans were aware of the various popular anecdotes spread by critics and supporters alike. Revolutionary leaders responded to rumors that their plans encouraged interracial mixing by saying that they would not force Cubans to dance with anyone, "as long as they danced with the revolution."[27] In a televised interview, Castro noted that some had said that "blacks had become *insoportable*" since his announcement. In response, he called for "everyone to be respectful to each other, and that blacks should be more respectful than before because they understand that the revolution is working to eliminate discrimination."[28] By requesting Afro-Cubans to be more respectful or patient with white anxieties Castro failed to see that the issue was white privilege, not black disrespect. Nevertheless, the frequent repetition of certain rumors and criticisms in popular discourses contributed to the perception held by all Cubans, and in particular people of color, that the "true start of the exodus" occurred after the revolutionary government initiated plans to build a new, integrated society.[29]

Racism as Counterrevolution

As the revolution progressed, national discourses sought to distinguish between "true" revolutionaries and counterrevolutionaries. Historian Marifeli Pérez-Stable notes that during the 1960s, "the revolution polarized Cuba and disallowed neutrality. *Con Cuba o contra Cuba* [for Cuba or against Cuba] was the battle cry."[30] Though often overlooked by scholars, a central component of this conversation was whether Cubans agreed with the campaign to eliminate racial discrimination. According to national discourses, revolutionaries supported plans to rid the island of racial inequity, while counterrevolutionaries did not.[31] Being labeled a counterrevolutionary carried considerable consequences. This was a significant shift, for while pre-1959 ideologies of "racelessness" and the legacy of the wars of independence might have led some Cubans to call the perpetrators of racial inequality unpatriotic, this label had few tangible penalties. Enthusiasm for the 1959 revolution and for Cuban sovereignty, however, meant that those who were seen as opposed to the revolution faced pressures to conform, remain silent, or leave the island. Further, the concept applied to both white and black Cubans. As one author noted, discriminatory practices "are, in the language of the moment, also counterrevolutionary practices. We have to continue as if we had an enemy in every racist, white or black."[32] Afro-Cuban leaders who seemed particularly interested in their individual advancement were labeled "opportunistic" or "counterproductive."[33] As we have seen, revolutionary leaders put black activists, including Juan René Betancourt, Walterio Carbonell, and Carlos Moore, into this category because their demands for racial equality threatened the established and appropriate parameters for discussions about white privilege.

Cuban leaders linked racism to counterrevolution to unify supporters and charge opposition groups with failure to accompany the new national project into the present day. Castro asserted publicly, "If on top of the division between rich and poor, we divide ourselves between black and white . . . we will fragment into a million pieces, and the oppressors will defeat us and we will return to the past."[34] An Afro-Cuban newspaper similarly condemned racial discrimination by calling establishments that refused to serve blacks and *mulatos* places where the "sentiment of slave discrimination" still lived.[35] Clearly there *was* fragmentation, and some businesses *did* discriminate; these statements reveal that the island's legacy of racial tension was still capable of dividing its people. Revolutionary leaders sought to diminish this possibility by maintaining that whoever succumbed to past ideas was an enemy of the revolution. A *mulato* representative of the revolutionary army, Jorge Risquet, accused critics of "using Machiavellian principles of 'Divide and Conquer' to destroy the revolution by dividing Cubans based on skin color." Calling these critics counterrevolutionaries, he stated that the "revolution does not have a color, except the olive green color of the revolutionary army."[36] In each of these sources Cubans publicly labeled counterrevolutionaries as oppressors, slave owners, and racists. This language was meant to discredit dissenters while suggesting to Afro-Cubans that the new government would protect their interests. Within such discursive parameters, it became impossible to disagree with certain revolutionary policies without being labeled a racist. Similarly, it was also unfitting to be a revolutionary leader or supporter and to continue to support (at least publicly) privileges based on skin color.

The case of Amaury Fraginals, the leader of the electrical workers' union, illustrates this point. In February of 1960, a controversy erupted when Cubaneleco, the private club associated with the electrical union, refused to allow Afro-Cubans entrance into its recreational facilities. Cubans vocally opposed this situation, using the language of the moment to paint Fraginals and the group's other leaders as racist counterrevolutionaries. One editorial accused the union of "not supporting the revolution" because it continued to discriminate against Afro-Cubans.[37] Another charged Fraginals with being "out of compliance" with the new goals of Cuba and committing "treason" against the revolution.[38] A single word, *discriminador* (discriminator), accompanied a photograph of the union leader to emphasize his rejection of the campaign to end racial inequality.[39] Ten months later, Fraginals was accused of plotting against the government and participating in bombings of critical electrical facilities. He and his associates fled to Miami to avoid imprisonment.[40]

Discourses linking racism to counterrevolution also allowed Afro-Cubans to pressure local authorities to make additional reforms. In the central province of Villa Clara, members of the Communist Party claimed that counterrevolutionaries were continuing the colonial custom of having whites and blacks walk on different sides of the park (*el paseo*). In a letter to local authorities, the two men said that they planned to "unmask these counterrevolutionaries . . . as enemies of the revolution, and that they wanted to encourage the [town] Commissioners not to march backward in their noble and just cause of building a new park."[41] This situation highlights the reach of racialized revolutionary discourses into the Cuban mainland; it also marks the new possibility for citizens to use revolutionary language and tropes publicly to critique those who continued to practice racial discrimination.

Even as emerging narratives about acceptable revolutionary behavior developed, disjunctures between national rhetoric and local practices, including acts of leaders affiliated with the new government, undermined the state's antiracist claims. Around the same time as the Fraginals Cubaneleco controversy, young editors in the student newspaper *Combate 13 de Marzo* expressed anger over the axing of a new *telenovela* (television soap opera) in which black and white artists collaborated. The author of the editorial blamed the cancellation of the program on "the caprices of counterrevolutionaries and reactionaries" and implied that only enemies of the project to end discrimination would terminate a show that fostered racial cooperation and broadcast its benefits.[42] Similarly, Afro-Cuban poet Georgina Herrera remembered that racism continued during the first years of the revolution at the radio station Radio Progreso, where she worked. On one occasion, the directors of the station worried that she and three colleagues were plotting a conspiracy because they were planning to air a show about the Caribbean poet Aimé Césaire and all of them were of African descent. After a tense meeting with the directors, the controversial radio story, following the integrated soap opera, was canceled. "A group of blacks were not able to get together to do art and celebrate a black figure, but the whites, they could," Herrera remembered.[43]

The notion of racist activities as counterrevolutionary created a complex relationship between many Afro-Cubans and the new government.

Revolutionary discourses provided the space to speak publicly about segregated practices such as divisions in provincial parks, but if "revolutionaries" canceled a popular television program or innovative radio segment it was difficult to voice critique because upper-level leaders' revolutionary commitment was supposed to be unquestionable. In these cases, blacks and *mulatos* were expected to be "respectful" and withhold critique of lingering ambiguities.

Nevertheless, during the first three years of the revolution, many Cubans came to see racial discrimination and segregation as counterrevolutionary. The sources suggest that once national discourses put public racism into the category of counterrevolution, the issue became a salient marker for the radicalization of the revolution. Moreover, once racism came to be accepted as a counterrevolutionary offense, the term "racist" was used to undercut dissenters. For example, many residents of the island would have agreed with Depestre's 1965 statement that "there are still some racists in Cuba, the major part of them are counterrevolutionaries."[44] Even Cubans writing in exile acknowledged this association. "The word 'revolution' came to symbolize liberty, justice, war against Batista and his criminals, dignity and honor. Counterrevolution came to mean return to Batista, slavery, injustice, and hunger."[45] The choice of the word "racist" reveals the intensity of racialized revolutionary discourses and the young leadership's commitment, at least publicly, to racial equality.

Discourses about Racial Discrimination in Exile

As other scholars have noted, Cubans went into exile for a variety of complex and diverse reasons, many of which were connected to the idea that the island and culture they knew and loved were being threatened by the revolution. A majority of this opposition moved to south Florida—a region of the United States with its own pressing racial struggles.[46] To say that racial conflicts composed a part of the transnational history of why some Cubans moved to the United States and how a particular type of politics developed in Miami does not discount other factors such as anticommunism or fear of radical change. Exploring how exiled Cubans participated in national debates over the definition of the revolution and the role racial politics should play in that concept, does, however, add another dimension to a story that is often told only in terms of economic concerns and explains why so many people in the contemporary moment imagine the Cuban Revolution as antiracist and the exile community as racist.

Deciding to leave the island of their birth was not an easy decision for any Cuban. And while immigration to the United States had been a pattern in Cuba since the late nineteenth century, most families moving north in response to Castro's revolution imagined that their relocation would be temporary.[47] One sign of this was that exiled Cubans in the early 1960s frequently responded to events occurring in Cuba and issued commentary on a variety of revolutionary actions. Although these exchanges rarely consisted of bodies traveling back and forth between Havana and Miami, contentious debates over who owned the revolution reveal how Cuban ideologies and concepts transcended national boundaries. Rather than seeing themselves as counterrevolutionary or racist, Cubans in the United States often imagined that they were the "true" revolutionaries. The most obvious area of dispute between the two communities was over the economic policies of the new government, although exile discussions of racial discrimination highlighted the ways that conflict also stemmed from diverging views of what Cuba was and should be. Notably, exiles dismissed the existence of racial problems in Cuba and claimed that Castro had invented them to solidify his power. Despite these efforts, the overall silence among Cubans in Miami about the needs of Afro-Cubans, their inaction regarding social justice struggles in the United States, and their favored status with the U.S. government led them to lose the discursive battle in Cuba and ultimately any claim to antiracist politics in the 1960s.

Only between 3 and 9 percent of the Cubans who immigrated to Miami were black or *mulato*.[48] As a result, the exile community did not feel compelled to acknowledge the demands of Afro-Cubans or work to integrate blacks and *mulatos* into their social spaces. The population demographics in the Miami neighborhoods in which Cubans settled allowed the exile community to remain silent in regard to the campaign to eliminate racial privileges occurring on the island. By re-creating an enclave community composed of mostly white middle- and upper-class residents, Cubans in south Florida constructed an idealized space where racial and class discrimination was an aberration of the distant past. In this space, they could entertain nostalgic memories of Cuba because they did not have to experience the realities some working-class black and *mulato* Cubans experienced on the island.

That nostalgia was reflected in the absence of substantive discourse on race in the exile press. The initial platform of the Movement for the Restoration of Democracy, which was founded in 1959, outlined the organization's goals, such as restoring democracy to Cuba, fair Agrarian Reform, and freedom of the press. Notably absent from the document was any direct reference to the need for racial equality.[49] Similarly, UR, the clandestine countergovernment group publishing in both Havana and Miami, demanded freedom of religion, travel, and work, without mentioning the need to equalize opportunity among Cubans of differing skin colors.[50] Rather than addressing racial issues, the leaders of these groups focused on fighting what they perceived as communist activities on the island and emphasized the need to restore democracy and other rights that they saw as being withheld by the revolutionary leadership.

Like critics of the civil rights movement in the United States, Miami Cubans framed calls for racial reforms in Cuba as communist.[51] By calling for the restoration of "democracy" to the island without mentioning the need to disrupt existing class and racial privileges in Cuba, exile discourses sought to define the goals of the revolution narrowly. For Cubans in Miami, the revolution had little to do with ending racial discrimination, opening private schools and beaches, or dismantling exclusive social clubs. Rather, exile discourses highlighted the need to restore freedom of the press and hold elections, changes that seemed to offer anti-Castro groups the best opportunity to regain control of the island. As historian Pérez-Stable notes, "their sudden appreciation of democracy too clearly belied their primary concern that the new Cuba would not attend to their interests."[52] By focusing their critiques of the revolutionary leadership on its failure to hold elections, exiles—like civil rights critics in the United States—showed their willingness to mobilize prodemocracy, anticommunist discourses at the expense of a racial justice project.

Conversations in exile at times paralleled those on the island in that both constantly referenced national heroes from the nineteenth-century wars for independence to legitimize plans for a new Cuba. The significance of Martí and Maceo for so many Cubans and the legacy of racial harmony coming out of independence struggles meant that leaders on the island and in exile had to engage with these ideas in defining the revolution. The predominantly white exile community, however, did not conclude that the founding fathers of the republic demanded the dismantling of racial inequality. Using popular quotations from speeches by Martí, exiled Cuban leaders planned to return and build an island "with all and for the good of all," free of the class and racial conflicts they perceived as *created* by Castro and his supporters.[53] In fact, some exile writers accused

Castro of "offending Martí" and others stated, "although the new government might dishonor Maceo's memory, we will honor it appropriately."[54] On the anniversary of Maceo's death, the editors of *Bohemia Libre* complained that the independence fighter must be "rolling in his grave" as a result of the communist infiltration in Cuba.[55] A scathing criticism of the revolutionary commander Juan Almeida, a prominent Afro-Cuban in the new leadership, accused the commander of wrongly "thinking [that] he was the Maceo of today." Calling Almeida Castro's "puppet" and "clown," reporter José Correa Espino refused comparisons made in Cuba between the revolution's popular Afro-Cuban leader and the beloved "bronze titan" of the nineteenth century.[56]

Exile charges that the revolutionary government had betrayed national ideologies reveal the continued salience of the legacies of Martí and Maceo. Both prorevolution and countergovernment groups on and off the island fought for ownership over the memories of the two men hailed as the founding fathers of the nation. In doing so, they participated in a transnational debate over the meaning of "racelessness" and the interpretation of Cuban history. In Cuba, the revolution believed that providing tangible opportunities for working-class blacks and *mulatos* through national social reforms best fulfilled the promises Martí and Maceo symbolized. Exiles argued that only democratic governance and race-blind policies in which "we are all Cubans" could realize the dreams of nineteenth-century patriots. It is notable that both groups were influenced and limited by the same historical discourses about racelessness. They differed over implementation and accused each other of betraying shared goals, but ultimately each position remained wedded to a raceless Cuba. The distinction lay in the process of getting there. Revolutionary discourses wanted to create a new Cuba through social reforms that would solve racism with a more equitable distribution of resources. Exile leaders romanticized a pre-Castro island where the unpleasantness of racial and social inequalities was not discussed. Cuban revolutionary discourses claiming ownership over plans to end racial discrimination, coupled with language depicting opposition groups as racists, helped to create this image of Miami's Little Havana, especially among black and *mulato* Cubans. The absence of meaningful discussion on racial equality within a large part of the Miami community did little to change this view, reinforcing the new government's claim that Miami exiles were unconcerned with racism and classism in Cuba.

Castro, Communism, and Race in Exile

Miami Cubans' nostalgia for their island home conflicted with the revolutionary government's portrait of exiles' disdain and rejection of the "Pearl of the Antilles." The exiles furthermore portrayed Cuba before M 26-7 and Castro's rise to power as a racial paradise, a component of a larger campaign by the exile community to show that the situation in Cuba after 1959 was worse than it had been before. In the discursive battle waged across the Straits of Florida, both the history and the future of Cuba were at stake. Leaders in exile romanticized pre-Castro Cuba as a place where all citizens interacted in a friendly atmosphere, casting the new government as betrayer of the nation.

Cubans living in exile responded to the revolutionary government's public campaign to end racial discrimination by arguing that the 1959 revolution invented tensions between racial groups and classes.[57] Some groups claimed that Castro had created a nation of "poor against rich, and blacks against whites." Others said that pre-Castro Cuba had been "a country known for its happiness and generosity," but was "now steeped in hate."[58] These arguments fed the (still widely accepted) narrative that racial tensions did not exist before Castro came to power. An oral history of an elderly group of exile Cubans, many born at the turn of the twentieth century, expressed this popular perspective that the island experienced racial unity during the fifty years prior to the revolution. These observers remembered a racially integrated and harmonious island where "relations between whites and blacks in Cuba were very cordial" and "racism did not exist because many people of color had white friends." While the interviewees admitted that black and white Cubans had attended separate social clubs and walked on different sides of the park, each of them, including an Afro-Cuban grandfather, maintained that racism did not exist on the island before they left and that blacks were appreciated and respected.[59] Tacit in these reminiscences was nostalgia for a time when Afro-Cubans knew their place and were not *insoportable*, as they supposedly became after 1959.

A 1960 exile editorial titled "The Myth of the Classes" argued that Castro transformed after 1959 from the leader of the "bourgeoisie" to the "redeemer of the proletariat and the friend of the blacks."[60] Rather than offering a positive portrayal of Castro as friendly, this editorial actually highlighted the new leader's supposed choice of one group (blacks) over another (whites). Similarly, the political cartoon "Blood of the Free Press" from an October 1960 edition of *7 Días del Diario de la Marina en el exilio* shows a darkly shaded Castro attacking a surprised white woman whose dress bears the name of the Havana newspaper, *Diario de la Marina*. The caption "The 'liberation' movement continues" is a sarcastic jab at what the editors saw as the revolution's attack on freedom of expression.[61] But even more than an attack on the revolution's censorship policies, this cartoon illustrates how Castro's body became conflated with his antiracist rhetoric. For some exiles, the young leader had so defined himself as the "redeemer the proletariat and the friend of the blacks" that they started to represent him as black—and with all the gendered and sexual overtones of the most toxic racist tropes of the day. *7 Días del Diario de la Marina en el exilio*'s critique of Castro's racial policies offers just one example of how ideas about Cuba's social changes traveled across the Florida Straits. Editors for the newspaper had reconstituted the well-known Havana daily, the original *Diario de la Marina*, in exile and claimed that the new edition offered the official news about Havana. After their staff went into exile, other Cuban newspapers also reopened in Miami (with similar names as their Havana editions) including *Bohemia Libre* and *El Mundo: Editado en exilio*.

Although these were the most prevalent attitudes in the Miami community, at times a few exiles acknowledged directly that blacks and *mulatos* had been treated unfairly, and promised that a better future lay ahead in Cuba once Castro was deposed. An editorial published in *Bohemia Libre* pledged that "after the disappearance of the red terror . . . we are not going to permit the rise of the white terror."[62] Others argued that rather than oppose Juan Almeida because he was black, Cubans needed to criticize him for being a communist.[63] In this way, some exiles conceded that racial prejudices existed, but countered that after the defeat of communism, leaders in Miami would be open to talking about these issues. Still, these gestures were presented almost always as secondary to the primary goal of overthrowing the Castro government and its communist supporters. In the exile community, the familiar notion prevailed that it was not yet the appropriate time to address the situation of Cubans of African descent. The May 1960 political cartoon "Street Talk" highlights this idea. In the sketch, a caricature of a black Cuban discusses politics with a white Cuban, saying, "Look, doc, the bad guy here is not the white, nor is it the black. . . . It is the red."[64] While problematic in its depiction of Afro-Cubans, this cartoon underscores the move frequently made in the exile press of turning away from racism and toward communism as the "bad guy" plaguing the island. This emphasis on anticommunism at the expense of racial equality limited the exile community's ability to reach out to Afro-Cubans or African Americans and reinforced the belief that Miami Cubans were unconcerned with ending racial discrimination.

Cuban exile attitudes toward African Americans did little to bridge racial divides. Revolutionary leaders had been successful, initially, in attracting African American support to the new government, and exiles won back few friends. They were more likely to alienate U.S. blacks who encountered their privileged position in the south Florida racial hierarchy. True, some black residents of the city were among those who welcomed the Cuban exiles and took pride in being able to play a role in the Cold War fight against communism.[65] But over time Miamians, especially blacks, encountered exiles' racism, came to resent the federal resources provided disproportionally to exiles over native working-class groups, and felt that they were losing jobs to incoming Cubans.[66] The revolutionary government encouraged further animus. As coverage about the arrival of Cubans displaced headlines about civil rights in Miami, Castro's administration openly denounced racial violence in the United States and invited African Americans to visit the island as a part of special tourist delegations.[67] The disjuncture between the exiles' disassociation with U.S. blacks and Castro's recruitment of African Americans signaled a fracture in the two Cuban groups' concepts of revolution.

As the recipients of nearly four times more financial aid than African Americans, Cuban exiles benefited from their status as Cold War refugees and nearly all of the early arrivals were middle- or upper-class white professionals. When African Americans complained that Cuban exiles were taking jobs and resources from working-class U.S. citizens, Cubans denied these accusations and claimed that they were fighting for the same rights as any other upwardly mobile group in the city. However, exiles could not deny their association with the U.S. government. As the beneficiaries of nearly $158 million in refugee aid between 1961 and 1966, Cubans in Miami were partnered with the U.S. government in ways that revolutionary leaders never would be.[68] Ultimately, it is not surprising that the exile community did not attack the racial hierarchies of the U.S. South given that exiles gained materially from sponsorship by the U.S. government. So while Cuban discourses on the island might have exaggerated racial violence in the United States to discourage Afro-Cuban migration and highlight the revolution's integration policies, their attention to these areas exceeded the lofty nods to racelessness heralded by the exile community. Together this rhetoric contributed to the narrative that those who elected to go into exile were the white racists Reynaldo Peñalver remembered.

Afro-Cubans in Exile: Revolution, Racism, and Unbelonging

Even as Cuban leaders on the island and in exile used the bodies of blacks and *mulatos* in their fights for the ownership of, and the future of, the revolution, both groups routinely ignored the small group of Afro-Cubans who left the island for the United States in the early 1960s. As noted earlier, Afro-Cubans did not compose a large portion of the first wave of exiles, but when they did leave Cuba they did so for different reasons than most whites. Once in the United States, Afro-Cubans faced particular challenges as both Spanish-speaking immigrants and blacks, especially in south Florida with its fierce racial segregation. Afro-Cuban Ricardo Gonzalez arrived in Miami in 1962 as a twelve-year-old; he was part of Operation Pedro Pan, a program run by the U.S. Catholic Church (with ties to the Central Intelligence Agency [CIA]) that sent 14,000 unaccompanied minors to south Florida to escape 'Castro's communism.'[69] He explained the situation succinctly: "Black Cuban exile is not the same as white Cuban exile. . . . [That difference] is like the hundred pound elephant in the room that no one wants to talk about."[70] Additional research is needed to unravel the invisibility of black exile experiences in the 1960s. Nevertheless, oral histories illustrate how the obstacles and privileges Afro-Cubans faced as they negotiated white North American, African American, *and* white Cuban American communities shaped transnational understandings of race, nation, and revolution.

Economics and fears about protecting families from domestic and international terrorism drove some Cubans of color to the United States. Diana, Ruben, and Pablo Foster recount their experiences as black youths in Cuba and the United States in the film *Cuban Roots/Bronx Stories* (2000). The three came from a large family consisting of seven siblings and their mother. Their father, Carlos Foster, was born in the town of Banes in Oriente province to Jamaican parents in the early twentieth century. Like other West Indian immigrants to Cuba, Foster's parents came to the island in search of work and better opportunities for their families.[71] Carlos worked on the Guantánamo naval base as a young man before moving to Havana where he found employment as a musical performer in Cuba's bustling 1950s tourist industry. After the 1959 revolution, tourism to the island decreased and Foster moved to the United States in 1960, once again in search of work. Ms. Foster, who had separated from Carlos before he moved to Havana, moved her remaining family of seven children to Havana and later the United States in 1962. But before leaving Cuba, the family witnessed the changes brought by the Urban Reform law, the campaign to eliminate racial discrimination, and counterrevolutionary violence against the new government. Remembering how Urban Reform saved them from being evicted from their apartment, Pablo pushed back against accepted narratives claiming that all first-wave Cuban exiles left because of disagreements with the revolution's redistribution agenda: "We didn't leave because we were against the revolution, we didn't leave because we had such a stake in Cuba and they were taking things from us. We would have been the beneficiaries of the revolution if we had stayed. We left because we had seven kids, a mother, and the U.S. threatening to invade Cuba—which they did with the Playa Giron [Bay of Pigs] invasion! And we had some family here and who doesn't want to be on safe ground?" His sister Diana recalled that once they landed in the Bronx she finally felt safe: "No bombs are going to fall here."[72] This narrative of fleeing Cuba to escape the ongoing civil war is frequently silenced in explanations about white exiles' decisions to leave Cuba. Moreover, the recognition that as a poor black family they might have benefited from some of the economic policies of the new government but still chose to leave provides insight into the agency that revolutionary leaders attempted to deny Afro-Cubans when they positioned them solely as loyal and grateful clients of the state.

Other Afro-Cuban families experienced similar attitudes of ambivalence about Cuba's new leadership and moved into exile with conflicting feelings about the United States and Cuba. Ricardo Gonzalez remembers that his family was not solidly anti-Castro when they decided to send him to the United States as a part of Operation Pedro Pan. Gonzalez's parents were distinct from many other Pedro Pan families not only by being Afro-Cuban, but also because they were working-class. His father was self-educated and held various jobs and his mother was a seamstress. The family lived ten miles outside of Havana and could not afford to join any of the elite black and *mulato* social clubs in the area—another indicator of their social situation before 1959. But Ricardo's mother, a devout Catholic, pressured his father, whom Ricardo described as very "anti-American" and suspicious of the U.S. government and the Catholic Church, to send their son to Miami. The tipping point came when armed revolutionary soldiers took over the private Catholic school Ricardo attended. Like other Cubans, his mother's fears about communism stemmed from her belief in Catholicism and local priests' claims that Castro planned to steal Cuban youth and send them to the Soviet Union. Family members were skeptical of the plan to send Ricardo to the United States alone: "My whole family thought that my mother was crazy. How are you going to let him go? When are you going to see him again? Who are you going to send him to? Who's going to take care of him?" Despite these misgivings, in 1962 Gonzalez boarded an airplane to the United States and was excited about going to a place where everyone had refrigerators full of Coca-Cola and delicious foods (at least that is what his friends' photographs showed). He found himself in a much less ideal environment, however, namely a segregated country where he had to navigate the politics of race alone until his parents arrived four years later.[73]

Afro-Cubans quickly recognized that just because they joined anti-Castro white Cubans in exile did not make them equals. Pablo Foster recalled that "Miami was unapologetic about its policy of racial segregation in that period," and he described how his family was immediately directed to a black hotel shortly after arriving in the United States. "After that, we didn't see any white Cubans."[74] Similarly, the Betancourt family only stayed in Miami one day before relocating to New York. "We didn't stay in Miami because the segregation was horrible," Lydia Mesa-Martí Betancourt Sharpe, Juan René Betancourt's wife, admitted in a 2011 interview.[75] In contrast to much of the publicity celebrating white Cubans' entrance into the United States, their welcome at the Freedom Tower, and relocation to friendly communities throughout the country, Foster's account illustrates how some black Cubans were instantly informed of their new positionality in the U.S. racial system through segregated immigration procedures. Once in New York, Betancourt characterized exile organizations in Miami as "short-sighted" groups composed of "white Cubans, members of the upper and middle class" who "do not exhibit the slightest interest in the fate of the Cuban Negro." Noting that black and *mulato* Cubans were "never mentioned in their pronouncements," he critiqued how "none of the exile groups have committed themselves to a nondiscrimination program should they get power."[76] That Betancourt launched his evaluation of white exile groups while living in New York, not Miami, provides insight into the politics of race and place for Cuban exiles. Afro-Cubans who disagreed with the new government were much less likely than white Cubans to move to the United States, a country known for its own racial tensions; but even fewer went to the South, reflecting the perception that there was little space for concerns about equality within the Miami exile community. Like the Betancourts and the Fosters, who moved to New York instead of Miami, the few Cubans of color who came to the United States before 1963 commonly relocated to the North because of both an awareness of the exile community's silence on racial issues and the prevalent segregation in the South.

As an unaccompanied youth, Ricardo Gonzalez had little choice but to live where the Pedro Pan Operation sent him. Consequently, he spent his teenage years in south Florida and one of his earliest memories speaks to the complexities of learning a new racial system and a new language in a new country. Gonzalez remembers an episode that occurred on the bus when he was en route to visit one of his mother's friends from Cuba who now lived in the United States. Having taken public transport in Cuba, he felt comfortable navigating Miami's bus system after the woman he was going to visit explained where to catch the bus and how much to pay. He recalled:

> I go on the bus. Put in my fare. And I sit on the front seat because I want to see the landmarks, I want to see where I'm going, this lady is telling me that when you see this building on the side of the other [I should get off]. So, the driver turns around and he starts mouthing at me. I'm sitting there going like this [shrugging]. You know I'm laughing and smiling because I don't know what the hell he's talking about. He got progressively more anger [sic]. Until, he finally got up and got in my face in front of me. Then this voice from the back of the bus said in Spanish, "You have to sit here." So, I got up and I sat there. But I thought: What happened? It was only much later I found out actually, because I thought maybe I stepped on some gum or something, but then I realized, of course, you have the color border. It was interesting. . . . We were dealing first of all with the language barrier, which was rough in itself. Then, all these other factors. . . . It's not that you were provoking or demanding your rights or anything like that, it's just that you don't know what the hell is going on. So that was rough, I have to admit.[77]

Even as someone who was familiar with racial inequality in Cuba, Gonzalez was unprepared to navigate segregation in the United States. Because while he knew the places where his family could and could not go on the island (such as the local white social club because of race or the black club because of class), the same rules did not apply in Miami. This episode also illustrates the disconnect between white and black experiences in exile. His mother's friend, who was not Afro-Cuban, explicitly told him the location of the bus stop and how fares were charged differently in Miami than in Havana, but she did not fathom that she needed to explain where he should sit on the bus. Whether this is because she assumed he knew or because she herself did not know is unclear. It was the unnamed stranger who was already sitting at the back of the bus—another Spanish speaker of African descent, potentially another Cuban—who mediated and translated the bus driver's demands to Gonzalez after first learning them himself at some prior moment. Gonzalez's ongoing confusion, both during and after the event, further highlights the limits of Operation Pedro Pan in preparing the few Afro-Cuban youth who participated in the program to navigate blackness in the United States. As Gonzalez himself noted, "the experiences we were seeing were unlike the experiences our counterparts [in Pedro Pan] were seeing. We had barriers that they didn't and that we couldn't even talk about because they wouldn't."[78]

In fact, social programs targeting incoming Cuban exiles frequently employed the same colorblind language, equating Cubanness with whiteness, that was popular on the island both before and after 1959. *Resettlement Re-cap: A Periodic Report from the Cuban Refugee Center* published quarterly newsletters about the successes of newly arrived Cubans as they acquired jobs, got married, and moved across the country. Written in English, each issue included images of Cuban nuclear families dressed in professional attire, smiling happily at the camera, and encouraged readers to accept Cuban Americans as new citizens. A November 1966 newsletter invoked traditional 1960s gender norms in "Steps in the Resettlement of Cuban Refugees" and reflected the values of the period. "The man needs a job. Try to find him one even though it might not be what he was doing in Cuba. . . . You help the refugee by encouraging him to help himself, and make sure to show his wife around the community (shopping, etc)."[79] *Resettlement Re-Cap*'s propaganda campaign emphasized the nuclear family to counteract negative attitudes in the United States about Cubans overrunning the country and taking jobs from North American citizens. Racializing Cubans as white was a major component of this project. The photographs in the newsletter reflected the image that officials in the Cuban Refugee Center wanted to distribute—clean-cut, professional Cubans who could easily integrate themselves into any (white) community. Only one issue featured an Afro-Cuban family, the Guevaras, and it did so in a way that highlighted their successful relocation to Illinois as marking fifteen thousand persons resettled by Church World Service. The brief article stated that "the Guevara case is significant since it [shows] the sponsorship by a white congregation of a Cuban Negro family."[80] But, the rarity of black exile—this is the only black or *mulato* family that appears in *Resettlement Re-Cap*—coupled with narratives about Cuban exiles as welcome Cold War citizens who placed themselves on the white side of the Jim Crow South, left little space for in-depth conversations about discrimination among Cubans in Miami.

In exile, blacks and *mulatos* faced discrimination from Cubans who distanced themselves from the island's racial heritage to more easily access whiteness in the United States. Gonzalez was the only black Cuban in his class attending the predominantly Cuban exile school Belén—a Miami version of the elite Havana institution that had been re-created in exile after its administration fled the island. Two other black boys, also from Operation Pedro Pan, Gerardo Sims and René Walker, were a year behind him at school. One of the challenges he faced in Miami came as a result of playing on the basketball team and enjoying the popularity of being a successful high school athlete. A white female classmate who admired the school's basketball program invited Gonzalez to a party at her house and he enthusiastically accepted the invitation: "I knock on the door and this dude comes. There are like bars on the door. He opens it . . . and he closes the door in my face. . . . Then the girl [who invited me] opens the door and she's crying her face out. 'I'm sorry. I'm sorry, but you have to go.' So you piece it together, because there is no other explanation."[81] In contrast to Gonzalez's experience with the white North American bus driver where he was puzzled by the racial restrictions of the segregated South, here he easily understood that the white Cuban man was barring his entrance to the party and his friendship with the young woman because of his race. Similar to the fears of interracial intimacy that pushed some Cubans into exile, this anecdote suggests that even in new spaces where Cubans of all colors faced similar challenges of national displacement racism persisted. But unlike Afro-Cubans on the island who frequently utilized the racialized rhetoric of the revolution to demand that Castro's government live up to its antiracist claims, blacks in exile (especially darker-skinned Cubans) often struggled to find tools for combating their marginalization from exile organizations or communities.

In fact, when blacks tried to become involved in exile politics they were often ignored or rejected. Afro-Cuban Juan René Betancourt reformatted his position as the president of black societies in Cuba after moving to the United States in 1961. Calling his new organization the Federation of Black Cuban Societies in Exile, Betancourt wrote at least two letters to the executive board of the Revolutionary Democratic Front (Frente Revolucionario Democratica, FRD) in Miami from his new home in New York. The FRD was the principal CIA-backed Miami organization in the early 1960s and it was led by the popular Cuban exile politician José Miró Cardona. Betancourt's second letter, directed to Miró Cardona and dated 24 March 1961, demanded that the FRD answer his initial request—where he had sought membership in the group—and make a public statement about its thoughts on racism in Cuba. After explaining that racial prejudice had always existed on the island and that black Cubans had played a significant role in national independence struggles, he attacked the prevailing belief that Castro had invented racial inequality. "To recognize the existence of this social ill is not to create it, and contrary to popular consensus, it [racial discrimination] will not cure itself by omission and silence." The entire letter, which spans five pages, shows an awareness of Cuban history and a clear idea about where blacks fit into the country's future. But unlike other Miami exile organizations, Betancourt's correspondence was not dominated by talk of anticommunism; rather, the word "communism" only appears twice in the document and on both occurrences the author asked the FRD to explain what its policy would be toward Afro-Cubans after communism was eliminated from Cuba. However, despite Betancourt's repeated requests and the links that he could have made between the exile group and other black club leaders, it appears that Miró Cardona never responded to his letters and the FRD remained a nearly all-white organization moving forward.[82]

People of color in Cuba, as well as Afro-Cubans in the United States, came to interpret this silence as a denial of their ongoing struggle for equal opportunity. Recognizing that he had been ignored, Betancourt turned to the National Association for the Advancement of Colored People's *Crisis* newsletter a few months later to express his frustration with white exile organizations. He noted that "those who affirm that the condemnation of the ills of the Negro and the demand for their elimination divides Cubans and creates racial problems are either naïve or unconsciously anti-Negro."[83] The prevailing "not yet" attitude among the Miami leadership estranged many blacks and *mulatos*, like Betancourt, who felt it revealed resistance to ending racial discrimination. For him and other Afro-Cubans it was unacceptable to postpone addressing racial inequalities until after the establishment of a noncommunist Cuba.

It was especially challenging for Afro-Cubans to obtain housing or employment as more and more white exiles assumed economic and political leadership in the community. "Many black Cubans are reluctant to talk about it because they somehow depend either socially or financially from the Cuban community," Gonzalez told me. His parents experienced this very concept when they joined him in Miami in 1966 and immediately encountered problems with a fair-skinned Cuban building owner. After learning from another exile, a neighbor from Cuba, that the apartment building across the street had a vacancy, they approached the landlord to rent. When they arrived, the super refused to lease a flat to the family because they were black. In our interview, Gonzalez described his frustration: "This is 1966. The civil rights laws had been passed. I became very vehement and very demanding that I was going to get that apartment or I'm going to bring the cops in here. And we got the apartment.... Interestingly, the [owner of the building] was Cuban and looked sort of like you. Maybe with hair a little less [kinky] (*quizás el pelo un poquito menos*). But, he obviously had, you know, *la mancha* (the stain)."[84] Like all of our conversations, this one occurred in Spanglish (a mixture of Spanish and English) and invoked both U.S. and Cuban racial systems to describe Gonzalez's experiences in the 1960s. Moreover, rather than identify the landlord as white, Gonzalez described him as *mulato*, indicating the nuances of racial discrimination in the Cuban diaspora where an exile whom most other Cubans would identify as being of African descent could discriminate against dark-skinned compatriots. White privilege worked in relational ways in Cuba and its diaspora. The landlord in this incident participated in policing the whiteness that the Cuban exile community desired even though he might not have been able to access all non-Cuban spaces himself.

Social venues in African American communities served as spaces of both acceptance and unbelonging for Afro-Cuban exiles. In light of the pervasive racism in Cuban and white North American public areas, black exiles frequently invoked the language of the civil rights movement as a way to fight back. In Miami, Gonzalez threatened the Cuban landlord with criminal proceedings under new civil rights laws if he refused to rent an apartment to his parents. Similarly, in New York, Diana and Pablo

Foster admired the Young Lords and watched enthusiastically as the group marched against social injustice with other black Latinos sporting natural Afros.[85] For Diana, becoming aware of and seeing the Young Lords helped her to understand and affirm her positionality as a black Latina. Describing how she was ostracized from African American and Puerto Rican social groups as a youth, she remembered a Latino friend in college asking her why she wore "black" clothes and styled her hair like a black girl. "You aren't black," the friend commented. Diana recalled responding, "If I'm not black, what am I?" When she discovered the Young Lords, Diana explained, "I felt like a person. . . . Yes, I belong here."[86] Similarly, civil rights literature and protests introduced Ricardo Gonzalez to the meaning of blackness in the United States. He devoured the writings of Martin Luther King Jr. and Malcolm X despite his parents' and other Cubans' misgivings that doing so made him a communist. Gonzalez credits his present-day social justice advocacy to his childhood formations in Cuba alongside the revolution and participation in U.S. civil rights struggles. Later, an African American basketball teammate at the predominately white St. Thomas University Gonzalez attended presented him to black women. "He opened the doors to African American women. That was very important. And, by definition, to African American life." Gonzalez later married a black Cuban woman whom he met in Miami, but his statement about women facilitating entrance into African American culture is telling of the ways that race and gender intersected in exile. Unlike some white Cubans, who feared and tried to prevent interactions between their daughters, sisters, and wives and black male exiles, African American women shared social spaces with black men and sometimes acted as a bridge between the two African diasporic cultures.

The questions of multiple identities and multiple ways of belonging and unbelonging impacted the social lives of Afro-Cuban exiles at every turn. Pablo Foster said, "I don't feel like a full-blown Cuban or a full-blown North American. There is a gap. I identify with the United States, especially from 1962 to now, so I feel more American than Cuban, but a strange type of American."[87] The strangeness of being a black exile especially in the 1960s had everything to do with the small numbers of Afro-Cubans who left the island, the racial politics of Cuban leaders in Cuba and in exile, and the United States' ongoing racial tensions. Some black exiles negotiated this convergence by joining African American communities or by trying to fit into the white exile enclave. In Miami, many black Cuban exiles settled in the Allapattah neighborhood in response to not being welcomed in other spaces. Gonzalez described the area as a "buffer" between the Cuban community and the African American neighborhoods. "I'm not going to say that all of the people were black, but the majority of the black Cuban people lived there." The neighborhood centered around Adán Jimeno's house—Gonzalez's future wife's father. Jimeno had been a high-ranking official in the Batista government and had left the island on the night of 31 December 1958 in the deposed president's airplane. His family joined him a year later. Despite being a lawyer and an influential person in the previous government, Jimeno was not rich and never planned to live in the United States because of the country's history of racial discrimination. Once in Miami, he initially worked as a carpenter before saving some money and opening a successful business. Jimeno and his family hosted parties and facilitated the development of a small black Cuban enclave that most scholarship about Miami's exile community ignores. In doing so, he created a space where black exiles would be welcomed. Addressing the problem of unbelonging, Gonzalez noted, "We were not really accepted by the black community. We were not really accepted by the Cuban community"; Afro-Cuban Allapattah developed physically and literally in the space between the two social groups.[88]

Ambiguous reasons for going into exile impacted the lived experiences of black Cubans in the United States. As the decades progressed Afro-Cuban exiles rarely held the polarizing positions against travel and trade with the island that white Cubans did. Both Gonzalez and Pablo Foster participated in return trips in the 1980s when they visited family members and reconnected with the country they had been forced to leave when they were young. This willingness to engage with Cuba is also reflected in how black exiles assess the revolution. Using a much more pragmatic approach than white Cubans, black and *mulato* exiles tend to be able to evaluate both the positive and the negative changes that have occurred on the island. Diana Foster even expressed regret over leaving and not working to construct a new Cuba: "We will always be known as the group of people who left. I'm a piece of that history in that way. I wish I could have stayed and struggled to help rebuild the country. To be one of the blacks who did that. And, as a woman of color, I would have been a part of that history of accomplishments of black Cubans. What they have done for that country. So I regret not being a part of that history. On the other hand I am a part of this country's history."[89]

Conclusions

In the early 1960s, both Cuban and exile leaders invoked the nameless, faceless figures of Cubans of color, not individual voices, as markers for political battles between the two countries. A transnational history of racial discourses from Havana to Miami reveals how these competing vocabularies of race and racelessness emerged as the two communities developed in opposition to each other. In Havana, the revolutionary government began a brief but public campaign to eliminate racial discrimination between 1959 and 1961. A central component of this plan included defining racism as counterrevolutionary and establishing the ideal that revolutionaries could not be racist. Integrating previously white-only spaces such as private schools, beaches, and recreational facilities also played a significant role in the new government's efforts to incorporate Cubans of color into the revolution. The prevalence of paternalistic attitudes, the closing of Afro-Cuban social clubs without an appreciation of their role in previous fights for racial equality, and the expectation of gratitude from black and *mulato* Cubans, however, undermined the revolution's antiracist claims. Nevertheless, the new government's racial discourses provided some tangible opportunities and languages for blacks and *mulatos* to challenge situations when national programs failed to achieve their integrationist goals.

Not all Cubans were comfortable with these changes. The evidence suggests that for some white middle- to upper-class Cubans revolutionary racial programs threatened traditional social hierarchies and generated anxieties over racial mixing. These fears influenced Cuban decisions to go into exile and aided in the creation of a particular exile politics as Cubans carried their apprehensions about the revolution with them to south Florida. In Miami, Cubans sought to create a heterotopic space that embraced the aspects of prerevolutionary Cuba that they loved, valued, and remembered. Within the context of the Cold War, this meant appropriating anticommunist language even before Cuba's official declaration of Marxist-Leninism and distancing themselves from African American civil rights struggles. But, it also meant redefining Cuban history to erase previous racial tensions and inequality. With claims that Castro had invented racial divisions and was befouling Martí's vision of racelessness, exiles invoked a romanticized past to legitimize their mostly white, U.S.-supported enclave. Their ideas, however, could not compete with the popular campaign to combat racial discrimination occurring on the island. Few Afro-Cubans went into exile during these early years, and those who did complained of being alienated from the leading groups in Miami. Black Cubans who elected to move to the United States in the 1960s faced a distinct set of challenges that white exiles routinely failed to recognize. Landing in the midst of power struggles between Cuban and exile leaders, some Afro-Cuban exiles chose to move to New York rather than stay in Miami where Cuban politics existed at an intense level. Others, especially black youth who arrived as a part of Operation Pedro Pan, remained in Miami and learned how identities based on race, class, and nation took new forms in south Florida.

Yet for all the ways that racial politics contributed to the emerging break between the two communities in the 1960s, a transnational history of conversations about race from Havana to Miami also reveals certain similarities. Both groups fought for ownership of the concept of revolution and struggled to redefine Cuban history to fit their goals and needs. In Cuba, that meant blaming the U.S. intervention in 1898 for bringing racism to the island, whereas in Miami, Castro was the racist villain. Such divisions did not apply only to conflicts over race and racism. The two communities frequently used similar notions in debates over economic and political policies, thereby participating in a moral battle over the ownership of a revolutionary vision of Cuba. The following chapter will discuss how Cuban leaders applied this rhetoric globally to combat U.S. criticism that the new government was communist, while attracting African American support for the revolution.

4

Cuba Calls!

Exploiting African American and
Cuban Alliances for Equal Rights

In September 1960, leaders from Havana's National Executive Committee of Orientation and Integration, among them Afro-Cuban communist Salvador García Agüero, declared a "Week of Solidarity with the U.S. Negro" after owners from a black hotel in Harlem opened their doors to Cuba's delegation to the United Nations (UN).[1] Members of the black social club the Women's Cultural Association recall being invited to a meeting where officials from the new revolutionary government encouraged them to support the week and welcome African American visitors into their institutions should they choose to visit Cuba. Because African Americans and Afro-Cuban social club leaders had collaborated in educational, tourist, and economic opportunities since the early part of the twentieth century, the women quickly voted to participate in the "Week of Solidarity."[2] However, unlike pre-1959 alliances between Cubans and African Americans, almost all of which had been initiated by blacks themselves, this 1960 event was organized by the National Confederation of Cuban Workers (Confederación de Trabajadores Cubanos, CTC) and supported by (predominantly white) former anti-Batista civic organizations across the island, including the 26th of July Movement (M 26-7), the Revolutionary Directorate (Directorio Revolucionario, DR), Communist Party (Partido Socialista Popular, PSP), University Students Federation (Federación Estudiantil Universitaria, FEU), and Association of Young Rebels (Asociación de Jóvenes Rebeldes, AJR).[3] In this way, relationships between Afro-Cubans and African Americans based on fighting racial oppression in their respective countries had a different focus after 1959. The new government nationalized historic diasporic alliances and transferred local antidiscrimination debates into a national rhetoric against imperialism, colonialism, and racism.

The first of January, 1960, was not the first time African Americans and Cubans shared common interests. Letters from black soldiers participating in the U.S. intervention in the Cuban wars for independence (1898–1902) reveal that young African American men were at first awed and later intrigued by the mixed racial composition of the island because they had been led to believe the population was white by U.S. standards. In the early twentieth century, Afro-Cuban students attended and sympathized with Booker T. Washington's Tuskegee Institute in Alabama as a means of obtaining an education and "advancing the race." Similarly, long-standing connections between Harlem poet Langston Hughes and Afro-Cuban author Nicolás Guillén resulted in over three decades of poetry and prose inspired by the social, political, and economic situations of people of color in the United States and Cuba. Most importantly for this chapter, elite African American institutions and Afro-Cuban social clubs had encouraged black tourist exchanges since the 1930s. By the 1950s, a select number of black entrepreneurs routinely sold tour packages and arranged trips for travelers to visit well-known black cultural sites in both countries.[4] When the mainstream North American press criticized the revolution and Cuba's normal tourism clientele decreased, Cuban political leaders actively built on these prior relationships by reaching out to U.S. black tourists.[5] The new revolutionary National Institute of Tourism (Instituto Nacional de Industria Turística, INIT) initiated a campaign in January 1960 inviting former world heavyweight boxing champion Joe Louis and other prominent African Americans to the island to experience "first class treatment—as a first class citizen."[6] Later, in September 1960, Castro moved Cuba's delegation to the UN to a black hotel in Harlem and spurred island-wide solidarity with African Americans as Cubans watched while U.S. blacks welcomed revolutionary leaders and white Manhattan hotel managers did not.

Inviting African American visitors to Cuba to experience "first class citizenship" was a key component of the revolution's antidiscrimination campaign, and it led to discussions of the similarities and differences in race relations between the United States and Cuba. Cuban leaders invoked the image of Louis as a strong, valiant, prorevolution boxer to highlight the contradictions of U.S. democracy and to solicit support from Afro-Cuban communities. In January 1960 while sitting with Louis, Castro told a group of U.S. blacks, "In Cuba we are resolving problems that the United States has not been able to resolve, such as that of racial discrimination. Here everyone lives together without problems."[7] Such rhetoric benefited revolutionary leaders, who were able to emphasize the progress made by the new government toward achieving racial equality in contrast to their neighbor to the north. These statements, however, also provided Afro-Cubans with an opening to demand additional improvements when they encountered inconsistencies in revolutionary promises of equality.

Afro-Cuban journalist Reynaldo Peñalver took this opportunity in July 1960 and published an article called "Discrimination in a Restaurant" in the popular Havana student newspaper *Combate 13 de Marzo*. He accused a tourist facility in central Cuba of racial discrimination for refusing to serve a group of black workers. The men were members of the Antonio Maceo Society in Mayajigua and had been admiring local tourist attractions when they decided to stop for lunch. Peñalver describes how the owner of the eatery rudely told the group that they could not dine in the restaurant because they were not members, even though it was supposedly a public venue. The black men immediately left the diner, but not before informing the owner that they planned to denounce the eatery to the press and that "the next time they or someone like them came to eat you will have to serve them because the revolution condemns discrimination."[8] Afro-Cuban outcries against public racism became more vocal following Castro's 1 January 1960 announcement to African American visitors that the 1959 revolution had eliminated racial discrimination. Cuban dailies printed denouncements like Peñalver's throughout the spring and summer as blacks and *mulatos* encountered racial discrimination in the very tourist hotels, restaurants, and recreational centers that the government promoted to African Americans. In denouncing this discrimination, Afro-Cubans both invoked revolutionary promises to demand domestic social reforms and threatened the new government's attempts to restructure historical diasporic linkages into alliances between the new state and U.S. blacks.

By September 1960, however, many of these Afro-Cuban protests against racial discrimination had disappeared from the Cuban press. Once Castro and the Cuban delegation to the UN moved into a black hotel in Harlem, Cuban newspapers, including articles by blacks and *mulatos*, rallied around revolutionary leaders' disgust with U.S. race relations and confirmed claims that racial discrimination had been eliminated in Cuba. The "Week of Solidarity with the U.S. Negro" described at the opening of this chapter was just one of many public actions that located continued racism in the United States while celebrating the success of Cuba's campaign against discrimination. Scholars exploring post-1959 exchanges between Cubans and African Americans, especially Castro's move to

Harlem, have tended to cast these relationships as examples of "Third World solidarity" and to use them to narrate civil rights events in the United States.[9] However, by describing the ways that African American leaders supported and allied with Cubans, these investigations do not question the imperfect images of the "other" that transnational alliances produce or to what ends such partnerships work. Nationalized transnational and diasporic linkages in post-1959 Cuba were discontinuous and occurred only at certain strategic moments, resulting in conscious instances of closeness and distance by both African Americans and Cubans. For Peñalver and countless other Afro-Cubans, visits by U.S. blacks were arguably more an opportunity to influence domestic fights against racism than to develop transnational partnerships. Previous scholarship has also failed to examine how these relationships changed rapidly over time, even just over the course of one year (1960), or investigate what those changes say about racial politics in Cuba. By exploring two episodes from the early revolutionary process, one where Afro-Cubans used a transnational moment to demand reforms and another where the majority of Cuba stood publicly behind Castro's claims of achieving a racial paradise, we can see how living in a "transnational social field" influenced and limited discussions about race on the island.[10] A close look at how Cuban encounters with African Americans constituted revolutionary discourses also allows us to push beyond the pattern of celebrating alliances among the aggrieved and begin to see the ways in which marginalized groups exploited one another to increase their respective visibility and further their cause on both a local and global scale.

Like the previous chapter's discussion of race between Havana and Miami, interactions between the revolutionary government and African American businessmen and activists in 1960 illustrate the process through which revolutionary racial discourses became racial politics. Cuban officials moved from debating how to eliminate racial discrimination to proclaiming that they had done so. At different moments throughout the year, Afro-Cubans both denounced continued racial discrimination by demanding that the revolution live up to its promises *and* supported the new government in its statements that Cuba was a racial paradise. These contradictory claims, made through and over declarations of "solidarity" with U.S. blacks, demonstrate the consolidation of revolutionary narratives about race and foreshadowed the closing of public spaces for debate.

The Brown Bomber Arrives in Havana

At midnight on 31 December 1959, former heavyweight boxing champion of the world Joe Louis celebrated New Year's Eve in the Havana Hilton. Sitting with his wife Martha to his left and Castro to his right, Louis expressed his sympathy with the Cuban Revolution by wearing a typical *guajiro* (farm or peasant) hat. A year earlier, neither Louis nor Castro might have imagined that they would mark the start of the 1960s together in a plush suite in Havana. Yet on this evening they celebrated their upcoming joint business venture, a plan to increase African American tourism to Cuba. Boxing was a popular sport in the Caribbean and many admiring Cubans had followed Louis's heavyweight career. In fact, black Caribbeans embraced Louis for the same reasons African Americans did—because he was an international black icon who had beaten and continued to beat white men in the ring. As Lara Putnam notes in her study of the early twentieth-century Caribbean, "No star mattered more in the circum-Caribbean migratory sphere than boxer Joe Louis. In a world in which sports heroes stood for nations of origins, Joe Louis stood for his people: Our People, the Negro Race."[11] Cuban newspapers built on Louis's celebrity while the African American tour group was in Havana in order to insert the boxer's voice into revolutionary debates about racial discrimination.

Joe Louis arrived in Havana on New Year's Eve as a representative of Louis, Rowe, Fisher, and Lockhart Enterprises, Inc., an all-black public relations firm. According to William Rowe's 1961 congressional testimony, the company had only recently expanded to include Al Lockhart, the advertising director of one of New York's most popular African American newspapers, the *Amsterdam News*. While managing the newspaper's fiftieth anniversary campaign, Lockhart approached Rowe, a private consultant working for the *New York Amsterdam News*, and suggested that he was on the verge of landing a "big account" with Cuba. Rowe responded, "If you can bring in a big account, we want you as a member of our firm." Lockhart then relayed how he had received a telegram from INIT inviting him on an all-expenses-paid trip to Havana to discuss a business endeavor that would encourage black Americans to visit Cuba. Rowe accepted Lockhart's invitation and traveled to the island with him and Charles Fisher, the last member of the team, on 19 December 1959.[12]

While in Havana, the three met with Jesús Martinez, the assistant director of INIT, and discussed plans to bring thirty U.S. blacks to Cuba to participate in the revolution's first anniversary festivities. The guest list reveals INIT's desire to showcase African American sports celebrities and to link these celebrities' voices to the revolution. Martinez specifically requested that Roy Campanella, Jackie Robinson, Willie Mays, and Joe Louis come to the island for New Year's Eve. Campanella, Robinson, and Mays were popular baseball players who had begun their careers in the Negro Leagues before debuting in the Major Leagues. In particular, Robinson was well known for breaking the color line in U.S. baseball, with Campanella and Mays further integrating the sport soon after. Of the four sports celebrities invited to Havana, only Louis made the trip.[13] While the firm was unable to produce all of the well-known African American sports figures requested by INIT leaders, the Havana meeting resulted in over fifty U.S. black journalists, intellectuals, and families traveling to Cuba on 31 December 1959. This group included prominent leaders such as John Sengstacke, publisher and editor of the *Chicago Defender*, O. D. Dempsey, pastor of Harlem Baptist Church, and Dr. James Cowan, who later served in President Richard Nixon's administration.[14] The visitors were welcomed in Havana as distinguished guests, and Cuban officials hoped they would promote tourism to Cuba once they returned home. However, throughout the short January visit, the Cuban press focused on Joe Louis more than any other individual as a spokesperson in national conversations about how the revolution had supposedly eliminated racial discrimination.

"The People of the United States Defend Cuba," an article published in *Combate 13 de Marzo* on New Year's Day 1960, heralded Louis as the "famous ex-champion" and reminded readers that "while his fighting days may be over, his fame continues. [Louis] is considered one of the most notable figures of color in the United States." The article also described Louis's impressions of the island: "This is my third trip to Cuba and I always leave highly content with the treatment I have received from Cubans. They are very hospitable."[15] By linking Louis's fame to quotations where he describes feeling comfortable in revolutionary Cuba, the reporter, Alvaro López Conde, connected the boxer's success in the ring to the new government's potential. Various prints of a photograph of Louis shaking hands with Castro while wearing a *típico sombrero de yarey de nuestros guajiros* (typical Cuban country hat) also reinforced the boxer's approval of the young Cuban leader and could be found in at least eight dailies in January 1960.[16] Another photograph of a smiling Louis boasted the caption, "There is no discrimination."[17]

The Cuban press quoted other African Americans to validate Cuban claims of racial egalitarianism. In "Black Journalists from the United States Analyze Our Revolution," *Revolución* confirmed that black North Americans "were impressed with the revolution . . . and thought that the U.S. press was screaming communism at a government that was doing right by its people, without regard to race or class."[18] *Combate 13 de Marzo* noted how the *Chicago Defender*, one of the most influential black newspapers of the time, had placed Castro on its 1959 "List of Honor" for his work toward abolishing discrimination in Cuba.[19] These articles underlined African American support for revolutionary reforms and contributed to ongoing conversations about race in Cuba. Outside viewpoints appeared frequently in the international news pages of most Cuban dailies, but commentary from popular U.S. black athletes and intellectuals highlighted the progress of the revolution and suggested that the situation of people of color on the island was better than that of U.S. blacks in their respective country. Inserting African American opinions about racial equality into public conversations about revolutionary politics also recalled initial gestures made in spring 1959 to locate and publish Afro-Cuban voices supporting the new government.[20]

By the second week of January, INIT had finalized its contract with Louis, Rowe, Fisher, and Lockhart, agreeing to pay the agency $286,000 in exchange for marketing and promotional materials targeting U.S. black communities. The four members of the firm returned along with the rest of the tour group to the United States, where many of the visitors wrote about their experiences. John Sengstacke, editor of the *Chicago Defender*, published the article "Castro Abolishes Race Bias in Cuba" on 23 January 1960, in which he wrote, "To be honest I saw nothing in Cuba which I [did] not like." Sengstacke also interviewed fellow travelers about their sentiments toward the revolution. He quoted Louis as saying, "[It] is really good for Cuba to invite American Negroes to the country. Colored people in the U.S. do not have any place to go in the winter except Cuba. And I think they are going to take advantage of the fact."[21] In many ways, Louis was echoing comments Castro had made previously to the tour group: "In Cuba we are resolving problems that the United States has not been able to resolve, such as that of racial discrimination. . . . You all have seen . . . that everyone is able to dance together."[22] Castro and Louis legitimized their business relationship by contrasting continuing discrimination against blacks in the United States with the supposed racial equality achieved in Cuba. Yet struggles for civil rights in the United States were invoked by

Cubans as much to celebrate the revolution's antiracist campaign as to highlight its inconsistencies.

Imagining the United States: "Woolworth Denies Democratic Rights to Black People"

Tensions between Cuba and the United States were high by spring 1960, and leaders of both countries condemned what they interpreted as inappropriate governance by the other. U.S. officials were suspicious of trade agreements signed in February between Cuba and countries in the Soviet bloc. They saw these events as evidence that Cuba leaned toward communist doctrine, even though the country's official declaration of Marxist-Leninism did not occur until April 1961. At the same time, the Cuban government felt pressured both by U.S. threats to cut long-standing sugar quotas and by the support anti-Castro exiles found in Miami, Florida.[23] One way for Cubans to deflect U.S. disapproval of their new government was to stress inconsistencies in the U.S. political and economic system by highlighting the treatment of African Americans. Cuban dailies published articles, editorials, and photographs describing the unfair treatment of U.S. blacks and their struggle for full citizenship ninety miles away. These sources have to be read and interpreted carefully, since most historians agree that by 1961 the Cuban press had become closely linked to the state. Nearly all oppositional newspapers, including *Avance*, *El Mundo*, *Diario de la Marina*, and *Prensa Libre*, "had been seized by the government or closed down altogether" by the end of 1960.[24] However, a close analysis of editorial letters by nonleaders such as students, women, and a variety of Afro-Cubans emphasizes the fluidity of opinion during the moment immediately following the African American visit and provides some insight into the continued incompleteness of state consolidation at the time.

Revolutionary discourses invoked examples of violence and discrimination against black Americans to contradict U.S. declarations of freedom and democracy. A front-page article in *Combate 13 de Marzo* titled "The Yankee Police Attack Blacks in the United States" was accompanied by photographs of police beating both male and female protesters attempting to gain entrance to a whites-only restaurant. The caption beneath the photograph reads "Democracy in the United States," drawing attention to the irony that the United States criticized Cuba for executing war criminals while simultaneously abusing its own black citizens.[25]

Similarly, a first-year medical student labeled the United States a *demo-kkkracia* (demokkkracy) and said it was "absurd for a country that values liberty like the United States to continue to be divided into blacks and whites."[26] These Cubans criticized racial violence in the United States on the grounds of both social justice and foreign policy, inasmuch as such violence rebuffed U.S. critiques of the Cuban Revolution. "Every day we are watching black North Americans try to achieve their deserved space, not just in life, but in a restaurant or a bus," Afro-Cuban poet Nicolás Guillén wrote. "Reader, do you think that there is anyone [in the United States] who can come and talk seriously to us about the free world? If there is, they should raise their hand and step forward, because we would like to meet them."[27] Likewise, revolutionary leader Rául Roa dismissed a statement made in the U.S. Congress that "90 miles from the United States is a communist regime" by replying, "Well, 90 miles from Cuba there is racial discrimination."[28] These statements reflected daily debates on the island. For many Cubans, the continued existence of racism in the United States refuted claims that the country was a genuine democracy and distinguished the 1959 revolution as a unique antiracist national project.

Given their awareness of race relations in the United States, it is not surprising that young Cubans supported the sit-ins that swept the U.S. South in the spring of 1960 by picketing the North American–owned Woolworth store in Havana.[29] Students from M 26-7, the DR, Socialist Youth, and the National Committee of Orientation and Integration marched outside the store located on the corner of Galiano and San Rafael holding signs that read "Woolworth Denies Democratic Rights to Black People."[30] Cuban student organizations argued that U.S. blacks and revolutionary Cubans were "fighting against a common enemy" and "that each victory here or there weakened the forces of bad everywhere."[31] After the Woolworth picket, *Combate 13 de Marzo* editorialist Casandra noted that the "protests against racial discrimination in the USA, taking place here in Cuba, reaffirm that for us [Cubans] this problem is beginning to have a just solution. And we owe this to the Revolution!"[32]

The Woolworth episode demonstrates the wide-ranging support for the U.S. civil rights movement among student leaders in Cuba. It also reveals both the pride some Cuban youth felt in being part of the revolutionary movement sweeping their country and their enthusiasm for international social justice causes. Some students compared the problems facing black Americans to racial tensions in Cuba and found that the latter

country was having more success in eliminating racism. Like the leaders of INIT, many Cuban youth thought that African Americans should
visit Cuba to experience true freedom. One elementary schoolteacher
was persuaded that "soon they [U.S. blacks] will triumph, but if this does
not happen, then I am sure that here [in Cuba], they will have a piece of
free land where equality exists for all men."[33] These opinions recalled
the claims made by Cuban leaders when they invited African Americans
to vacation on the island and worked to reinforce public discourses that
imagined Cuba as a racial paradise.

Not all Cubans agreed with this official rhetoric, however. Afro-Cubans
in particular challenged the revolution's claims of achieved racial equality,
most notably in regard to access to national tourist and recreational facilities. Writing in *Noticias de Hoy*, *mulato* author Nicolás Guillén addressed
these contradictions in the article "Discrimination and Literature." "It
would be unfair to say that we are like we were in 1912," he wrote, referring to the 1912 Independent Party of Color massacre. "But, the other
extreme is equally false, that which . . . we have heard more than once
recently, that racial discrimination does not exist '*anymore*' in Cuba."[34]
For Guillén, there was a discrepancy between the rhetoric proclaimed to
and for African American visitors and the lived experience of people of
color on the island. Similarly, other individuals and groups wrote letters
and articles to popular Cuban dailies describing the unfair treatment of
black Cubans between January and June 1960. Editors and citizens claimed
that they wanted to denounce (*denunciar*) a certain group or individual
for racism and frequently asked the government to sanction (*sancionar*)
discrimination against Cubans of color. These conversations about racial
equality reveal an opening after 1959 for both white and black Cubans to
challenge white supremacy on the island. They also show how in seeking
access to white-only spaces such as social clubs and tourist centers, Afro-
Cubans exploited the rhetoric popularized during the African American
visits to Cuba.

Echoing revolutionary leaders who compared the island to the United
States, ordinary Cubans frequently structured complaints about domestic
racial discrimination by asking the government to fulfill its promise to
have better race relations than the U.S. South. The Afro-Cuban recreational association the Victoria Society wrote to *Combate 13 de Marzo* to
"denounce" the opening of a new "Ten Cents Cubano" in Camagüey. The
society described how, much like Woolworth in the United States, the
new store planned to refuse service to blacks. This prompted the society

to argue that "Cuba cannot support the actions of those who are trying to copy here the situation existing in our neighbor to the north. This is why the Revolution has to continue to advance."[35] Similarly, Afro-Cuban journalist Reynaldo Peñalver compared classified advertisements in Cuban newspapers seeking employees of a specific race to the divisive techniques used by the Ku Klux Klan. Describing how *Diario de la Marina* continued to print advertisements soliciting a "white" girl as a domestic worker or a "white" man as a chauffeur, Peñalver questioned whether the editors of the newspaper were "aware that Cuba is undergoing a revolution."[36] Authors and readers struggled to make the racial paradise promised by the revolution a reality by contrasting Cuban practices to those of the United States. Interestingly, blacks and *mulatos* mobilized the same language used to fight formal segregation in the United States when attacking informal practices in Cuba. This was not the first time that Afro-Cubans had faced discrimination or used this comparative strategy to denounce it. However, the combined use of hemispheric comparisons and revolutionary discourses to fight racial inequality provided a unique opening in the early part of 1960.

Other Cubans also recognized the disjuncture between the promise that their island was an ideal place for U.S. blacks to visit and the persistence of racial discrimination, especially in provincial tourist centers. In the town of Banes, in Oriente province, a dentist wrote a letter reporting that employees in the local tourist center practiced discrimination and turned Cubans of color away from a popular soda fountain. After calling this accusation "extremely grave," *La Calle*'s editors asked INIT to investigate immediately because "the Cuban Revolution is an example to the world of humanism and generosity and cannot allow representatives of the tourist centers to act in a way that is not fitting with revolutionary ideals."[37] As we saw at the beginning of this chapter, Reynaldo Peñalver critiqued a similar event in Mayajigua, a small town in central Cuba, in "Discrimination in a Restaurant."[38] In the article, Peñalver accused a tourist diner of refusing service to a group of black men solely based on their race and publicly called for a government investigation. A few days later, the local workers' union in Mayajigua, of which the men were members, demanded sanctions against the restaurant's owner for racial discrimination.[39]

It is unclear how the revolutionary government responded to these critiques. However, the very act of denouncing and attempting to sanction businesses and facilities perpetuating racial divisions showed an awareness among Cubans that 1960 was a moment when it was publicly unacceptable to be a racist. Cubans of color used a combination of new transnational and old domestic discourses to express the racism they experienced when attempting to use the very tourist centers INIT heralded as perfect vacation destinations for African Americans. In fact, black and *mulato* Cubans undermined revolutionary plans to use the highly publicized visit of Joe Louis to discredit the U.S. government by openly stating that Cuba had not yet achieved racial equality. Their actions reveal the complexities of comparing the situation of African Americans to that of blacks in Cuba. Once revolutionary leaders highlighted the distinctly un-American racial paradise allegedly available on the island, they created the space for Afro-Cubans to manipulate this discourse for their own needs. Such manipulation shows how the conditions facing most Afro-Cubans were much more complicated than the romanticized version that INIT presented to Joe Louis and other African American tourists. Promises to African Americans that they would receive hospitable treatment in Cuban tourist centers legitimized Afro-Cuban demands that recreational and tourist attractions be open to them as well. While it is not clear how INIT resolved complaints about discrimination, these political openings and the hopes they raised helped to racialize the rhetoric of the Cuban Revolution.

Imagining Cuba: "Come and Discover the Real Cuba for Yourself, You'll Love the Difference!"

In the United States, Louis, Rowe, Fisher, and Lockhart Enterprises, Inc. published advertisements depicting the beauty of Cuba and its people in prominent African American periodicals such as the *Pittsburgh Courier, Chicago Defender, Washington Afro-American, New York Age, Crusader, New York Amsterdam News, Cleveland Call and Post, Ohio Sentinel,* and *Jet* magazine. "Come to Cuba—The tourist paradise, where you get: First class treatment— as a first class citizen," the full-page advertisements announced, urging readers to "Come and Discover the Real Cuba for Yourself, You'll Love the Difference!"[40] Filled with photographs of integrated schoolrooms and black and white youths playing soccer in public parks, these advertisements implicitly compared the racial integration in Cuba with the injustice of the Jim Crow South, where Woolworth continued to refuse to serve blacks.

Many of these promotions contained visual images contrasting darker- and lighter-skinned Cubans and North Americans mingling together at leisure. Images of swimsuit-clad *mulata* women flirtatiously inviting readers to the island mirrored how Cuban women had been portrayed historically in the U.S. media. However, the inclusion of darker-skinned women in the photographs departed from the traditional focus on the *mulata* in U.S. promotions and made these advertisements peculiar to the African American press.[41] A May 1960 advertisement titled "Cuba Calls!" celebrated the revolution's desegregation of golf courses with a photograph of African American golfer Teddy Rhodes shaking hands with the son of a white INIT official, Jesús Montane.[42] Another full-page announcement, "Racial Integration Advances in Cuba," included images of black and white children playing with the caption, "The termination of racial discrimination in Cuba has been singled out as an outgrowth of the revolution, headed by Fidel Castro. According to reports, integration is now practiced in all of the official centers and different institutions on the island."[43] The public relations firm used the data they had collected during their January visit to Havana to promote Cuba as an integrated and racially mixed society where all shades of African Americans could enjoy leisure activities like golf, soccer, and swimming. Joe Louis and other black leaders insisted upon their return from Cuba that the island was one of the few destinations where African Americans could vacation freely, in sharp contrast to most U.S. resorts. The images used in the firm's marketing campaign sought to appeal to disgruntled African Americans searching for a sunny vacation from segregation.

Even though some Cubans might have disagreed with how the public relations firm portrayed their island, the campaign had sufficient credibility with African Americans both to generate responses in the black press and to warrant exploration by the Federal Bureau of Investigation (FBI). The FBI, purportedly concerned with the potential for communist infiltration of African American communities, began to probe Louis and his partners' connection with Cuba as early as January 1960. The FBI traced Louis's phone calls, tracked his travels throughout the United States, and put a "discrete mail cover" on his mailbox to inspect incoming correspondence.[44] In April, news of Louis's Cuba affiliation became public after his firm registered as a foreign agent with the U.S. Department of Justice, a necessary step for conducting business in another country. Critics of Cuba reacted immediately, and U.S. newspaper headlines in May and June 1960 were full of anticommunist and paternalistic rhetoric against the boxer. Columnist Jimmy Cannon's article in *American Weekly*, "Say It Ain't So, Joe," criticized Louis for being duped by Castro. Claiming that the business venture with Cuba was "evidence of how far he has fallen" from his days as a poster boy for American soldiers in World War II, Cannon called Louis weak and said that he "pitied him."[45] The author also argued that only Louis's naïveté allowed him to dismiss the fact that the Cuban government was using his name for "anti-American" and "communist friendly" purposes. Similarly, the *New York Times* labeled Louis a "foreign agent," while the *New York Mirror* called the heavyweight champion a "drumbeater for Fidel Castro's Cuba."[46]

In each of these examples, U.S. newspapers dismissed claims that African Americans could only find first-class treatment outside of their own country and assumed that blacks were duped by communist manipulators. Many U.S. critics read Cuban invitations to African American tourists as communist attempts to infiltrate domestic racial politics. Facing such allegations, Louis responded that his firm was not involved in Cuban politics and that their agreement was with INIT only and not with Castro. He also pointed out that a white-owned public relations agency had been hired at the same time by INIT to promote travel to Cuba among white Americans, and yet no one was criticizing them.[47]

African Americans felt that the white press vilified Louis and his partners because they were black, and these African Americans supported the firm's decision to work with Cuba. *Chicago Defender* editorial columnist Masco Young suggested that "those folks who're criticizing Joe Louis and his associates for accepting the $287,000 fee for publicizing Cuba are apparently forgetting that Joe, and no other Negro, could get a similar job at home in the good old U.S.A."[48] Similarly, Jackie Robinson questioned why no one was challenging the "propriety" of companies like General Motors, Coca-Cola, Esso Standard Oil, and many others that continued to conduct business in Cuba.[49] Louis, Rowe, Fisher, and Lockhart also received dozens of letters from supporters encouraging them to continue providing travel opportunities for the black community.[50]

Despite this support, Louis ended his association with the public relations firm in June and denied any further connection with Castro. Initially, Lockhart and Rowe planned to continue the business venture without Louis as the headliner. However, continued pressure from critics soon forced the other men to terminate the contract as well. Firm president William Rowe sent a letter to Baudilio Castellanos, director of INIT, on 7 July 1960 to explain: "We understood and appreciated the banning of discrimination in Cuba, and felt prone to publicize Cuba as a new Utopia, where the promise of first-class treatment as first-class citizens would be a reality for American Negroes. . . . However, the conflict of interest, of which you are familiar, has continued to multiply, and the failure of (INIT) [*sic*] to overcome its financial problems leaves us no alternative except to resign."[51]

After this decision, the debate over Louis's relationship to Cuba calmed down in the United States, but consequences remained. Louis's reputation as the American hero who encouraged U.S. soldiers to fight in World War II was tarnished permanently in the eyes of those who questioned his patriotism, politics, and dedication to capitalism. U.S. critics of communism saw the Cuban solicitation of African American tourists as further proof of the divisive and radical nature of the new Castro regime. Many African Americans, however, continued to be fascinated by reports that Cuba had eliminated racial discrimination, a fascination that foreshadowed visits to Cuba by Monroe, North Carolina, National Association for the Advancement of Colored People (NAACP) president Robert Williams, black intellectual Harold Cruse, and many others during the summer of 1960.[52] Most importantly, however, African Americans became familiar with images and rhetoric portraying Cuba as a racial paradise. As we will see, these ideas resurfaced when Castro and the Cuban UN delegation relocated to Harlem in September 1960 to stay in the black-owned Hotel Theresa. The *New York Amsterdam News* reported how Malcolm X visited Castro in his hotel and reassured the Cuban leader that U.S. blacks did not believe the negative propaganda written about Cuba in the white press.[53]

Louis's "Low Blow": A Short-Lived Business Venture

Cuban officials learned of Louis's decision to distance himself publicly from the new government in June 1960. And while the former boxer did not speak directly against the revolution, Cubans expressed their surprise and disappointment over his resignation in a variety of ways. Some blamed his actions on pressure from the U.S. government and remained supportive of the ex-champion. Others, however, disapproved of Louis's weakness in succumbing to U.S. coercion, and they portrayed Louis as a fallen hero.

Many Cubans struggled to explain the change in Louis's thinking and his rejection of the revolution without tarnishing his celebrated iconic status. One high school student found that "the declarations of Joe Louis attacking the revolutionary government of Cuba are a consequence of the racial problem in the United States. This is nothing more than pressure that has been exercised [on him] by the discriminating Americans which causes him to lie to win the indulgences of Uncle Sam."[54] INIT director Baudilio Castellanos issued a public statement explaining the position of the Cuban government regarding Louis's resignation. He argued that Louis was a "victim of U.S. oppression" and that the boxer had only renounced his agreement after enduring a public "character assassination" in the U.S. press. Castellanos emphasized that it was well known that Louis was a "great friend and sympathizer" of Castro and Afro-Cuban commander Juan Almeida, but intense pressure from the U.S. government forced him to deny those associations.[55] Additionally, the INIT leader highlighted how Louis had enjoyed his previous visits to Cuba and the enthusiasm the boxer felt for the new government's moves to eliminate racial discrimination. By labeling Louis as a victim who continued to support the revolution privately if not publicly, Cubans assumed that the racist democracy of the United States forced his reversal. Castellanos's choice to stress the continued personal connection between Louis, Castro, and Almeida also suggests that he wanted to repair the relationship between African Americans and Cubans, which might have been damaged by the boxer's hasty cutting of his Cuban ties.

Cuban newspapers published opinions from African American leaders to support their claim that racism fueled the disapproval Louis encountered in the United States. NAACP leader Montgomery Reynolds noted that he was "disgusted" by the Louis situation and mockingly called the pressure on Louis an example of the "racial equality" that exists in the United States. "This sin of discrimination should be eliminated in the United States, in the same way it has been eliminated in Cuba."[56] Similarly, the Havana-based newspaper *El Mundo* reprinted Jackie Robinson's editorial from the *Chicago Defender* that contrasted how some white companies were allowed to continue their business in Cuba without comment while Louis and his associates were called traitors to their country.[57] Not only do these examples demonstrate the transnational conversation about racial politics occurring between Cubans and African Americans, but they also reveal how the Cuban press located and circulated U.S. black voices to legitimize Cuban racial politics and to denounce the United States. Together with official statements by Castellanos, these articles represent a faction of Cubans who viewed Louis and his partners as victims of forces beyond their control and who defended the ex-champion even though he could no longer openly support Cuba.

Other Cubans focused on the personal weakness of Louis as the reason behind his resignation. Building from the assumption that Louis faced significant pressure from the U.S. media, some critics portrayed the former boxer as craven and old for succumbing to such tactics. One writer described Louis as having an "expression of defeat" on his face during a press conference. Saying that he looked "unhappy and incapable of resisting," the journalist seemed to pity Louis.[58] Another contributor depicted a "confused" Louis who, having spent most of his earnings from boxing, was now "impoverished," in debt for delinquent taxes, and forced to renounce his contract with INIT.[59] These accounts portray a man without the strength to stand up for himself or his beliefs, and they contrast sharply with the descriptions of Louis published in January when he celebrated the New Year with revolutionary leaders. Rather than seeing him as the glorified former heavyweight champion of the world who had posed proudly with Castro in a Cuban farm hat, these Cubans viewed Louis as the epitome of black helplessness against U.S. influence and pressure.

Political cartoons demonstrated these attitudes in visual form. Published shortly after Louis and his partners renounced their contract with INIT, the cartoon "Without Words" shows a small character waving his arms and shouting at a much larger Statue of Liberty.[60] The small figure in the sketch, drawn using characteristics similar to those in depictions of Afro-Cubans in other political cartoons, represents Louis and his associates. Reflecting how Louis was powerless to pursue his economic and political interests in the United States, the title of the cartoon highlights how Louis and other U.S. blacks were voiceless in their nation. The title also implies that readers would have understood the cartoon without a caption because Cubans were already familiar with the unequal and second-class status of African Americans.

Some Cubans felt that Louis was not only weak and powerless, but that he also lacked dignity. A writer for *La Calle* agreed that Louis had encountered formidable pressure from the U.S. media; however, he argued, so had many others before him. The columnist claimed that in the face of oppression and challenges some chose the solitariness of exile, others went to prison, and even more resisted, but that many, like Joe Louis, gave in. In the case of Louis, this writer concluded that "the old, the great, the valiant gladiator of the ring has no more weapons with which to fight . . . tied to the good life, he prefers to sell his decorated dignity in exchange for the ability to play golf in the afternoon."[61]

Another cartoon, titled "Ex Campeón en Apuros" ("The Jammed-Up Ex-Champion"), linked Louis's resignation with his desire for material wealth and poked fun at the former heavyweight champion. This cartoon shows two men observing Louis in the boxing ring. One asks the other, "Do you think they knocked him out or that he threw himself onto the floor?" The second man responds, "In my opinion, it was a fixed fight."[62] The discussion between the onlookers implies that the U.S. government paid Louis to renounce his contract with INIT in order to neutralize any positive comments the fighter had made about the Cuban Revolution. The disapproving look on the faces of the two men, coupled with language labeling the situation a "fixed fight," the ultimate insult to a boxer, demonstrates both a growing disgust with Louis for his renunciation of the INIT scheme and a rejection of his glorified boxing past. It is unknown how Cuban readers reacted to these cartoons; however, the themes of betrayal, anger, and shame they express suggest that many Cubans expected more from Louis and were disappointed in his sudden turnaround. Persistent references to Louis choosing money over revolution signaled a shift in revolutionary relationships with African Americans. The failure of the Louis business venture suggested that after 1959 Cubans might more easily establish revolutionary relationships with less mainstream elements of the African American community. Focusing on U.S. blacks' helplessness also allowed revolutionary leaders to send certain messages to Afro-Cubans about what was (or was not) possible in the United States and Cuba. The pressure applied to Louis by the U.S. media highlighted for Afro-Cubans how in the United States white supremacy limited the economic and political mobility of African Americans. But in Cuba, responses to Louis's decision reflected how turning away from the revolution could lead to humiliation.

INIT, however, continued to encourage African Americans to visit Cuba despite the termination of the public relations contract with Louis, Rowe, Fisher, and Lockhart. The Cuban press claimed that INIT director Castellanos sent a public letter to the United States inviting people to the island: "Cuba was a place without segregation or discrimination," he wrote, where all people were welcome.[63] Consequently, Monroe NAACP president Robert Williams traveled with Richard Gibson from the Fair Play for Cuba Committee (FPCC), Amiri Baraka (then LeRoi Jones), Julian Mayfield, and Harold Cruse to Cuba in June 1960. In "Why I Am Going to Cuba," published in the *Crusader*, Williams explained how he wanted to see Cuba for himself "because I cannot accept the reports of the respectable American press which has proven itself a galvanized conductor of lies here when reporting incidents involving Negroes. . . . It is hard to believe that Cuba is worse than Mississippi."[64] Interestingly, while many of the African Americans who traveled to Cuba in June 1960 wrote extensively about their impressions of the island and its race relations upon their return home, Cuban newspapers featured few, if any, articles about this trip.[65] The absence of press coverage about African Americans in Cuba in the summer of 1960 demonstrates the strategic nature of national attention to U.S. blacks. In January 1960, when Joe Louis was visiting the island and INIT was trying to promote African American tourists, it was important to publicly celebrate U.S. blacks who were willing to travel to Cuba in the face of discouragement from their government. But, by June 1960, with Afro-Cubans mobilizing the language Cuban leaders had used to welcome Louis's contingent to demand additional reforms, revolutionary leaders returned to writing about domestic concerns rather than publicize the Williams, Gibson, Baraka, Mayfield, and Cruse trip.

After the resignation of Louis, Rowe, Fisher, and Lockhart, revolutionary leaders remained committed to appealing to African Americans. This included plans for a letter-writing campaign to congratulate Dr. Martin Luther King Jr. on receiving the "Most Decorated Man of the Year" award from a Baptist Church organization in the United States. In correspondence between high-ranking Cuban officials, the chief of protocol wrote the presidents of the CTC, FEU, and National Executive Committee of Orientation and Integration saying, "Since it is of great importance for our Revolution to capture [the support of] black North Americans, permit us to suggest that you send a message to Dr. Luther King in the name of your organization."[66] This purposeful recognition of the importance of gaining African American support for the revolution persisted throughout the 1960s, although Cuban leaders increasingly turned their attention to more marginalized sectors of the U.S. black population. New exchanges occurred primarily between white representatives of the Cuban government and radical or militant black leaders and groups in the United States. Cuban officials became less interested in working with black entrepreneurs (who were financially vulnerable to pressure by the U.S. government) and shifted their focus to building relationships with allies who could support both their antiracist and anti-imperialist stance. Similarly, African American leaders who risked association with the Cuban Revolution, such as Malcolm X, Robert Williams, and Richard Gibson, did so with the knowledge that any involvement between them and the Castro government could lead to public criticism.

On the Corner of 125th St. and 7th Ave.: Internationalizing Racial Politics, September 1960

After July (and the height of press coverage about Louis's resignation), the number of articles in *Revolución*, *Noticias de Hoy*, *La Calle*, and *Combate 13 de Marzo* about either U.S. blacks or the civil rights movement declined. However, this silence was abruptly broken when the Cuban delegation to the UN, led by Fidel Castro, packed their bags and departed in a motorcade from their suites in the Manhattan Shelburne Hotel for the UN headquarters at 7 P.M. on 19 September 1960. The reason for the after-hours visit was simple. Castro and his group were dissatisfied with their treatment at the midtown hotel and went to the UN to demand a more hospitable residence.[67] Threatening to sleep in Central Park if the issue was not resolved, Castro filed a complaint, returned to his Oldsmobile, and headed to lodging where he felt his group would be more welcome—in Harlem. UN officials were mystified by this sudden departure and ordered various police cars to follow the Cuban caravan to its unknown destination, both to provide security to the delegates and to monitor their actions. Thus, 10 P.M. arrived with a mob of traffic spilling into uptown Harlem, including police cars, the eighty-person Cuban delegation, and an assortment of newspaper reporters. This diverse group was met by a cheering, albeit surprised, crowd of African Americans, Puerto Ricans, Dominicans, and Cubans standing on the corner of 125th Street and 7th Avenue, outside of the aging Hotel Theresa. The Theresa was well known in the African American community for housing popular black figures and celebrities during the twentieth century; international star Josephine Baker, congressional representative Adam Clayton Powell, and boxer Joe Louis all had stayed there. However, that evening in September was the first time in history that its suites were occupied by a foreign head of state.

Cuban and African American audiences were already acquainted with each other when Castro landed on Harlem's doorstep in September 1960. Advertisements encouraging U.S. blacks to travel to the island, combined with North American press coverage about the events occurring in the neighboring country, provided many Harlem residents with an awareness, at least partially, of revolutionary programs targeting people of color. Similarly, Cubans were sensitive to the reality of racial segregation and violence in the United States and the desire of some African Americans to visit the island, encouraged by recent encounters with Joe Louis. However, the Cuban delegation's move from the Shelburne Hotel in Manhattan to the Theresa in Harlem brought international attention to the new government's racial politics. Unlike the previous exchange that occurred in Cuba and in a space mostly controlled by revolutionary leaders, this new interaction between Cubans and African Americans occurred on U.S. soil, a situation that immediately escalated tensions between the two governments. Revolutionary leaders proclaimed to African American crowds, world leaders attending the UN, and Cuban readers at home that the new government had eliminated racial discrimination and would support other oppressed groups fighting for equality. This section investigates this moment in Harlem to provide a better understanding of the evolution of revolutionary discourses on racism and the changing relationship between Cubans and African Americans in the latter part of 1960.

Both contemporary journalists and recent scholars have offered various interpretations of the motivations behind Castro's surprising move to Harlem. Most often these readings focus on assessing the successes and failures of the Cuban campaign to attract African American support for the revolution and the role U.S. blacks played in defending the post-1959 Cuban government.[68] Yet, concentrating on whether or not U.S. blacks supported Castro fails to explain why the two groups sought out each other and what they gained through constructing particular images of one another. Similar to the conversations occurring during Joe Louis's visit to Havana, newspaper articles generated throughout the Cuban delegation's stay in Harlem suggest that both African Americans and Cubans invoked a particular concept of the other to further their domestic agendas.[69]

Cuban leaders used the UN meeting as an opportunity to assert internationally that their policies toward people of color were different from previous administrations. The Cuban press highlighted the revolution's stance against racial segregation in the United States with visual images of the new leadership in a black hotel, eating in a "colored" restaurant, and leading crowds of U.S. citizens to shout "Cuba, Sí!, Yankee, No!" By enthusiastically accepting lodging in a black-owned business, despite their ability to stay in a more prestigious Manhattan hotel, the new government announced its growing interest in global racial politics and transferred ongoing domestic conversations about black and *mulato* Cubans to debates about racism in the United States and anticolonialism in Africa. However, the evidence also reveals that alongside positive images of revolutionary leaders surrounded by cheering African Americans, Cuban readers also encountered representations of U.S. blacks as juvenile and helpless. Similar to photographs published in 1959 depicting Afro-Cubans as downtrodden, poor, and in need of reform before they could become citizens, images of African Americans in the Cuban press perpetuated notions of black inferiority in contrast to white revolutionary might.

Most importantly, the Harlem event highlights a crucial shift from open conversations about how to best eliminate racial discrimination to a public consensus that the new government had achieved this goal. As discussed earlier, in the spring of 1960 Afro-Cubans wrote articles calling for additional reforms and denouncing establishments that continued to practice racial prejudice in response to promises made to African American tourists. However, Cuban newspapers published very few criticisms disturbing the idea that racial discrimination had been removed from the island while Castro and the delegation were in Harlem. Most histories of Cuba identify 1962 as the official closure of conversations about racial equality. Alejandro de la Fuente finds that "the initial campaign against racial discrimination waned after 1962, leading to a growing public silence on the issue—except to note Cuba's success in the area."[70] And political scientist Mark Sawyer concurs that the "revolution's early dialogue on race ended in 1962 when the problem was declared officially solved."[71] The silence about domestic racism occurring in the Cuban press while the delegation was in Harlem reveals that debates about ending racial discrimination closed long before 1962. Afro-Cubans on the island could not and did not publicly contradict the official stance that the revolution had achieved racial equality in September 1960. In fact, most Afro-Cuban leaders participated in the national consensus celebrating the revolution's elimination of racial discrimination. Only exiles in Miami criticized publicly the move to the Hotel Theresa as a propaganda stunt.

The immediate suppression of racial issues and a closing of debates about racial equality after the initial opening in 1959 foreshadowed future problems for Afro-Cubans. By failing to create a positive language for talking about race and inequality, the Cuban leadership silenced future dialogues and limited possibilities for progress. Yet, these were tough decisions made by both revolutionary leaders and Afro-Cubans as criticism from the United States grew and the threat of intervention seemed imminent. Revolutionary leaders found it more important to discredit U.S. democracy and protect national cohesiveness than talk about lingering racial prejudices. Cuban newspapers expressed outrage for the plight of U.S. blacks without mentioning the situation of people of color in Cuba because by the latter part of 1960 it was easier to discuss the troubles of blacks in the United States than disturb the romanticized image of Cuban racial equality. Talking about instances of global racism also opened doors for alliances with the newly independent African countries, which some Cuban leaders saw as an important partner in the battle against U.S. aggression.

Prelude to Harlem

Leaders in the United States and Cuba knew that the 1960 New York meeting of the UN General Assembly would be unique. For the first time, representatives from newly liberated African countries attended the summit, along with increasingly popular leaders from the Soviet bloc and revolutionary Cuba. However, until a few weeks before the meeting, the U.S. government believed that President Osvaldo Dorticós would head the Cuban delegation, not Fidel Castro. Growing tensions between the two countries changed this plan and Castro decided to travel to New York to represent Cuba and respond to U.S. criticisms of the new government. Events occurring prior to the Cuban delegation's arrival in Harlem foreshadowed the highly publicized conflict that eventually occurred between leaders from the two countries during the international summit. The insertion of conversations about which country provided the best opportunities to people of African descent might have been expected given the debates that occurred while Joe Louis was working with INIT; however, the physical relocation of the Cuban delegation to a black-owned hotel was a radical move that generated much excitement and speculation from onlookers in New York and readers on the island.

Cuban representatives went to the UN to challenge the Declaration of San José, a document approved by the Organization of American States (OAS) on 28 August 1960 in San José, Costa Rica. The declaration was a proposal sponsored by the United States and passed by a majority of other Latin American leaders that condemned the nationalist character of the Cuban Revolution and agreed to enact sanctions against the country if Cuba aligned itself with the Soviet bloc. At the OAS meeting, Raúl Roa, Cuba's foreign minister, offered a scathing rebuttal of the declaration but was unable to prevent the passing of the agreement. Cuba responded by issuing its own proclamation, the Declaration of Havana, on 2 September

1960. Announced in front of a crowd of over one million Cubans, the Declaration of Havana summarized the politics of the revolution and condemned imperialist actions, reactionary interest groups, large landowners and corporations, and those who discriminated against "Blacks, Indians, and women." Castro asked the massive audience if they approved the declaration and with shouts of "Si" and "Ya, votamos con Fidel" (We vote with Fidel) the crowd gave its answer.[72] Cuban leaders asserted that the declaration had been voted for and approved by the "National General Assembly of the Cuban People," and took it as a mandate to continue with their revolutionary programs. In the following weeks, organizations and individuals across the island wrote to national newspapers to express support for the Declaration of Havana.[73] The declaration served to express Cuban discontent with U.S. interference in domestic affairs and set the tone for the upcoming UN meeting. And while little specific attention was paid to the concerns of Afro-Cubans, the declaration highlighted racial discrimination among a list of important injustices that the revolution planned to fight internationally.

A few weeks later, Castro led the Cuban delegation to the UN to convey this message to the world. Castro's decision to head the group surprised the U.S. State Department and they retaliated by restricting the Cubans' movements to the island of Manhattan. This limitation was applied to Nikita Khrushchev, leader of the Soviet Union, and representatives from the Hungarian and Albanian delegations as well; however, in Cuba it was interpreted as another insult in a growing trend of hostilities between the two nations. One cartoonist used this situation to undermine U.S. democracy by sketching the statue of liberty crying after becoming aware of the travel restrictions imposed by the State Department.[74] With these competing decisions, leaders from both countries began what would become a cycle of reacting to one another's actions with excessively theatrical countermeasures. This push-and-pull dynamic ultimately spilled over into Harlem.

When the manager at the Shelburne Hotel asked the Cuban delegation to pay an additional $5,000 deposit for their rooms, increasing the total amount to $10,000, the conflict reached a critical peak. Castro said that he would rather sleep on the lawns of Central Park than continue to be treated as an unwelcome guest in New York and proceeded to file a formal complaint with the UN secretary general. Following the meeting with UN leaders, the Cubans packed their bags and moved to the Hotel Theresa in Harlem, where they were met by crowds of cheering African

Americans. Competing stories describe how the Cuban delegation came to stay in the Theresa. Some critics characterized the move as a purposeful, propaganda-seeking choice,[75] while others claimed that the delegation received poor treatment at the Shelburne and moved to Harlem to find more hospitable accommodation.[76] An article in *Verde Olivo*, the national Cuban publication for the revolutionary armed forces, reported that prior to arriving in New York the Theresa had offered lodging to the delegation. Castro initially refused this invitation because of existing plans to stay at the Shelburne; however, once free of those obligations, he decided to accept the offer.[77]

While it remains unclear who initiated the move to Harlem, it is apparent that residing in the Hotel Theresa became a significant metaphor for speaking to domestic issues faced by Cubans on the island. The move allowed revolutionary leaders to compare the mistreatment that the Cuban delegation felt they had received in Manhattan to the discrimination African Americans and other groups felt daily. Castro addressed this issue in his speech in front of the UN General Assembly when he criticized the "humiliating and degrading measures" the Cuban delegation had faced upon coming to the United States.[78] Similarly, *mulato* author Nicolás Guillén wrote an editorial pondering how the leader of the Cuban nation could be invited to an international meeting and then repeatedly bothered by the police and denied a simple room in a hotel.[79]

Revolutionary leaders quickly realized that in order to build relationships with U.S. blacks and representatives from newly liberated African countries, the delegation needed to appear as racially integrated as possible. Initially the delegation, like the governing coalition, was composed of white leaders, but after moving to Harlem, Castro immediately invited Afro-Cuban commander Juan Almeida to join the group in New York.[80] "I want the black leaders of Harlem to meet the leader of our armed services," Castro declared.[81] The request for Almeida to come to New York reveals an awareness among revolutionary leaders of the importance of not simply stating that the revolution had eliminated racial discrimination, but of showing how new policies had allowed Afro-Cubans to obtain prestigious positions in the government. An editorial in the magazine *Verde Olivo* contrasted the opportunities the revolution had provided for qualified black and *mulato* Cubans with the unfair limits imposed on African Americans. "The people of Harlem have to ask themselves: How is it that in our *demokracia* there is not one Black Minister, high executive in the armed forces, or ambassador? Is it because in twenty thousand people there is not one capable one?"[82] Articulations such as this demonstrate a consciousness among leading Cubans that the unequal treatment of U.S. blacks was an exploitable weakness of the United States.

Harlem through Cuban Eyes

The Cuban delegation occupied its rooms in the Hotel Theresa for ten days. During this period, Cubans on the island published numerous editorials and articles that worked to give the event multiple meanings. These discourses routinely inserted African Americans and the Harlem community into ongoing conversations about the hypocrisies of U.S. democracy, the popularity of revolutionary leaders, and the success of the campaign to eliminate racial discrimination. The most prominent theme throughout national conversations in 1960 was the claim that the Cuban Revolution had achieved racial equality in the island. Opinions printed in the national press while Castro was in Harlem sought to speak to Cuban audiences about these topics and other domestic issues through the lens of the U.S. black community. Similarly, African American leaders described the Cuban residence in the Hotel Theresa in ways that benefited them. This event shifted Cuban discourses about race between 1959 and 1961: instead of talking about how to eradicate domestic racism from the island, revolutionary leaders began to focus on battling global racial injustices. As a result, Cubans were inundated with press about the positive reception their leaders received from blacks in Harlem to show all readers, but especially Afro-Cuban audiences, the revolution's continued investment in racial equality. Similar to the discursive gestures discussed in previous chapters, the Castro government repeatedly sought ways to highlight its racial politics without alienating white Cubans. Dialoguing with African Americans allowed the young revolutionary regime to demonstrate its support of racial equality without undermining national solidarity.

Post-1959 racialized discourses invoked and emphasized U.S. race relations to ridicule the hypocrisies of U.S. democracy. The move to the Hotel Theresa in Harlem served as an occasion to reiterate these inconsistencies, especially as U.S. and counterrevolutionary criticism of the revolution increased. As the first half of this chapter showed, this was not the first time U.S. race relations served as a poignant example of the limits of North American democracy. Nevertheless, Cuban journalists emphasized the comfort the new leadership felt surrounded by people of color in Harlem, in contrast to unwritten rules keeping black and white Americans from socializing together, to distinguish their progressive racial politics from those of U.S. leaders. A political cartoon titled "Demokkkracia" and featuring a black silhouette hanging from a large cross surrounded by a group of hooded men highlighted the United States' long history of racial violence.[83] Another titled "The Ku Klux Klan Is Like That" featured a Klansman undressing to reveal the figure of Uncle Sam beneath the hood.[84] These cartoons, along with a sketch of Castro's beard strangling a Klansman, compared racial violence in the United States with revolutionary claims of equality.[85]

Images of Klansmen, blacks swinging from nooses, and Uncle Sam's tall hat had meaning for Cuban readers because of the cultural closeness between the United States and Cuba. These images also contributed to the popular belief that the Cuban Revolution had achieved racial equality while the United States had not. Castro voiced these contradictions in his speech to the UN. Cuban newspapers printed transcripts of both his talk and ones given by Raúl Castro as a means of showing readers how their leaders confronted the inconsistencies of U.S. ideals while in Harlem. Cuban journalists also proposed relocating the UN to another country since the U.S. State Department had neglected to guarantee suitable lodging for attending foreign leaders.[86] Each of these actions was a part of an ongoing project to inform readers of the myth of U.S. democracy. Such articulations were familiar to Cuban audiences, but the Harlem trip served as the immediate reworking of accepted ideas.

In a similar strategic manner, U.S. blacks inserted the delegation's residence at the Theresa into contemporary calls for desegregation and full citizenship. African Americans, including those who denounced the Cuban Revolution as communist, argued that its appeal to black America endangered democracy. These authors used the September event as further proof of why blacks deserved equal rights. They concluded that failure to treat all Americans as citizens was an embarrassment to U.S. articulations of liberty and democracy and increased the risk of communist infiltration into disillusioned black communities. One anti-Castro columnist warned against "dangling democracy" in front of U.S. blacks without following through. "It cannot be denied that a color-struck democracy is fighting against fearful odds," he wrote, especially with Khrushchev and Castro "forcing themselves into the forefront" of the debate.[87] The African American press used the Cuban Revolution as a metaphor to express long-standing arguments for equal rights. With Castro in the Hotel Theresa, the Cold War opened a new front in Harlem. And while this was not the first time black intellectuals had draped civil rights rhetoric in anticommunist rhetoric, the events of September 1960 served as a salient example of the potential dangers of ignoring the African American community. Similar to the tactical ways in which Cubans mobilized the event, African Americans also used it as a means of making additional demands for an integrated society.

Cuban writers frequently used military references when talking about the delegation's move to Harlem to connect the event to the ongoing fight against U.S. imperialism. A recurring column in *Revolución*, "Zona Rebelde" ("Rebel Zone"), printed an article titled "The Battle of New York" to identify the UN meeting as another "historic battle of the Cuban Revolution." The United States would receive "a great defeat" and Harlem was to be a "victory for Cuba."[88] Similarly, *Noticias de Hoy* identified the event as the "Battle of Harlem" and said that Castro would triumph as the true "liberator" of U.S. blacks.[89] Like arguments over Joe Louis's loyalty, the delegation's move to Harlem firmly placed racial politics at the center of conflicts between the United States and Cuba. It is significant that Cuban authors used military language to describe the UN meeting and imagined Harlem as the newest front in the battle for Cuban sovereignty, because it reveals a willingness on the part of revolutionary leaders to use racism as a moral weapon against the United States. Doing so, however, was only valuable if the new leaders could demonstrate that they were not racists and did not practice racial discrimination. Residing in a black-owned hotel legitimized this claim and allowed Cubans to link pledges to eliminate racial discrimination to other revolutionary battles. President Osvaldo Dorticós explained this idea in front of thousands of Cubans during a mass rally outside of the presidential palace. "The actions of the U.S. government [at the UN meeting] are its response to the Cuban Revolution, the Agrarian Reform, the nationalization of exploiting Yankee businesses, the revolutionary government's politics of independence and sovereignty, the measures to benefit popular [groups], the defense of racial equality and the respect of the dignity of man."[90] By claiming that the restrictions placed on the Cuban delegation were a part of the United States' reaction to revolutionary principles, including programs to eliminate racial privilege, Dorticós aligned the United States with oppression and Cuba with freedom and justice. With their residence at the Hotel Theresa, the Cuban delegation showed that it viewed African Americans, and implicitly Afro-Cubans, as part of the revolutionary fold.

African American leaders utilized similar metaphors to encourage radical black mobilization against racial inequality in the United States. One article in the *Washington Afro-American* noted how, prior to January 1959, Afro-Cubans had been discriminated against in the same way African Americans were. The author wrote, "On a recent visit to the island I saw proof that it doesn't take decades of gentle persuasion to deal a death blow to white supremacy."[91] In a direct attack on the nonviolent tactics of the NAACP, some U.S. intellectuals held up the Cuban Revolution to legitimize aggressive action in the struggle for civil rights. Other writers chastised African Americans for continuing to pursue peaceful steps toward political inclusion. According to a black councilman in New York, "Even the Africans, the Caribbeans and other foreign colored people feel superior to American Negroes because of their apparent willingness to accept second-class citizenship without fighting hard enough to achieve full equality."[92] On one hand, this statement compares African Americans to people of color throughout the world and suggests a race or phenotypically based link to African-descended people in other places. However, the author is also arguing for immediate and direct action from within the U.S. black community to combat racial inequality. These articles utilized the presence of the Cuban delegation in Harlem to rearticulate reasons for meeting violence with violence. Writers were willing to invoke an international community of color to make comparisons about their situation, yet like Cubans they envisioned potential solutions on the national level.

The Cuban press also emphasized the warm welcome Castro received in Harlem to demonstrate the revolution's ability to win allies in international politics. Images of crowds applauding the delegation were communicated to audiences on the island as a means of legitimizing the young government and its leadership. National dailies favored photographs of Cuban leaders surrounded by large crowds repeating revolutionary slogans. This imagery implied that Castro could entice hundreds of black Americans to chant "Cuba, Sí!, Yankee, No!" in the same way he commanded Cuban demonstrations outside of the presidential palace in Havana.[93] These visuals made sense to Cuban audiences familiar with mass mobilization as a means of showing political support. In particular, a full-page layout titled "Harlem: Police vs. the People" showed six different images of police officers harassing crowds fighting to get close to the Theresa Hotel to catch a glimpse of the popular Cuban leader. Captions under the photographs note that in "the zone where the most humble and poor citizens (*los humildes*) live, is where you find Fidel Castro."[94] When describing the crowds of African Americans who applauded the Cuban delegation in Harlem, authors repeatedly referred to blacks as *los humildes*.[95] For Cubans, identifying people of color in the United States as *humildes* signified that blacks were poor, humble, and uneducated, but also hard-working and honest. Authors invoked this language because Castro identified himself and the 26th of July Movement (M 26-7) "as a rebellion of *humildes* and for *humildes*."[96] This conceptualization transferred the relationship between the two groups from the sphere of race to that of class and allowed poor Cubans of all colors to relate to the struggles facing African Americans. Moreover, by repeatedly printing photographs of Castro surrounded by large crowds, newspapers dared readers to doubt the legitimacy of the new government and showed that the appeal of the revolution superseded national boundaries. Castro and his administration were natural leaders wherever they went since a majority of people throughout the Western hemisphere, especially people of color, supported the 1959 revolution.

Cuban journalists published details from meetings between revolutionary leaders and well-known African Americans to show that black intellectuals supported the new government as strongly as the crowds of *humildes* gathered outside of the hotel. On the same evening that the Cuban delegation arrived, Malcolm X visited Castro at the Theresa and the two men spoke about the relationship between their countries. Castro asked the black leader why African Americans had rejected the propaganda published in the U.S. media and welcomed his group to Harlem. Malcolm X responded that U.S. blacks were "aware that Fidel was against discrimination and in favor of the oppressed people in the world."[97] In response, Castro praised the savviness of African Americans and extended an invitation to Malcolm X to visit Cuba. Revolutionary leaders also met with other U.S. blacks while at the Theresa, including the hotel's manager Love B. Woods. In an interview with Reynaldo Peñalver, Woods compared the mistreatment the Cubans had faced at the Shelburne Hotel to the discrimination he encountered throughout his life in the United States: "I do not care what they do against me or the people of Harlem for giving Castro the lodging he deserves ... [because] in every way, with or without Castro, we have suffered from repression since we were born."[98] For Cubans reading such statements, the implied message was that revolutionary leaders had earned an international reputation for fighting U.S.

imperialism, implementing social justice projects, and eradicating racial prejudices. When printed in national Cuban newspapers, stories of these encounters also worked to show readers that the delegation had succeeded in forging alliances with African Americans based on their parallel positions as outcasts from mainstream U.S. society.

In addition to being a moment to ridicule U.S. democracy and show Cuban readers the international popularity of revolutionary leaders, moving to Harlem also announced, internationally, that the new government had abolished racial discrimination. This claim dominated Cuban conversations in September 1960. Castro stated in an interview that "in nineteen months the revolution has terminated racial discrimination" by eliminating privileges.[99] At the same time, to the applause of thousands of onlookers in front of the presidential palace, President Dorticós explained how revolutionary leaders would show the blacks in Harlem how "every man and woman [in Cuba], regardless of the color of their skin has equal rights."[100] Another journalist argued that staying in the Theresa demonstrated to African Americans the "true and just character of the Revolution," namely its ability to "fix" inequalities between blacks and whites.[101] These comments departed from previous Cuban discourses by portraying racial problems in Cuba as resolved rather than a work in progress. And while many would have argued, at least privately, that racial discrimination had yet to be eliminated, the announcement met little resistance from Cubans on the island.

Cuban journalists invoked popular U.S. president Abraham Lincoln as a metaphor for the revolution's successful elimination of racial discrimination. Images of Lincoln had meaning for Cuban audiences because many readers were familiar with his role in freeing American slaves. While in Harlem, Castro received a bust of Lincoln from the FPCC, during a reception with FPCC members and employees from the Hotel Theresa. The African American president of the committee, Richard Gibson, said "it is only fair that we give you this bust of Lincoln, the liberator of the slaves in this country, because you are the liberator of our friends the Cuban people."[102] Cuban newspapers highlighted this reception by repeatedly printing articles describing the event, but also through visual images linking Castro and Lincoln. A political cartoon titled "Happy" shows Castro talking to a small black figure in the foreground and Lincoln in the background commenting, "At last someone who understands me"[103] (figure 4.1). Similar to 1959 discourses connecting Castro to José Martí,

Felix   Por Blanco

LINCOLN—¡Por fin alguien me comprende...!

Figure 4.1 "Happy"; "Lincoln—'At last someone who understands me!'" From *El Mundo* (23 September 1960).

these characterizations suggest that the young revolutionary leader was the contemporary heir of the abolitionist president.

Another cartoon, "We Want Castro," depicted the Cuban leader sitting at a table dining with U.S. blacks with a poster of President Lincoln watching over the meal, giving the meeting his blessing.[104] Comparisons between Castro and Lincoln reiterated that the Cuban leader had eliminated racial discrimination in the same way that the U.S. president had freed the slaves. Suggesting that the revolutionary government acted in the spirit of Lincoln also worked to undermine critiques about its economic policies while demonstrating a solid commitment to racial equality.

The UN meeting served as an opportunity to announce to the world that two years of revolutionary programs had eliminated racial discrimination. In addition to photographs and articles describing African American support for the revolution's racial politics, Cuban newspapers also reprinted translated articles written by U.S. blacks to defend the existence of racial equality on the island. *Revolución* ran excerpts from an article in the *Crusader*, a U.S. black newspaper, that described the advantages of living in Cuba, and implied that the island was a racial paradise. According to the black activist Robert Williams, "Cuba was a land where brotherhood is available to everyone, without taking into account skin color."[105] Editorials by African American journalist and civil rights activist William Worthy appeared in national newspapers as well, and praised the equalizing advances made by the revolution in contrast to the limited democracy practiced in the United States.[106] When reprinted in Cuban dailies, these claims showed readers that U.S. blacks recognized that the revolution had achieved racial equality. The statements portrayed the Cuban leadership in a positive manner to all Cubans; nevertheless, the frequency of articles supporting the cause of African Americans also appealed to black Cubans without overtly talking about race on the island. For revolutionary leaders, the Harlem episode permitted the island to have a conversation about racial injustice through the issues of U.S. blacks that did not jeopardize national unity.

Unlike spring 1960, when Afro-Cubans had contested openly absolute claims of equality, by September national dailies published few articles or editorials disputing this image of Cuba as a racial paradise. The lack of printed materials contesting the achievement of racial equality reveals the closing of public discourses about race in Cuba in favor of constructing both an external and internal image of national unity. Most articles highlighted how Castro, despite being a "white man," did not hold any racial prejudices, nor believed in the separation of people based on skin color.[107] Raúl Castro stressed this point by saying, "The Cuban nation knows that among its people there flows a fraternity based on blood kinship and identity" with "our black brothers in the North" and independence fighters in the Congo.[108] Yet, despite such claims the sources suggest that Cuba had not eliminated racial discrimination. In fact, this very discourse was littered with paternalistic references and metaphors imagining African Americans and Afro-Cubans as dependent clients of the state, rather than equal partners in an alliance or full citizens in the nation. The following section explores these contradictions to highlight the paradoxes that arose when pledges to eliminate racism were structured in inherently unequal ways.

Visual Contradictions in Revolutionary Promises of Solidarity

Harlem was well known among many Cubans as an energetic and lively artist center. Intellectuals such as Langston Hughes and Arturo Schomburg, an Afro-Puerto Rican, strengthened the connection between African Americans and Afro-Cubans in the 1920s through their writings and visits to the island. One historian noted that "to race-conscious Afro-Cubans, Harlem—the race capital of African Americans—epitomized the struggle taking place in the United States."[109] Links such as these offered Afro-Cubans a lens for understanding the African American struggle and the economic situation in Harlem. But Cuban rhetoric in 1960 invoked the neighborhood only as an explicit example of everything that was wrong with U.S. race relations, namely segregation and poverty. At the same time that revolutionary leaders claimed to respect and belong with African Americans in New York, they also belittled them by portraying U.S. blacks as inferior and in need of Cuban aid.

Political cartoons depicting the friendship between revolutionary leaders and African Americans frequently contradicted Cuban claims of racial equality and demonstrated lingering prejudicial attitudes toward people of color. In contrast to images celebrating the artistic and cultural creativity of Harlem that might have been expected given the historic relationship between Cubans and African Americans, cartoonists applied paternalistic metaphors to illustrate the revolution's relationship to U.S. blacks. Cartoons featuring black characters with exaggerated features disrupted notions that revolutionary leaders saw people of color as equal partners in the growing alliance.

In a cartoon printed three days after Castro arrived in New York, a sleeping African American child dreams of Castro wielding the liberty torch[110] (figure 4.2). Like the cartoons associating the revolutionary leader with Abraham Lincoln, this cartoon positioned Castro as the source of liberty and freedom for U.S. blacks. The following day a very similar cartoon appeared, with the same childlike figure stroking his smooth chin while imagining a bearded Castro and thinking "I want Castro."[111] Titled "A Child from Harlem," this cartoon contrasted the maturity of the beaded Cuban leader with the naïveté and inexperience of the young black

Figure 4.2 Political
cartoon from *Revolución*
(21 September 1960).

boy (figure 4.3). Santiago Armada (pen name Chago Armas), the cartoonist for *Revolución* who authored these images, sketched six other cartoons
illustrating African Americans as underdeveloped children while Castro
was in New York.[112]

Cartoonists for other national newspapers used comparable imagery.
"In Harlem" appeared in *Verde Olivo* and depicts a black child wearing a
fake beard while carrying a popgun and a poster with the phrase "Dignity

Figure 4.3 "A Child from Harlem: 'I Want Castro.'" From *Revolución* (22 September 1960).

NIÑO DE HARLEM

or Death" spelled incorrectly.[113] The child's parents appear shocked to see him passionately mimicking revolutionary leaders. Some cartoons showed Castro shaking hands or patting small black figures on the head.[114] Another has a smiling minstrel-looking character waving a Cuban flag above the caption "Fidel, this is your house"[115] (figure 4.4). The prevalence of paternalistic gestures in Cuban political cartoons suggests a belief among the press and the leadership that African Americans should admire and ultimately imitate the Cuban Revolution. Cartoonists simplified the complex and often tenuous political association between the two groups by employing the trope of a happy, black, simpleton eager for Castro's

Fiesta en Harlem   Por Blanco

¡Fidel, ésta es tu casa...!

Figure 4.4 "Party in Harlem: Fidel, this is your house!" From *El Mundo* (20 September 1960).

attention. Moreover, this type of imagery undermined reports celebrating meetings between African American leaders and revolutionary authorities by portraying the alliance between Cubans and U.S. blacks as inherently unequal.

To convey these skewed images of the Harlem community, cartoonists drew political sketches of U.S. blacks in the same style they used when illustrating Afro-Cubans. In the past, Afro-Cubans had appeared in political cartoons as childlike, with markedly dark coloring, and exaggerated features.[116] The UN meeting and the delegation's residence in an African American hotel allowed cartoonists to transfer these notions beyond Cuban borders. Such images suggest that revolutionary leaders did not see people of color as equals in any alliance, domestic or international. By drawing both groups in similar ways, cartoonists reinforced prerevolutionary prejudicial attitudes labeling people of African descent as immature, ignorant, and in need of salvation. Photographs depicting African Americans as beneath and reaching up to Cuban leaders mirrored the imagery in political cartoons.[117] Such portrayals of U.S. blacks suggested a hierarchal distinction between the two groups. Cuban editors routinely imagined and pictured their leaders as potential saviors for the African American community. This gesture succeeded in producing favorable images of Castro, but also characterized Harlem blacks as downtrodden, childlike, and in need of aid. These types of characterizations were a familiar aspect of revolutionary discourse about blacks in Cuba, and their projection onto African American leaders reveals the prevalence of norms linking blackness to inferiority even among the most ardent revolutionaries.

Friendship and Solidarity: Responses by Workers, Women, and Afro-Cubans

While the delegation was in Harlem, Cuban newspapers routinely printed letters to the editor supporting Castro's move to the black-owned hotel and publicly praising U.S. blacks for providing their leader with hospitable lodging. Published alongside speeches by revolutionary leaders and daily columns written by high-ranking officials, these pieces offer a more popular perspective on how the Harlem event was interpreted by some Cubans. These sources have to be read and interpreted carefully since by 1960 there was a restricting of Cubans' ability to contradict government claims.[118] However, because letters to the editor are among the few existing written materials revealing the voices of nonleaders, exploring how workers, women, and Afro-Cubans envisioned their government's solidarity with African Americans provides some insight into what was important to these groups at the time. For the most part, Cubans writing to national dailies agreed with the rhetoric expressed by the government. The existence of such overwhelming public support for the achievement of racial equality in the same newspapers that six months earlier had denounced lingering racial prejudices and pushed for additional reforms shows an increase in revolutionary control over the press and conversations about racism. On one hand, such a consensus highlights the success of the campaign to eliminate racial discrimination because of the overwhelming acceptance among different Cubans that racism did not belong in revolutionary Cuba. However, the silence on the part of Afro-Cubans, in particular, foreshadowed the closure of debates about racial equality and their inability to push the new government to act when it was needed.

Cuban unions and trade associations frequently echoed revolutionary discourses by pledging support to U.S. blacks. Workers and employees from a hotel in Vedado wrote to *Noticias de Hoy* explaining how they had changed the name of their establishment to the Hotel Theresa in honor of the community that offered lodging to revolutionary leaders.[119] Shortly afterward, a sugar mill in Santiago was rechristened the "Mina Harlem."[120] Renaming was an accepted revolutionary tool used to remove U.S. markers from the island and replace them with meaningful symbols of the people. However, the move by workers to change the name of a hotel located in the middle-class white neighborhood of Vedado to celebrate a black establishment in Harlem was unprecedented and showed the popularity of revolutionary antiracist discourses. Other groups, such as the CTC and the Federation of Cuban Women (Federación de Mujeres Cubanas, FMC), also wrote letters thanking the Harlem community for its efforts and expressing solidarity with the African American fight for equal rights.[121] In one letter, CTC representatives assured their "dear friends in Harlem" that Fidel Castro represented the Cuban Revolution that had eliminated "all forms of discrimination" from the island and that he would fight to end the injustice throughout the world.[122] And while these outcries of support did not make their way to Harlem, their frequent presence in Cuban dailies demonstrates how the delegation's move to the Theresa resonated with some readers.

As we saw at the start of this chapter, Cuban organizations also declared the period Castro was in Harlem as a "Week of Solidarity with the U.S. Negro." Similar, to the Havana Woolworth protest that coincided with civil rights boycotts in the United States, the week of solidarity emphasized Cuban support for equal rights for all North Americans.[123] Leaders of the National Executive Committee of Orientation and Integration, among them Afro-Cuban Salvador García Agüero, initiated this move in a letter to the editor of *Noticias de Hoy*. They claimed that the week would commemorate the African American struggle for democratic rights and salute Castro's decision to move to Harlem.[124] Popular appreciation thanking Harlem for welcoming the Cuban revolutionaries ranged from specific letters to the manager of the Hotel Theresa, to more general expressions of gratitude to the entire U.S. black community. These gestures reflected an increasing trend to extend support to African Americans while at the same time agreeing that the Cuban Revolution had eliminated racial discrimination.

Editorials and short stories located on women's pages of popular dailies reveal the opinions held by some Cuban women about the move to Harlem. A letter by Vilma Espín, the highest-ranking female revolutionary and president of the FMC, criticized the treatment the delegation received in New York, while offering words of encouragement to U.S. blacks: "All the people of Cuba are aware of the discriminatory politics imposed by the financial oligarchy that governs that country and [works] against the black population of the United States. We condemn repeatedly the inhumane conditions in which live thousands and thousands of black North American citizens. Keep your faith that the same way in which Cuba has achieved its liberation from these reactionary interests, black North Americans, you will find together with all your people the true road to dignity and liberty as well."[125] The letter mirrored revolutionary discourses by discrediting U.S. claims of providing democracy and freedom to all and condemning the unfair treatment of African Americans. Espín also encouraged blacks in Harlem to find comfort in knowing that they could overcome their situation in the same way that Cubans had managed to eradicate racial injustice from the island, thereby highlighting the revolution's success in an area where the United States continued to fail. Another letter to the editor came from a woman who identified herself as a mother ready to defend her country against a U.S. invasion. She thanked the Harlem community for its hospitality to the delegation and celebrated Castro's efforts to tell the UN General Assembly the truth about the Cuban Revolution.[126] Both women represented a growing movement to denounce U.S. democracy and racism at the same time and show the different ways various Cuban factions mobilized revolutionary discourses about race.

The short story "La Niña Negra" ("The Little Black Girl"), published on the women's page of *Noticias de Hoy*, offers another, more subtle, example of this trend. In the story a group of white children are playing outside when one of them begins to talk about a particular girl in their class. An older male classmate inquires, "Isn't she black? ... my grandmother said that blacks are not like us." Immediately, one of the other children interrupts, "You are behind the times, everyone knows blacks are like us ... they just have different skin color, hair, and noses, but in regard to intelligence and nobility they are just like us. ... My grandfather said so, and he is smarter than you, because he fought with the guerrillas." As the play group is having this conversation, the little black girl in question arrives, "looking sweet, nicely dressed, and with a beautiful smile."[127] Each child is quickly enamored of her and offers her a piece of candy. The story ends with the whole group playing together happily. This narrative shows how some women imagined fiction as an ideal way of discussing changing racial norms and revolutionary programs among themselves and with their families. The story readily credits the "guerrillas" and the new revolutionary government with teaching Cubans to accept people of varying skin colors and labels racial prejudices as outdated. While the narrative concurred with government claims that "everyone knows blacks are like us," the fact that at least one character in the story maintained preconceived notions about people of color suggests awareness by the author that certain Cubans had yet to change. The others correct the boy and persuade him to discard prejudices about Afro-Cubans based on revolutionary principles. However, this story also defines an acceptable code of black behavior, another component of revolutionary discourses about race. The author pointedly notes that the little girl is embraced due to revolutionary teachings about equality and because she is pretty and kind, with luminous dark eyes, and a starched white dress. For her and other Afro-Cubans, impeccable standards of behavior and appearance were required before they could be welcomed into the nation.

Most Afro-Cubans also applauded the delegation's move to Harlem and mirrored the attitude of revolutionary leaders who saw the event as a component of the battle against the United States. During a rally with over a million Cubans, Raúl Castro linked the discrimination faced by the Cuban delegation to the unfair treatment suffered previously by Afro-Cubans.[128] Carlos Moore claims that the crowd, which was composed almost entirely of blacks and *mulatos*, responded to Raúl Castro by demanding that he tell his brother Fidel to "free American Negroes too!" and "turn Harlem into another Sierra Maestra!" They also chanted, "Fidel, Sí, Ku Klux Klan, No!"[129] For these Cubans of African descent the opportunities provided by the revolution and Castro's move to a black-owned hotel inspired enthusiasm and support. Similarly, in a letter announcing the week of solidarity with African Americans, Salvador García Agüero highlighted the Cuban residence at the Theresa as an example of the new "antiracist" and "revolutionary" policies of the government.[130] Another Afro-Cuban leader, Jesús Soto, agreed that the revolution had removed racism from the island in a telegram sent to Commander Almeida, who was with the delegation in New York. The note asked Almeida, the black leader of the Cuban armed forces, to tell the people of Harlem that "Castro represented the Cuban Revolution which had eliminated all forms of racial discrimination."[131] Nicolás Guillén reinforced this idea by saying that "the population of Harlem saw in Castro a defender of their rights; a white man without racist prejudices, an integral revolutionary, for whom the separation of human beings by skin color does not exist nor can exist."[132]

These statements represented a near consensus among some Afro-Cuban leaders that the Cuban delegation was correct in telling African American audiences in Harlem and foreign leaders at the UN that the revolution had eliminated racial discrimination. Such statements conflicted, however, with critiques published by blacks and *mulatos* six months earlier asking the new government to provide Afro-Cubans with the same rights they promised U.S. black visitors. In April, Guillén had argued, "It would be unfair to say that we are like in 1912 [Race War]. But, the other extreme is equally false, that which . . . we have heard more than once recently, that racial discrimination does not exist '*anymore*' in Cuba."[133] It is unlikely that in just six months these Afro-Cuban leaders had come to agree that the revolution had eliminated racial discrimination completely, even with the gradual opening up of private clubs, schools, and beaches. Rather their responses are most likely evidence of the consolidation of the Cuban press, a growing inability to discuss racism in late 1960, and strategic choices made by Afro-Cuban leaders to support the revolutionary national project. Each of these men was also a member of the PSP, a group that had previously been vocal in pressuring Cuban governments before 1959 for racial equality. When members of M 26-7 assumed power in January 1959, they continued that struggle and even criticized revolutionary leaders who did not act quickly enough to resolve racial tensions. However, by September 1960, García Agüero, Soto, and Guillén each held high-ranking positions within either the CTC or the PSP, and were connected heavily to the new government. It is possible that such associations also kept them from questioning, at least publicly, the rhetoric claiming that the revolution had achieved its goal of racial equality.

By September 1960 national conversations reveal an almost complete silence among Cubans who previously had used government claims of creating a racial paradise to push for access to tourist centers, trade associations, and leadership positions. This silence represents the closing of public domestic debates about racial discrimination, but also the foregrounding of pledges to fight racism abroad. The battle shifted from being about Afro-Cubans to being about fighting the United States and forging alliances with people of color around the world. Privately, some Afro-Cubans might have expressed concern over government claims and criticized the hypocrisies they saw in revolutionary discourses. For example, some testimonies agree that racism continued to exist after 1960 in the form of "fear of the black," discomfort in the workplace, or difficulties obtaining certain influential positions. National discourses on the island, however, did not reflect these attitudes.[134]

Ninety miles away in Miami, however, Cuban exiles disagreed with claims made by revolutionary leaders while in Harlem. Calling the event the "Harlem Show," popular countergovernment groups said, "Obviously this was an act to discredit and humiliate the United States in its own territory."[135] Another writer claimed that Castro had not faced any hardship at the Shelburne Hotel; rather he had orchestrated the move to Harlem to "inflame" negative sentiments toward the U.S. government.[136] In attempts to undermine pledges of solidarity between African Americans and Cuban officials, Miami exiles also suggested that revolutionary leaders had bribed U.S. blacks to cheer outside of the Hotel Theresa and that other groups were simply there to protest the communist infiltration of their neighborhood, not support Castro.[137] Mirroring revolutionary discourses that reprinted positive feedback from African American leaders, Miami publications also published the dissenting voices of Adam Clayton Powell and Jackie Robinson to demonstrate that not all U.S. blacks supported the new Cuban government.[138] Comments in the exile press, however, did not declare or deny the existence of racial discrimination on the island. Instead, they saw September 1960 as another moment to link the new Cuban government with communism. As one author noted, at the UN General Assembly "Fidel celebrated his wedding with communism" by meeting with Nikita Khrushchev and other socialist leaders.[139] Some of these newspapers probably made their way back to Cuba and were circulated clandestinely, thereby adding to conversations about the meaning of the delegation's stay in a black North American community. However, since they too failed to interrogate claims of racial harmony, it is unlikely that they could have served as an outlet for any Afro-Cubans frustrated by their inability to publicly discuss lingering racial prejudices.

Conclusions

Cuban leaders used the 1960 UN meeting to announce to the world that their revolution had successfully achieved racial equality. For Cubans, this meant a closing of debates about racial prejudice on the island. The year 1960 also signaled the shift in revolutionary racialized discourses from their previous focus on Afro-Cubans to a global battle based on the situation of Africans and African Americans. Yet, despite declarations that the campaign to eliminate racial discrimination had been resolved, Cuban leaders continued to imagine people of color as inferior clients of the nation. The termination of the brief business venture between INIT and the Louis, Rowe, Fisher, and Lockhart public relations firm and the vocal chastising of Louis foreshadowed the paternalistic rhetoric that the new Cuban government used in Harlem and had numerous lasting consequences. For one, extensive press coverage in Cuba of African Americans' second-class citizenship fit with and contributed to revolutionary discourses about race introduced by Castro's March 1959 speech. Echoing the message of *Revolución*'s editorial blaming the 1898 U.S. intervention for the failure of nineteenth-century plans for racial equality, Cuban leaders celebrated the revolution's antiracist stance and located continued racism solely in the United States. This situation benefited revolutionary leaders by providing a response to U.S. and counterrevolutionary disapproval of the changes occurring on the island and turned into a lasting critique about the character of U.S. democracy. Moreover, discussions about the violent and segregated conditions faced by U.S. blacks encouraged Afro-Cubans to be grateful for the new opportunities provided by the revolution and discouraged blacks and *mulatos* from joining the growing exodus to Miami. As Micol Seigel suggests in her 2005 essay "Beyond Compare: Historical Method after the Transnational Turn," tracing the movement of racial discourses between Cuba and the United States reveals how transnational dialogues reinforce national ideologies.[140] Ideas about race did not just cross borders between Cuba and the United States in 1960. Rather, they constituted and constructed those borders by portraying Cuba's revolutionary egalitarian project as the opposite of its northern neighbor.

Ultimately, exchanges between African Americans and Cubans after 1959 were both similar and distinct from previous ones. In many ways, they built on over fifty years of shared battles against racial discrimination, especially during the Jim Crow era. Some might say that once Cuban revolutionary leaders nationalized these relationships and sought to make them work for a state that claimed to be both anti-imperialist and anti-racist, possibilities for alliances based solely on race became limited and diasporic dialogues disappeared. However, post-1959 interactions with African Americans are significant moments to recapture because they show the shift from racial discourses to racial politics, as Afro-Cubans used government claims to reposition themselves within the revolution. Choosing to mobilize the stories of African Americans for state purposes foreshadowed the 1961 strategic iconization of a murdered Afro-Cuban teacher as a soldier for the yearlong literacy campaign. The following chapter investigates this episode to see how propaganda celebrating the death of a black youth represented the symbolic end of public conversations about racism in Cuba.

5

Poor, Black, and a Teacher

Loyal Black Revolutionaries and the Literacy Campaign

When questioned about the 1961 Literacy Campaign, Cubans recount stories of national highs and lows, fears and opportunities, and excitement and estrangement. Teenage *alfabetizadores* (literacy teachers) remembered Fidel Castro's call to join the revolutionary literacy army, traveling to far-flung areas in the rural countryside, and the joy of sharing their knowledge with other Cubans. But, the most common story I heard when I inquired about this period of the Cuban Revolution was a recounting of the brutal murder of an eighteen-year-old volunteer teacher named Conrado Benítez. More than one literacy teacher recalled how counterrevolutionaries assassinated Benítez outside of his schoolhouse in Escambray because he was "poor, black, and a teacher." Using nearly identical wording, these now elderly Cubans remembered that a band of countergovernment rebels tortured and killed Benítez because of his support for the revolution *and* his marginalized race and class status.[1] It is not surprising that Cubans retell almost verbatim the story of Benítez's death since a large proportion of the island's population participated in the Literacy Campaign (either as members of national teaching brigades or as students learning to read) and even more Cubans attended one of the memorial services held in the fallen teacher's honor. During the spring of 1961, community events and Literacy Campaign publicity created and solidified a lasting narrative of Benítez's life and death, fondly remembered today, that described a young man who sacrificed himself for the nation. Revolutionary leaders held mass rallies where they proclaimed that the murder of Benítez epitomized Cuba's ongoing struggles against imperialism, counterrevolution, and social injustice. National media outlets repeated the words announced by Prime Minister Fidel Castro, explaining how the young man had been murdered for being a "poor, black, teacher."[2] By linking Benítez's assassination to counterrevolutionary distaste for Afro-Cubans, the new government created and transmitted a narrative of the young man's life that both declared the successful end to the campaign against racial discrimination and further discredited counterrevolutionaries as racists.

The 1961 Literacy Campaign was a foundational moment for the Cuban Revolution. Over the course of the year, the campaign dramatically reduced illiteracy from 23.6 percent to 3.9 percent with the help of some 270,000 literacy teachers. Nearly half of these volunteer teachers were youth members of Conrado Benítez brigades—as the groups named after the fallen youth were called—who taught in rural areas, while adults (the other half) offered instruction in urban settings after work and in their free time.[3] Afro-Cuban participation in the campaign was high and blacks and *mulatos* composed nearly 19 percent of the brigades.[4] However, the "Year of Education" was a national mobilization that taught Cubans more than simply how to read.[5] The Literacy Campaign also provided Cubans with a new "political education," spreading the values and ideals of the revolutionary government.[6] *Brigadistas* (a common term for the literacy teachers) carried textbooks that included sections about the perils of U.S. aggression, the benefits of the Agrarian Reform, and information about how the new government planned to fulfill the dreams of José Martí.[7] Teaching manuals also taught lessons about the need to eliminate racial discrimination and the Literacy Campaign encouraged Cubans to open their homes to Afro-Cuban volunteer teachers. At the end of the year, when the young teachers returned to Havana for the December celebration where Castro announced that Cuba was a "territory free of illiteracy," Cubans celebrated the movement's achievements and solidified fond memories of 1961 that have endured for over fifty years.

The life and death of Conrado Benítez played a central role in the construction of these memories and in Cuba's political education in general. The literacy movement coincided with the end of the public campaign to eliminate racial discrimination. Celebrations honoring the martyred Afro-Cuban teacher gave revolutionary leaders a means of asserting that they had achieved a raceless nation where blacks, like Benítez, could be seen as the counterparts to other national icons like José Martí and Camilo Cienfuegos.[8] The national press even linked conversations about Benítez's murder with reports about the assassination of two other black men, Afro-Cuban communist Jesús Menéndez and Congolese leader Patrice Lumumba, to create a pantheon of revolutionary black male icons.[9] Popularized images of these men allowed the revolutionary government to insert darker-skinned faces into a national leadership cohort that was almost completely white, with the exception of rebel army leader Juan Almeida. Revolutionary leaders invoked the story of Benítez in particular to vilify countergovernment groups by labeling them as racist murderers willing to kill innocent teachers. Blaming his death on counterrevolutionaries funded by the U.S. Central Intelligence Agency allowed Cuban leaders to depict the Year of Education not only as a movement against illiteracy, but as a battle against U.S. imperialism, coded as "white" and "racist" as well.

Similar to moments discussed previously when national rhetoric about race, racism, or people of color was at its highest, certain contradictions underlie the iconization of black martyrs and signaled the incomplete end of the campaign to eliminate discrimination. In fact, despite its impressive accomplishments in teaching Cubans to read and the unprecedented move to use a black man's face on revolutionary visual materials, revolutionary leaders also used the Literacy Campaign to stand in for additional conversations about blackness. The Literacy Campaign epitomized the contradictory end to official debates about racism in post-1959 Cuba. On one hand it included racially integrated brigades, celebrated Afro-Cuban revolutionaries, and produced dramatic education reforms. At the same time, the stories revolutionary leaders used to explain the deaths of Benítez, Menéndez, and Lumumba fashioned lasting impressions about appropriate Afro-Cuban behavior and acceptable black contributions to the new nation that allowed stereotypes about black gratefulness to persist. The emphasis placed on Benítez's humble background and his loyalty to the revolution celebrated a vision of patriotic blackness that highlighted a particular, nonthreatening Afro-Cuban citizen who was both grateful to and dependent on the new government. Cuban leaders created an image of a safe, strong, committed black patriot that left little space for other (living) Afro-Cubans to disagree or challenge the course of the revolution. Benítez was nonthreatening because he was a martyr and could not contest the revolution's portrayal of him or his life. The limited number of women—white, *mulata*, or black—invoked in these conversations also suggests the limits of who could serve as a symbol for the nation in the 1960s.[10] In many ways, the 1959 antiracist movement that began when Castro publicly declared the new government's plans to tackle the "hated injustice" of discrimination ended in 1961 with indirect suggestions about revolutionary loyalty and undefined paths for future debates about blackness.

1961: The Year of Education

Revolutionary leaders announced plans for a campaign to educate all Cubans while attending the 1960 United Nations (UN) meeting in New

York. "In the coming year, our people intend to fight the great battle against illiteracy, with the ambitious goal of teaching every single inhabitant of the country to read and write in one year." Noting that student organizations, teachers, and workers were preparing for the task, Castro promised that "Cuba will be the first country in the Americas which, after a few months, will be able to say it does not have one single illiterate."[11] Back on the island, the Ministry of Education established a National Literacy Commission (Comisión Nacional de Alfabetización, CNA) to oversee the project, recruit teachers from urban youth groups, and create new teaching manuals and workbooks for the campaign.[12] Conrado Benítez volunteered for one of these pilot brigades and spent the final two months of 1960 training with 1,400 other new teachers in the Sierra Maestra. The culmination of their preparation occurred on New Year's Eve 1960, when Benítez's group along with nearly ten thousand other Cuban youth attended a large rally in Havana. Castro announced the goals of the Literacy Campaign and gave the students certified diplomas identifying them as official *brigadistas* in Cuba's national education drive.[13] A *Verde Olivo* article, "From the Peaks of the Sierra Maestra to the Heights of Havana," described the challenges the youth faced sleeping in hammocks, camping in the rain, and working with the rural poor before being welcomed as heroes into the capital. Revolutionary officials arranged for the *brigadistas* to stay in the Havana Hilton, much in the same way Castro and other M 26-7 rebels had returned from the rough life of guerrilla warfare in eastern Cuba to the comforts of the famed Havana hotel two years before. Photographs of these pilot brigades captured racially integrated groups laughing and posing together in smart uniforms and wearing beads from the celebration.[14] Like so many other young Cubans who volunteered for the campaign, Conrado Benítez was a part of this merriment. Unbeknownst to him or his proud *compañeros*, the continuation of the civil war, now against Castro rather than Batista, soon changed the campaign against illiteracy into a battle for revolutionary hearts and minds.

The murder of Benítez by countergovernment rebels supplied this battle with its first and most famous martyr. Benítez was killed on 5 January 1961. The official narrative—that he was tortured and murdered by counterrevolutionaries—went uncontested in 1961 and fit with persistent attacks both internally and externally against the new government. Yet, while the circumstances of Benítez's death remain unclear due to the lack of access to classified archival materials, revolutionary leaders quickly publicized a narrative about how the teacher died that celebrated his unwavering commitment to the revolution and his humble class and racial background. According to published testimonies from his friends and family, Benítez missed and wanted to return to his students in Villa Clara and left the capital shortly after the New Year's celebration. A band of counterrevolutionaries captured and assassinated Benítez while he was traveling to his school along with a local worker and a militia member.[15] A few weeks later, revolutionary leaders and the increasingly consolidated national press swiftly named the young black man a national hero and the official symbol of the Literacy Campaign. Having a black youth serve as the representative for the Year of Education was an unexpected turn of events, since the Ministry of Education had planned for nineteenth-century nationalist José Martí to act as the figurehead for the campaign. Before Benítez's death, posters of Martí decorated rallies celebrating volunteer teachers and quotations from the historical figure repeatedly accompanied newspaper articles announcing the upcoming campaign. Revolutionary leaders even set 28 January, Martí's birthday, as the official kickoff date for the battle against illiteracy in honor of the nineteenth-century intellectual.[16]

After the murder of Benítez, however, Cuban leaders changed these plans and made the young teacher and the story of his brutal death the rallying force for the campaign. To be fair, the image of Benítez did not erase completely Martí's presence from the Year of Education. Quotations from the intellectual along with signs with his photograph continued to decorate some literacy rallies and materials. Yet, revolutionary leaders named future groups of volunteer teachers after Benítez, not Martí, and framed calls for youth to join the movement as "Honor the Teacher Martyr! Join the Conrado Benítez García brigades!"[17] (figure 5.1) The image of the young teacher dressed in a suit and tie became the standard representation of the Literacy Campaign and endured in Cuban memories throughout the twentieth century.[18] Selecting a dark-skinned working-class youth from outside of Havana as the symbol of a national education movement over a white independence leader was a strategic decision in line with previous discourses about incorporating Afro-Cubans into the nation.[19] The swiftness with which a young black man, who barely participated in the campaign, became the face of the movement highlights the willingness of revolutionary leaders to consciously and purposely build on prior invocations of loyal Afro-Cuban soldiers and construct narratives that

Figure 5.1 "Honor the Teacher Martyr! Join the 'Conrado Benítez García' Brigades!" From *Noticias de Hoy* (18 February 1961).

¡HONRA AL MAESTRO MARTIR!
INSCRIBETE EN LAS BRIGADAS
"CONRADO BENITEZ GARCIA"

celebrated their racial politics in comparison to those of the United States and Cuban exile groups.

This was not the first time, however, that republican or revolutionary officials had emphasized black heroes. The representations of Benítez, Menéndez, and Lumumba celebrated by revolutionary leaders emphasized a particular set of characteristics that scholars of nineteenth-century Cuba have referred to as the "ideal black insurgent" or "patriotic blackness."[20] In the 1880s, Cuban intellectuals, both white and black, promoted a narrative of the ideal black insurgent to challenge Spanish claims that independence from Spain would lead to a race war, like the Haitian Revolution. The ideal black insurgent was a selfless and unthreatening patriot who believed in raceless nationalism and willingly sacrificed himself for Cuba's independence.[21] In 1961, Castro and other M 26-7 leaders recycled this nineteenth-century rhetoric and applied it to the new revolutionary context. As earlier chapters have discussed, the pattern of locating and publicizing Afro-Cuban voices to support the new leadership had occurred since 1959. Similarly, frequent visits from African Americans had provided the revolution with opportunities to show how people of African descent from the United States admired and enjoyed the equalizing measures implemented since the new government came to power. And while publishing commentaries by Afro-Cuban intellectuals and African American leaders demonstrated the popularity the revolution had achieved with some people of color, the limits of this strategy quickly became apparent when these same men and women attacked the revolution's policies. For example, when Afro-Cuban Juan René Bentancourt, the leader of the National Federation of Black Societies, went into exile and vocally criticized claims that the new government had eliminated racial discrimination, Castro lost the potential support of an influential leader of color. Likewise, Joe Louis's public denouncement and distancing from revolutionary leaders showed the danger of highlighting the opinions of blacks and *mulatos*, who were as capable of changing their minds and choosing not to support the new government as any other citizen.[22] In contrast, revolutionary leaders had successfully invoked the memories of black men like nineteenth-century nationalist Antonio Maceo and Amardo Mestre, an M 26-7 member killed in the 1953 attack on the Moncada barracks, to reach out to Afro-Cubans without increasing white anxieties about black social mobility. By calling upon the memories of slain Afro-Cuban men to legitimize their authority, revolutionary leaders signaled awareness that black support was necessary to the success of the new government. The iconization of young Benítez followed from this history and constructed contradictory lessons about the great potential a nationally integrated Cuba had for overcoming social inequalities and what revolutionary leaders believed to be the appropriate space for blackness in the revolution.

Black Martyrs and Lessons from the Literacy Campaign

On 7 February 1961, Cubans attended a massive demonstration to protest the murder of Benítez. Leading the parade, two Afro-Cuban students carried a large poster of the slain teacher with the words "Glory to the Martyr" written in black ink and decorated with white flowers. Thousands of other young people marched behind this poster carrying signs, flowers, and Cuban flags to the presidential palace where they listened to speeches by Fidel and Raúl Castro and President Osvaldo Dorticós.

The next day, almost every national newspaper printed the text of these speeches along with a photograph of Benítez ringed with carnations and a caption reading, "We cannot let the living memory of Conrado Benítez, the volunteer teacher assassinated by counterrevolutionaries, falter. . . . The young sacrificed teacher is now a guide and an example for all revolutionary youth."[23] With these sentences, *La Calle* contrasted Benítez's commitment to the national project with the misplaced intentions of counterrevolutionary groups. Revolutionary leaders used rallies such as this one along with other visual media and editorials in Cuban publications to create a lasting symbol of the slain Benítez that promoted a new set of values in the new nation. Cubans learned lessons about national sacrifice and racial and class inclusiveness through their work in the Literacy Campaign and the commemoration of black martyrs.

The official organ of the CNA, *Arma Nueva*, popularized what later became the iconic photograph used to honor Benítez on the cover of its January–March 1961 issue, which the editors dedicated to the young man. The image showed a clean-cut, dark-skinned Benítez wearing a neat button-down shirt, suit jacket, and tie.[24] The Ministry of Education used this photograph to decorate literacy badges, identification cards, education workbooks, and the pages of national dailies throughout 1961. The image of the slain teacher differed from the typical revolutionary archetype of a white-bearded man in army fatigues, suggesting a hesitation to portray black men as dangerous, armed combatants. Benítez's photographs also clashed with the regular portrayal of impoverished Afro-Cuban law breakers featured on the crime pages of national dailies. Rather, revolutionary discourses emphasized his well-kempt appearance and respectability.

Public demonstrations celebrating Benítez allowed Cubans across the island to become familiar with his story and the principles with which he was identified. Mothers of volunteer teachers attended meetings where they signed petitions condemning Benítez's assassination and demanding the execution of his murderers.[25] Youth in the Havana neighborhood of Regla marched through the streets shouting, "Firing wall!" for his killers and "Long live the revolution!"[26] The National Confederation of Cuban Workers hosted an event where President Dorticós, his wife, and Minister of Education Armando Hart spoke against counterrevolutionary activity in front of a large banner bearing the teacher's face and repeating the words "Glory to the Martyr."[27] Each of these gatherings memorialized Benítez and speakers referred to the young man as a national hero who was killed because he was "poor, black, and a teacher." Repeatedly, the publicity accompanying the Literacy Campaign stressed that counter-revolutionaries killed the young black man due to his dark skin color and economic status. Cubans attending state-sponsored events learned a particular narrative of Benítez's death that demonized enemies of the revolution as racists while celebrating humble supporters who were committed to the new government. Even Cubans unable to go to a memorial service would have been familiar with how Benítez died, since the national press repeatedly highlighted his class, race, and occupation to contrast the demographics of the masses, many of whom were poor and black, with the growing opposition movement, depicted as rich and white.

After the murder of Conrado Benítez in January 1961, Cuban discourses about the Literacy Campaign became increasingly militarized.[28] Revolutionary leaders invoked the martyred teacher as a soldier for the nation, especially in the ongoing discursive and physical battles against counterrevolutionaries and U.S. aggression. One way of doing so was to claim that countergovernment groups killed innocent Cubans simply because they were black, poor, and loyal to the new government. This move created an "us" versus "them" mentality, where Cubans of color were pushed to support revolutionary leaders, since according to popular representations countergovernment groups murdered blacks. Cuban leaders associated themselves with the minority position, since they too were outcasts from exile groups funded by the United States and thus open to attack from "imperialists," even though they were not black.

Literacy Campaign publicity invoked Benítez as a soldier for the nation in a literal sense as well. Across Cuba, young volunteer teachers joined Conrado Benítez brigades, wore army-like uniforms, saw themselves as members of an educational army, and marched to spirited lyrics about defeating the counterrevolution.[29] *Brigadistas* wore patches on their sleeves identifying them as members of the Benítez "Army of Literacy Teachers."[30] Additionally, most descriptions of the Literacy Campaign imagined it as a "battle" against ignorance, and encouraged Cubans to equate acquiring an education with defeating the enemy who wanted to keep the island illiterate. Lyrics to a song popularized by *brigadistas* claimed that the literacy teachers were "fighting for peace" and encouraged them to "bring down imperialism and lift up liberty."[31] Imaging the Literacy Campaign as a national battle against both illiteracy and countergovernment forces raised the intensity of the movement. Stories of Benítez and other slain black martyrs along with revolutionary discourses encouraging Cubans to "overcome or die" served to push Cubans to interpret the revolution in increasingly militarized ways.

Revolutionary leaders combined stories about Jesús Menéndez, an Afro-Cuban union organizer murdered in 1948, with the commemoration of Benítez in 1961 to highlight the historic contributions of Afro-Cuban citizens to the nation. It is likely that Cubans would have celebrated the anniversary of Menéndez's death on 22 January even if Benítez had not been murdered during the same month, since the slain union leader's commitment to racial equality and anti-imperialism fit with ongoing revolutionary projects. However, with the assassination of the young teacher, Cuban leaders inserted plans to commemorate Menéndez's life into a larger national conversation about black patriotism. Cuban journalists frequently portrayed the union organizer as the predecessor to Benítez, and emphasized his humble background and blackness as well. For example, a political cartoon honoring the union leader labeled him as an unassuming man whose grandparents had fought alongside Maceo in the wars of independence.[32] Like comments reporting Benítez's personal history, highlighting that Menéndez was from a poor family, albeit one with a strong revolutionary background, worked to teach Cubans that the revolution respected commitment and hard work.

Black icons also appealed to certain spiritual beliefs by relating the assassination of Benítez to how Jesus Christ was crucified on the cross. Fidel Castro characterized the dead teacher as "a martyr whose blood will erase ignorance."[33] Claiming that Benítez had "noble blood," Castro offered to construct a monument to honor the spot where the youth's blood fell.[34] An interviewed literacy teacher concurred, saying that the blood of Benítez had made Cubans more eager to "rise up" and end illiteracy during the Year of Education.[35] In each of these comments, the blood of the slain youth was called upon to work for the revolution and the Literacy Campaign. It was Benítez's sacrifice, like that of Christ, which was going to allow Cubans to achieve literacy, fight imperialism, and become better people. Other spiritual references concluded that the soul of the young martyr continued to live on and encouraged Cubans to see his death as a light that would brighten the way for future revolutionaries.[36] By labeling Benítez as a martyr and discussing his legacy using religious metaphors, Cuban leaders substituted traditional Catholic icons with revolutionary ones. A line from the chorus of the Conrado Benítez brigade song, "Estudio, trabajo, fusil" ("Study, work, gun"), illustrated this point.[37] In 1961, Raúl Castro proclaimed the phrase the "new trinity" to replace the Catholic version of the "Father, Son, and Holy Ghost."[38] The narrative of Benítez's life, as popularized by revolutionary leaders, celebrated each of these elements along with sacrifice to the government as the new national ideology.[39]

Cuban revolutionaries iconized another black figure, Patrice Lumumba, less than one month after the public martyring of Conrado Benítez. When antigovernment forces captured and murdered thirty-five-year-old Lumumba, the nationalist leader of the newly independent Congo, Cubans returned to the streets to express solidarity with the man known as the "African Fidel."[40] Cuban leaders applied the same tropes used in creating the narrative of Benítez's death to memorialize Lumumba. The Congolese revolutionary was depicted with a clean-shaven face and wearing respectable clothing like the popularized images of the young teacher[41] (figure 5.2). The wire-rimmed eyeglasses worn by Lumumba signaled his intelligence and offered a model of blackness based on propriety and a commitment to revolutionary values of hard work and education. Revolutionary leaders also used religious metaphors to honor Lumumba. Echoing the Christian references used to comment on Benítez's murder, Nicolás Guillén said that Lumumba had been "crucified" by the Yankees.[42] *Noticias de Hoy* suggested that the soul of the Congolese nationalist would endure by calling him an "immortal symbol of African rebellion."[43] And a poet writing in *Bohemia* claimed that in death Lumumba would be "more grand and victorious" than in life.[44] Repeated allusions to the spiritual longevity of black martyrs solidified their position in Cuban memories as symbols of revolutionary blackness.

Celebrating Lumumba, a global figure, linked Cuba to its African ancestors and legitimized the revolution's future participation in global social struggles. An editorial titled "Two Martyrs, the Same Idea" epitomized this connection by applying the language used to explain Benítez's death to discuss Lumumba's murder in the Congo. "Why did they kill Patrice Lumumba? Because he was a leader, a teacher of his people, and a black. . . . Conrado Benítez and Patrice Lumumba are not two martyrs of distant lands . . . they are two brothers in the same fight, two martyrs fallen for the same cause, two teachers."[45] In this piece, the editorialist related the common phrase "poor, black, and a teacher" to Lumumba by claiming that he was targeted by Congolese counterrevolutionaries for being a "teacher of people" and a black man. Doing so both offered an explanation for the leader's assassination and connected Cubans to their "brothers" in Africa. Similarly, *Noticias de Hoy* claimed that messages of

Figure 5.2 Popularized photograph of Patrice Lumumba printed in *Hoy Domingo* (19 February 1961).

support sent to the Congo after Lumumba's death "are not routine pieces of diplomacy." "Cuba is interested in strengthening relationships with all the young states from which many of our grandfathers came . . . whose sons were the Maceos, the Moncadas, the Quintíns and whose grandsons were named Jesús Menéndez, [Juan] Almeida, and Conrado Benítez."[46] This statement reminded readers of the ancestral connection between Cuba and black Africa by identifying people of color as the grandfathers of the nation. It also linked popular black revolutionary figures like Lumumba, Menéndez, Almeida, and Benítez to Afro-Cuban independence heroes, thus legitimizing their roles as contemporary icons.

Ultimately, adding an international figure to the pantheon of revolutionary black icons continued the linking of the Cuban Revolution to global racial struggles. Like the measures taken by the government to reach out to African Americans in 1960, these gestures made sense to Cubans because they fit with ongoing narratives about the revolution's conflict with U.S. imperialism, often depicted as white and racist. Moreover, most Cubans found meaning in the celebrated story of Lumumba's assassination because it paralleled the familiar narrative of Benítez's death. The revolutionary rhetoric surrounding the lives and deaths of these martyrs reiterated the most common components of post-1959 revolutionary discourses, especially efforts to undermine counterrevolutionary movements and combat claims that the revolution was communist.

In a speech before the Communist Party (Partido Socialista Popular, PSP) committee, *mulato* Blas Roca discussed how counterrevolutionaries claimed they killed Benítez because he was a communist. Roca disagreed: "The young teacher was no communist." He continued, "With anticommunism they want to preserve the imperialist regime, colonial oppression, inhumane exploitation, racial discrimination, and unemployment."[47] *Noticias de Hoy* concurred, saying that the "*gusanos* (worms) assassinated him for being a worker, for being black, and for being poor," not because he was a spy.[48] Castro, meanwhile, called the murder of Lumumba a few months later a mixture of "imperialism, colonialism, and savagery."[49] Articulations such as these demonized countergovernment groups as savage racists and created a paradigm whereby anyone who disagreed with the revolution was as well. The case of the principal of the private school La Luz illustrated this point. Eight students from the school wrote letters to *Noticias de Hoy* saying that they had been expelled for holding a rally protesting the murder of Lumumba. In the letter, they characterized the principal as a counterrevolutionary whose entire family lived in exile and called for his termination because he did not support their demonstration against imperialism.[50] Revolutionary journalists also condemned other private schools for failing to participate in activities objecting to the assassination of Benítez. One editorialist claimed that members of the privileged classes remained silent unless threatened with losing their "precious private" institutions.[51] By linking counterrevolutionaries to the killings of Benítez and Lumumba, these Cubans further vilified opposition to the state. This move allowed the new government to identify other whites as racists without having to respond to questions about their personal preferences. Moreover, these conversations continued to divide the island into two groups: those who supported the revolution and therefore publicly embraced black martyrs; and those who did not, namely counterrevolutionaries. By spring 1961, these camps had already been forged, but inserting the death of the young teacher and the Congolese leader into national debates served to reiterate previous ideas.

Discussions such as these contrasted the disdain counterrevolutionaries held for people of color with the new government's claims to have eliminated racial discrimination. Castro summarized these comments in a speech where he argued that counterrevolutionary forces would use anticommunism as a justification to assassinate every "worker, *humilde*, and black."[52] Others argued that the UN forces, led by the United States, must only protect whites, since they allowed Lumumba to be assassinated while occupying the Congo.[53] *La Calle* meanwhile concluded that Uncle Sam only approved of people of color when they conceded the sidewalk to white women or played the guitar in tourist venues in Havana. According to this piece, "imperialists" sought to eliminate blacks and latinos when they tried to learn, teach, or rebel against the status quo.[54] By popularizing the idea that the opposition movement would murder innocent people of color because they feared change, revolutionary leaders worked to solidify Afro-Cuban loyalty to the new government. Yet, implicit in these conversations was the view that prejudicial attitudes belonged to the "other side," not to Cuban revolutionaries who had waged successfully the war against racial discrimination.

The iconization of Conrado Benítez and other black martyrs that occurred in 1961 served as a public celebration of the end of the campaign to end racial discrimination and the rhetorical move to transform Afro-Cubans into citizens. By the start of the Literacy Campaign, national discourses about racism claimed that the problem had been solved. The growing threat of U.S. intervention and counterrevolutionary opposition pushed Cubans toward national unity. However, publicly announcing the completion of national projects was a familiar aspect of revolutionary moves to consolidate state control. In December 1961, in front of crowds holding flags decorated with Benítez's name, Castro declared "Cuba a territory free of illiteracy."[55] For the youthful, mixed-race audience, the moment came to be remembered as a turning point in Cuban race relations. And while racial prejudices continued to exist privately, revolutionary leaders used the figures of black martyrs and the integrated work of the Literacy Campaign to conclude the debate over racial equality opened in 1959.

Literacy Campaign teaching manuals created by the Ministry of Education were effective tools in this form of "political education" and spread new claims about achieving racial equality in 1961. *Trabajo*, the official organ of the Ministry of Labor, published an article describing why the government printed the new manuals: "To teach literacy they had to begin by making the workbooks and manuals, because it wouldn't have been worth it to teach half the country to read, if they were going to continue to learn the lies that the *Histories of Cuba* told us, like for example, one said, 'the Americans helped us in our independence' or 'North America is a bulwark of democracy.' They had to build consciousness. They had to awaken the sleeping man inside each Cuban who could not read. They had to give something more than eyes to the blind man in our civilization. They had to give him the weapon of knowledge, but also show him the path."[56]

Consequently, Conrado Benítez *brigadistas* used lessons from *Alfabeticemos*, the official manual for literacy instruction, to reeducate their students about different topics in Cuban history, including the Agrarian Reform, U.S. imperialism, and the role the new National Institute of Tourism (Instituto Nacional de Industria Turística) played in opening private beaches to the public. A photograph accompanied each of the twenty-four themes. Trainers instructed volunteer teachers to begin conversations with learners by asking them to discuss the photograph as a means of gauging prior knowledge about a given topic. Theme Ten was about "Racial Discrimination" and included a full-page photograph of four children of different skin colors sitting on a park bench. And while we cannot know what types of conversations emerged between *brigadistas* and new readers about the manual's integrated scene (showing a white boy, a black boy, an Asian boy, and a little *mestiza* girl), the explanation for Theme Ten promoted a raceless national identity and blamed racism on "exploitative countries." The first line of the theme, "Racial discrimination always has economic origins," framed discrimination as a social problem and linked it to colonialism and slavery. The last line told Cubans never to forget "the joint struggles of Martí and Maceo, Guillermo Moncada and Calixto García, Fidel Castro and Juan Almeida, and as Martí has said, 'There is no racial hatred because there are no races.' "[57] The Ministry of Education published *Alfabeticemos* before the announcement about the socialist nature of the revolution in April 1961. Therefore, the book's analysis of racism was more a result of Cuba's racial past (and the ways revolutionary leaders invoked it, namely by blaming continued discrimination on the 1898 U.S. intervention while applauding the joint work of black and white nineteenth-century patriots) than the coming turn to socialism.

It was not a coincidence that racial discrimination was a prominent theme in Literacy Campaign teaching manuals. As we have seen, Benítez's death and the narrative constructed by revolutionary leaders about the role race played in counterrevolutionary hostility toward the young teacher (and other blacks) guaranteed a collaboration between the campaigns to eliminate racial discrimination and illiteracy. Literacy teaching materials fit with previous state rhetoric about race in Cuba and used the national mobilization to spread those ideas across the island. These lessons taught both *brigadistas* and their students that Afro-Cubans were a key component of the country, especially when they served as soldiers in national battles. Both the *Alfabeticemos* manual and *Producir, Ahorrar, Organizar*, the textbook for arithmetic, explicitly contrasted the racial violence and continued discrimination facing African Americans in the United States with the lack of racial prejudice in Cuba. For example, the math textbook included the following word problem: "There have been 3,000 lynchings in the United States in the last 20 years. What has been the average number of lynchings per year in that country?"[58] In the index for *Alfabeticemos*, Cubans learned that the "KKK, Ku Klux Klan" was a "Racist North American organization that persecuted black citizens." Literacy Campaign resources fully proclaimed that Cuba had accomplished the goal set in 1959 of ridding the island of racial discrimination and employed references to Cuba's past and the United States' present in doing so. A poem by Afro-Cuban author Nicolás Guillén, printed on the last page of *Venceremos* (*We Will Overcome*, another literacy campaign workbook), sat alongside a photograph of José Martí and reinforced this idea: "Fidel came and achieved that which Martí had promised."[59] In the end, the Literacy Campaign and the paraphernalia that accompanied it acted as commemoration of the government's declared victory against racism and positioned Cuba for its newest battle against counterrevolution and the increasingly hostile United States.

National dailies echoed these sentiments by publishing pieces that marked the end of racial discrimination and expressed gratitude for the work of Cuban leaders. One article described how "thanks to the Revolution" Cubans have this "marvelous example of human solidarity," and included images of a small black child visiting a predominantly white school to show the progress of racial integration. Throughout the article, the author attributed the prevalence of racially integrated classrooms and groups to the successes of the revolutionary government.[60] In doing so, he portrayed white leaders and the white Cubans who had fulfilled their demands as the heroes of racial equality. An article by Afro-Cuban journalist Reynaldo Peñalver in *Combate 13 de Marzo* shows the ways some blacks and *mulatos* agreed with these new claims. Peñalver applauded revolutionary efforts to eliminate racial discrimination and argued that the martyred Benítez believed that the new government had accomplished this feat as well. Benítez, the journalist wrote, "looked to the future with faith, having the security that the new country was free of racial prejudices and constructed for everyone."[61] By invoking the popular black martyr to thank the new government for creating a more positive future for Afro-Cubans, this author linked the voice of Benítez to the successful elimination of racial discrimination.

Images further emphasized the success achieved by the campaign to eliminate racial divisions in favor of Cuban unity. The billboard for the 1961 Congress on Literacy recycled imagery from 1940s PSP advertisements and the recent 1959 May Day parade publicity by illustrating black and white hands coming together[62] (figure 5.3). The text of the poster, "For every illiterate, a literary teacher and for every literary teacher, an illiterate: We will overcome!," highlights the potential for interracial organizing. A drawing that appeared regularly in *Noticias de Hoy* shows four Cubans (two white men, a dark-skinned black man, and a white woman) walking together with linked arms and dressed in army fatigues, the implication being that the Cuban army is inclusive of all citizens.[63] Such visuals differed from images produced at the start of 1959, because rather than encouraging Cubans to begin a conversation about racial equality, 1961 representations celebrated its achievement. The act of glorifying a black martyr as a symbol of the nation fit into this trend.

Memories of the Literacy Campaign confirm that young Cubans took life lessons from their experiences as volunteer teachers in Conrado Benítez brigades. For many black *brigadistas*, the national education movement allowed them to invoke revolutionary antidiscrimination rhetoric to gain entrance into rural homes where white farmers were initially uncomfortable with racial integration. In Holguín, a city on the eastern corner of the island, a young *guajiro* (farmer) described how his grandfather was hesitant to offer a black *brigadista* quarters in their home during the campaign. Noting that the electric lanterns the literacy teachers carried were appealing, the young man said that his grandfather finally allowed the "sweet black girl" to sleep in their house simply so the family could use her lamp.[64] Another volunteer teacher told a similar story about the debate over lodging that occurred when his group arrived in Guantánamo: "We met to divide up the available rooms. Some men did not want boys sleeping in the house with their women. Some women

Figure 5.3 "For every illiterate, a literacy teacher and for every literacy teacher, an illiterate: We will overcome!" From the cover of the Second National Literacy Congress pamphlet.

refused to provide lodging for pretty girls from Havana, who they feared would seduce their husbands. And another group would not agree to accept the three or four blacks, who were as dark as the night. I resolved the situation by reminding the group of the words of the Commander in Chief [Castro], where he highlighted the role the popular masses had to play in defending and spreading the Revolution. In this work especially, age, sex, nor race were as important as overall unity."[65] These situations reveal the continued anxieties toward racial integration existing in Cuba in 1961, especially in private spaces such as the home. In each case, certain aspects of revolutionary antidiscrimination rhetoric worked to settle the issue and create positive memories of *brigadistas* overcoming adversity. In the first, the girl was allowed entrance into the house because she was an acceptable type of Afro-Cuban; she was "sweet" and came bearing an electric lantern, technology that the rural family did not possess. The literacy teacher in Guantánamo invoked the very language used by M 26-7 and national calls for unity to encourage reluctant elements to admit Afro-Cubans, but not without pointing out that the four literacy teachers in question were "black as the night" and belonged to the "popular masses." Another young *brigadista* remembered the shock rural farmers expressed when she said she was going to interview a black family to see if any illiterates lived in their house:

Brigadista: Who lives in that little house?
Farmer: Oh just some blacks.
Brigadista: Can they read and write?
Farmer: I don't know, they are blacks.
Brigadista: Well, I'll just drop in and see if they have illiterates in the house.
Farmer: No, no, you can't go there! I tell you, they're blacks.
Brigadista: All right, I heard you, but I'm going.

They tried to stop me, but seeing my mind was made up, the old man said, 'Elias will take you on horseback and wait for you outside.' It was then I realized the country people were a lot more prejudiced than city people. They discriminated brutally against blacks. They never visited them and feared for my safety. They hinted that the black boys might molest me and also said they practiced bestiality. Later I learned that this was true. After a time, I realized everybody here practiced it. Frankly I was scared, but I said to myself, 'Buck up kid, be brave,' and I went to visit them. I found that nearly every one of the blacks was illiterate, so I decided to give two classes a day, and, wanting to make people go to the blacks' house, I chose that one for afternoon classes. My hosts of course were shocked.[66]

Like other volunteer teachers, this young girl describes having to overcome her own fears and prejudices about blacks and rural Cubans to accomplish the goals of the Literacy Campaign. The young woman's story gives insight into how anxieties about black male sexuality took both similar and different forms in the countryside. Rather than being concerned about whites and blacks dancing together in social clubs, some rural Cubans assumed that black boys were sexually deviant and feared that they abused animals and young women. But, in telling herself to "buck up" and in refusing to accept the antiblack advice of the older farmer, the young *brigadista* illustrates how the collective efforts of the campaign to eliminate racial discrimination, the literacy movement, and the national celebration of Benítez taught a new generation of Cubans revolutionary values and pushed them to try to construct a more inclusive society.

Ironically, however, revolutionary rhetoric about race could also be used to hinder integration. A dark-skinned woman named María remembered how she encountered resistance when she sought lodging from a white rural family as a *brigadista* in 1961: "I was going to stay with one family, a white one, but they decided that it would be best for me to stay in a black house, so that the counterrevolutionaries would not notice my arrival to the region."[67] By referencing the threat countergovernment militants presented to María, this household was able to deny lodging to the black youth without facing the stigma of being labeled racist. In fact, the family invoked the very paranoia revolutionary leaders had publicized when claiming that the counterrevolutionaries wanted to kill black teachers to steer the Afro-Cuban girl to another residence. In both of these stories, *brigadistas* worked to make sense of their prior prejudices, lived experiences, and state rhetoric. The young woman who was afraid of teaching in the countryside made herself approach the black family's house because the revolution told her to do so, but in the end she reaffirmed her previous beliefs about the lack of civilization in rural Cuba by saying that everyone practiced bestiality. Similarly, María discursively bridged her uncomfortable experiences of prejudice with her hope that the revolution had eliminated racist thinking by framing her story in a way that excused the white family for their failure to open their home to a black woman out of a supposed fear for her safety. The contradictory messages in revolutionary racial rhetoric and the challenges of creating a new Cuba from the island's colonial, slave past required such discursive gymnastics.

Despite, or maybe because of overcoming, these challenges, Cuban literacy teachers interviewed nearly fifty years after the end of campaign had strong memories about the Year of Education. Afro-Cuban poet Georgina Herrera told me in 2007 that "those were years of so much movement.... We broke all the norms. The world turned upside down. But everyone won something. Because the young people who went to teach learned about the difficulties people faced in the countryside. These were productive years for everyone."[68] One of the norms broken by the literacy movement was the decision to send young Cubans, some of whom had not reached their teenage years, into the countryside to teach. Afro-Cuban Graciela Chailoux, who is now a professor at the University of Havana, recalled that she was eleven when she joined the Literacy Campaign and spent eight months away from home. On 22 December 1961, when Castro declared, "Cuba was an illiteracy free territory," Chailoux participated in the mass mobilization of volunteer teachers marching in Revolution Plaza. In an emotional interview about her involvement, she described the campaign as one of the revolution's greatest achievements. Chailoux, with tears in her eyes, explained, "Yes, I think so, I think so, [this was Cuba's finest moment] because Fidel said that everybody had to study.... It was a special moment and everyone's strength was put into it."[69] Norma Guillard, another black Cuban, concurred in the 2013 documentary *Maestra*, saying, "I have many years left, but until today, in my fifty-eight years I don't have another experience as enormously powerful as this one [the Literacy Campaign]. It evokes this feeling ... it is the most important thing that I have done." Guillard was a fifteen-year-old girl from Santiago when she decided to join the literacy movement. Like Chailoux, today she is a university professor, specializing in social psychology.[70] For each of these women, participating in the Literacy Campaign had profound effects on their childhood memories, investment in the revolution, and future careers as intellectuals and teachers.

Volunteer teachers also conveyed their gratitude to the revolution for exposing them to the inequalities that existed on the island and offering them the chance to make a difference in other Cubans' lives. In many ways, participating in the Literacy Campaign allowed young Cubans to join the revolution and show their fidelity to the leaders who had fought against Batista.[71] One Conrado Benítez *brigadista* wrote a letter to Fidel Castro thanking him for the opportunity to serve the nation. "I feel very grateful and proud as one of the *compañeras* that taught. Do you want me to tell you why? Because now I feel more human, more revolutionary, more Cuban for having helped my *semejantes* [equals or people like me] and also because I have learned that people don't only exist in the city, they exist in the rural areas too."[72] A young Afro-Cuban girl from the Las Yaguas community in Havana shared the same sentiments and told a journalist from *Verde Olivo* that she has always wanted to teach, but had never had the opportunity until after the revolution. According to this young woman, brigade members learned "the pain of the rest" and "gave back" to their nation by teaching in the countryside.[73]

One Campaign Replaces Another: Contradictions and Silences about Blackness

Cubans remember 1961, the Year of Education, as one of the most important moments in their lives because as a whole the year highlighted the potential of revolutionary Cuba. But sitting alongside the many possibilities of racially integrated teaching brigades, celebrations honoring black martyrs, and Cuba's defeat of U.S.-backed exile forces in the April Bay of Pigs invasion lay remnants of an old, republican Cuba that had yet to embrace blackness on equal footing. Literacy Campaign publicity and commemorations about black martyrs replaced direct debates about antidiscrimination in 1961. Moreover, rather than make efforts to answer the demands of black consciousness thinkers and insert black history into the national culture, revolutionary leaders silenced future debates about racism. In fact, as we have seen, state leaders declared that the revolution had resolved the problem of racism and used the iconization of black heroes to do so. But even as depictions of the three men taught Cubans lessons about humility, sacrifice, and revolutionary loyalty, it is telling that revolutionary leaders constructed these ideas using the stories of the dead Afro-Cubans. Unlike in the 1880s, when Cuban intellectuals worked with black and *mulato* Cubans to carve a space for living war veterans, in 1961 state leaders held up these martyrs as the ideal black insurgent.

Popular representations asserted a particular type of patriotic blackness that used martyrs, not living Afro-Cubans, as soldiers for the nation while appealing to standing perceptions about the inherent physical strength of black men. As one historian has noted, Conrado Benítez's blackness "carried specific messages that promoted black militancy as an exclusive arm of the state."[74] A poster advertising the "Week of Cuban Youth" illustrated the role revolutionary figures allocated to Benítez and other black martyrs as soldiers in national battles.[75] Unlike most images of the teacher, this poster, created by the Association of Cuban Youth, depicted Benítez without his customary suit. Rather he is a warrior for the nation, wielding a large pencil as a weapon to stab, and thus defeat, Cuban illiteracy. This image redirected stereotypes about black masculinity away from threatening the state—as in the threat of the Independent Party of Color (Partido Independiente de Color, PIC)—and toward the revolution's current enemy, illiteracy and the counterrevolutionaries who attacked the education campaign. Cubans had used the bodies of black men to fight national battles previously during the wars of independence, where national journalists often referred to Maceo as the strength behind Martí's leadership. In 1961, revolutionary discourses invoked a similar trope of strong, black masculinity through the image of Benítez to undermine counterrevolutionary movements. However, both Maceo and Benítez had died before revolutionary leaders applied their muscle to Cuban battles. The attention given to black martyrs as loyal revolutionaries in this period suggests an underlying belief among some Cuban leaders that blacks and *mulatos* were safest when they could be controlled and their stories manipulated.

A central component of the Literacy Campaign and the values it promoted among literacy teachers was the idea that it was noble to fight and die for the fatherland. Audiences across the island repeatedly encountered articles and editorials explaining how the counterrevolutionaries had offered to free Benítez and allow him to live if he would only join their forces. "Conrado said no! 'I am a revolutionary and will not betray my people. Do to me what you will!' "[76] Publicity about the young teacher repeated this narrative and encouraged Literacy Campaign volunteers to remain faithful to the revolution, regardless of the sacrifices requested of them. In the same way, the code for the Conrado Benítez brigades pledged, "We will not abandon our task no matter how great the deprivations, difficulties, or sacrifices. A Conrado Benítez *brigadista* never will be a deserter."[77] This code and a photograph of the slain teacher appeared on the back of every identification card carried by members of the Benítez brigades to remind young Cubans of their obligations to the revolution. National publicity for the Literacy Campaign coded these responsibilities as universal characteristics found in "true revolutionaries" of all colors;

however, because revolutionary leaders taught these values through the story of a black martyr, promises to never desert reaffirmed expectations of loyalty for Afro-Cubans (namely staying on the island) as well.

Cuban newspapers also highlighted Benítez's modest origins to promote the new government as a revolution of *los humildes*. Revolutionary leaders repeatedly identified themselves and M 26-7 "as a rebellion of *humildes* and for *humildes*" as a means of redefining what it meant to be Cuban after 1959. For Cubans, *los humildes* signified that someone was working-class, humble, and possibly uneducated, but also determined and honest. This was the formula for the new man and representations of black martyrs glorified the concept.[78] Cuban leaders specifically named Benítez a *"humilde* teacher" and used examples from his background and work ethic to outline this new type of citizen.[79] Castro told crowds of graduating teachers that the slain youth was just like them and others said he was a "man of the people," to link the dead teacher to the popular masses.[80] Editors for *La Calle* recounted Benítez's life history and celebrated his willingness to sacrifice to get an education. He was from a black working-class family in Matanzas, where his father was an agricultural worker and his mother a domestic servant. Distinguishing the young teacher as "a shoeshine boy, a bread maker, and a student who went to night school because he worked during the day," the same article noted that Benítez had not been to Miami, did not drive a Cadillac, and was not the son of a businessman. Literacy Campaign materials like this one contrasted Benítez's modest life to the supposed extravagant existence of counter-revolutionaries and exiles.[81]

While such editorials and photographs might have elevated a new idea of national character dependent on humility, continual references to the meager class background of the black martyr depicted Afro-Cubans as indigents in need of government aid. Photographs of Benítez's parents crying in a crumbling apartment depicted a black family that was helpless due to its limited economic power and inherently grateful to Cuban leaders for the opportunities they provided. These associations routinely depicted people of color in safe and harmless ways that emphasized their poverty and allegiance to the new government. By celebrating the stories of working-class Afro-Cubans who had dedicated themselves to the revolution, M 26-7 prescribed the ideal type of black citizen, namely someone who had come from nothing, was indebted for the opportunities provided after 1959, and faithful to the new government as a result. Notably, this conceptualization left little space for black intellectuals, especially those proposing a black consciousness approach, to be ideal revolutionary citizens. Cuban leaders demanded loyalty from all citizens during this period; therefore this practice was not uncommon and was applied frequently to white working-class Cubans as well. However, publicity celebrating two black centenarians who learned to read during the Literacy Campaign illustrates how revolutionary leaders used stories about loyal Afro-Cubans in particular to stand in for direct conversations about racism and position the new government as the solution to previous inequalities.

Verde Olivo published front-page feature articles about Isidra Pupu y Ponce de Leon and María Sentmanat in July 1961 that used the lives of Afro-Cuban women to connect the Literacy Campaign to revolutionary achievements. In "Why Isidra Wanted to Go to Playa Girón," a 102-year-old dark-skinned woman laments how she had fought in the Ten Years' War, but that after the War of 1895 her life changed little, saying, "I had to fight hard against the Spanish and afterward, you know, nothing." The journalist for *Verde Olivo* expanded on her comment in a way that positioned racism as a problem of the past: "Nothing. The people got almost nothing [out of the wars for independence]. New foreign masters—more voracious than the old ones—they appropriated all the riches of Cuba. The poor continued to be poor. The black continued to be discriminated against.... Isidra is now in a new position to fight because the people have come into real power, because now the Revolution has brought real justice for all." *Verde Olivo* represented Isidra's life story within prevalent revolutionary narratives about race. Racism was a legacy of the colonial past aggravated by U.S. intervention and eliminated by the revolution, in this case through the work of the Literacy Campaign. In the concluding lines of the article, the author tied Isidra's gratitude to the revolution to her willingness to sacrifice her life fighting against the Bay of Pigs invasion. "In a hundred years of existence no one has tried to take away her ignorance. Today the Revolution brought her a way to illuminate her hard life. It's for this reason that she wanted to fight."[82] The story told by *Verde Olivo* about the older woman's past directly positioned revolutionary leaders as the heirs and saviors of Cuba's nineteenth-century past because her life spanned the century.

Like the 1966 book *Biography of a Runaway Slave*, where Cuban anthropologist Miguel Barnet interviewed another centenarian, Esteban Montejo, stories produced after 1959 about Afro-Cubans who had survived slavery centered on comparing horrors of racial discrimination in the late nineteenth century to opportunities provided by the revolution.[83] But even as the articles about the two Afro-Cuban women invoked previous racial inequalities, they also intentionally silenced parts of black Cuban history like the government massacre of the PIC in 1912 or any reference to persistent racism in the present.[84] The journalist's comments also epitomized the complex package that was revolutionary discourse on race because at the same time that the article celebrated Isidra as a revolutionary citizen, it also called attention to her "ignorance" in a way that did not fit with the wealth of knowledge she had surely acquired from over a century of living.

Verde Olivo iconized a second black woman, this time a 106-year-old, after Castro spoke with María Sentmanat during a public rally in July 1961. Castro invited Sentmanat to the podium and they discussed her experiences learning to read. Fitting with the gratitude portrayed in the lives of black martyrs, Sentmanat thanked the young Cuban leader for the Literacy Campaign and invoked religious imagery to do so. She called Castro an "apostle," and he said, "No, Martí was the apostle, I am only the disciple." To which she responded, "No, you are Jesus Christ."[85] Sentmanat, however, was more than simply appreciative of the revolution for her reading lessons because she viewed education as a right, not a gift to be bestowed. She made Castro repeat her name out loud to the crowd and said that she was only willing to act as a "mascot" for the campaign if revolutionary leaders told her story and sent someone to her house to transcribe her life.[86] It is unknown whether the stenographer Sentmanat requested ever visited her home in Havana, but *Verde Olivo* sent a journalist to interview her a few days after the magazine printed its feature on Isidra.

In the resulting article, "Maria Sentmanat, You Are Free," editors for *Verde Olivo* presented the Afro-Cuban woman as an ideal black revolutionary. Rather than highlight her agency in learning to read or her terms for being the revolution's mascot, however, the journalist framed Sentmanat's story as a linear progression from slavery to freedom as a revolutionary citizen. Saying that "at last Maria de la Cruz can learn to read and write! Now, there aren't masters who impede, nor slaves chained to exploitation and ignorance. Our patria is free! Now, you are free Maria de la Cruz!," this piece attributed Sentmanat's "freedom" to the revolution and again juxtaposed nineteenth-century oppression to 1960s opportunities. The article also referenced racism in the United States, following trends linking the Literacy Campaign to battles against imperialism:

Journalist: What do you think about the persecution of blacks
   in the United States?

Sentmanat: Look, there, they have a regime that isn't interested in
   anything but gold; there is not democracy, there is not liberty,
   and as long as there is exploitation, slavery, and this thing called
   discrimination there can be no liberty. They—*referring to the
   Yankee imperialists* [editors' note]—said to us that the Russians
   continue to have slavery, that the Russians are communists, and
   that the communists are bad. . . . Lies! . . . lies, all this is lies. The
   bad ones are them. The Russians help us, if the Russians are
   communists, well then the communists are good.[87]

Here, Literacy Campaign publicity, revolutionary narratives about U.S.
racism, and the lives of Afro-Cubans collided to legitimize the new government's alliance with the Soviet Union and shift to socialism. The attention given to the stories of elderly Afro-Cuban women mirrored the
emphasis revolutionary leaders placed on the sacrifice, gratitude, and
loyalty of black martyrs because like dead Afro-Cuban heroes, female
centenarians appeared safe and nonthreatening to the revolution. This is
not to say that these women were duped or that they did not appreciate
their interactions with Literacy Campaign volunteers. The images, letters,
and stories memorialized in documentaries and films about the movement, some housed in the Literacy Campaign museum that sits outside
of Havana and hosts school children, tour groups, and others interested
in learning more about one of Cuba's most ambitious and impressive
achievements, say otherwise. Nevertheless, the ways that photographs of
Benítez and framed articles about these two Afro-Cuban women disproportionally decorate the walls of the museum (and decorated the Cuban
press in 1961) illustrate how narratives about blacks as beneficiaries of
the Literacy Campaign replaced direct debates about continued racism
and conversations revaluing blackness in 1961. And while closing one
door might have opened another, the rhetoric of black gratefulness and
loyalty left little space for Afro-Cuban intellectuals, workers, or exiles to
participate in the revolution on equal footing.

Conclusions: Incomplete Racial Revolutions

Cubans I interviewed in 2007 claimed that there was a black man among
those that invaded and were captured on the island at Playa Girón (Bay of

Pigs) on 17 April 1961, just four months after Benítez's death. According to the informal account told by these now elderly Cubans, when Fidel Castro caught a glimpse of the dark-skinned prisoner during a public interview, the young leader became enraged. Castro called the black prisoner over, and asked, "What are you doing here? With everything that I have given you blacks, why are you fighting against the revolution?" In response, the black man stepped forward and answered, "No sir, I didn't board the boat to fight, I'm just the cook!"[88] Older Cubans recounting this humorous narrative follow the punch line with laughter, saying, "You get it? He was the cook; he was not helping the invaders."

An estimated fifty Afro-Cubans participated in the exile expeditionary force Brigade 2506. Official transcripts of the interrogations tell a story of a puzzled and angry Castro demanding to know why an Afro-Cuban would attempt to reinstall a government that had supported racial discrimination, but they do not show anyone trying to avoid being punished by claiming to be a domestic laborer:

> *Castro:* You have the audacity to . . . land here on the beaches of Playa Girón to fight the Revolution, but you were not allowed on the beaches for recreation. Nevertheless, you came together with that gentleman who never cared whether or not you were let into the club to bathe, as if the seawater could be stained by your skin color!
> *Black prisoner:* The fact is that I did not come to Cuba out of considerations of whether or not I could be allowed on the beach . . .
> *Castro:* Very well, that is not the point.[89]

National discourses highlighted that white leaders expected black clients to be appreciative of revolutionary integrationist policies while not understanding that Cubans of color might have their own independent political ideas. The contemporary, altered version of this story—the joke I described above—demonstrates the ways revolutionary leaders shaped conversations about race in Cuba and how those narratives shifted, grew, and became legend as they fit with existing preconceived notions about blackness. In fact, Cubans I interviewed in 2007 told me this "humorous" anecdote whenever I asked about race during the first years of the revolution without any prompting on my part about Playa Girón or Conrado Benítez. Rather, this joke was the de facto or automatic means through which my interviewees remembered the changes that occurred on the island in those years. Castro's questioning of the black combatant reveals the common belief that the revolutionary government "gave" Afro-Cubans unprecedented opportunities, including access to education, employment, and health care. Reminiscent of the way the white Communist Party of Cuba (PCC) official in the introduction to this book criticized his Afro-Cuban neighbors for having a party after the announcement of Castro's failing health in 2006 by saying that the "Revolution had made blacks into people," the Bay of Pigs joke reinforced Afro-Cuban loyalty and gratitude. The early 1960s joke and the 2006 statement both contend that blacks and *mulatos* owed something to the revolutionary government and that Afro-Cubans needed to pay that debt with unquestioning loyalty. And finally, the joke's punch line, which identifies the Afro-Cuban as a cook, positions him in the familiar role of a nonthreatening, domestic servant. The comedic story mocks the political naïveté of the black member of the invading brigade, and depicts him as someone incapable of forming his own critical opinions. The brigade member and the Afro-Cuban neighbors end up being helpless, if amusing figures, open for manipulation by *both* counterrevolutionaries and the Castro government.

This anecdote and its nuances resonated with Cubans because of the government's public campaign to tackle racial discrimination between 1959 and 1961. When M 26-7 entered Havana in 1959, they recognized the importance of solidifying their power by enlisting popular support. One way they accomplished this goal was by reaching out to Cubans of color and pledging to fulfill nineteenth-century promises of racial equality. This strategy opened a brief dialogue across the island about racism that coincided with the radicalization of the revolution. *Antiracism in Cuba* has looked closely at racialized revolutionary discourses to show how Cuban leaders constructed their new antidiscrimination campaign using old symbols, images, and ideas. This contradictory process allowed racism to coexist with antiracism from the very start of the revolution.

Revolutionary leaders repeatedly invoked history to justify the campaign to eliminate racial discrimination. The new government mobilized the legacies of José Martí and Antonio Maceo to press for integration and to demonstrate Afro-Cuban capabilities. This strategy reveals the continued salience of the two independence heroes as fathers of the nation in 1959, so much so that Castro and other revolutionaries sought to portray themselves as the heirs of these icons. Yet, maybe one of the most fascinating aspects of national discourses about race was how they employed a "new" version of the Cuban past to blame the U.S. intervention in 1898 for the failure of racial democracy in the republic. Cuban leaders deemphasized how white privilege had contributed to continued inequality, thereby erasing the historical role white Cubans played in limiting black and *mulato* social mobility in the twentieth century.

Racial violence in the United States was also a central component of revolutionary discourses used to discredit enemies in the United States and internationalize racial struggles. Revolutionary leaders were able to discourage black emigration to the United States and show the progress of Cuban battles against racial discrimination by comparing the situation of African Americans to that of Afro-Cubans. Incorporating the plight of U.S. blacks into national conversations also allowed Cubans to portray North American hostility, and any opposition group linked to U.S. interests, as white and racist. Doing so gave revolutionary leaders a moral weapon to use in the battle against U.S. criticism, and a focal point for solidifying Afro-Cuban and popular support. In the 1970s, these early events provided the social context for Cuban contributions to African anticolonial movements and the island's willingness to offer sanctuary to African American militants hiding from the U.S. government.

Revolutionary leaders celebrated the end of the campaign to eliminate racial discrimination with the iconization of black male martyrs. Afro-Cuban teacher Conrado Benítez emerged as an icon of both the Literacy Campaign and the defense of the revolution more broadly. The narrative of his murder enabled the new government to cast its opponents as racist, and racism as antirevolutionary. National conversations about the slain teacher continued to declare public racism as unacceptable in the same manner that conversations had previously identified countergovernment groups as antiblack. This tactic depicted revolutionary leaders as the defenders of Afro-Cubans without having to address lingering instances of racial discrimination directly. The story of Benítez's life and death also appropriated black contributions to the nation. Similar to the ways that revolutionary leaders invoked the legacy of Maceo, Benítez represented a suitable black role model due to his loyalty to the nation and humble background.

Despite public celebrations about the elimination of discrimination, racism still existed in Cuba after 1961. However, the available space to address these concerns was continually diminished in favor of a more unifying national rhetoric. The continuing presence of racial discrimination despite government attempts to address the injustice occurred for a number of reasons. Primarily, it was an ambitious and possibly unachievable goal to try to abolish attitudes and practices that had been a part of the Cuban daily existence for so long through such a brief conversation. Secondly, certain contradictions existed within revolutionary racialized discourses that undermined Cuban commitments to racial equality.

At the same time that revolutionary leaders highlighted the blackness of Afro-Cubans to construct a supportive constituency that could fight U.S.-funded countergovernment groups, they also worked toward a goal of a raceless Cuba. The frequent repetition of comments about transforming "blacks into citizens" or "*negritos* into Cuban children" reveals strategic intentions to open a discussion about racism, "achieve" the elimination of discrimination by reforming blacks and *mulatos*, and then close these national conversations by declaring that "we are all Cubans." Yet, revolutionary leaders frequently imagined these same Afro-Cuban citizens as dependent clients of the state. National discourses portrayed people of color as indigents in order to promote popular acceptance of social programs among critical audiences and decrease fears about black uplift. And while light-hearted political cartoons might have sought to encourage Cubans to welcome blacks and *mulatos* into the national fold, they also undermined promises of racial equality by depicting Afro-Cubans as childlike and infantile. Portraying blacks and *mulatos* in this way helped form the opinion that people of African descent, both domestically and internationally, needed the revolutionary government to rescue them from their blackness before becoming acceptable citizens.

Another paradox within conversations about eliminating racial discrimination was the ways revolutionary leaders solicited Afro-Cuban support while simultaneously prescribing a type of acceptable black contribution to the nation. Blacks were encouraged to participate in the revolution as loyal and grateful citizens. Like the question Castro posed to the black counterrevolutionary at the Playa Girón interrogation, asking why he would undermine a government that had provided Afro-Cubans with so many opportunities, national discourses highlighted the appreciation white leaders expected from black clients. Such attitudes led to frustration among some Afro-Cubans and African Americans. Intellectuals like Juan René Betancourt, Carlos Moore, and Walterio Carbonell interpreted these interactions as evidence of underlying sentiments of black inferiority among white leaders. Ultimately, constructing the campaign to eliminate racial discrimination around the tropes of parent-child or state-client relationships foreshadowed an early and unfinished end to the program once the new leadership proclaimed the project achieved.

As discussed, Cubans responded to and influenced how revolutionary leaders constructed national discourses on race. In particular, Afro-Cubans living in the Havana neighborhood of Las Yaguas were hesitant to accept the interference by a mostly white government in their daily lives. Black consciousness thinkers proposed alternative narratives for including African and black history and culture into revolutionary nationalism. We have also seen how Cubans living in exile engaged with these discussions by denying that racial inequality existed, claiming that revolutionary leaders created the problem, and pledging to tackle the issue themselves after the removal of communism from the island. The centrality of charges of racism to revolutionary critiques against countergovernment groups in the United States forced the exile community to address how to incorporate Afro-Cubans in the nation. Likewise, this book has examined how some Afro-Cubans mobilized revolutionary racialized discourses at different times to press for additional opportunities, such as entrance into recreational and tourist facilities. In each of these cases, the sources clearly show how rhetoric initiated by the state was open for manipulation by residents. Popular involvement reveals the impossibility of separating conversations about ending racial discrimination from understandings of what it meant to be a Cuban between 1959 and 1961. The considerable participation in these discussions by students, workers, intellectuals, and Cubans from different geographical, class, and racial backgrounds highlights the pervasiveness of race in revolutionary culture.

Moreover, the common narratives remembered by diverse Cubans fifty years later that identify the exile community as racist, Harlem residents as Fidelistas, and Benítez as a martyr assassinated for his race and class status demonstrate how particular representations about racial equality and its meaning to the revolution not only took hold between 1959 and 1961, but endured and became a central component of Cuban national memory. However, as seen in the anecdote about the black Playa Girón prisoner and the exaggerated solidarity attributed to African Americans, these popular recollections do not always correspond to historical events. If anything, such fascinating inconsistencies suggest that Cuban conversations about race worked more to support the state, unify the masses, and demonize the United States than to describe actual occurrences.

The end of the campaign to eliminate racial discrimination in 1961 told through the story of black martyrs created spaces for the coexistence of racism and antiracism, especially in private attitudes seen in jokes and humor. In many ways, this story about race and revolution in Cuba has been a story about what was said and what was left unsaid. The impressive accomplishments that the revolution made and continues to make disguise the nearly 100-year-old subtext that frequently devalued blackness in the pursuit of a raceless nation. That many blacks and *mulatos* (in Cuba and globally) participated in and celebrated the revolution's unprecedented integration efforts in education and obtained new professional positions reveals how the dream, the reality, and all of the in-between of race in Cuba worked together to make the revolution in 1959. Yet, revealing the limits of the new government's actions to eliminate racism does not discount the overall project. If anything, the many opportunities pursued by Cubans of color, often in private, to continue conversations about the centrality of blackness and black experiences in Cuba show how M 26-7 leaders sometimes unknowingly facilitated a "revolution inside of the revolution."

Epilogue

A Revolution inside of the Revolution:
Afro-Cuban Experiences after 1961

After the closing of the campaign to eliminate racial discrimination in 1961, Cubans of African descent faced considerable challenges tackling lingering racism in the late 1960s. In addition to Castro's public claims that racial discrimination had been eliminated and the dismissal of black critics as ungrateful, in June 1961 (two months after declaring the Marxist-Leninist nature of the revolution) Cuba's leader declared, "Within the Revolution, everything! Outside of the Revolution, nothing!" In this speech, titled "Some Words to the Intellectuals," Castro argued that artists and intellectuals had creative freedom to do whatever work they desired, but that the revolution had the right—the greater right—to review (and prohibit if necessary) any art form that would ideologically damage Cubans: "We have the responsibility to lead the people and to lead the Revolution, especially in the midst of a revolutionary struggle."[1]

The speech did not mention socialism or try to validate its claims with Soviet ideology; instead Castro depicted the revolution as a battle for the reeducation or decolonization of Cuban minds. In addition to being an attempt to unify the country after the Bay of Pigs invasion in April 1961, Castro's speech was also a part of a series of meetings and public forums between intellectuals, the National Cuban Film Institute (Instituto Cubano de Arte e Industria Cinematográficos, ICAIC), and the National Culture Council (Consejo Nacional de Cultura, CNC) in response to the censuring of the film *P.M.* (1961). Directed by two young filmmakers, *P.M.* was a short, less than ten-minute documentary showing Afro-Cubans partaking in the nightclub scene in Havana. A British traveler to the island described the film as showing black and *mulato* Cubans "drinking, arguing, loving, quarrelling, [and] dreaming. A blurred negress stands in front of the lens, and the camera moves back to take in the whole jostling, sweating scene. . . . The only sound is the roar of so many Cuban voices, the clink of glasses and ice from the bar, and the music."[2] More pointedly, Bob Taber highlighted the difference between the Cubans portrayed in the film and the revolution's famous literacy martyr by saying, "I didn't see a single Conrado Benítez among them, with a rifle in one hand and a book in the other."[3] Scholars continue to debate why the revolution banned *P.M.* Some argue that the ICAIC and CNC found its focus on black nightlife counterrevolutionary and in conflict with the celebratory rhetoric that had consumed the island since the April 1961 defeat of U.S.-backed forces in the Bay of Pigs invasion. Others see the banning as the first step in what would soon be a state-supported censorship campaign that only valued positive portrayals of the revolution for both domestic and international consumption.[4] Significantly, for this book's story about race and revolution, film historian Susan Lord concludes that "the story of *P.M.* is more than a story of the censorship of a film that coincidentally has black content; it is a story about the struggle over how to tell the story about race."[5]

After 1961, the debate over how to tell the story about race, especially in relation to blackness, in Cuba continued even though official narratives claimed that the revolution had eliminated racial discrimination and silenced further national debate about the issue. The censuring of art featuring Afro-Cuban life, the closing of black social clubs that had existed since the late nineteenth century, and, as we will see, ICAIC's later choice not to screen filmmaker Sara Gómez's documentaries reflected national conflicts over who could define Afro-Cuban roles in the new state and what images of blackness were acceptable in the 1960s. The state's distaste for *P.M.* centered on the fact that the blacks in the film, while obviously working-class—later interviews even identified them as revolutionaries—did not accept the new government's plans to reform them. The Afro-Cubans caught on camera for *P.M.* saw little reason to give up their nightly leisure activities nor did they fit into the parameters of appropriate revolutionary blackness, which valued clean-cut and grateful workers and *brigadistas*. Instead, these dancers were individuals who dared to pursue their own destiny and definition of the revolution.

After activists such as Juan René Betancourt, Carlos Moore, and Walterio Carbonell were silenced by the revolution (either via exile or censorship), young black and *mulata* women (Afrocubanas), including poet Georgina Herrera, author Nancy Morejón, literary critic Inés María Martiatu Terry, and filmmaker Sara Gómez, carved out spaces for continued debates about racial inequality. These Afrocubanas worked to both support and challenge the revolution's agenda in the late 1960s and beyond—basically setting their own agenda by using art to offer a more expansive understanding of black contributions to the nation.[6] Sara Gómez directed her first solo documentary, *Iré a Santiago* (*I'm Going to Santiago*) in 1964, three years after the *P.M.* controversy.[7] *Iré a Santiago* employs wide shots of the city's colonial streets, cathedral, and university, with Gómez as narrator explaining to the audience that "the first blacks [in Cuba] were brought to Santiago and General Antonio Maceo was born here." In doing so, she emphasized the city's rich past and Afro-Cuban contributions to the nation. But in 1964, Gómez was not only aware of Santiago's past; she also had a stake in its future. The narrator claims that "history is beginning again in Santiago [with the revolution]" as Afro-Cuban women outfitted with batons, drums, and marching band uniforms move across the screen. As the only female and one of three black directors working at ICAIC in the 1960s, Gómez routinely stood out by producing documentaries that showcased the daily experiences of blacks and *mulatos* in revolutionary Cuba—she showed how blacks in neighborhoods, factories, and rural areas participated in and questioned the new government's policies. This work sat in stark contrast and offered an alternative to the paternalistic images we have seen in revolutionary visual culture portraying blacks in need of salvation and reform. It also contradicted recent moves by state cultural institutions, ICAIC included, to position blackness in the past, as folklore.[8] Gómez's claim that history was beginning again in Santiago mirrored statements made by revolutionary leaders who imagined 1959 as a new start for the island; however, the young filmmaker saw Cuba's renewal, its revolution, in the lives of black men and women in Santiago, Guanabacoa, and other sites far removed from the accepted centers of white, male power.

Unlike revolutionary leaders and some Afro-Cubans who saw little need for black and *mulato* social clubs after 1959, Gómez recognized the importance of, and the challenges facing, Afro-Cuban clubs in the late 1960s. She dedicated a quarter of *Iré a Santiago* to tracking a funeral procession for Esperanza, the president of a "French society." "In Santiago, there are blacks who call themselves French," she says, "because their ancestors arrived in Cuba when white planters fled Haiti to escape the neighboring island's revolution which had freed its slaves." And even as the documentary notes that there are no longer any French in Cuba and that the coffee plantations they owned have long disappeared, Gómez employs footage of over fifty Afro-Cubans marching behind Esperanza's casket to demonstrate the cultural significance that black social clubs like the French society had in structuring life in Santiago. In *Guanabacoa: Crónica de mi familia* (*Guanabacoa: Chronicle of My Family*, 1964), Gómez continued to draw attention to black social clubs, this time through the example of members of her own middle-class family.[9] She describes how her aunts did not attend public dances because they were "decent women." Instead, they supported events and dances at El Progresso and El Provenir—two Afro-Cuban societies—that Gómez says were clubs only for "certain blacks."

Combined with the scenes of the French society in *Iré a Santiago*, Gómez's accounts of Afro-Cuban associations in *Guanabacoa* reflect on the controversial closing of black and *mulato* social clubs discussed in chapter 2. Most private clubs (both black and white) were gone by the mid-1960s when Gómez made this documentary. Therefore, for her to mention these clubs in her films, in a positive way no less, while highlighting her middle-class roots, is likely one of the reasons her works were not screened in Cuba in the first decade of the revolution. *Guanabacoa*, however, was not a simple statement in support of Afro-Cuban clubs. While Gómez warmly remembered the dances her family members had attended, she also acknowledged that the societies were only for "certain blacks." At the end of the short film, Gómez asks, "Will we have to fight against the necessity of being a better and superior black?—to come to Guanabacoa and accept a complete or total history; a complete picture of Guanabaoca and to tell it all." With these words, Gómez recognized and questioned the tensions between working-class and middle-class blacks, something the revolution's antiracist campaign often failed to do. These documentaries suggest that she saw something to be admired in the popular French society of Santiago and the refined clubs of Guanabacoa, but she also questioned how Afro-Cuban associations perpetuated class hierarchies. In trying to paint a "complete picture" of black Cuba—using case studies from cities outside of Havana—Gómez's work marked continuities between pre- and postrevolutionary life. She celebrated her family's history even as she felt compelled not to be a "middle-class girl who played the piano" and struggled to meld her own class background with revolutionary ideals.[10] Gómez insisted on using routine images of black life, including its contradictions (such as shots of Catholic religious idols sitting next to Santeria altars or M 26-7 paraphernalia in the French society's funeral procession), to portray Afro-Cubans as normal human beings. In doing so, Gómez built on the work of previous Afro-Cuban activists and challenged notions of grateful, simplistic, revolutionary blackness seen in other aspects of popular culture while positioning black cultural practices as a part of present-day Cuba, not the far-off past.

By 1968, Gómez was using her camera to expose contradictions in the government's claims to have eliminated racism and her work stands out as an example of the ways Afro-Cubans continued debates about discrimination past the official end of the campaign. However, spaces for critiquing of the revolution continued to decrease as the decade progressed. Over four hundred intellectuals from seventy different countries gathered in Havana in January 1968 for Cuba's first Culture Congress. The meeting, which celebrated the growth of a revolutionary and anti-imperialist consciousness in the developing world, was a congress of contradictions. On one hand, the Cuban government invited foreign intellectuals (often paying for their travel) and presented them with an image of cultural openness and opportunity on the island. Domestically, however, the congress marked the beginning of a five-year interlude Cuban historians have now characterized as the "grey period" in Cuban culture because of the limits placed on what was considered revolutionary art.[11] According to Afrocubana author (and close friend of Goméz) Inés María Martiatu Terry, one of the topics challenged at the congress was the work of black intellectuals, like Walterio Carbonell, who had fought to insert the history of Africa and blacks in Cuba into the public school curriculum. Revolutionary leaders accused Carbonell, along with other Afro-Cubans, of fomenting "black power."[12] Similarly, in 1968 the Minister of Education called Gómez and two of her colleagues, black playwright Tomás González and ethnologist Alberto Pedro Díaz, into his office under the suspicion "of organizing activities diverging from the Revolution's ideological line and encouraging black power."[13] These charges point to the shrinking space for intellectual creativity in the late 1960s, but also the ways that the revolutionary government targeted some Afro-Cuban artists as counterrevolutionaries.

Race added an additional layer to the contradictions of the 1968 Cultural Congress and raised the stakes for black and *mulato* intellectuals who questioned the new government. The three Afro-Cuban directors at ICAIC each experienced this period in different ways. When describing a film that he had made that was considered "inopportune" and therefore not released in Cuba until years later, Sergio Giral said, "That was hard to take, because I've always felt a sense of political and social responsibility and wanted what I do to serve the revolutionary process. You exercise a form of self-censorship in not wanting to destroy the cake by sticking your fingers in it too much."[14] Giral's comment, though brief, explains why slavery and the lives of blacks in the nineteenth-century colonial period became the content of the majority of his films. Rather than risk having his work not shown, he chose topics that featured Afro-Cubans and educated audiences about blackness, without intervening into contemporary affairs. Giral had a long and successful career in Cuba until 1991 when he moved into exile for economic reasons. In contrast, the second black director at ICAIC, Nicolás Guillén Landrián, nephew of national poet Nicolás Guillén, made documentaries questioning contemporary issues explicitly, using banned Beatles music in the background of one and poking fun of Castro in another. Revolutionary leaders jailed Guillén Landrián, and after attempts to "rehabilitate" him with excessive electric shock therapy failed, the young director escaped into exile as well.[15] In this high-risk environment, only Gómez directed documentaries and films that questioned the lingering inequalities on the island and demanded that the revolution meet its own social justice claims. And while she did not face the physical persecution that Guillén Landrián encountered, ICAIC did not screen her work at the time when it might have been most useful; and until recently, Gómez was largely unknown on the island. Other than her feature film *De Cierta Manera* (*One Way or Another*, 1974), which was released to international acclaim after her death in 1977, ICAIC censored her documentaries, leaving them untouched in the institute's archives until 2007.[16]

In 1968 and 1969, Gómez completed a series of three documentaries questioning why so many black and *mulato* youth were sent to reform camps on the Isle of Youth, including *Una isla para Miguel* (*An Island for Miguel*, 1968), *En la otra isla* (*On the Other Island*, 1968), and *Isla del Tesoro* (*Treasure Island*, 1969). She took on the role of ethnographer in these pieces and juxtaposed interviews with teenagers on the island with statements from revolutionary leaders describing the purpose of the reform camps. For *En la otra isla*, Gómez interviewed two dark-skinned youths: a girl named Maria who was studying to be a hairdresser and a former opera singer, Rafael. Martiatu recalls that Gómez was interested in visiting the Isle of Youth because it had been featured prominently in the Cuban press. Revolutionary leaders portrayed the island as a utopic space where young people could construct a revolutionary consciousness without the bourgeoisie prejudices of adult Cubans. However, its residents were predominantly black and *mulato* because revolutionary authorities sent kids to the island if they got into trouble with the law, if they failed to show the appropriate ideological formation, or if their parents could not care for them.[17] By questioning how these criteria led to so many Afro-Cubans residing on the island, Gómez showed how social inequalities of the past invaded and were reproduced in the present. She also challenged the revolution's claims to have eliminated racial discrimination and suggested an alternative path for Cuba.

In his interview, Rafael described his love of music and the numerous concerts he gave in Havana until the "problems" began. Rafael had studied music for two and a half years at the National Art Institute and sang tenor in the National Opera in Havana before coming to the island:

Rafael: Then the problems started.

Gómez: Which ones?

Rafael: Problems with some of the *compañeras* (women) in the group. A lot of them didn't want to work with me anymore. It didn't feel right to be working in a scene with me anymore. I didn't know why, what was happening to me.

Gómez: Did they not like you because you came from the National Art Institute or because of your political formation?

Rafael: No, I don't think so.

Gómez: Were they political problems? What type of problems? . . .

Rafael: [looking directly at Gómez] I think the problem was race.

Gómez: They were prejudiced against you? . . . Weren't they revolutionaries?

Rafael: Yes. . . . [pause] They were revolutionaries, some not, but most were, but the fundamental problem was to tell you more concretely that the only black man was me. . . . [pause] Look, Sara, this wasn't about color. It was about aesthetics. They needed someone to work with a white woman in love scenes in the opera. And imagine it . . . [pause] if I might have to give her a kiss? When I took this problem of race to my supervisor, they said maybe it was there before but not now; that it must have been some error.

After this dialogue, Gómez cut to images of Rafael performing agricultural work, before a final close-up of him speaking again. Nodding his head affirmatively, he says, "I have confidence in the revolution that things will get better. So, now I'm doing agriculture, I'm doing something to help the revolution . . . being on the island has helped me a lot, they treat me well, and it is not like there. [pause] I have a question for you, Sara: Do you think one day, a black man could sing *La Traviata?*"[18] This uncomfortable exchange highlights how many of the contradictions inherent in the 1959 campaign to eliminate racial discrimination followed Cubans into the late 1960s. On one hand, Rafael benefited from the opportunity to break into a predominantly white space of opera having studied and worked with the National Opera in the early 1960s, something that would likely not have been available before 1959. On the other hand, the public silence around racism after 1961 not only left him with few spaces to denounce the discrimination he faced but also meant that he was ashamed of what happened to his career and had internalized it as his fault that white women did not want to sing with him.

In choosing to highlight the stories of youth like Maria and Rafael in 1968, Gómez suggested that there were things that revolutionaries could learn from the supposed deviants of society. As she told Rafael during their discussion, "The Revolution can't do everything for you. You have to make it, the Revolution, yourself."[19] These young men and women were not delinquents to Gómez. Rather their perseverance, commitment to revolutionary equality, and willingness to sacrifice for Cuba positioned them as potentially more revolutionary than the Cuban authorities who were unwilling to see past their race and class status. A scene of working-class women performing a rumba in 1969 at a work camp in Camagüey reinforced Gómez's message. As a well-dressed white female revolutionary leader looked on, a *mulata* woman started singing impromptu rumba lyrics while black women drummed and acted as a chorus. The spontaneous song celebrated Castro's leadership, communism, and the revolution. Nevertheless, in a fascinating Afro-Cuban interpretation of national rhetoric, the *mulata* brushed her forearm with her other hand, to refer to blacks, while saying, "We are the *columnistas*," or "We are the revolutionaries."[20] This image, filmed ten years after the announcement of the campaign to eliminate racial discrimination, portrayed all of the contradictions within revolutionary pledges of equality discussed in this book: a white paternalistic onlooker smiling in a motherly manner at Afro-Cuban playfulness; and poor black women (many of whom were former prostitutes) residing in a labor camp outside the city where they had been sent to learn appropriate modes of behavior from communist youth leaders.[21] The young women's words, however, relocated blackness to the center of the revolution. Rather than seeing themselves as revolutionary deviants, the Afro-Cuban women at the camp mocked the white leadership and called themselves the "true revolutionaries." In doing so, these women participated in public debates over building a new Cuba and the question of where blacks and *mulatos* fit into the revolution.

Afro-Cubans negotiated the changing landscape of revolutionary Cuba throughout the 1960s. Every day blacks and *mulatos* challenged the official declaration that racial discrimination had been eliminated and fought state attempts to silence public debates about lingering racisms. Cuban conversations about racism did not end after 1961; instead, they were reconstructed in areas outside of the public sphere, in art, poetry, literature, and film. Additional research is needed on the seemingly large role black and *mulata* women artists played in this continued struggle and the ongoing transnational connections they invoked. Rather than trying to impede the goals of the new Cuba, Gómez and other Afro-Cuban artists who continued debates about inequality wanted to make it better; Gómez believed in a "perfectible revolution" and used her art and her own intersected positionality as a black woman to push the revolution in a more equitable direction.[22] After her death, her colleague Tomás González wrote that when he first met Gómez her hair was straight "under the neocolonial process of a relaxer," but that by 1973 she sported a small Afro. "Hers was the first natural black head in my country. A Revolution inside of a Revolution!" he claimed. This comment invoked Castro's claim that women's entrance into the workplace was a "revolution within a revolution," but it does so in a way that directly highlights Gómez's contributions to national debates about black aesthetics and Afro-Cubans' role in the revolution in the late 1960s and 1970s.[23] Knowing that her films would not be shown publicly, Gómez continued to write and direct innovative scripts about pressing social concerns, often mixing narratives about racism, sexism, and class hierarchies together in ways that raised more questions than answers until her death from an asthma attack in 1973.

Martiatu concludes that "ICAIC had a very special politics with Sara. They left her to make her documentaries, but they didn't exhibit them. They didn't show the documentaries. They didn't appear at the film festivals, but she worked, and kept working and working."[24] It was the perseverance to keep working and creating a revolution inside of the revolution that distinguishes Gómez from Cuban leaders. By refusing to accept paternalistic representations of blackness that imaged Afro-Cubans as only beneficiaries of the revolution, Gómez implied that youth like Maria and Rafael and Afro-Cubans who continued to practice black cultural rites would be the ones to make the real revolution. Moreover, the content of her films, often drawing attention to lingering racism, revealed the missteps leaders of M 26-7 took in applying a moderate colorblind plan to eliminate racial discrimination in a postcolonial former slave colony. Yet, these contradictions also show that within these failures were opportunities. Gómez is just one of the many men and women who used revolutionary institutes, funding, and resources to push for additional reforms—it was in this gray space of compromising with and redefining the revolution that radical change occurred.

21st-Century Afrocubana Revolutionaries

Today in Cuba, nearly sixty years after M 26-7's triumphant entrance into Havana, race and revolution have remained inextricably linked in the national imaginary. After the fall of the Soviet bloc in 1989, Cuba underwent a series of economic challenges that forced the restructuring of the economy and a turn toward a more capitalist-oriented system. This period of economic crisis shook the foundations of the revolution as for the first time the Cuban government struggled to maintain the education, health care, and social security reforms implemented in 1959. For its part, the United States, instead of aiding Cuba, decided to tighten the embargo in hopes that starving children, limited transportation to get to work, and a lack of basic goods and medicines would force Cuban leaders to renounce socialism. Rather than walk away from their revolution, politics, or social project, Cubans adapted. They turned to tourism and joint business ventures with European and Canadian enterprises and made new strategic hemispheric partners (most recently exchanging doctors for oil with Venezuela) to bolster the flagging economy. Tourism and remittances from Cuban exiles became two of the most profitable ways for the government to make money. For the most part, these modifications worked and now one rarely sees the long bus lines, electrical blackouts, and empty shelves that were commonplace in the 1990s and early 2000s.

Unfortunately, blacks and *mulatos* suffered disproportionately in the new economic structure. Tourist jobs often rejected Afro-Cuban applicants due to informal appearance guidelines that gave hiring preference to light skin and straight hair and blacks received significantly less income from the exterior than their white counterparts. Yet, along with a tightening of the economy came openings in public conversations about race. As noted in the Introduction, new discriminatory practices led multiple scholars to describe this moment as the "return of racism." However, the idea that racism reappeared in the 1990s silences the history told in this book and obscures the ways that state rhetoric imagining blacks as infantile, grateful, and/or loyal Cubans in the early 1960s allowed racism to persist even after social reforms had provided Afro-Cubans opportunities for education and employment. Nor does the "return of racism" claim leave space to examine how Afro-Cubans continued to battle racism into the late 1960s, albeit in different ways that deserve future attention.

Nevertheless, the post-1990s period has seen a resurgence in public conversations about race. Hip-hop musicians or *raperos* combine African American beats and Cuban rhythms to critique their inability to find hotel jobs despite speaking multiple languages. Afro-Cuban academics publish articles, hold community forums, and give lectures about the history of racism in Cuba, the island's cultural connections to Africa, and potential solutions moving forward. Revolutionary leaders have responded to these denouncements and the growing black activist sentiment in a variety of ways. For example, the Cuban Rap Agency is a state-sponsored organization that employs Afro-Cuban *raperos* and provides performance venues and recording space. That the rappers are often making music critiquing discrimination and some aspect of the revolution while receiving a government paycheck and ration book is an irony not lost on the participants.[25] Both Fidel and Raúl Castro have recognized publicly that racism still exists in Cuba and is one of the most pressing concerns on the island today.

Unfortunately, emerging official discourses about race on the island continue to be plagued by a commitment to a raceless Cuba and a fear that talking about racism will divide the revolution, or worse yet encourage black rebellion.[26] In May 2010, I returned to Cuba to do additional research for this book. When I landed in Havana, immigration officials pulled me out of the line and questioned me about my intentions for visiting and previous trips I had taken and searched my bags for forty-five minutes. I was a little perplexed about the scrutiny given my arrival after leaving the airport, but dismissed it as a routine check for someone who traveled to the island a lot—my host family even suggested they might have thought I was a drug mule. Within the first week of my trip, as I waited to obtain the coveted research visa that I needed to enter the National Archive, I received an "official immigration citation" inviting me to the immigration office for an interview. During the interview, a white Cuban man grilled me about my work: How did you come to this topic?

Do you think the revolution has eliminated racial discrimination? Why or why not? I answered as truthfully as possible, always knowing that if I gave the wrong response, I would most likely be denied the piece of paper I needed to conduct my research. I was also becoming aware that while this interview was about me it was also about a recent statement signed by over fifty African American and Caribbean scholars condemning the revolution as racist. Their letter, "Acting on Our Conscience: A Declaration of African American Support for the Civil Rights Struggle in Cuba," had been circulated by Afro-Cuban exile Carlos Moore and called for the release of Dr. Darsi Ferrer, a black political prisoner in Cuba.[27] My interviewer, of course, asked if I had seen the "Acting on Our Conscience" letter. I told him I had, but that I had not signed it because I did not think it was my place to tell the Cuban government what to do without a thorough investigation into contemporary race relations. Besides, I said, "I'm trained as a historian, not an anthropologist or sociologist. I don't have the tools to evaluate race in Cuba today." Now, this was only half true, because while I am a historian, I am also a woman who has been mistaken as a tourist-hustling prostitute (*jinetera*) due to the color of my skin when dining in a Havana hotel with a white U.S. university official. Another time, while traveling with my husband, who is also African American, we were refused entrance into the Hotel Havana Libre. The guard took one look at us and tried to block the door. When we explained that we were Americans and wanted to use the computer station in the business center, he grimaced and said we could not enter because my husband was wearing a sleeveless shirt. As I glimpsed past him into the lobby of the popular tourist hotel, I saw at least four white guests sporting tank tops to stay cool in the July heat. It was my partner's brown color, not his shirt, that barred our entrance into the popular hotel—because of his blackness the guard thought he was Cuban and therefore not allowed in the tourist (i.e., white) space. Even as all these thoughts raced through my head, I stuck to my thesis: "I'm a historian who doesn't deal with contemporary issues," I told the official. We concluded our conversation and he promised that my visa would be ready soon.

A few days later, while attending a conference on Afro-Cuban religions in Old Havana where scholars and practitioners spoke about the recent demise of predominantly black religious houses and churches, another Cuban official invoked the African American protest letter. After the presentations, a white Communist Party of Cuba leader who had been sitting toward the back of the room, observing the event, stood up and spoke.

He thanked everyone for their presentations and wondered aloud how a conference that was supposed to be about religion had turned political. He cautioned the men and women in the room to remember that African American scholars had recently sent a letter accusing the revolution of being racist and that they needed to be aware that counterrevolutionaries were using race as a tool to attack the government. Immediately, hands when up around the room, and one young woman began to speak: "We are *not* African Americans and we are *not* counterrevolutionaries," she said. The friend who had invited me to the event looked over and put a finger to his lips—I was not supposed to let anyone know at that moment that I was not Cuban. The woman continued, "This is our country and we are revolutionaries who are trying to make the revolution better." Others chimed in, explaining how they had stayed and struggled with the revolution for years and that they wanted to be heard about the issues they were facing. As the meeting ended and I left with my colleague, I marveled over everything that I had heard. Using the same fifty-year-old trope often mobilized in the early years of the revolution against black intellectuals who pointed out racism in the new government, this young communist had claimed that Cubans needed to unify against attacks from the United States. This time, the white official had tried to invoke the African American critique to threaten Afro-Cubans into silence. In doing so, he built on the many transnational moments of closeness and distance that had occurred between Cubans and African Americans since the late nineteenth century. The black and *mulato* scholars, however, immediately recognized and dismissed his rhetorical attempt to bring their conversation about the plight of black religious houses to an end—silencing them was not going to be as easy today as it was in 1959. By stating that they were revolutionaries and affirming that they had stayed on the island and were trying to make the nation a better place for all, these Cubans of color, like many before them, refused to allow others to deny their race or define their revolution.

It is not surprising that black and *mulata* women (Afrocubanas) were the most vocal respondents to the Cuban official's analysis. Today, Afrocubana scholars, activists, and musicians are leading the way in Cuba's antiracist *and* antisexist movements. These women are building on the work done by black and *mulata* women in the 1960s who stayed on the island and continued to fight discrimination in indirect ways once Castro and other revolutionary leaders claimed that Cuba had eliminated racism. The legacy of filmmaker Sara Gómez, in particular, has played a central role in this new movement. In November 2007, a special three-day colloquium in Havana titled "Sara Gómez: Multiple Images: The Cuban Audiovisual from a Gendered Point of View" celebrated Gómez and pushed for the digitalization of her short films. The recent availability of her fifteen short documentaries has led Afro-Cubans to begin publishing and talking about Gómez's work as they find ways to perfect their own twenty-first-century revolutions. Black blogger Sandra Álvarez Ramirez wrote an essay in 2007 analyzing feminist themes in Gómez's *De Cierta Manera* and later featured Gómez on her blog *Negra cubana tenía que ser* (*Black Cuban Woman I Had to Be*) in 2012.[28] Afro-Cuban women responded to the blog post "Sara Gómez in Her Own Voice" and spoke about Gómez's significance to their contemporary lives. One commenter, Aymée Rivera, said, "Sara taught me that there is beauty and art in the marginal [*lo marginal*]. . . . Far from denying me [*negarme*] (or should I say, denying me through blackness) [*o debí decir: negrarme*] the right to my marginality, she reaffirms it. . . . Thank you, Sara."[29] Aymée's words show how Afro-Cuban women today fight for recognition and equality and how the recent release of Gómez's documentaries is key to these debates. Álvarez and her readers are a part of a new movement of black women who are proud to be black and refuse to be ashamed of their skin color, sexuality, or gender; hence the title of the blog, *Negra cubana tenía que ser*.

In the past five years, a number of antiracist organizations have emerged to fight inequality in light of Cuba's new economic challenges. The Afro-cubanas Project (founded by Daisy Rubiera Castillo and Inés María Martiatu Terry) is one of most prominent groups in Havana. Its members hail from a variety of professions, ages, and sexual orientations and meet regularly in each other's houses or available cultural spaces. What they have in common is that all of them are black women who are interested in challenging negative stereotypes about blacks and women in Cuba. The *Estatutos* (*Bylaws*) of the Afrocubanas Project state that the group's objectives are to "1) Recognize the contribution and the work of black Cuban women and 2) to stimulate the existence of a counterdiscourse to dismantle the negative, racist, and sexist stereotypes [that exist in Cuba] about black women." The *Estatutos* state that persons of any race, gender, sexual orientation, or political leaning can join the group, but they also emphasize that the project has been "created for afro-descended women and by afro-descended women."[30] Their decision to use terms like *afrodescendiente* (Afro-descended) and "Afrocubana" reflects the group's politics of intersectionality, specifically acknowledging a black and female positionality that is often silenced in historical and contemporary narratives about race in Cuba. Inés María Martiatu Terry explains in the prologue to the group's first published collaborative project, a 2011 book titled *Afrocubanas: Historia, pensamiento y prácticas culturales (Afro-Cuban Women: History, Thought, and Cultural Practices)*, that one of the goals of the Afrocubanas movement is to "feminize negritude and to blacken feminism."[31] Similarly, Rubiera, Martiatu's coeditor, notes that today activists like herself are reclaiming the word *afrodescendiente* as a political move to connect their work to hemispheric movements against racism and discrimination. The title of their new organization and the book *Afrocubanas* stemmed from a desire "to talk about the racial diversity that is marked by women. It is a word that is in defense of diversity."[32]

The Afrocubanas Project is creating an intersected revolutionary agenda that advocates for black Cuban women's racial and sexual rights. The organization emphasizes collectivity, uncovers hidden historical narratives, and provides paths for later generations to follow. Martiatu and Rubiera dedicated *Afrocubanas* in the following way:

To the African women and their Afro-Cuban descendants, for
their arduous battle for liberty, justice, and equality. Women who
since immemorial times have transmitted to us in diverse ways their
sufferings, needs, achievements, all this that has arrived to us and
that has served to light our way.
    To the Afro-descendants of today who maintain this flag up
high in order to light the way for the generations to come.
    To all the women, irrespective of their skin color.[33]

This dedication invokes the past, present, and future to show the consistency between Afrocubana rebels and activists. It links Antonio Maceo's mother Mariana Granjales and women who supported the Independent Party of Color (Partido Independiente de Color, PIC) in 1912 to post-1959 activists like Sara Gómez, her contemporaries Martiatu and Georgina Herrera, and future generations. The dedication also gestures to the diaspora and Cuba's African past by thanking African women as well. Both the book and the Afrocubanas Project are collective projects that mirror Cuban revolutionary attitudes about working together for a common goal. Members of the Afrocubanas Project might come from a variety of professions but are joined in their commitment to construct an intersected revolution. For example, at a December 2012 meeting a black theatre director invited members of the organization to view and comment on a play she was exhibiting for the first time geared toward teaching Cuban children about the PIC. The women in the group agreed to attend the play to support the director and offered other suggestions about how to publicize the event. Similar to some U.S. black 1970s feminist organizations whose motto was "Lift as we climb," the Afrocubanas Project imagines their new revolutionary agenda as a collaborative one where they support community events, brainstorm ideas, and workshop creative pieces together.[34] Women expressed a common attitude of "It is our responsibility" to work on this project or achieve that goal throughout the December 2012 meeting.[35] By "light[ing] the way for generations to come," this collection of black women activists combines revolutionary sensibilities with new radical feminist and antiracist agendas.

Like the work of pioneering black activists in the twentieth century who wanted to rid Afro-Cubans of the "inferiority complex" associated with blackness, the Afrocubanas Project is working to establish a counternarrative to accepted discourses about race and gender on the island. Pushing back against jokes like "One white woman is more valuable than twenty black women," the authors of *Afrocubanas* are determined to insert black women's voices into Cuban national histories and dismantle negative stereotypes that undervalue black womanhood while oversexualizing *mulatas*.[36] A *mulata* artist denounced the terrible portrayal of Afrocubanas on television at the December 2012 meeting—"*negras* are either absent or represented as slaves," she said—and brainstormed with the group a plan to write and film her own *telenovela* (soap opera) featuring black female protagonists in more positive roles. To this same end, Rubiera has authored *testimonios* (memoirs) about black women and their experiences in twentieth-century Cuba (*Reyita: The Life of a Black Cuban Woman in the Twentieth Century*, 2000; *Golpeando la memoria: Testimonio de una poeta cubana afrodescendiente*, 2005). When discussing *Reyita*, a testimony that she wrote based on interviews with her own mother, Rubiera homed in on the way her work fills a gap in current narratives about race in Cuba: "I wanted to add the voice of a black woman to the national discourse. Reyita is the other side of what it means to be Cuban."[37]

To combat low self-esteem among Afrocubanas, the new organization is actively running a public relations campaign encouraging women to love their black bodies and their hair. Music, film, and television have been the main mediums for spreading this message. Similar to the work of Sara Gómez, who appropriated the white male power that was associated with filmmaking in the 1960s by picking up her own camera and turning it on black subjects, Afrocubana activists produced a short documentary titled *Negra Luz* that mobilizes the voices and images of women of all ages, sizes, and skin colors to show the diversity of blackness on the island. The opening scenes of the documentary flash through headshots of black women with locks, Afros, braids, straight hair, curly hair, and hair of all colors while a song, "Eres bella" ("You Are Beautiful"), by the black lesbian rap group Las Krudas plays in the background. Cuban historian and bibliographer Tomás Fernández Robaina characterizes Las Krudas as a central part of the black movement today in Cuba. In a community workshop held at the National Union of Writers and Artists, one of Havana's premier cultural institutions, Olivia, a member of Las Krudas, described the situation facing women today: "Black women are the cockroaches of the world. We have to do something already, already! It is the time for us to exercise our rights to change things; to do something. Each system, capitalism, socialism, etc., is macho. We have to create a new one."[38] Afrocubanas are doing just that. Between Sandra Álvarez's blog *Negra cubana tenía que ser* and the Afrocubanas Project's plans to script a television advertisement to publicize their work, black women in Cuba are using their revolutionary education, new technology, and intersected ideologies to create a new revolution inside of the revolution.

In the end, the campaign to eliminate racial discrimination in the 1960s was a central part of the many dynamic changes happening in Cuba after 1959. Revolutionary leaders literally opened doors for Cubans of African descent by integrating public spaces, opening private beaches, and providing more equitable access to education and employment. Despite these gains, the premature proclamation that the new government had eliminated racism and the uncritical acceptance of nineteenth-century raceless ideologies failed to dismantle racial prejudices. In fact, revolutionary visual materials contradicted themselves by reinforcing ideas of Afro-Cuban immaturity and positioning blacks as clients of the new state. In the face of such challenges, black and *mulato* artists like Gómez continued to attack racism in subtle ways after the official closure of the campaign in 1961. Often using the very language of revolutionary nationalism or pressing the government to live up to its promises to African Americans, black and *mulato* Cubans worked to create a "revolution inside of the revolution," both on the island and in exile. In the 1960s and again today in the twenty-first century, black women have played a central role in these struggles. That their story is often overshadowed by other national, masculinist narratives does not negate their work. Today, local organizations are recovering this history and pushing back about the contradictory narratives about race in Cuba using both new and old methods and technologies. This new movement will have an intersected agenda, one that finally encompasses the many ways blacks and *mulatos* have made and continue to make Cuba's many revolutions.

Notes

Introduction

1. José Hernández Artigas, "¡Negros No . . . Ciudadanos!," *Revolución*, 20 January 1959, 16.

2. See Louis A. Pérez, *Cuba*.

3. De la Fuente, *Nation for All*.

4. Alexander, *New Jim Crow*.

5. One of the earliest theorists to try to explain the coexistence of racism and antiracism in the Caribbean was Frantz Fanon: see Fanon, "Racism and Culture." In this 1956 speech, Fanon describes how outright racism has evolved into a cultural racism that devalues a whole group's way of being or existing. While he is talking specifically about the relationship between the native and the colonizer, his warnings against seeing racism as only an individual attitude that will be eliminated with time expose how proponents of colorblind theories fail to see how racism works in the modern era, namely that it devalues whole cultures (blackness) and pushes oppressed groups to deny that their culture has any value or knowledge as they try to be accepted by the dominant society. Also see Bonilla-Silva, *Racism without Racists*, and Lipsitz, *How Racism Takes Place*, for treatment of the same question in the United States.

6. The "Special Period in times of peace" (*período especial en tiempos de paz*) was the official name given to Cuba's economic collapse after the fall of their main trading partner, the Soviet Union, and referred to the austerity measures taken by the state to try to overcome the crisis—hence the idea of warlike economic rationing, but in a time of peace.

7. Rodríguez López, "La Revolución." Emphasis added.

8. Ibid.

9. See Murray, *Odious Commerce*, 244.

10. For nineteenth-century slave rebellions see Duharte Jiménez, *Nacionalidad e historia*; Paquette, *Sugar Is Made with Blood*; Gloria García, *Conspiraciones y revueltas*; Childs, *1812 Aponte Rebellion*; and Finch, *Rethinking Slave Rebellion in Cuba*. For the role that *cabildos* (ethnic societies) played in organizing slave rebellions see Ortiz, *Los cabildos*; Howard, *Changing History*.

11. Childs, *1812 Aponte Rebellion*, 178.

12. Céspedes, "Manifiesto de la Junta Revolucionario"; Céspedes, "Decreto de 27 de Diciembre de 1868." For slavery and abolition in Cuba see Scott, *Slave Emancipation in Cuba*; Knight, *Slave Society in Cuba*; Carreras, *Esclavitud, abolición, y racismo*; Portuondo Zúñiga, *Entre esclavos y libres*.

13. See Scott, *Slave Emancipation in Cuba*, 56; and Francisco Serrano's "Ley de vientres libres," found in the appendix to Ortiz, *Los negros esclavos*, 452.

14. García Pérez, "El Valle de Yaguajay," 23.

15. Riera Hernández, *Ejército Libertador de Cuba*, 93.

16. Barnet, *Biography*, 151.

17. O'Kelley, *Mambi-Land*, 221.

18. See Sartorious, *Ever Faithful*, for the participation of Afro-Cubans in Spanish military forces during the wars of independence.

19. Scott, *Slave Emancipation in Cuba*, 114.

20. "Ley de abolición."

21. Martí, "Con todos y para el bien de todos," 700.

22. Louis A. Pérez, *Cuba*, 147.

23. Martí, "Con todos y para el bien de todos," 704.

24. On the formation of the raceless ideology during the wars of independence see Ferrer, *Insurgent Cuba*, 122–38; Cepero Bonilla, *Azúcar y abolición*; Ortiz, "Cuba, Martí, and the Race Problem"; Armas, "José Martí"; Martí, *La cuestión racial*.

25. For the U.S. intervention into the Cuban wars for independence see Louis A. Pérez, *War of 1898*.

26. Barnet, *Biography*, 194. For another black Cuban soldier's testimony criticizing the lack of equality and access to resources after 1898, see Sanders, *Black Soldier's Story*.

27. For the iconization of Antonio Maceo in the republic see Nathan, "Blood of Our Heroes."

28. Guerra, *Myth of José Martí*, 2–3. With the exception of Nathan, "Blood of Our Heroes," the ways Cuban governments have used and repurposed Maceo's legacy in the twentieth century remain underexplored in the existing literature.

29. Similarly, other Latin American independence leaders built integrated fighting forces and promoted racially mixed nations in the early nineteenth century, but in each of these cases, with or without U.S. intervention, racial discrimination and black marginalization continued after independence because of long-standing attitudes linking blackness to savagery and whiteness to civilization. See Lasso, *Myths of Harmony*; Vasconcelos, *Cosmic Race*; Gilberto Freyre, *Masters and the Slaves*.

30. See de la Fuente, *Nation for All*, 56–66; and Pappademos, *Black Political Activism*, for black electoral participation.

31. See Guridy, *Forging Diaspora*.

32. De la Fuente, *Nation for All*, 55.

33. Pappademos, *Black Political Activism*.

34. De la Fuente, *Nation for All*, 79–80.

35. Helg, *Our Rightful Share*, 100.

36. De la Fuente, *Nation for All*, 51. Also see ibid., 100–105; and Putnam, *Radical Moves*, for restrictions against black Caribbean immigration in Cuba.

37. For the 1912 conflict see Helg, *Our Rightful Share*; Louis A. Pérez, "Politics, Peasants, and People of Color"; Fermoselle, *Política y color en Cuba*; Castro Fernández, *La masacre*; Fernández Robaina, *El negro en Cuba*.

38. Helg, *Our Rightful Share*, 240.

39. Nathan, "Blood of Our Heroes," 68–121.

40. See Pappademos, *Black Political Activism*; Guridy, *Forging Diaspora*.

41. See Guridy, *Forging Diaspora*; Brock and Castañeda Fuertes, *Between Race and Empire*.

42. See Guridy, *Forging Diaspora*; de la Fuente, *Nation for All*; Robin Moore, *Nationalizing Blackness*.

43. As quoted in de la Fuente, *Nation for All*, 200.

44. Guridy, "'War on the Negro.'"

45. De la Fuente, *Nation for All*, 218.

46. Smart, *Nicolás Guillén*.

47. See Ring, *How Cuba Uprooted Race Discrimination*; Casal, "Race Relations in Contemporary Cuba"; Thomas, *Cuba*, 1117–26, 1432–34. With the exception of Thomas, who provides only minimal attention to this topic in his 1,500-page monograph, these other works are based almost solely on personal visits to Cuba and informal conversations with residents of the island.

48. See Booth, "Cuba, Color, and the Revolution"; Clytus and Rieker, *Black Man in Red Cuba*; Fox, "Race and Class."

49. Carlos Moore, *Castro, the Blacks, and Africa*.

50. See Sawyer, *Racial Politics*, 164–65, for a discussion of Carlos Moore's reception in Miami in 1986.

51. Young Afro-Cubans of working-class backgrounds frequently contributed to this new conversation through the medium of hip-hop. Rap lyrics became a way for nonacademics to discuss racial profiling, including the way dark-skinned Cubans were refused entrance into tourist centers and hotels more often than those with a fairer skin color. See Fernandes, *Cuba Represent!*

52. Cuban scholarship about race written prior to the 1990s typically investigated topics covering slavery in the nineteenth century or racial discrimination in the early republic. With support and funding from the Cuban government, these scholars built a solid literature that interrogated Afro-Cuban experiences in the colonial period and the republic before 1959. However, this work for the most part did not question the effectiveness of revolutionary policies toward people of color after 1959 until the 1990s. See Serviat, *El problema negro*. Serviat's work, written before the collapse of the Soviet Union, argues that the post-1959 government eliminated racial discrimination. For a more nuanced perspective of how the revolutionary government has tackled racial disparities since 1959 see Fernández Robaina, *El negro en Cuba*; Morales Domínguez, *Desafíos de la problemática racial*; Martínez Fuentes, "Siglo XXI"; Alvarado, "Relaciones raciales en Cuba."

53. Morales Domínguez, "Un modelo para el análisis," 70. Morales Domínguez further develops this argument in his *Desafíos de la problemática racial*.

54. In my interviews with Cuban anthropologist Lourdes Serrano, writer Daisy Rubiera Castillo, and political scientist Esteban Morales, each recounted the same metaphor of "running a race" to describe the continued inequity between black and white Cubans in contemporary Cuba.

55. De la Fuente, *Nation for All*.

56. De la Fuente, "New Afro-Cuban Cultural Movement," 714.

57. For other studies using similar time frames see Casavantes Bradford, *Revolution Is for the Children*, 2–3; Chase, *Revolution within the Revolution*.

58. Putnam, *Radical Moves*, 9. I am indebted to and build on trends in African Diaspora Studies that investigate transnational racial formations by exploring how Cuban exchanges with African Americans, exiles in the United States, and neighboring Caribbean nations shaped understandings of racism and racial discrimination in Cuba. See Scott, *Degrees of Freedom*; Guridy, *Forging Diaspora*; Seigel, *Uneven Encounters*; and Putnam, *Radical Moves*.

59. Most of the Cubans with whom I conducted oral histories I encountered through informal connections I made during my research trips. Once I told archivists, librarians, and university faculty members about my topic, people willingly suggested relatives, scholars, and neighbors whom I could follow up with in Havana and in Miami. This process then led to other interviews and invitations to Afro-Cuban activist meetings and cultural events. Unfortunately, I am unable to include a list of my interviewees' real or full names because the approval I received for this project from the Institutional Review Board only allows me to use pseudonyms (first name only) for the Cubans I spoke with unless they were public intellectuals who gave me permission to cite their real names.

60. Previous scholarship on Afro-Cuban activism in the republic has also been largely from the perspective of male leaders. For the main exceptions to this see Brunson, "Constructing Afro-Cuban Womanhood" and Morrison, *Cuba's Racial Crucible*.

61. Sanders, *Black Soldier's Story*, xi.

62. Rubiera Castillo and Martiatu Terry, *Afrocubanas*.

Chapter 1

1. "A ganar la batalla de la discriminación," *Revolución*, 20 March 1959, 1.

2. De la Fuente, *Nation for All*, 261. De la Fuente appropriately notes that some Afro-Cuban intellectuals and communist leaders began pushing the new leadership to address these issues as early as January 1959.

3. "Piden castiguen discriminación racial en Cuba," *Revolución*, 11 February 1959, 4.

4. "Un millón de trabajadores: ¡Más unidos que nunca!," *Revolución*, 23 March 1959, 1.

5. "Las cuatro grandes batallas por el bienestar del pueblo," *Revolución*, 23 March 1959, 24.

6. "A este pueblo nuestro, de Maceo y Martí, no lo volverán a oprimir," *Noticias de Hoy*, 24 March 1959, 1. "La Semana," *Nuevos Rumbos*, March 1959, 3, also published various excerpts and long quotations from the same speech.

7. Castro, *La historia*, 83. The original speech was given at his trial on October 16, 1953.

8. Thomas, *Cuba*, 1117–26.

9. *Nuestra Razón*, 20.

10. Ibid., 31.

11. Letter from Daniel to Aly, 1 August 1957, Documentos del Movimiento 26 de Julio, May 1957–December 1958, 2, Princeton University Latin American Pamphlet

Collection, Princeton, N.J. See de la Fuente, *Nation for All*, 238–41, for how Cuban president Carlos Prío Socarrás issued a decree in 1951 in response to pressure from Afro-Cuban groups to try to enforce the antidiscrimination article in the Cuban Constitution. The next chapter explores further how M 26-7's silence on race contrasted not only with popular representations of blackness but also with other political movements in the 1950s.

12. See Documentos del Movimiento 26 de Julio, May 1957–December 1958, Princeton University Latin American Pamphlet Collection, Princeton, N.J., for letters written between rebel commandants.

13. For examples of these photographs see Segundo Ceballos Pareja, "La Ciencia económica y la desocupación," *Bohemia*, 25 January 1953, 32; Jorge Mañach, "Carta abierta a Don Jose Vasconcelos," *Bohemia*, 22 February 1953, 48; Herminio Portell Vila, "Barrio Suburbano," *Bohemia*, 15 March 1953, 46.

14. For Afro-Cuban domestic labor organizing see de la Fuente, *Nation for All*, 231.

15. "Problema doméstico," *Bohemia*, 4 January 1953, 2.

16. Versions of this advertisement are repeatedly printed in *Bohemia*. For a few examples see "Ese mejor sabor de Tu-py!," *Bohemia*, 9 November, 1952, 145; "Ese mejor sabor de Tu-py!," *Bohemia*, 1 March 1953, 145. A few of the advertisements featured an elegant-looking white woman wearing a silk blouse and pearls sipping from a small coffee cup to promote the coffee. The black Tu-py figure is in a bottom corner of these advertisements, still clad in the waiter outfit, suggesting that he served the woman the coffee that she is now enjoying. See "Ese mejor sabor de Tu-py!," *Bohemia*, 16 November 1952, 161.

17. "Triunfa: La maravillosa crema Allyn's!," *Bohemia*, 2 November 1952, 89.

18. For articles about Antonio Maceo and Afro-Cuban participation in the wars of independence see Rafael Soto Paz, "El ayer que vive aun: La muerte de Acea," *Bohemia*, 9 November 1952, 138; Luis Rolando Cabrera, "Maceo visto por Martí," *Bohemia*, 7 December 1952, 68; Leopoldo Horrego, "Maceo: Personalidad y destino," *Bohemia*, 7 December 1952, 20.

19. Rolando Cabrera, "Maceo visto por Martí."

20. Soto Paz, "El ayer que vive aun."

21. See Helg, *Our Rightful Share*, 118, for mambises' (Cuban independence soldiers) complaints after the war. She argued that while many veterans struggled, Afro-Cuban mambises had a particularly hard time upon returning to their homes to find their jobs and homes gone, and new positions being given to those who had sided with Spain.

22. Vicente Cubillas Jr. and Oswaldo Salas, "Sugar 'Ray' Robinson, bailarin," *Bohemia*, 16 November 1952, 30; Vicente Cubillas Jr. and Oswaldo Salas, "¡Joe Louis retorna al ring!," *Bohemia*, 12 April 1953, 74; Rene Molina, "Las Glorias de Talua han hecho olvidar sus pecados," *Bohemia*, 11 January 1953, 82; Eladio Secades, "Esos Yankees Negros de Puerto Rico!," *Bohemia*, 1 March 1953, 86; Eladio Secades, "La catástrofe del club Cienfuegos," *Bohemia*, 14 December 1952, 92; Raúl Vales, "Gavilan, un campeón que mira al futuro," *Bohemia*, 21 December 1952, 150; Harold Rosenthal, "Chuck Devey, El Retador de Kid Gavilan," *Bohemia*, 8 February 1953, 78.

23. Vicente Cubillas Jr., "Habla Arsenio Rodriguez: ¡Ese Maldito Mambo!," *Bohemia*, 7 December 1952, 24. Similarly, an article about comparsas (masked companies of street dancers in Cuban carnival processions) linked Afro-Cuban drummers and performers to the annual carnival celebration. See Lisandro Otero González, "La Comparsa en el ensayo: Lo que usted no ve en el Prado," *Bohemia*, 22 February 1953, 54.

24. De la Fuente, *Nation for All*, 253.

25. Pappademos, *Black Political Activism*, 198, for *sorteros*, and 65 for black brokers.

26. For examples of this cartoon see Silvio, "El Reyecito Criollo," *Bohemia*, 2 November 1952, 67; 9 November 1952, 67; 1 March 1953, 67; 8 March 1953, 59. This caricature is published in different situations throughout *Bohemia* in the 1950s.

27. Franqui, *Twelve*, 28.

28. Thomas, *Cuba*, 1122.

29. Interview with Lydia Mesa-Martí Betancourt Sharpe, 16 January 2011, New York, CHC, Luis J. Botifoll Oral History Project, interview 5212.0043, University of Miami Libraries. This interview can be found online at http://merrick.library .miami.edu/cdm/compoundobject/collection/chc5212/id/586/rec/74 (accessed 11 April 2015).

30. See Guridy, "'War on the Negro'"; Barnet, *Biography*.

31. "Untitled," *Bohemia*, 16 November 1952, 162.

32. Louis A. Pérez, *Cuba*, 313–36.

33. Louis A. Pérez, *War of 1898*, 126.

34. Louis A. Pérez, *Cuba*, 313.

35. "Explicó Fidel Castro a la prensa la verdadera acción revolucionario," *Revolución*, 23 January 1959, 14.

36. De la Fuente, *Nation for All*, 261.

37. "De Estudiante a soldado de la libertad," *Adelante*, 16 February 1959. *Adelante* was the Órgano Cívico de Combate de la Juventud (official newspaper for Rebel Youth civic organization).

38. "En Cuba no debe existir la discriminación," *Adelante*, 16 February 1959, 1.

39. "Es preciso acabar con la discriminación racial en la UAAC," *Adelante*, 16 February 1959, 6.

40. "Playas para el pueblo," *Adelante*, 2 March 1959, 3; "Sin Discriminaciones," *Adelante*, 9 March 1959, 3.

41. José Villalata Piedra, "El Obrero negro y las grandes industrias," *Adelante*, 2 March 1959, 1.

42. "Piden castiguen discriminación racial," 4.

43. "Discriminan a cuatro soldados por ser negros," *Noticias de Hoy*, 26 February 1959, 4; "Que se defina el caso de racial la Fed. De Sociedades Cubanas," *Noticias de Hoy*, 26 February 1959, 3. Also see "Precisa acabar con la discriminación racial," *Adelante*, 16 February 1959, 4.

44. Butterworth, *People of Buena Ventura*, 5. For previous campaigns to transform Las Yaguas see Horst, "Shantytown Revolution."

45. José Hernández Artigas, "La Revolución transforma 'Las Yaguas,'" *Revolución*, 18 February 1959, 15.

46. Ibid.

47. José Hernández Artigas, "2,000 Niños viven en el barrio Las Yaguas," *Revolución*, 23 February 1959, 28.

48. José Hernández Artigas, "!Negros No . . . Ciudadanos!," *Revolución*, 20 January 1959, 16.

49. Artigas, "La Revolución," 15; Artigas, "2,000 Niños," 28.

50. José Hernández Artigas, "Barrio de pobres en Santiago de Cuba," *Revolución*, 2 March 1959, 24.

51. Butterworth, *People of Buena Ventura*, 6–12.

52. "Lázaro Benedí Rodríguez," found in Lewis, Lewis, and Rigdon, *Four Men*, 48.

53. See Horst, "Shantytown Revolution."

54. Butterworth, *People of Buena Ventura*, 12–15.

55. Ibid., 19–20.

56. "Lázaro Benedí Rodríguez," found in Lewis, Lewis, and Rigdon, *Four Men*, 86.

57. See "Vecinos de Las Yaguas con la Reforma Agraria," *Revolución*, 21 March 1959, 12, for an example of Las Yaguas's supposed support of the revolution.

58. "Lázaro Benedí Rodríguez," found in Lewis, Lewis, and Rigdon, *Four Men*, 86.

59. Artigas, "La Revolución," 15.

60. Ibid., 15.

61. Butterworth, *People of Buena Ventura*, 19–20.

62. Alcibíades Poveda, "Un problema social en Santiago de Cuba," *Revolución*, 9 February 1959, 2.

63. Andrés Collazo Duany and Efrain Vinent Rodríguez, "La Integración nacional consolidará la revolución," *Sierra Maestra*, 5 February 1959, 1.

64. Andrés Collazo Duany and Efrain Vinent R., "Frente de Integración Nacional Cubana," *Sierra Maestra*, 20 February 1959, 1.

65. Andrés Collazo Duany and Efrain Vinent Rodríguez, "Integración racial, no; Integración nacional, sí," *Sierra Maestra*, 10 March 1959, 6.

66. Juan René Betancourt, "La cuestión racial," *Revolución*, 17 January 1959, 4. Afro-Cuban Betancourt denounced accusations from a competing journalist, Masferrer, calling Castro prejudiced as "slanderous lies." For 1950s claims that Castro was antiblack see de la Fuente, *Nation for All*, 253.

67. See Pérez-Stable, *Cuban Revolution*, 2nd ed., 74–81, for a discussion of the role the *clases populares* played in consolidating M 26-7 as the leaders of the post-1959 government.

68. "Un millón de trabajadores," 1. "A este pueblo nuestro," 1. This speech was reprinted in its entirety in the *Revolución* and *Noticias de Hoy*. "La Semana," 3, also published various excerpts and long quotations of the same speech.

69. Ibid. "Nuestro obra revolucionario es sembrar comprensión y confraternidad entre todo los Cubanos, dice Fidel," *Sierra Maestra*, 26 March 1959, 1.

70. "Un millón de trabajadores," 1.

71. "La integración social ahora si será realidad," *Surco*, 23 March 1959, 1; "Raciales: Raúl en Atenas," *Nuevos Rumbos*, March 1959, 15.

72. "La unidad de blanco y negros esencial para la revolución," *Noticias de Hoy*, 25 March 1959, 1.

73. "La Semana," 3.

74. See the editorial "Cuatro cosas . . . que son ciertos," *Surco*, 30 March 1959, 6, for more agreement that Castro was speaking about something that others would not dare to talk about.

75. Nicolás Guillén, "Una revisión entre otras," *Noticias de Hoy*, 29 March 1959, 1.

76. René Depestre, "Carta a Cuba sobre el imperialismo de la mala fe," *Casa de las Américas*, January–February 1966, 96.

77. Castro responded to critics in an interview that played on national TV and radio, and excerpts from the conversation were published in the following articles as well: " 'Esta revolución no se hizo para conservar privilegios ni para acobardarse ante nadie en particular, ni para venderse a nadie en particular,' dijó Fidel Castro en la TV," *Noticias de Hoy*, 26 March 1959, 1; "A ganar la batalla," 1; Nemesio Bustamante, "Declaraciones en un programa televisado," *Oriente*, 26 March 1959, 1.

78. "El espíritu renovador va a superar al tradicionalista," *Revolución*, 26 March 1959, 2.

79. " 'Esta revolución no se hizo para conservar privilegios,' " 1.

80. Alcibíades Poveda, "Un problema social en Santiago de Cuba," *Revolución*, 9 February 1959, 2.

81. Manuel Rey Araque, "Discriminación vs. Desarrollo," *Nuevos Rumbos*, 9 April 1959, 19.

82. " 'Esta revolución no se hizo para conservar privilegios,' " 1.

83. Diego González Martín, "Los reflejos condicionales y la discriminación racial," *Noticias de Hoy*, 31 March, 5 April, and 7 April 1959, 1. *Verde Olivo* reprinted the first article, describing "conditional responses" as "La lucha contra el prejuicio racial" (the fight against racial prejudice), *Verde Olivo*, 20 April 1959, 10.

84. Elías Entralgo, "Fórum sobre prejuicios étnicas en Cuba," *Nuevos Rumbos*, 9 August 1959, 26.

85. Carlos Rafael Rodríguez, "¡A las filas!" *Noticias de Hoy*, 27 March 1959, 1.

86. As quoted in Someillan, "Cartooned Revolution," 124.

87. Adigio, "Cubano es más que blanco, más que negro," *Noticias de Hoy*, 24 March 1959, 1.

88. Adigio, *Noticias de Hoy*, 31 March 1959, 1.

89. Adigio, "La unidad nacional: El héroe negro y el héroe blanco," *Noticias de Hoy*, 27 March 1959, 1.

90. "La unidad de blancos y negros esencial para la revolución," *Noticias de Hoy*, 25 March 1959, 1.

91. Carlos Franqui, "La discriminación racial," *Revolución*, 23 March 1959, 1.

92. "El Titán de bronce vive en los hechos de la Revolución," *Verde Olivo*, 7 December 1959, 11.

93. C. Valerino, "Voces del Pueblo," *Oriente*, 27 March 1959, 5.

94. "El espíritu renovador," 1.

95. "Inician campaña de integración," *Verde Olivo*, 20 April 1959, 4; "Integrarán el 4 Comité Nacional de Integración," *Noticias de Hoy*, 31 March 1959, 1.

96. "Hablará hoy García Agüero por el Canal 7 sobre discriminación," *Noticias de Hoy*, 24 March 1959, 1; "Acabaremos la discriminación declare por Augusto Martínez Sánchez," *Combate 13 de Marzo*, 25 March 1960, 1. *Combate 13 de Marzo* was the official periodical of the Directorio 13 de Marzo (March 13th Directorate). The directorate, composed mostly of university students, had been part of the coalition to overthrow Fulgencio Batista in the 1950s, and its leadership was separate from Fidel Castro's M 26-7, thus representing a distinct arm of the revolutionary movement.

97. Sadie Caballero, "Fue una poderoso demonstración de unidad el mitin de anoche," *Surco*, 24 April 1959, 1.

98. Ibid., 1.

99. Las Hermanas Benítez, "Angelitos negros," *Hermanas Benítez* (Discophon 1959; 2nd edition 1965).

100. Rosendo Gutiérrez (pen name Rosen), *Verde Olivo*, 4 May 1959, 4. In an interview with the author, ninety-seven-year-old Afro-Cuban Rafael Mestre, a former minister of agriculture, sang the lyrics to the song perfectly when I showed him the political cartoon. See website for the cartoon: http://antiracism-in-cuba .squarespace.com.

101. *Revolución*, 2 April 1959, 16.

102. "Sucesos," *La Calle*, 23 July 1960, 2.

103. For additional examples of Afro-Cubans featured in this column see "Luis Herrera: víctima de horror de la 1a.," *Noticias de Hoy*, 21 January 1959, 1; "El Capitán Peñate y sus cómplices deben pagar las torturas y el asesinato de Carlos Hernández," *Noticias de Hoy*, 7 February 1959, 2; "Hector Jiménez, luchador de la Juventud Socialista desde que tenía 16 años, dio un ejemplo de firmeza revolucionaria," *Noticias de Hoy*, 24 February 1959, 2.

104. "'Déjalo, que este es comunista y no tiene miedo.' Así dijo un Capitán René Wilson golpeado y torturado brutalmente," *Noticias de Hoy*, 28 February 1959, 2; "Oscar Fernández Padilla fue golpeado salvajemente siete horas seguidas en la 7ma.," *Noticias de Hoy*, 4 March 1959, 2.

105. "Se honora Mestre con un Creche," *Revolución*, 20 February 1959, 4; *Revolución*, 5 March 1959, 4.

106. "Inician obra de la Creche 'A. Mestre,'" *Noticias de Hoy*, 19 April 1959, 1.

107. "'Esta revolución no se hizo para conservar privilegios,'" 1.

108. Someillan, "Cartooned Revolution," 114–15. Chago Armas, *Revolución*, 24 January 1959, 8, was the first "Julito 26" cartoon in *Revolución*, but the figure had been popular during the war against Batista when Armas initially published it in Guevara's *El Cubano Libre*.

109. Chago Armas, *Revolución*, 28 March 1959, 4.

110. Chago Armas, *Revolución*, 2 April 1959, 6. For another example see Chago Armas, *Revolución*, 14 March 1959, 4. http://antiracism-in-cuba.squarespace.com.

111. Bipohia, "Tiro al Blanco," *Revolución*, 31 March 1959, 14.

112. Miko, *Revolución*, 20 April 1959, 2.

113. *Bohemia*, 19 January 1953, 128. See http://antiracism-in-cuba.squarespace .com for image.

114. For additional images of Afro-Cuban poverty see the Hernández article series in *Revolución* mentioned earlier in the chapter and *Verde Olivo*, 4 May 1959, 14; "Sucesos," *La Calle*, 23 July 1960, 8.

Chapter 2

1. Betancourt, *El Negro*, 175.

2. Existing scholarship, including de la Fuente, *Nation for All*; Helg, *Our Rightful Share*; Ferrer, *Insurgent Cuba*; Guridy, *Forging Diaspora*; Bronfman, *Measures of Equality*; Pappademos, *Black Political Activism*; and Morrison, *Cuba's Racial Crucible*, has shown how Afro-Cubans fought for racial equality in the context of a raceless colony/republic in 1895, 1912, 1933, and 1940.

3. Pappademos, *Black Political Activism*, 14, 42.

4. Additional research is needed on the circulation of black consciousness in the Caribbean because Cuban *negrismo* had similar ideas about revaluing blackness and linking Cuba to Africa found in Aimé Césaire's Negritude movement or C. L. R. James's black Marxism. See Césaire, *Discourse on Colonialism*; James, *Black Jacobins*, 391–418.

5. See Pappademos, *Black Political Activism*, 73.

6. Ibid., 5, 42, 45, 52. For the patronage networks between black leaders and national politicians also see Guridy, "'War on the Negro,'" 60.

7. See Helg, *Our Rightful Share*, 121, for analysis of how Gómez did not mention racial issues while a delegate for the 1901 Constitutional Convention; rather his main political talking points were "nationalism and cross-racial union of all Cubans."

8. Guridy, *Forging Diaspora*, 34–75. Also see Morrison, "Civilization and Citizenship."

9. Pappademos, *Black Political Activism*, 125–39.

10. As quoted in Morrison, "Civilization and Citizenship," 82. *La Prensa* was a Havana-based newspaper that frequently published Afro-Cuban journalist Ramón Vasconcelos's column "Palpitaciones de la raza de color" (1915–16).

11. Serra, *Para blancos y negros*, 144–53. Also see Guridy, *Forging Diaspora*, for a discussion of Serra's transnational ties.

12. Serra, *Para blancos y negros*, 135–44.

13. Ibid., 93.

14. For more on the formation and repression of the PIC see Helg, *Our Rightful Share*.

15. See ibid., 155–56, for a discussion of PIC membership.

16. Pappademos, *Black Political Activism*, 58.

17. "Programa político del Partido Independiente de Color" and "Acta de la constitución de la Agrupación Independiente de Color," found in Fernández Robaina, *El negro en Cuba*, 192–95, 195–96.

18. Portuondo Linares, *Los independientes de color*, 119.

19. Ibid., 166.

20. For black social clubs see Pappademos, *Black Political Activism*; de la Fuente, *Nation for All*; Guridy, *Forging Diaspora*; and Montejo Arrechea, *Sociedades negras en Cuba*.

21. "Estatutos de la Asociación cultural femenina," November 1935, Registro de Asociaciones, leg. 1111, exp. 23246, fol. 56, ANC.

22. Guridy, "'War on the Negro.'"

23. Pappademos, *Black Political Activism*, 5.

24. Urrutia, *Puntos de vista del nuevo negro*, 31.

25. Robin Moore, *Nationalizing Blackness*, 197.

26. For use of the term "Afro-Cuban" in this period see Pappademos, *Black Political Activism*, 15.

27. Urrutia, *Puntos de vista del nuevo negro*, 13.

28. Urrutia, "Racial Prejudice in Cuba," 473–74.

29. De la Fuente, *Nation for All*, 193, says that it is likely that these numbers were exaggerated, but the perception that the Communist Party was a black party remained.

30. "¿Nación negra? ¡No!," *Adelante*, 18 November 1936, 12, as quoted in de la Fuente, *Nation for All*, 193.

31. De la Fuente, *Nation for All*, 190. For the early Communist Party see Instituto de Historia del Movimiento Comunista y de la Revolución Socialista de Cuba, *Historia de movimiento obrero cubano*.

32. Aguirre, *La Unidad juvenil*, 26.

33. Peña, *¡La unidad es Victoria!*, 30.

34. Ibid., 16.

35. Brunson, "Constructing Afro-Cuban Womanhood," 273.

36. Lipman, *Guantánamo*, 67; de la Fuente, *Nation for All*, 222.

37. De la Fuente, *Nation for All*, 225. Blas Roca, Salvador García Agüero, and Jesús Menéndez were all elected.

38. Peña, *¡La unidad es Victoria!*, 38.

39. De la Fuente, *Nation for All*, 218. Articles about the complementary law can be found in Communist Party newspapers like *Liberación Social* and black club newspapers like *Rumbos*.

40. De la Fuente, *Nation for All*, 227.

41. Aguirre, *La Unidad juvenil*, 3; Peña, *¡La unidad es Victoria!*, 30; Roca, *Los Fundamentales del socialismo*, 164.

42. Aguirre, *La Unidad juvenil*, 38.

43. The first issue of *Azúcar*, published in July 1942, had Jesús Menéndez on the cover and claimed that the purpose of the *Azúcar* was to "fight to defend the salaries and standards of living of sugar workers and not to be divided."

44. Cover and "Nuestra Portal," *Azúcar*, January 1943.

45. Jesús Menéndez, "En pos de la organización," *Azúcar*, March 1943, 5.

46. Cover, *Azúcar*, April 1943.

47. Cover, *Azúcar*, June 1943. See http://antiracism-in-cuba.squarespace.com for image.

48. Cover, *Azúcar*, April 1943; cover, *Azúcar*, June 1943.

49. Peña, *¡Unidos por la defensa!*, 30.

50. Brunson, "Constructing Afro-Cuban Womanhood," 269.

51. Pinto Albiol, *El Pensamiento filosófico de José Martí*, 8.

52. Roca, *Los Fundamentales del socialismo*, 5. Marinello was also a member of the multiracial committee that advocated for justice after the 1933 murder of the *mulato* Trinidadian youth and rioting against black businesses.

53. Pinto Albiol, *El Pensamiento filosófico de José Martí*, 10.

54. Ibid., 131.

55. Ibid., 83.

56. Ibid., 17. Pinto reprints the entirety of the reply from Julio Le Riverend, dated 18 February 1942.

57. Ibid., 76–77.

58. De la Fuente, *Nation for All*, 250. Peña was not involved in the 1953 attack on Moncada and after questioning was released.

59. Lazara Rodríguez Alemán, "Sobre el progreso de Las Villas," *Combate 13 de Marzo*, 20 February 1960, 4.

60. Esther Ayala, "Sobre Santa Clara: Tras el triunfo de la Revolución," *Combate 13 de Marzo*, 16 February 1960, 4.

61. "Programa del Candidatura No. 2," 12 December 1956, Gobierno Provincial, Club Aponte: Agrupación Orientación Social Gobierno Provincial file, leg. 2731, exp. 12, Archivo Histórico Provincial de Santiago de Cuba.

62. "Los circulos sociales obreros: Un privilegio de los humildes," *Trabajo*, February 1961, 84–85.

63. "Erradicado el racismo de un club militar," *Noticias de Hoy*, 19 March 1959, 4.

64. "Siboney: Playa abierta," *Surco*, 31 March 1959, 1.

65. "Baile en la Vivien House," *La Calle*, 28 January 1961, 20. The full title of this newspaper was *La Calle: El Diario de la Revolución Cubana* (*The Street: The Cuban Revolution's Daily*); it also published a shorter weekly version under the same name, but with "Weekly" added to the end. This was not an official government newspaper; rather it chronicled a variety of news and events (and included a sports and editorial page) after 1959.

66. Wilson, "Mami, ¿Qué cosa es la discriminación racial?," *Mujeres*, 15 October 1962, 101. *Mujeres* was the official magazine of the Federation of Cuban Women (FMC), a women's organization closely tied with the new government and composed of many former female M 26-7 combatants and supporters. The FMC first published the magazine in 1961 after the nationalization of the popular, middle-class *Vanidades* (Vanities).

67. "Letter from Dra María Teresa Ramírez Medina to Gobernador Provincial de la Cuidad de la Habana," 1957–1960, Registro de Asociaciones, leg. 1111, exp. 23248, fol. 79, ANC; "Valiosos donativos para el plan de la reforma agraria," *Surco*, 4 May 1959, 1; "La operación aviones y el Club Aponte," *Sierra Maestra*, 4 December 1959, 3; "Apoyo el Club los XXX la justicia revolucionario," *Sierra Maestra*, 4 March 1959, 8; Dr. Arnaldo Portuondo Valdés and Dr. José G. Castellanos González, "Una Carta de la Federaciones de Soc. Cubanas de Ote," *Oriente*, 30 March 1959, 5. This last

letter is reprinted in *Surco* as Dr. Arnaldo Portuondo Valdés and Dr. José G. Castellanos González, "Apoyo de la Federación de Sociedades Cubanas de Oriente," *Surco*, 30 March 1959, 6.

68. Valdés and Castellanos González, "Una Carta de la Federaciones," 5. Valdés and Castellanos González, "Apoyo de la Federación," 6.

69. De la Fuente, *Nation for All*, 252.

70. Pappademos, *Black Political Activism*, 198.

71. "Integrada la Directiva de 'Unión Fraternal,'" *Revolución*, 30 January 1959, 6; Sadie Caballero, "Coronada la reina del 'Trabajo Agrícola,' en el Club 'Aponte' anoche," *Surco*, 4 May 1959, 1. Ousting old leaders in favor of new ones to gain favor with a recently elected government was a familiar practice for Afro-Cuban clubs. See de la Fuente, *Nation for All*, 201, for how black youth took over clubs in 1933 to purge them of any association with ex-president Machado.

72. "Letter from José A. Valdés Diago to José Cortina," 24 March 1959, Registro de Asociaciones, Club Atenas, leg. 1112, exp. 23268, March 24, 1959, ANC.

73. "Minutes, Unión Fraternal Meeting, July 22, 1960," 22 July 1960, Registro de Asociaciones, leg. 729, exp. 18528, 19/5/1966-30/4/1966, ANC.

74. Caballero, "Coronada la reina del 'Trabajo Agrícola,'" 1.

75. "La integración racial en Santiago," *Surco*, 23 December 1959, 4. This is the second time the image was published. Here it stands alone, but in an earlier edition, *Surco* printed it with an article about the event; see "Ingresa el comisionado municipal en el 'Aponte,'" *Surco*, 17 December 1959, 1.

76. "La integración racial en Santiago," 4.

77. Melba Marsilli, "Integración en el Club Aponte ciclo de conferencias y adoctrinamiento: Entrevista con dos dirigentes," *Surco*, 11 December 1959, 1.

78. Letter of final closure, 20 October 1961, Gobierno Provincial, Sociedades de Recreo (1938–1960), sociedad instrucción y recrea 'Antonio Maceo' (Manzanillo), leg. 2734, exp. 8, Archivo Histórico Provincial de Santiago de Cuba.

79. Registro de Asociaciones, Club Atenas, leg. 1112, exp. 28270, p. 1, ANC.

80. De la Fuente, *Nation for All*, 281–82.

81. Manuel Cuéllar Vizcaíno, "Discriminación," *Nuevos Rumbos*, 26 April 1959, 5.

82. De la Fuente, *Nation for All*, 281. See also Carlos Moore, *Castro, the Blacks, and Africa*, 48.

83. Pappademos, *Black Political Activism*, 201–2.

84. Juan Betancourt, "Castro and the Cuban Negro," *Crisis: A Record of the Darker Races*, May 1961, 272. See Guridy, *Forging Diaspora*, 1, for how Betancourt built on historical relationships between Afro-Cubans and African Americans in exile when he published this article attacking Castro's antidiscrimination campaign in the United States.

85. Author's interview with Berta, May 2010, Artemisa.

86. Guerra, "Self-Styled Revolutionaries."

87. "Llegó a Cuba Nicolás Guillén," *Noticias de Hoy*, 24 January 1959, 1. See de la Fuente, *Nation for All*, 261, for more information on *Noticas de Hoy*'s reopening.

88. "Blas Roca en la televisión (final): La Revolución no necesito freno, sino avance, progreso; sobran las retrancas," *Noticias de Hoy*, 8 May 1959, 5. This is the

continuation of an interview that Roca gave on television. *Noticias de Hoy* published the first part of the interview on 6 May 1959, 1.

89. Guerra, *Visions of Power*, 64.

90. Juan Marinello and Blas Roca, "El derrocamiento de la tiranía y las tareas inmediatas," *Noticias de Hoy*, 7 January 1959, 2.

91. "Unidad republicana en la Casa de Cultura," *Revolución*, 23 March 1959, 2.

92. "Habló Ernest Guevara en el acto de Integración Nacional," *Noticias de Hoy*, 7 April 1959, 1.

93. "Un comité de Integración en la 'Beck,'" *Noticias de Hoy*, 12 May 1959, 1; "Crean un Comité de Integración Nacional en Bauta," *Noticias de Hoy*, 20 May 1959, 1. Black women also formed revolutionary committees; see "Dán esta tarde almuerzo a la comité de la 'Richards,'" *Noticias de Hoy*, 16 May 1959, 3; photograph, *Noticias de Hoy*, 20 May 1959, 3.

94. María Arguelles, "El Avance de la Revolución y la lucha contra la discriminación racial," *Noticias de Hoy*, 2 August 1959, 4.

95. Nicolás Guillén, "Una revisión entre otras," *Noticias de Hoy*, 29 March 1959, 1. Also see Juan Marinello and Blas Roca, "Carta al ciudadano presidente," *Revolución*, 31 January 1959, 15.

96. Lázaro Peña, "Debemos combatir prácticamente la discriminación racial desde los sindicatos," *Noticias de Hoy*, 29 March 1959.

97. "Un triunfo arrollador y pleno de Ejército Rebelde ha sido el paso decisivo para dar una nueva vigencia a los ideales mambises," *Noticias de Hoy*, 24 February 1959, 1.

98. Guillén, "Una revisión entre otras," 1.

99. "Blas Roca en la televisión (final)," 5.

100. See Ferrer, *Insurgent Cuba*, 126–27, for how Cubans distinguished their interracial brotherhood achieved through fighting side by side in the wars of independence with Latin American notions of biological *mestizaje*. Also see Vasconcelos, *Cosmic Race*; Freye, *Masters and the Slaves*; Fernando Ortiz, *Cuban Counterpoint*.

101. Adigio, *Noticias de Hoy*, 30 April 1959, 1. An article directly below this sketch titled "Union juvenil contra la discriminación" furthered the connection between the parade and antiracist organizing. See http://antiracism-in-cuba.squarespace.com for images.

102. Raúl Castro, "¡Sepan que hoy el estado tiene más fuerza que nunca!," *Noticias de Hoy*, 8 February 1961, 11. In this speech and another poem (Indio Nabori, "Al son de la historia," *Noticias de Hoy*, 8 February 1961, 6), the trinity "trabajo, estudio, fusil" (work, study, gun) is introduced. For the revolution as the new religion see Guerra, *Visions of Power*.

103. Back cover, *Verde Olivo*, 27 April 1959, 12. For other examples of May 1 advertising featuring black and white figures together see a CTC advertisement with a row of Cubans standing with their arms linked over the caption "!Marchemos unidos!" (We march united!). It includes white and black men and women dressed in a variety of attires to demonstrate their different class/work/geographic statuses. Cabezas, *Oriente*, 29 and 30 April, 1959, 3.

104. Cabezas, *Oriente*, 29 and 30 April 1959, 3.

105. Cabezas, "Todos al desfile del 1 de mayo / apoyo a las leyes revolucionarias," *Oriente*, 21 April 1959, 2; Cabezas, "En apoyo a la reforma agraria," *Oriente*, 22 April 1959, 2; Cabezas, "Pedimos tribunales de trabajo . . . / para la justa solución de los / conflictos laborales . . . / trabajadora desfile el 1 de mayo," *Oriente*, 24 April 1959, 2; Cabezas, "Por un trato más humano reforma de la ley de accidente al desfile del 1 de mayo," *Oriente*, 27 April 1959, 7; Cabezas, "Por el mantenimiento de la política de altos salarios / para elevar el nivel de vida del pueblo / marchemos todos en el desfile de 1 de mayo," *Oriente*, 28 April 1959, 7.

106. Cabezas, *Oriente*, 20 April 1959, 7; and Cabezas, *Surco*, 22 April 1959, 1. Santiago's FGTO was one of the oldest and most respected unions on the island and precursor to the founding of the CTC in 1939. Afro-Cuban Juan Taquechel was the leader of this organization until inspectors from the Prío government replaced him in October 1948. See de la Fuente, *Nation for All*, 235.

107. Lillian Guerra argues in *Visions of Power*, 104–5, that the PSP infiltrated M 26-7 and pushed out anticommunist revolutionaries. Others have suggested that M 26-7 strategically aligned with the communists in the face of U.S. hostility (Louis A. Pérez Jr.) or, as Carlos Moore argues in *Castro, the Blacks, and Africa*, 129, that Moncada fighters took over the leadership of the PSP. Santiago's May Day celebration examines these ideas through the topic of racial discrimination. Rather than "infiltration" going in any one direction, M 26-7 leaders and black communist leaders came together and influenced each other's language about equality.

108. César Marin, "Hablan los organizadores del Primer de Mayo," *Surco*, 30 April 1959, 1.

109. Ibid.

110. "Uníos!," *Noticias de Hoy*, 30 April 1960, 3.

111. José A. Marin, "Los discursos," *Surco*, 2 May 1959, 1.

112. Roca, *Los Fundamentales del socialismo*, 163.

113. Peña, *Discurso pronunciado por el Sec. General*.

114. Roca, *Los Fundamentales del socialismo*, 174.

115. Carlos Moore, *Castro, the Blacks, and Africa*, 47.

116. Nicolás Guillén, "Racismo y Revolución," *Granma*, 18 December 1966, 1. *Revolución* and *Noticias de Hoy* combined to form *Granma* in 1965.

117. Fernández Robaina, *Cuba*, 23.

118. De la Fuente, *Nation for All*, 311. The current version of Cuba's Communist Party, the PCC was founded in 1965 and consolidated M 26-7, the PSP, newly formed mass organizations like the Federation of Cuban Women (FMC), and other anti-Batista / pro-Castro groups.

119. "Un millón de trabajadores: ¡Más unidos que nunca!," *Revolución*, 23 March 1959, 1.

120. See Guerra, *Visions of Power*, 150–57. Guerra defines "black *fidelismo*" and "revolution *con pachanga*" as "political shorthand" for black support of the revolution that imagined 1959 as an opening for "turning the world upside down" and inverting "Eurocentric values and white dominated culture" (150). She shows how revolutionary leaders shut down this black alternative because of the need to consolidate power around Fidel Castro. While this is a significant intervention,

it is important to see post-1959 dismissals and fears of autonomous black political organizing and devalorizations of black culture as fitting with previous discourses about blackness that Castro inherited from the colonial and republican periods.

121. See Carlos Moore, *Castro, the Blacks, and Africa*, 35–36; and Carlos Moore, *Pichón*, 178.

122. Juan René Betancourt, "La cuestión racial," *Revolución*, 17 January 1959, 4.

123. In *Nation for All*, de la Fuente notes that outside of the FNSN, the ONRE was the largest Afro-Cuban organization on the island before 1959 (281).

124. Betancourt, *El Negro*; Carbonell, *Crítica*.

125. Betancourt, *El Negro*, 36.

126. Carbonell, *Crítica*, 79.

127. Ibid., 108–10.

128. Ibid., 19, 21.

129. Betancourt, *El Negro*, 34.

130. For examples see Césaire, *Discourse on Colonialism*; James, *Black Jacobins*; and Fanon, "Racism and Culture."

131. Carbonell, *Crítica*, 32.

132. Ibid., 33.

133. Betancourt, *El Negro*, 51.

134. Ibid., 179.

135. Ibid., 34–35. It is unknown if Betancourt read or was familiar with the work of Áime Césaire or Malcolm X but his use of the term *negrista* and the ways he describes the group's goals are similar to Césaire's Negritude movement and U.S. black nationalism. For additional reading on Negritude, see Áime Césaire, *Discourse*.

136. Carlos Moore, *Pichón*, 173–81. In *Pichón*, Moore describes how he spent most of his time at the National Memorial African Bookstore in Harlem, what he calls the "headquarters of Harlem's black nationalists during the 1960s" (ix). There he met and interacted with U.S. black radicals, including U.S. poet Maya Angelou (110–14), black Garveyites (117), and Nation of Islam leaders like Malcolm X (132). He was also working at the Congolese Embassy when Patrice Lumumba was killed (135–37).

137. Interview with Lydia Mesa-Martí Betancourt Sharpe, 16 January 2011, New York, CHC, Luis J. Botifoll Oral History Project, Interview 5212.0043, University of Miami Libraries; Betancourt, *Sociología integral*.

138. Guerra, *Visions of Power*, 157. Also see Carlos Moore, *Castro, the Blacks, and Africa*, 99.

139. As quoted in Guerra, *Visions of Power*, 274. Also see Guerra, *Visions of Power*, for additional reading on UMAP camps.

140. Betancourt, *El Negro*, 57.

141. In a 2013 conversation, Cuban historian and bibliographer Tomás Fernández Robaina told me that he plans to write his next book on Pinto, Betancourt, Carbonell, and Moore because of how important they are for the new black rights movement in Cuba and how little work has been done on them. For other works that have briefly discussed these authors, although rarely all together, see Carlos Moore,

Castro, the Blacks, and Africa; de la Fuente, *Nation for All*; Bronfman, *Measures of Equality*; and Guerra, *Visions of Power*.

142. See de la Fuente, *Nation for All*, 288–90, for the establishment of the Department of Folklore in 1960.

Chapter 3

1. Peñalver, "Under the Streetlamp," 48.

2. Fagen, *Cubans in Exile*, 17.

3. For the anti-Batista coalition and the political and economic changes occurring after 1959 see Pérez-Stable, *Cuban Revolution*, 2nd ed., 62–63; Boswell and Curtis, *Cuban American Experience*, 19.

4. Lisandro Pérez, "Cubans in the United States," 129.

5. De la Fuente, *Nation for All*, 278. Similarly, in *Castro, the Blacks, and Africa*, 58, Carlos Moore finds that "toward the end of 1959 Castro began to refer to the 'Negro question' to discredit his enemies" in relation to the trial and imprisonment of revolutionary leader Commander Huber Matos. Like de la Fuente, Moore's analysis begins to explore this connection between racism and counterrevolution, but reveals little about how the revolution constructed this link or how it was interpreted by Cubans both living on and leaving the island in the early 1960s.

6. María Cristina García, *Havana USA*, 1, 15. In *Havana USA*, García explains how over half of the Cuban exiles who left the country in the first wave of emigration before 1963 settled in south Florida. She notes that others went to Mexico, Spain, Venezuela, and Puerto Rico because they were leery of living in the United States, but that the majority went to Miami because of historic connections to the city from before 1959.

7. Hoffnung-Garskof, *Tale of Two Cities*, xi–xvii.

8. Dudziak, *Cold War Civil Rights*, 12; see also Borstelmann, *Cold War*. Dudziak and Borstelmann explore the ways international criticism about racial violence in the United States, especially from newly independent African countries and Communists in the Soviet Union, forced U.S. leaders to make limited concessions to black Americans.

9. De la Fuente, *Nation for All*, 83. For example, after the massacre of thousands of Afro-Cubans in 1912, both Conservative and Liberal Party members portrayed their opponents as the "butchers" and "assassins of the noble [black] race" to undermine the other group's legitimacy with voters.

10. The opposing tactic, the antiracist demand for "human rights," was also not new, and was often rejected by U.S. cold warriors as associated with the Soviet Union; see Anderson, *Eyes Off the Prize*, 5.

11. María Cristina García, *Havana USA*, 44. García includes one paragraph about these issues.

12. This chapter builds on and contributes to a rapidly growing body of literature about Afro-Latinas/os in the United States. The Afro-Cuban exiles discussed in this chapter are a part of a broader history of Afro-Latino experiences of "belonging and unbelonging" in both U.S. Latino and African American communities

where their skin color excludes them from being accepted fully in white Miami Cuban spaces and different cultural and language backgrounds makes the African American community initially seem foreign as well. See Glasser, *Puerto Rican Musicians*; Grillo, *Black Cuban, Black American*; Greenbaum, *More than Black*; Dzidzienyo and Oboler, *Neither Enemies nor Friends*; Burgos, *Playing America's Game*; Jiménez Román and Flores, *Afro-Latin@ Reader*; López, *Unbecoming Blackness*; Guridy, "Private Evelio Grillo."

13. "Esta revolución no se hizo para conservar privilegios ni para acobardarse ante nadie en particular, ni para venderse a nadie en particular," *Noticias de Hoy*, 26 March 1959, 1. This article is printed in *Revolución* as well.

14. Fagen, *Cubans in Exile*, 14. See ibid., 16–28, for demographic information about the Cubans who went into exile between 1959 and 1963. Fagen finds that 23.5 percent of the exiles in Miami at the end of 1962 graduated from high school, compared to only 3 percent of all Cubans on the island as reported by the 1953 census. Cubans who left for Miami also earned about four times the income of residents on the island.

15. For more on Ruston Academy see Baker, *Ruston*.

16. Author's interview with Marta, May 2007, Havana.

17. Unidad Revolucionario, *Letter to American Students*, 23.

18. René Depestre, "Carta a Cuba sobre el imperialismo de la mala fe," *Casa de las Américas*, January–February 1966, 123.

19. Eire, *Waiting for Snow in Havana*, 3–4.

20. *Mujeres*, 15 December 1961, 83.

21. "Plan Contrarrevolucionario," *Combate 13 de Marzo*, 15 April 1960, 4.

22. Depestre, "Carta a Cuba," 96.

23. Ibid., 123. These comments were found initially in the Depestre text and verified as common during oral histories with the author.

24. "Puede ser hermano, pero no hermano!": repeated in oral histories with author, May 2007.

25. Depestre, "Carta a Cuba," 124.

26. Pérez Sarduy and Stubbs, *AfroCuba*, 9.

27. "Esta revolución no se hizo," *Noticias de Hoy*, 26 March 1959, 1.

28. Ibid.

29. Peñalver, "Under the Streetlamp," 48.

30. Pérez-Stable, *Cuban Revolution*, 1st ed., 77.

31. "Esta revolución no se hizo," 1.

32. "Punto 2," *Combate 13 de Marzo*, 20 January 1960, 8.

33. "Fidel Castro invitado por el Comité de Integración," *Noticias de Hoy*, 2 April 1959, 1. And while few people of African descent were identified as racist, the story of Afro-Cuban dissident Carlos Moore reveals how some black Cubans faced persecution for calling attention to racial discrimination in ways that went beyond official parameters. After confronting revolutionary leaders for failing to eliminate racial discrimination despite international claims to have done so, Moore was interrogated and jailed before escaping into exile in 1963. For more information see Carlos Moore, *Pichón*.

34. "Esta revolución no se hizo," 1.

35. "En Cuba no debe existir la discriminación," *Adelante*, 16 February 1959, 4.

36. Sadie Caballero, "Fué una poderoso demostración de unidad el mitin de anoche," *Surco*, 24 April 1959, 1.

37. "Discriminación eléctrica," *Combate 13 de Marzo*, 2 February 1960, 4.

38. "Renuncian líderes de los eléctricos," *Combate 13 de Marzo*, 5 February 1960, 10.

39. "Discriminación eléctrica," *Combate 13 de Marzo*, 23 March 1960, 4.

40. "Gran asamblea de la CTC," *Revolución*, 15 December 1960, 1. The immediate charges that forced Fraginals and his partners into exile were allegations of sabotage, but arguments connecting the union leaders to racist activities, made almost ten months earlier, contributed to the perception that they were counterrevolutionaries.

41. "Contra la discriminación en Cruces se manifiesta el PSP," *Noticias de Hoy*, 1 April 1959, 1.

42. "Novela integracionista," *Combate 13 de Marzo*, 4 February 1960, 4.

43. Rubiera Castillo and Herrera, *Golpeando la memoria*, 99.

44. Depestre, "Carta a Cuba," 123.

45. Artime, *Traición*, 112–13.

46. María Cristina García, *Havana USA*, 15. In the early 1960s, Miami was already a global city with a more complex, albeit equally entrenched, racial order than other southern cities. The commonness of Latin American tourists visiting the city meant that stores and restaurants in Miami Beach often served both black and white customers before the end of legal segregation. Despite these cracks in racial separation, which were sometimes mobilized by civil rights activists to demonstrate the ridiculousness of Jim Crow, violence against African Americans and forced divisions among ethnic groups were common when Cubans arrived after 1959. For racial tensions in Miami during the 1960s see Shell-Wise, *Coming to Miami*; Croucher, *Imagining Miami*.

47. Lisandro Pérez, "Cubans in the United States," 127–29.

48. Sawyer, *Racial Politics*, 157. Also see María Cristina García, *Havana USA*. Competing numbers exist about this population before 1963, but most agree that over 90 percent of the first wave of exiles were white Cubans.

49. "Plataforma inicial del MRR," *7 Días del Diario de la Marina en el exilio*, 1 October 1960, 12.

50. Unidad Revolucionario, "Letter to American Students," 5.

51. Anderson, *Eyes Off the Prize*, 5.

52. Pérez-Stable, *Cuban Revolution*, 1st ed., 75.

53. Virgilio Campaneria, "Letter from Prison," *Trinchera: Órgano Oficial del Directorio Revolucionario Estudiantil* 1, no. 18, n.d., 3.

54. Radio Swan, "Lo dijo El Mundo," *El Mundo: Editado en el exilio*, 30 November 1960, A4; "7 de diciembre," *El Mundo: Editado en el exilio*, 7 December 1960, A1.

55. "Asi se forjo la democracia en América," *Bohemia Libre*, 4 December 1960, 88–89. *Bohemia Libre* was published in Caracas, Venezuela; however, it was distributed and read in Miami as well.

56. José Correa Espino, "Cartas a El Mundo: Almeida cree que es Maceo," *El Mundo: Editado en el exilio*, 5 October 1960, A4.

57. "Cubanos-Rusos en Estados Unidos," *Patria: El periódico de Martí, sin Martí*, 21 June 1960, 3.

58. "Un documento para la historia," *Bohemia Libre*, 4 December 1960, 59.

59. Fernández, *Los abuelos*, 95–96.

60. Álvaro Santiago, "El mito de las clases," *El Mundo: Editado en exilio*, 30 November 1960, A4.

61. Facha, "Sangre de prensa libre," *7 Días del Diario de la Marina en el exilio*, 1 October 1960, 3. See http://antiracism-in-cuba.squarespace.com for image.

62. "Todos somos soldados con meritos iguales," *Bohemia Libre*, 23 October 1960, 48.

63. "El hecho y los hechos," *Comandos*, October 1960, 3.

64. "Diálogo Callejero," *Patria: el periódico de Martí, sin Martí*, 10 May 1960, 2. See http://antiracism-in-cuba.squarespace.com for image.

65. Croucher, *Imagining Miami*, 64.

66. Scholars debate the accuracy of the claim that Cubans stole employment opportunities from African Americans. The common perception that this was the case, however, coupled with the distance exiles put between themselves and Americans in general, and U.S. blacks in particular, increased tensions between the two groups. For black displacement after Cuban emigration see Egerton, *Cubans in Miami*, 15; Croucher, *Imagining Miami*; Grenier and Stepick, *Miami Now*.

67. Shell-Wise notes in *Coming to Miami*, 170, that at a time when civil rights news was the "major headline" in other cities, the Miami press focused on Cuba and the incoming exiles.

68. Rose, "Neither Southern nor Northern," chaps. 8, 11.

69. For Operation Pedro Pan see Conde, *Operation Pedro Pan*; Torres, *Lost Apple*; Casavantes Bradford, *Revolution Is for the Children*.

70. Author's interview with Ricardo E. Gonzalez, 29 July 2012, Miami. "El exilio negro cubano no es igual que el exilio blanco cubano. Y las cosas que son se caen de la mata. Es como el hundred-pound elephant in the room that nobody wants to talk about." I spent a month of summer 2012 in Miami doing additional research about Afro-Cuban exiles. I had worked previously at the University of Miami's CHC gathering materials for this chapter, so I decided to return there to begin my search for black exiles. While looking through the files of the Operation Pedro Pan Collection (CHC0350), I came across photographs of a few black children who had arrived in south Florida in the 1960s. Some of the photographs had names on them, but many were unidentified. Determined to track down at least one of the boys I saw in the photographs (the collection is mainly images of boys living in either the Matacumbe or Opalocka Camps), I asked everyone if they recognized Ricardo Gonzalez, Gerardo Sims, or René Walker (three names that were listed). Finally, in an interview with Enrique Patterson, an Afro-Cuban scholar who arrived in the United States in 1992, I acquired Gonzalez's phone number. I first met Gonzalez on the University of Miami campus and we talked for over three hours, switching between English and Spanish during our first meeting. I asked

him about his life in Cuba, including his family, school, and social worlds, and his family's decision to send him to the United States and leave Cuba. I also asked about his time in the Pedro Pan camps, first experiences in the United States, and reunification with his parents four years after he arrived. The interview was largely unstructured with Gonzalez choosing which memories to share about his life after I had told him the general topics that interested me. A few days after our first interview, I met with Gonzalez again, this time at his office (he was retired, but doing consulting work at the County Commissioner's office) to follow up and ask more questions. He also gave me articles he had written or been interviewed for in Miami newspapers and offered to put me in touch with other Afro-Cubans in Miami. See Ricardo E. Gonzalez, "Reflexiones de un Pedro Pan," *El Nuevo Herald*, January 1996; Mohamed Hamaludin, "Black Cubans Are Getting Ready to Be More Visible," and "Top Priority for Black Cubans Is to Preserve Their Culture," *Miami Times*, 22 November 1990, 1.

71. For Caribbean migration to Cuba in the early twentieth century see Putnam, *Radical Moves*.

72. *Cuban Roots/Bronx Stories*.

73. Author's interview with Gonzalez, 29 July 2012, Miami.

74. *Cuban Roots/Bronx Stories*.

75. Lydia Mesa-Martí Betancourt Sharpe, 16 January 2011, New York, CHC, Luis J. Botifoll Oral History Project, Interview 5212.0043, University of Miami Libraries.

76. Juan Betancourt, "Castro and the Cuban Negro," *Crisis: A Record of the Darker Races*, May 1961, 274.

77. Author's interview with Gonzalez, 29 July 2012, Miami.

78. Ibid.

79. "Steps in the Resettlement of Cuban Refugees," *Resettlement Re-Cap: A Periodic Report from the Cuban Refugee Center*, November 1966.

80. Ibid.

81. Author's interview with Gonzalez, 29 July 2012, Miami.

82. "Juan R. Betancourt to José Miró Cardona," 24 March 1961, CHC, José Miró Cardona Papers, box 2, folder 12 (Other Associations in Exile), University of Miami Libraries.

83. Betancourt, "Castro and the Cuban Negro," 274.

84. Author's interview with Gonzalez, 29 July 2012, Miami.

85. For the Young Lords see Torres and Velázquez, *Puerto Rican Movement*; and Whalen and Vázquez-Hernández, *Puerto Rican Diaspora*.

86. *Cuban Roots/Bronx Stories*.

87. Ibid.

88. Author's interview with Gonzalez, 29 July 2012, Miami. Additional research needs to be done on the Allapattah community. There is no mention of it in the CHC and Marvin Dunn's book, *Black Miami*, only sparsely deals with the community and does not recognize it as an Afro-Cuban space.

89. *Cuban Roots/Bronx Stories*.

Chapter 4

1. "Semana de solidaridad con el pueblo negro de EEUU," *Noticas de Hoy*, 22 September 1960, 1. For another letter describing the week see "Clausuran semana de solidaridad con el pueblo negro de los Estados Unidos," *Revolución*, 26 September 1960, 1.

2. "Acta de la Asociación Cultural Femenina," 8 October 1960, Registro de Asociaciones, leg. 1111, exp. 23246–48, ANC.

3. In *Forging Diaspora*, Frank Guridy discusses pre-1959 alliances between Afro-Cubans and African Americans and shows that they usually took place through black social clubs and recreational societies.

4. The physical and cultural proximity of Cuba and the United States allowed for relationships between African Americans and Cubans in the late nineteenth and early twentieth centuries. For general cultural connections between the United States and Cuba see Louis A. Pérez, *On Becoming Cuban*. For prior exchanges between Afro-Cubans and African Americans see Gatewood, *"Smoked Yankees"*; Guridy, *Forging Diaspora*; Brock and Castañeda Fuertes, *Between Race and Empire*. Guridy, *Forging Diaspora*, 152, delineates the growth of black tourist exchanges from the 1930s to the 1950s and argues that while Afro-Cuban and African American travelers faced discrimination in both places, the story of these tours is not just one of racism, but also a "form of adaptation" as black elites built travel networks and businesses to negotiate racial restrictions.

5. See Louis A. Pérez, *On Becoming Cuban*, 167. Pérez notes that a record number of North American tourists—356,000—visited Cuba in 1957. This number dropped dramatically after the 1959 revolution after civil unrest, executions of Batista supporters, and the spreading of rumors of communism.

6. *Chicago Defender*, 7 May 1960, 45. This slogan was a part of an advertising campaign that ran in U.S. black newspapers.

7. "EU no comprende a Cuba," *Combate 13 de Marzo*, 3 January 1960, 6.

8. Reynaldo Peñalver, "Discriminación en restaurant," *Combate 13 de Marzo*, 20 July 1960, 5.

9. Gosse, "The African-American Press," 277. Also see Young, *Soul Power*; Rodriguez, "'De la Esclavitud Yanqui'"; Tyson, *Radio Free Dixie*; Gosse, *Where the Boys Are*; Plummer, "Castro in Harlem"; Reitan, *Rise and Decline of an Alliance*.

10. Hoffnung-Garskof, *Tale of Two Cities*, xi–xvii. For how the United States built its Cold War strategy toward race relations with an "international audience in mind" see Dudziak, *Cold War Civil Rights*, 12; Borstelmann, *Cold War*.

11. Putnam, *Radical Moves*, 140. Putnam describes stories of Louis's fame spreading in the Caribbean through newspapers and film, leading people in Trinidad, St. Vincent, and Costa Rica to write letters and put up posters of the boxer. For more on Louis's international reach see Roberts, *Joe Louis*. Roberts notes how Louis was a popular figure in advertising campaigns in the United States in the 1930s and 1940s.

12. *Communist Threat to the United States*, 772 (testimony of Joe Louis Barrow and William Rowe).

13. Ibid., 774. According to Rowe, Mays agreed to the visit but canceled at the last minute because his wife was ill; Campanella, who was in a wheelchair after a car accident two years earlier left him paralyzed, claimed the trip would be too "strenuous." Robinson refused the offer outright, saying that he had to be home with his children.

14. "EU no comprende a Cuba," 1.

15. Alvaro López Conde, "El pueblo de EU defiende a Cuba," *Combate 13 de Marzo*, 1 January 1960, 1.

16. For examples see *Diario de la Marina*, 2 January 1960, 9B; the full page of photographs in *Revolución*, 2 January 1960, 20; "Celebra el fin de año el Doctor Fidel Castro en el Hotel Habana Hilton," *El Mundo*, 2 January 1960, B6; "Grupo de Visitantes Norteamericanos invitados por el INIT," *El Mundo*, 5 January 1960, B8; López Conde, "El pueblo de EU," 1; "EU no comprende a Cuba," 1.

17. "En Alemania," *Combate 13 de Marzo*, 12 February 1960, 4.

18. Vicente Cubillas Jr., "Analizan nuestra revolución periodistas negros de EE.UU," *Revolución*, 6 January 1960, 5.

19. "Lista de honor," *Combate 13 de Marzo*, 20 January 1960, 2.

20. See chapter 1 for examples.

21. John H. Sengstacke, "Castro Abolishes Race Bias in Cuba," *Chicago Defender*, 23 January 1960, 1.

22. "EU no comprende a Cuba," 6.

23. Louis A. Pérez, *Cuba*, 324–25.

24. Ibid. Also see Guerra, "'To Condemn the Revolution," 83–91. Guerra shows how by late 1960 workers, with or without state support, took over national newspaper offices and forced editors and administrators who published articles critiquing the revolution to resign. They then replaced those editors with journalists more aligned with the state's new policies.

25. "Ataca a los negros la policía yanqui en EEUU," *Combate 13 de Marzo*, 17 March 1960, 1.

26. "La juventud opina: Sobre la discriminación racial en Estados Unidos," *Combate 13 de Marzo*, 8 March 1960, 4.

27. "Cintillos," *Combate 13 de Marzo*, 19 March 1960, 4.

28. "A 90 millas de Cuba, lo que hay es discriminación racial," *Combate 13 de Marzo*, 26 March 1960, 6.

29. For the sit-in movement in the American South see Chafe, *Civilities and Civil Rights*, 79–101.

30. "Contra la discriminación en 'USA,'" *Combate 13 de Marzo*, 3 June 1960, 1.

31. "¿Por qué no boycotear también en la Habana a la Woolworth?," *Combate 13 de Marzo*, 26 March 1960, 1.

32. Casandra, "Contra discriminación en USA," *Combate 13 de Marzo*, 3 June 1960, 4.

33. "La juventud opina sobre: La discriminación racial en EEUU," *Combate 13 de Marzo*, 5 June 1960, 4.

34. Nicolás Guillén, "Discriminación y literatura," Noticias de Hoy, 19 April 1960, 2. The original quotation in Spanish is especially interesting because of the quotation marks emphasizing "ya" (anymore).

35. "Discriminación," *Combate 13 de Marzo*, 8 January 1960, 2.

36. Reynaldo Peñalver, "Los anuncios clasificados: Se solicita una joven 'pardo' como en los tiempos de la colonia," *Combate 13 de Marzo*, 29 January 1960, 1.

37. "Discriminación racial, no," *La Calle*, 5 June 1960, 16.

38. Peñalver, "Discriminación en restaurant," 5.

39. "Piden castigo por discriminación en San José del Lago," *La Calle*, 22 July 1960, 4.

40. *Chicago Defender*, 7 May 1960, 45.

41. In particular, one editorialist for a U.S. black newspaper commented that "Joe Louis is hunting for dark-skinned girls to send to Cuba on a tourist promotion deal." Ole Nosey, "Everybody Goes When the Wagon Comes," *Chicago Defender*, 7 May 1960, 18.

42. "Cuba Calls!," *Chicago Defender*, 7 May 1960, 44.

43. "Racial Integration Advances in Cuba," *Chicago Defender*, 10 May 1960, 12; and 21 May 1960, 7A.

44. Memo, 9 March 1960, Joe Louis file, Federal Bureau of Investigation, http://vault.fbi.gov/joe-louis (accessed 15 November 2012).

45. Jimmy Cannon, "Say It Ain't So, Joe," *American Weekly*, 17 April 1960.

46. "Joe Louis Agency Engaged by Cuba," *New York Times*, 26 May 1960, 4; "Louis Works for Cuba," *New York Mirror*, 26 May 1960.

47. "Joe to Continue Tourist Work," *Chicago Defender*, 31 May 1960, 2.

48. Masco Young, "They're Talking About," *Chicago Defender*, 31 May 1960, 16.

49. Jackie Robinson, "Editorial," *Chicago Defender*, 13 June 1960, A11.

50. "Joe's Firm 'Not Yielding' on Cuba," *Chicago Defender*, 18 June 1960, 1.

51. Letter to Baudilio Castellanos dated 7 July 1960, found in *Communist Threat to the United States*, 782 (testimony of Joe Louis Barrow and William Rowe).

52. See Tyson, *Radio Free Dixie*, 224–28.

53. James Booker, "Bars White Press; He Calls Himself 'African American,'" *New York Amsterdam News*, 24 September 1960, 1.

54. "La juventud opina sobre," 4.

55. This statement was printed in all three of the following newspapers: "Agresión a Cuba la actitud de Joe Louis," *Revolución*, 3 June 1960, 1; "Declaraciones de Baudilio Castellanos," *Combate 13 de Marzo*, 4 June 1960, 1; "Nueva agresión a Cuba la actitud de Joe Louis," *El Mundo*, 3 June 1960, A11.

56. "La Revolución Cubana es la más linda que he visto," *Noticias de Hoy*, 4 June 1960, 7.

57. "Enjuicia Robinson la actitud de Joe Louis," *El Mundo*, 7 June 1960, A2.

58. "Joe Louis en apuros," *La Calle*, 5 June 1960, 7.

59. Rogelio Caparrós, "Louis se rajo o lo rajaron," *Revolución*, 2 June 1960, 1.

60. Chago, "Sin palabras," *Revolución*, 3 June 1960, 2. See http://antiracism-in-cuba.squarespace.com for image.

61. Siquitrilla, "Un pobre ex-campeón acosado," *La Calle*, 3 June 1960, 16. See http://antiracism-in-cuba.squarespace.com for image.

62. Blanco, "Ex campeón en apuros," *El Mundo*, 3 June 1960, A4.

63. "Declaraciones de Baudilio Castellanos," 1.

64. Robert Williams, quoted in Tyson, *Radio Free Dixie*, 224. The Cuban press reprinted Williams's article as "Prominente líder negro de EEUU viene a Cuba a conocer a la Revolución," *La Calle*, 12 June 1960, 16.

65. For African American experiences in Cuba in summer 1960 see Cruse, "A Negro Looks at Cuba" (written but not published in 1960); Jones, "Cuba Libre."

66. "Letter from Manuel Yepe to Odón Alvarez de la Campa," 31 August 1960, Ministerio de Relaciones Exteriores, exp. 180, fol. 10, ANC.

67. Max Frankel, "Cuban in Harlem," *New York Times*, 20 September 1960, 1. This article provides a detailed description of why Castro left the Shelburne Hotel. Frankel notes that initially the Cuban delegation had difficulty finding a place to stay in New York. Once they arrived at the Shelburne, the manager asked for $10,000 in cash as insurance on the room. Since the Cubans did not have the money and were insulted that this was asked of them and not of other guests, they refused to pay. The last complaint resulted from the hotel's refusal to fly the Cuban flag over the building, a common courtesy for diplomatic guests. Alvin White, "Historic Theresa in News Again," *Washington Afro-American*, 24 September 1960, 2.

68. Carlos Moore offers one interpretation in his work *Castro, the Blacks, and Africa*, 77–88. He labels the event the "Harlem Show" to emphasize what he sees as the theatrical quality of Castro's move. In contrast to Moore's focus on Castro, Van Gosse, in "The African American Press," describes how the support the African American press demonstrated toward the Cuban Revolution in its early years "reflected an impulse toward Third World solidarity that in 1959 . . . ran deep in black America." Brenda Gayle Plummer argues in "Castro in Harlem" that the Cuban delegation's stay in Harlem was a watershed moment that altered the way the U.S. government understood its foreign policy in relation to people of color and led African Americans to situate the civil rights movement in the international arena.

69. Both presses generated an extensive paper trail that reached many readers. Cuban newspapers printed articles from all parts of Cuba, including pieces describing how cities as far east as Santiago pledged their support for African Americans. See Gosse, "The African American Press" for how the *Washington Afro-American* was the most widely circulated black newspaper in the United States in 1960. The *Carolinian*, the southernmost U.S. newspaper in the sample, helped spread ideas by reprinting articles from the *Washington Afro-American* and running advertisements for businesses in New York and other northern states.

70. De la Fuente, *Nation for All*, 279.

71. Sawyer, *Racial Politics*, 60. Sawyer notes that "discussions of race . . . shifted from being a domestic issue to being an international issue." However, he fails to fully explore how and when this happened, or more importantly its effects on Afro-Cubans.

72. "Con las banderas de nuestra patria desplegadas, Camaguey proclama: Patria o Muerte! Venceremos!," *Noticias de Hoy*, 20 September 1960, 10.

73. "Untitled," *Noticias de Hoy*, 17 September 1960, 1.

74. "Como ven los caricaturistas extranjeros el confinamiento de Fidel y Jruschov," *Noticias de Hoy*, 18 September 1960, 2.

75. Comment by Andrew Berding found in "La voz de la Revolución: Un reportaje de la sección en Cuba," *Bohemia*, 25 September 1960, 69. In *Castro, the Blacks, and Africa*, 79, Carlos Moore argues that originally Castro wanted to leave the Shelburne and camp in front of UN headquarters to embarrass the United States for its inhospitable actions. However, before this could occur, supporters from the FPCC proposed that the delegation move to Harlem. According to Moore, Castro enthusiastically agreed and said, "We will deal the Americans a strong blow" by moving to Harlem.

76. Peñalver, "Under the Streetlamp," 47. The Afro-Cuban journalist Reynaldo Peñalver was also in Harlem as a correspondent for the *Prensa Latina* news agency. He describes how Foreign Minister Raúl Roa spoke with Malcolm X about the possibility of the Cubans staying at the Hotel Theresa and attributes the move to this conversation.

77. "Cuba en las Naciones Unidas," *Verde Olivo*, 8 October 1960, 26–34.

78. Fidel Castro, "Vinimos a la ONU a hablar muy claro," *Revolución*, 27 September 1960, 3.

79. Nicolás Guillén, "Si hubiera boniatos," *Noticias de Hoy*, 22 September 1960, 2.

80. "Cable between Olivares (Subsecretatio Político) and Cuban Delegation to the United Nations," 1960, Ministerio de Relaciones Exteriores, exp. 2, fol. 18, ANC. This cable indicated that Dr. Regino Boti, an Afro-Cuban intellectual, traveled with Almeida on the special flight to New York; however, there is no other mention of Boti in either Cuban or U.S. press coverage or memoirs about the event. Also see Carlos Moore, *Castro, the Blacks, and Africa*, 81; and Peñalver's testimony, "Under the Streetlamp," for information about an Afro-Cuban journalist who traveled with the all-white official delegation.

81. "La voz de la Revolución: Un reportaje de la sección en Cuba," *Bohemia*, 25 September 1960, 55.

82. "Punteando," *Verde Olivo*, 1 October 1960, 18.

83. "Demokkkracia," *Revolución*, 4 October 1960, 2. See http://antiracism-in-cuba.squarespace.com for cartoon.

84. Frémez, "El Ku Klux Klan es así," *Bohemia*, 25 September, 1960, 76. See http://antiracism-in-cuba.squarespace.com for cartoon.

85. "Untitled," *Lunes de Revolución*, 3 October 1960, 16. See http://antiracism-in-cuba.squarespace.com for image.

86. "Organizaciones negras con nuestra revolución," *Revolución*, 20 September 1960, 1.

87. Gordon Hancock, "In Between the Lines: Tribulations of a Color-Struck Democracy," *Washington Afro-American*, 1 October 1960, 4. This editorial and another one by the same author were reprinted in the *Carolinian*, 1 October 1960, 4.

88. "Zona rebelde: La batalla de New York," *Revolución*, 20 September 1960, 1.

89. "La batalla de Harlem," *Noticias de Hoy*, 1 October 1960, 1. For other articles labeling the event as a battle see "Fidel ganó dos batallas: La de la ONU y la de Harlem," *Verde Olivo*, 8 October 1960, 4; and "Primerias Victorias," *El Mundo*, 20 September 1960, A8.

90. "'El imperialismo carece hasta de la capacidad moral para ofender,'" *Noticias de Hoy*, 21 September 1960, 8.

91. Julian Mayfield, "Cuba Has Solution to Race Problem," *Washington Afro-American*, 1 October 1960, 20.

92. Earl Brown, "Visitors to Harlem," *New York Amsterdam News*, 1 October 1960, 11.

93. "Organizaciones negras con nuestra revolución," *Revolución*, 20 September 1960, 1. In Cuba, the chant was "Cuba, Sí! Yankee, No!" The English translation, "Cuba, Yes! Yankee, No!," was used in the United States.

94. *Revolución*, 23 September 1960, 18.

95. "Almorzó Fidel con empleados del Teresa," *Revolución*, 23 September 1960, 1. The headline above this reads, "Es un honor comer con los humildes (It is an honor to eat with the humble people)."

96. Pérez-Stable, *Cuban Revolution*, 2nd ed., 81.

97. Robert Taber, "Visita Fidel un líder negro de EEUU," *El Mundo*, 20 September 1960, A1.

98. Reynaldo Peñalver, "Tengo un caballero en mi casa," *El Mundo*, 27 September 1960, A11.

99. Robert Taber, "Invita el Dr. Castro a 300 personalidades negras para que visiten a Cuba," *El Mundo*, 22 September 1960, A10.

100. "'El imperialismo carece,'" 8.

101. "Fidel ganó dos batallas," 4.

102. *El Mundo*, 24 September 1960, A2.

103. Blanco, "Feliz," *El Mundo*, 23 September 1960, A4.

104. "We Want Castro," *Noticias de Hoy*, 21 September 1960, 1.

105. J. M. Vázquez Mora, "Lo que no pudieron impedir," *Lunes de Revolución*, 3 October 1960, 13.

106. William Worthy, "Cuba triunfará," *El Mundo*, 23 September 1960, A4.

107. Nicolás Guillen, "El cancer y la tisana," *Noticias de Hoy*, 29 September 1960, 8.

108. Raúl Castro, "Speech," *Noticias de Hoy*, 21 September 1960, 8.

109. Schwartz, "Cuba's Roaring Twenties," 109.

110. Chago, *Revolución*, 21 September 1960, 7.

111. Chago, "Niño de Harlem," *Revolución*, 22 September 1960, 3.

112. See http://antiracism-in-cuba.squarespace.com for additional examples.

113. "En Harlem," *Verde Olivo*, 1 October 1960. See http://antiracism-in-cuba.squarespace.com for cartoon.

114. See http://antiracism-in-cuba.squarespace.com for additional cartoons. "Sin Palabras," *Verde Olivo*, 1 October 1960; "Untitled," *Verde Olivo*, 1 October 1960, 79.

115. Blanco, "Fiesta en Harlem," *El Mundo*, 20 September 1960, A8.

116. See cartoons in chapter 1 for examples of how Afro-Cubans were sketched before and after the revolution.

117. For an example of these photographs see *Revolución*, 28 September 1960, 16. In a series of images, the first picture shows Castro and Almeida waving to crowds from the balcony of their hotel. In the second photograph, black supporters stand

cheering in the street below, holding a sign saying, "Stand-Up for the Struggle of Negro Liberation in America."

118. For how the Cuban press was linked closely to the revolutionary government by 1961 see Louis A. Pérez, *Cuba*, 324–25; and Guerra, "'To Condemn the Revolution,'" 83–91.

119. "Denominan 'Theresa' al hotel St. John's," *Revolución*, 22 September 1960, 16. Front cover, *Noticias de Hoy*, 22 September 1960, 1.

120. "'Mina Harlem' la de Charco Redondo," *Revolución*, 3 October 1960, 3.

121. For examples of letters see "Protestan mujeres Cubanas," *Noticias de Hoy*, 22 September 1960, 8; "La carta de hoy," *Noticias de Hoy*, 29 September 1960, 8.

122. "Llevó Almeida mensaje de la CTC a la población de Harlem," *Noticias de Hoy*, 22 September 1960, 3.

123. "Clausuran semana de solidaridad," 1.

124. "Semana de solidaridad con el pueblo negro de EEUU," 1. For another letter describing the week see "Semana de solidaridad con el pueblo negro estadounidense," *Noticias de Hoy*, 24 September 1960, 3. This letter was signed by members of M 26-7, DR, PSP, CTC, FEU, and AJR.

125. Vilma Espín, "Protestan mujeres Cubanas," *Noticias de Hoy*, 22 September 1960, 8.

126. Celia Delgado, "La carta de Hoy," *Noticias de Hoy*, 29 September 1960, 8.

127. Renata Vigano, "La niña negra," *Noticias de Hoy*, 4 October 1960, 8.

128. Raúl Castro's speech was reprinted in "Qué no digan luego que exportamos la Revolución a los Estados Unidos," *Revolución*, 20 September 1960, 1.

129. Carlos Moore, *Castro, the Blacks, and Africa*, 80.

130. "Semana de solidaridad con el pueblo negro de EEUU," 1.

131. "La Solidaridad de los pueblos: Envía la CTC un mensaje a vecinos del barrio de Harlem," *Revolución*, 23 September 1960, 4.

132. Guillen, "El cancer y la tisana," 2.

133. Guillén, "Discriminación y literatura," 2.

134. For examples see Rubiera Castillo and Herrera, *Golpeando la memoria*. Also see Juan Betancourt, "Castro and the Cuban Negro," *Crisis: A Record of the Darker Races*, May 1961, 273. Betancourt, an Afro-Cuban who left the island and went into exile in 1961, remembered how surprised some blacks and *mulatos* were when Castro returned from Harlem and said that he was going to invite three hundred more African Americans to the island to see the "terrestrial paradise": "Cuban Negro Leaders merely looked at each other when they heard this announcement. They asked: What's he going to show them?"

135. "Harlem Show de Show en 'Tecnicolor,'" *Patria: El periódico de Martí, sin Martí*, 20 September 1960, 4. For articles calling the event a "show" see "'Declara' a Fidel el Show de la ONU," *Patria: El periódico de Martí, sin Martí*, 27 September 1960, 4.

136. "Tributan 'Cálido' recibimiento a Fidel en Nueva York," *7 Días del Diario de la Marina en el exilio*, 24 September 1960, 20.

137. Ibid; "Actos Anticastristas en Nueva York," *Avance Criollo*, 30 September 1960, 1.

138. "El lamentable viaje del tirano comunista de Cuba Fidel Castro a New York y los shows escarnecedores que causan estupor," *7 Días del Diario de la Marina en el exilio*, 8 October 1960, 12.

139. " 'Declara' a Fidel el Show de la ONU," 4.

140. Seigel, "Beyond Compare."

Chapter 5

1. From interviews with the author conducted spring 2007.

2. " 'El maestro asesinado es un mártir cuya sangre servirá para borrar la incultura e ignorancia,' " *Combate 13 de Marzo*, 25 January 1961, 3.

3. Fagen, *Cuba*, 11.

4. Fagen, *Transformation of Political Culture*, 45.

5. Each year since 1959 has had a particular focus and was named as such; 1961 was the Year of Education.

6. Fagen, *Cuba*, 11. See Guerra, *Visions of Power*, 158, for additional discussions of how the Literacy Campaign worked to "free Cuba from its patriarchal past."

7. Gobierno Revolucionario, Ministerio de Educación, Comisión Nacional de Alfabetización, *Producir, Ahorrar, Organizar: Segunda Parte* (Havana, 1962), found in Fagen, *Cuba*.

8. Camilo Cienfuegos was a revolutionary figure close to Fidel Castro and Che Guevara. He was aboard the *Granma* when it sailed to Cuba to overthrow Batista and later became part of the ruling coalition until his tragic death in October 1959. He has been celebrated by the post-1959 government as an exemplary revolutionary and held up as one of the revolution's first martyrs. See "Muerte al invasor!," *Noticias de Hoy*, 1 January 1961, 15, for a full-page image of Castro, Cienfuegos, and Martí. At the start of 1961, these men were the most glorified contemporary Cuban icons.

9. Jesús Menéndez was an Afro-Cuban communist leader in the 1930s and 1940s before he was assassinated in January 1948. See García Galló, *Esbozo biográfico*. Patrice Lumumba was the nationalist leader of the newly independent Congo before being captured and murdered by antigovernment forces in January 1961. He was thirty-five years old.

10. Mariana Grajales Coello, the mother of Antonio Maceo, is the notable exception to this trend of male icons. She was at times held up as an example of Cuban motherhood. Additional research needs to be done on how prevalent this discourse was during the first few years of the revolution.

11. Fidel Castro, UN speech, 1960, Castro Speech Data Base, http://www1.lanic.utexas.edu/project/castro/db/1960/19600926.html (accessed February 2012).

12. Fagen, *Cuba*, 9.

13. Ibid.

14. Senande, "De los picos de la Sierra a las alturas de la Habana," *Verde Olivo*, 8 January 1961, 36–38. See http://antiracism-in-cuba.squarespace.com for images.

15. Montalván, *De Conrado a Manuel*.

16. "Iniciará el pueblo hoy el censo de analfabetos," *Noticias de Hoy*, 15 January 1961, 1. "Alfabeticemos," *Noticias de Hoy*, 21 January 1961, 6. Even though Conrado

Benítez was killed on 5 January, news of his death did not reach official news sources or become popularized until later in the month. See the http://antiracism-in-cuba .squarespace.com for "Inscribiendo alfabetizadores," *Noticias de Hoy*, 21 January 1961, 6, an advertisement printed on the "Literacy Campaign" page of *Noticias de Hoy* before information about Benítez's death had become widely known that encouraged Cubans to honor Martí by joining the brigades.

17. *Noticias de Hoy*, 18 February 1961, 6.

18. Ibid. Again, interviews with a variety of Cubans who lived through the 1960s demonstrate a common awareness of what Benítez looked like and why he was killed.

19. It is significant to note that the other two men who were murdered alongside Benítez, a white worker and militia member, remained unnamed and faceless in the national narrative about his death and the Literacy Campaign.

20. See Ferrer, *Insurgent Cuba*, 117–22, for the making of this trope in the Ten Years' War; and Nathan, "The Blood of Our Heroes," for how Cubans mobilized the legacy of Antonio Maceo in the republic.

21. Ferrer, *Insurgent Cuba*, 117–18.

22. The case of Robert Williams also comes to mind. He visited Havana in June 1960 and received a hero's welcome. He returned to live in Cuba in 1962 to escape imprisonment in the United States. Like some others, he ultimately became disillusioned with the revolution and broke with its leadership in 1965, after realizing that racial discrimination had not been eliminated and that the new leaders refused to talk publicly about its continuation.

23. "Gráficas del desfiles estudiantil," *La Calle*, 9 February 1961, 9; "El acto estudiantil: Gran Victoria a Cuba," *Noticias de Hoy*, 8 February 1961, 1.

24. Popularized photograph of Conrado Benítez from the cover of *Arma Nueva*, January–March 1961. *Arma Nueva* was the official organ of the CNA published by the Ministry of Education. See http://antiracism-in-cuba.squarespace.com for image.

25. "Celebran concentración los padres y familiares de maestros voluntarios," *Noticias de Hoy*, 5 February 1961, 5.

26. "Jovenes rebeldes y patrulleros," *Combate 13 de Marzo*, 28 January 1961, 4.

27. "Lealtad a la memoria a Conrado Benítez," *Verde Olivo*, 12 February 1961, 12–15.

28. See Pérez-Stable, *Cuban Revolution*, 2nd ed., 99. Pérez-Stable notes that "the struggle to survive infused these mobilizations with a military mission" when talking about the Literacy Campaign. However, her analysis does not explore how certain black figures were used as national warriors in these battles.

29. *Historia de una batalla: Recuerdo de 1961, el año de educación*, directed by Manuel Octavio Gómez (Instituto Cubano de Arte e Industria Cinematográficos, 1962) is a film depicting the experiences of the literacy teachers. In the film the young men and women are shown in uniform singing the Conrado Benítez song.

30. Cover of a pamphlet used as publicity in Literacy Campaign, *Brigadas Conrado Benítez*, in Archivo del Museo de Alfabetación. See http://antiracism-in-cuba .squarespace.com for image.

31. Eduardo Saborit, "Conrado Benítez Brigade Song," found in the appendix of Serra Robledo et al., *El pueblo dice.*

32. *Noticias de Hoy*, 11 February 1961, 2. See http://antiracism-in-cuba.squarespace.com for image.

33. "'El maestro asesinado es un mártir,'" 3.

34. Núñez Jiménez, "Antes la patria era una teoría una simple idea y ahora la patria es una realidad," *La Calle*, 28 January 1961, 6.

35. Pedro J. Riesgo Lujan, "'Voy con la tranquilidad de dejar a mis hijos en buenas manos,'" *Noticias de Hoy*, 4 February 1961, 6.

36. Gerado Sábado Lago, "Mensaje de Luz," *Noticias de Hoy*, 8 February 1961, 6. The discourse of glorifying death and sacrifice for the nation dates back to the nineteenth-century wars of independence. See Louis A. Pérez, *To Die in Cuba.*

37. Eduardo Saborit, "Conrado Benítez Brigade Song," found in the appendix of Serra Robledo et al., *El pueblo dice.*

38. Raúl Castro, "¡Sepan que hoy el estado tiene más fuerza que nunca!," *Noticias de Hoy*, February 8, 1961, 11.

39. For the revolution as the new religion see Guerra, *Visions of Power.*

40. "Un comentario: Lumumba," *Noticias de Hoy*, 14 February 1961, 1.

41. Popularized photograph of Patrice Lumumba from *Hoy Domingo*, 19 February 1961, 11; example of cartoon series honoring Jesús Menéndez from "Heroes del Pueblo: Jesús Menéndez," *Noticias de Hoy*, 19 February 1961, 2. There were over ten parts to this series published over a course of two months.

42. Nicolás Guillén, "Un ejemplo dramático," *Noticias de Hoy*, 15 February 1961, 2.

43. "Sobre el vil asesinato de Patricio Lumumba," *Noticias de Hoy*, 14 February 1961, 1.

44. "Lumumba: Canto al negro heroico," *Bohemia*, 9 April 1961, 106–7.

45. "Una opinión: Dos mártires y un mismo ideal," *Noticias de Hoy*, 16 February 1961, 8.

46. "Cuba junto al Congo," *Noticias de Hoy*, 17 February 1961, 1. The quotation refers to the black heroes of the Cuban wars of independence: Antonio Maceo, Guillermo Moncada, and Quintín Banderas.

47. "Lo que determina y condiciona la actual situación de cuba, son los éxitos alcanzados por la revolución," *Noticias de Hoy*, 2 February 1961, 8.

48. "Con cien ojos," *Noticias de Hoy*, 3 February 1961, 2.

49. "Fidel y el asesinato de Lumumba," *Noticias de Hoy*, 15 February 1961, 1.

50. "La Gomilla," *Noticias de Hoy*, 17 February 1961, 7; Benito, "Expulsan a estudiantes de 'la Luz,'" *Noticias de Hoy*, 17 February 1961, 7.

51. Casandra, "Escuelas privadas para qué?," *Combate 13 de Marzo*, 26 January 1961, 4.

52. "El maestro asesinado es un mártir," 3.

53. "Servicio para blancos," *La Calle*, 25 January 1961, 14.

54. "Tambien en México asesinaron maestros," *La Calle*, 26 January 1961, 14.

55. Fidel Castro speech, *Revolución*, 23 December 1961, 1.

56. Carmen Villar, "El ejercito de cien mil jóvenes que derrotara al analfabetismo," *Trabajo*, February 1961, 68–73. Villar includes only one example from the

Alfabeticemos manual in her article—she reprints all of "Theme Ten: Racial Discrimination" and links it to her discussion of Conrado Benítez as the Literacy Campaign's first martyr.

57. Gobierno Revolucionario, Ministerio de Educación, Comisión Nacional de Alfabetización, *Alfabeticemos*, 41.

58. Gobierno Revolucionario, Ministerio de Educación, Comisión Nacional de Alfabetización, *Producir, Ahorrar, Organizar*, found in Fagen, *Cuba*, 68.

59. Gobierno Revolucionario, Ministerio de Educación, Comisión Nacional de Alfabetización, *Venceremos*.

60. Oscar F. Rego, "Del campo llegó la Revolución, del campo llegan los niños," *Bohemia*, 9 April 1961, 56.

61. Reynaldo Peñalver, "Llevar hasta el último rincón de la patria la luz de la enseñanza, será el mayor homenaje a la memoria de Conrado," *Combate 13 de Marzo*, 1 February 1961, 8.

62. Congreso Nacional de Alfabetización, *Segunda Congreso*, cover page.

63. *Noticias de Hoy*, 23 February 1961, 4. See http://antiracism-in-cuba.squarespace .com for image.

64. Serra Robledo et al., *El pueblo dice*, 173.

65. Ibid., 112.

66. Lewis, Lewis, and Rigdon, *Four Women*, 71.

67. Author's interview with María, May 2007.

68. Author's interview with Georgina Herrera, May 2007.

69. "Cuba: The Next Revolution," *Black in Latin America*, produced by Henry Louis Gates Jr. (Public Broadcasting Services, 2011).

70. *Maestra*, directed by Catherine Murphy (Literacy Project, 2013), http://www .maestrathefilm.org (accessed 7 December 2013).

71. Guerra, *Visions of Power*, 167.

72. Julia Aranda, "Letters to Fidel: Volume 2," December 1961, Ministerio de Educación, Museo Nacional de la Campana de Alfabetización.

73. Georgina Duvallon, "Hablando con los maestros voluntarios," *Verde Olivo*, 12 February 1961, 46–48.

74. Guerra, *Visions of Power*, 160.

75. "Muerte al Anafabetismo," publicity for Literacy Campaign found in Archivo del Museo de Alfabetización. See http://antiracism-in-cuba.squarespace.com for image.

76. *Conrado Benítez García: Síntesis Biográfica*, found in Archivo del Museo de Alfabetización.

77. "Decalogo del Brigadista," found in Archivo del Museo de Alfabetización.

78. Pérez-Stable, *Cuban Revolution*, 2nd ed., 81.

79. "El maestro asesinado es un mártir," 3.

80. Ibid., 3; "Diario de un maestro voluntario," *La Calle*, 27 January 1961, 2.

81. "Diario de un maestro voluntario."

82. Jaime Soler, "Por qué Isidra quiso a ir a Playa Girón," *Verde Olivo*, 2 July 1961, 46–47.

83. Barnet, *Biografía*.

84. See Luis, "Politics of Memory," for what was left out of Montejo's account, especially how it stops at the end of the wars of independence and does not discuss the 1912 PIC massacre or blacks in revolutionary Cuba even though the narrator lived through those periods as well.

85. "Nunca es tarde para aprender: Fidel vencimos, leemos, y escribimos," *Verde Olivo*, 5 July 1961, 36–39.

86. Ibid. See Guerra, *Visions of Power*, 168, for more on the ways Sentmanat pushed back against revolutionary narratives.

87. Rosendo Gutierrez, "Maria Sentmanat, eres libre," *Verde Olivo*, 9 July 1961, 24–25. In the article, the interview is in italics and the editor's note is in roman type.

88. As told to author in multiple interviews, May 2007.

89. *Playa Girón*, 455–59.

Epilogue

1. Castro, *Palabras a los Intelectuales* (a pamphlet).

2. Nicolás Wollaston, quoted in Chanan, *Cuban Cinema*, 134.

3. Bob Taber, "En defensa de PM," in Jiménez Leal and Zayas, *El Caso de PM*, 14.

4. For this debate see Jiménez Leal and Zayas, *El Caso de PM*; Chanan, *Cuban Cinema*, 133–36; Guerra, *Visions of Power*, 162–64, 342–44; Lord, "Acts of Affection," 184–85; Quiroga, *Cuban Palimpsests*, 251. Guerra, in particular, describes how, five years later, black filmmaker Nicolás Guillén Landrián made a film resembling *P.M.* Titled *Los del baile* (*Those of the Dance*), it showed Afro-Cubans dancing and drinking in the streets of Cuba during the day. Saying that "it might well have been called *A.M.*," she describes how revolutionary leaders also banned this film for its supposed "counterrevolutionary" content (343).

5. Lord, "Acts of Affection," 184–85.

6. See Sanmartín, *Black Women*, for a discussion of how the 1959 revolution was in fact of revolution in black women's writings.

7. *Iré a Santiago*, directed by Sara Gómez Yera (Instituto Cubano de Arte e Industria Cinematográficos, 1964).

8. For the ways revolutionary cultural institutions imagined blackness and African cultural practices as a part of the Cuban past see de la Fuente's discussion of the creation of the Department of Folklore in 1960 in *Nation for All*, 285–96. See Lord, "Acts of Affection," 175, for how unlike her ICAIC colleagues' films Gómez's were; they were not about "the 'past' of racial identity."

9. *Crónica de mi familia*, directed by Sara Gómez Yera (Instituto Cubano de Arte e Industria Cinematográficos, 1964). For information about Gómez's background see Chanan, *Cuban Cinema*, 341–52; and Martiatu Terry, "Una Isla para Sara Gómez."

10. Martiatu Terry, "Una Isla para Sara Gómez."

11. For censorship in the late 1960s see Abreu Arcia, *Los juegos de la escritura*; Barquet, *Ediciones El Puente*.

12. Lord, "Acts of Affection," 185. Martiatu Terry, "Una Isla para Sara Gómez," 13.

13. As told to Martiatu Terry in "Una isla para Sara Gómez," 14.

14. Pérez Sarduy and Stubbs, *AfroCuba*, 266.

15. See Guerra, *Visions of Power*.

16. Martiatu also noted that one of the reasons Gómez was able to continue working was because she had influential protectors at ICAIC.

17. Author's interview with Inés María Martiatu Terry, Spring 2010; Martiatu Terry, "Una Isla para Sara Gómez," 15.

18. *En La Otra Isla*, directed by Sara Gómez Yera (Instituto Cubano de Arte e Industria Cinematográficos, 1968).

19. Ibid.

20. Original Reel 15, *Columna Juvenil de Centenario* (1969), found in Cuban Revolution Collection, Latin American Collection, box 38U, Yale University Library, New Haven, Conn. This is unedited footage filmed by Adolfas Mekas and Barbara Stone for the making of the documentary *Compañeras y compañeros* (1970). However, only a small percentage of the footage went into the film; the rest has recently been acquired by the Yale University Library. Afro-Cubans frequently brush their forearms to indicate that they are talking about people of color. At times this gesture replaces actually saying *negro* or *mulato* aloud; other times it is accompanied by verbal references to people of African descent.

21. In 1961, the revolution began a program to rehabilitate prostitutes. It lasted six years and was organized to reform the forty thousand prostitutes on the island in 1959. See Pilar's testimony in Lewis, Lewis, and Rigdon, *Four Women*, 237–319, for an account of someone who participated in this process.

22. Martiatu Terry, "Una Isla para Sara Gómez," 15.

23. In a speech on 9 December 1966, Castro announced that women's emerging roles in Cuba were a "revolution within a revolution."

24. Author's interview with Mariatu Terry, Spring 2010.

25. De la Fuente, "New Afro-Cuban Cultural Movement."

26. The controversy about Roberto Zurbano's 23 March 2013 *New York Times* article, "For Blacks in Cuba, the Revolution Hasn't Begun," is revealing in this area. I arrived in Havana on 6 April 2013 and a number of people I talked to (all well-educated revolutionaries) immediately compared Zurbano's critique to the PIC in 1912. They suggested that he wanted to start his own black political party. From my reading of Zurbano's work, that is not the case; but the repeated connection to 1912 illustrates how many Cubans still fear that any critique of the revolution by a black Cuban is a radical position that threatens national unity, and thus is a cause for alarm.

27. "Acting on Our Conscience: A Declaration of African American Support for the Civil Rights Struggle in Cuba," 30 November 2009, http://www.afrocubaweb .com/actingonourconscience.htm (accessed 11 April 2015).

28. Sandra Álvarez Ramirez, "De cierta manera feminista de filmar," *La Jiribilla: Revista de Cultura Cubana*, 3–9 November 2007. Negracubana [Sandra Álvarez Ramirez], "Sara Gómez en su propia voz," *Negra cubana tenía que ser* [blog], 29 May 2012, http://negracubanateniaqueser.com/2012/05/29/sara-en-su-propia-voz/ (accessed 4 April 2015). Gómez is a frequent topic of this black feminist blog, with at least four specific articles about the filmmaker in the 2013–14 year.

29. Aymée Rivera, comment on Negracubana, "Sara Gómez en su propia voz."

30. Proyecto Afrocubanas, *Estatutos*. Copy in the author's possession. Received 2 April 2013. Bold emphasis is used in the original.

31. Rubiera Castillo and Martiatu Terry, *Afrocubanas*, 2.

32. Daisy Rubiera Castillo, Lecture to Williams College History and Politics in Cuba course, 16 January 2012.

33. "Dedication," *Afrocubanas*, n.p.

34. Combahee River Collective, *A Black Feminist Statement*. April 1977. The statement was found in Eisenstein, *Capitalist Patriarchy*, 362–72.

35. Meeting of Afro-Cubanas Project, Centro Havana, 5 December 2012.

36. Rubiera Castillo and Martiatu Terry, *Afrocubanas*, 12.

37. Rubiera Castillo, Lecture.

38. Union of Escritores y Artistas panel, 16 January 2012, Havana.

Bibliography

Archives and Libraries

Havana, Cuba
  Archivo del Museo de Alfabetación
  Archivo Nacional de Cuba
    Fondo Registro de Asociaciones
  Biblioteca Nacional José Martí
  Instituto de Historia de Cuba
  Instituto de Literatura y Lingüística
Miami, Fla.
  University of Miami Libraries
    Cuban Heritage Collection
      Cuban Refugee Center Collection
      José Miró Cardona Papers
      Pedro Pan Collection
New Haven, Conn.
  Yale University Library
    Latin American Collection
      Cuban Revolution Collection
New York, N.Y.
  New York Public Library
    Schomburg Center for Research in Black Culture
Princeton, N.J.
  Princeton University Latin American Pamphlet Collection
    Documentos del Movimiento 26 de Julio, May 1957–December 1958
Santiago de Cuba, Cuba
  Archivo Histórico Provincial de Santiago de Cuba
    Fondo Gobierno Provincial
      Biblioteca Provincial de Oriente Elvira Cape
      Sociedades de Recreo (1938–60)

Periodicals

Adelante
American Weekly
Arma Nueva
Avance Criollo
Azúcar
Bohemia

Bohemia Libre
Carolinian
Casa de las Américas
Chicago Defender
Comandos
Combate 13 de Marzo

Crisis: A Record of the Darker Races
Diario de la Marina
El Mundo
El Mundo: Editado en el exilio
El Nuevo Herald
Granma
Hoy Domingo
La Calle
La Jiribilla: Revista de Cultura Cubana
Lunes de Revolución
Miami Times
Mujeres
New York Amsterdam News
New York Mirror
New York Times
Noticias de Hoy
Nuevos Rumbos
Oriente
Patria: El periódico de Martí, sin Martí
Resettlement Re-Cap: A Periodic Report
    from the Cuban Refugee Center
Revolución
7 Días del Diario de la Marina en el exilio
Sierra Maestra
Surco
Trabajo
Trinchera: Órgano Oficial del Directorio
    Revolucionario Estudiantil
Verde Olivo
Washington Afro-American

Primary and Secondary Sources

Abreu Arcia, Alberto. *Los juegos de la escritura o la reescritura de la historia.* Havana: Casa de las Americas, 2007.

Aguirre, Severo. *La Unidad juvenil contra el imperialismo.* Havana, 1940.

Alexander, Michelle. *The New Jim Crow: Mass Incarceration in the Age of Colorblindness.* New York: New Press, 2012.

Alvarado, Juan A. "Relaciones raciales en Cuba: Notas de investigación." *Temas* 7 (July–September 1996): 37–43.

Anderson, Carol. *Eyes Off the Prize: The United Nations and the African American Struggle for Human Rights, 1944–1955.* Cambridge: Cambridge University Press, 2003.

Armas, Ramón de. "José Martí: La verdadera y única abolición de la esclavitud." *Anuario de Estudios Americanos* 43 (1986): 333–51.

Artime, Manuel F. *Traición: Gritan 20,000 tumbas cubanas.* Mexico City: Editorial Jus, 1960.

Baker, James D. *Ruston: From Dreams to Reality.* Miami: Ruston-Baker Educational Institution, 2007.

Barnet, Miguel. *Biografía de un cimarrón.* Havana: Academia de Ciencias de Cuba, Instituto de Etnología y Folklore, 1966.

———. *Biography of a Runaway Slave.* Translated by W. Nick Hill. Rev. ed. Willimantic, Conn.: Curbstone Press, 1994.

Barquet, Jesús J., ed. *Ediciones El Puente en la Habana de los años 60: Lecturas críticas y libros de poesía.* Chihuahua, Mexico: Ediciones del Azar, 2011.

Betancourt, Juan René. *El Negro: Ciudadano del futuro.* Havana: Cardenas y Cia., n.d.

———. *Sociología integral: La Superación científica del prejuicio racial.* Buenos Aires: Editorial Freeland, 1964.

Bonilla-Silva, Eduardo. *Racism without Racists: Color-blind Racism and the Persistence of Racial Inequality in America.* 4th ed. Lanham, Md.: Rowman and Littlefield, 2014.

Booth, David. "Cuba, Color, and the Revolution." *Science and Society* 11, no. 2 (Summer 1976): 129–72.

Borstelmann, Thomas. *The Cold War and the Color Line: American Race Relations in the Global Arena.* Cambridge, Mass.: Harvard University Press, 2001.

Boswell, Thomas, and James R. Curtis. *The Cuban American Experience: Culture, Images, and Perspectives.* Totowa, N.J.: Rowman and Allanheld, 1984.

Brock, Lisa, and Digna Castañeda Fuertes, eds. *Between Race and Empire: African-Americans and Cubans before the Cuban Revolution.* Philadelphia: Temple University Press, 1998.

Bronfman, Alejandra. *Measures of Equality: Social Science, Citizenship, and Race in Cuba, 1902–1940.* Chapel Hill: University of North Carolina Press, 2004.

Brunson, Takkara Keosha. "Constructing Afro-Cuban Womanhood: Race, Gender, and Citizenship in Republican-Era Cuba, 1902–1958." Ph.D. diss., University of Texas at Austin, 2011.

Burgos, Adrián. *Playing America's Game: Baseball, Latinos, and the Color Line.* Berkeley: University of California Press, 2007.

Butterworth, Douglas. *The People of Buena Ventura: Relocation of Slum Dwellers in Postrevolutionary Cuba.* Urbana: University of Illinois Press, 1980.

Carbonell, Walterio. *Crítica: Cómo surgió la cultura nacional.* Havana, 1961.

Carreras, Julio Angel. *Esclavitud, abolición, y racismo.* Havana: Editorial de Ciencias Sociales, 1989.

Casal, Lourdes. "Race Relations in Contemporary Cuba." In *The Position of Blacks in Brazil and Cuban Society*, edited by Anani Dzidzienyo and Lourdes Casal, 11–27. London: Minority Rights Group, 1979.

Casavantes Bradford, Anita. *The Revolution Is for the Children: The Politics of Childhood in Havana and Miami, 1959–1962.* Chapel Hill: University of North Carolina Press, 2014.

Castro Fernández, Silvio. *La masacre de los Independientes de Color en 1912.* Havana: Editorial de Ciencias Sociales, 2002.

Castro, Fidel. *La historia me absolverá.* Havana: Editora Política, 1964.

——. *Palabras a los Intelectuales.* Havana: National Cultural Council, 1961.

Cepero Bonilla, Raúl. *Azúcar y abolición.* Barcelona: Editorial Crítica, 1976.

Césaire, Aimé. *Discourse on Colonialism.* Translated by Joan Pinkham. New York: Monthly Review Press, 2000. Originally published in 1955.

Céspedes, Carlos Manuel de. "Decreto de 27 de Diciembre de 1868 sobre la esclavitud." In *Documentos para la historia de Cuba*, edited by Hortensia Pichardo, 1:370. Havana: Editorial de Ciencias Sociales, 1977.

——. "Manifiesto de la Junta Revolucionario de la Isla de Cuba, dirigido a sus compatriotas y a todas las naciones." 1868. In *Documentos para la historia de Cuba*, edited by Hortensia Pichardo, 1:358. Havana: Editorial de Ciencias Sociales, 1977.

Chafe, William H. *Civilities and Civil Rights: Greensboro, North Carolina, and the Black Struggle for Freedom*. New York: Oxford University Press, 1980.

Chanan, Michael. *Cuban Cinema*. Minneapolis: University of Minnesota Press, 2004.

Chase, Michelle. *Revolution within the Revolution: Women and Gender Politics in Cuba, 1952–1962*. Chapel Hill: University of North Carolina Press, 2015.

Childs, Matt. 2006. *The 1812 Aponte Rebellion in Cuba and the Struggle against Atlantic Slavery*. Chapel Hill: University of North Carolina Press, 2006.

Clytus, John, and Jane Rieker. *Black Man in Red Cuba*. Coral Gables: University of Miami Press, 1970.

Communist Threat to the United States through the Caribbean: Hearing before the Subcommittee to Investigate the Administration of the Internal Security Act and Other Internal Security Laws of the Committee on the Judiciary, Part 11, 87th Cong., 1961. Washington, D.C.: U.S. Government Printing Office, 1961.

Conde, Yvonne. *Operation Pedro Pan: The Untold Exodus of 14,048 Cuban Children*. New York: Routledge, 1999.

Congreso Nacional de Alfabetización. *Segunda Congreso de Consejos Municipales de Educación*. Havana, 1961.

Croucher, Sheila L. *Imagining Miami: Ethnic Politics in a Postmodern World*. Charlottesville: University Press of Virginia, 1997.

Cruse, Harold. "A Negro Looks at Cuba." In *The Essential Harold Cruse: A Reader*, edited by William Jelani Cobb, 8–20. New York: Palgrave, 2002.

Cuban Roots/Bronx Stories. DVD. Directed by Pam Sporn. Grito Productions, 2000.

de la Fuente, Alejandro. *A Nation for All: Race, Inequality, and Politics in Twentieth-Century Cuba*. Chapel Hill: University of North Carolina Press, 2001.

———. "The New Afro-Cuban Cultural Movement and the Debate on Race in Contemporary Cuba." *Journal of Latin American Studies* 40 (2008): 697–720.

Dudziak, Mary L. *Cold War Civil Rights: Race and the Image of American Democracy*. Princeton: Princeton University Press, 2000.

Duharte Jiménez, Rafael. *Nacionalidad e historia*. Santiago de Cuba: Editorial Oriente, 1989.

Dunn, Marvin. *Black Miami in the Twentieth Century*. Gainesville: University Press of Florida, 1997.

Dzidzienyo, Anani, and Suzanne Oboler, eds. *Neither Enemies nor Friends: Latinos, Blacks, Afro-Latinos*. New York: Palgrave, 2005.

Egerton, John. *Cubans in Miami: A Third Dimension in Racial and Cultural Relations*. Nashville: Race Relations Information Center, 1969.

Eire, Carlos. *Waiting for Snow in Havana: Confessions of a Cuban Boy*. New York: Free Press, 2003.

Eisenstein, Zillah, ed. *Capitalist Patriarchy and the Case for Socialist Feminism*. New York: Monthly Review Press, 1979.

Fagen, Richard R. *Cuba: The Political Content of Adult Education*. Stanford: Stanford University Press, 1964.

——. *Cubans in Exile: Disaffection and the Revolution*. Stanford: Stanford University Press, 1968.

——. *Transformation of Political Culture in Cuba*. Stanford: Stanford University Press, 1969.

Fanon, Frantz. "Racism and Culture." In *Toward the African Revolution: Political Essays*, translated by Haakon Chevalier, 30–44. New York: Monthly Review Press, 1967.

Fermoselle, Rafael. *Política y color en Cuba: La guerrita de 1912*. Montevideo: Ediciones Géminis, 1974.

Fernandes, Sujatha. *Cuba Represent! Cuban Arts, State Power, and the Making of New Revolutionary Cultures*. Durham, N.C.: Duke University Press, 2006.

Fernández, José B. *Los abuelos: Historia oral cubana*. Miami: Ediciones Universal, 1987.

Fernández Robaina, Tomás. *Cuba: Personalidades en el debate racial*. Havana: Editorial de Ciencias Sociales, 2007.

——. *El negro en Cuba, 1902–1958: Apuntes para la historia de la lucha contra la discriminación racial*. Havana: Editorial de Ciencias Sociales, 1990.

Ferrer, Ada. *Insurgent Cuba: Race, Nation, and Revolution, 1868–1898*. Chapel Hill: University of North Carolina Press, 1999.

Finch, Aisha K. *Rethinking Slave Rebellion in Cuba: La Escalera and the Insurgencies of 1841–1844*. Chapel Hill: University of North Carolina Press, 2015.

Fox, Geoffrey. "Race and Class in Contemporary Cuba." In *Cuban Communism*, 4th ed., edited by Irving Louis Horowitz, 309–30. New Brunswick, N.J.: Transaction Books, 1981.

Franqui, Carlos. *The Twelve*. New York: Lyle Stuart, Inc., 1968.

Freyre, Gilberto. *The Masters and the Slaves: A Study in the Development of Brazilian Civilization*. Translated by Samuel Putnam. New York: Alfred A. Knopf, 1946.

García, Gloria. *Conspiraciones y revueltas: La actividad de los negros en Cuba, 1790–1845*. Santiago de Cuba: Editorial Oriente, 2003.

García, María Cristina. *Havana USA: Cuban Exiles and Cuban Americans in South Florida, 1959–1994*. Berkeley: University of California Press, 1996.

García Galló, Gaspar Jorge. *Esbozo biográfico de Jesús Menéndez*. Havana: Editora Política, 1978.

García Pérez, Gladys Marel. "El Valle de Yaguajay, Barrio Africa y Bofil Narcisa: Descendencia generacional de esclavos y colonos (siglos XIX y XX)." Paper presented at Encuentro-Cultura y Sociedad: "El Valle de Yaguajay," Yaguajay, Cuba, December 2002.

Gatewood, Willard. *"Smoked Yankees" and the Struggle for Empire: Letters from Negro Soldiers, 1898–1902*. Urbana: University of Illinois Press, 1971.

Glasser, Ruth. *Puerto Rican Musicians and Their New York Communities, 1917–1940*. Berkeley: University of California Press, 1995.

Gobierno Revolucionario, Ministerio de Educación, Comisión Nacional de Alfabetización. *Alfabeticemos: Manual para el Alfabetizador*. Havana: Imprenta Nacional de Cuba, 1961.

——. *Venceremos*. Havana: Imprenta Nacional de Cuba, 1961.

Gosse, Van. "The African-American Press Greets the Cuban Revolution." In *Between Race and Empire: African-Americans and Cubans before the Cuban Revolution*, edited by Lisa Brock and Digna Castañeda Fuertes, 266–80. Philadelphia: Temple University Press, 1998.

——. *Where the Boys Are: Cuba, Cold War America, and the Making of a New Left*. London: Verso, 1993.

Greenbaum, Susan. *More than Black: Afro-Cubans in Tampa*. Gainesville: University Press of Florida, 2002.

Grenier, Guillermo J., and Alex Stepick III, eds. *Miami Now: Immigration, Ethnicity, and Social Change*. Gainesville: University Press of Florida, 1992.

Grillo, Evelio. *Black Cuban, Black American: A Memoir*. Houston: Arte Público Press, 2000.

Guerra, Lillian. *The Myth of José Martí: Conflicting Nationalisms in Early Twentieth-Century Cuba*. Chapel Hill: University of North Carolina Press, 2005.

——. "Self-Styled Revolutionaries: Forgotten Struggles for Social Change and the Problem of Unintended Dissidence." Paper presented at Williams College, Williamstown, 11 March 2010.

——. "'To Condemn the Revolution Is to Condemn Christ': Radicalization, Moral Redemption, and the Sacrifice of Civil Society in Cuba, 1960." *Hispanic American Historical Review* 89, no. 1 (2009): 73–109.

——. *Visions of Power in Cuba: Revolution, Redemption, and Resistance, 1959–1971*. Chapel Hill: University of North Carolina Press, 2012.

Guridy, Frank Andre. *Forging Diaspora: Afro-Cubans and African Americans in a World of Empire and Jim Crow*. Chapel Hill: University of North Carolina Press, 2010.

——. "Private Evelio Grillo and Sergent Norberto González: Afro-Latino Experiences of War and Segregation." In *Latinas/os and World War II*, edited by Maggie Rivas-Rodriguez and B. V. Olguín, 43–58. Austin: University of Texas Press, 2014.

——. "'War on the Negro': Race and the Revolution of 1933." *Cuban Studies* 40 (2009): 49–73.

Helg, Aline. *Our Rightful Share: The Afro-Cuban Struggle for Equality, 1886–1912*. Chapel Hill: University of North Carolina Press, 1995.

Hoffnung-Garskof, Jesse. *A Tale of Two Cities: Santo Domingo and New York after 1950*. Princeton: Princeton University Press, 2008.

Horst, Jesse. "Shantytown Revolution: Slum Clearance, Rent Control, and the Cuban State, 1937–1955." *Journal of Urban History* 40, no. 4 (July 2014): 699–718.

Howard, Philip A. *Changing History: Afro-Cuban Cabildos and Societies of Color in the Nineteenth Century*. Baton Rouge: Louisiana State University Press, 1998.

Instituto de Historia del Movimiento Comunista y de la Revolución Socialista de Cuba. *Historia de movimiento obrero cubano 1865–1958*. Vol. 1, *1865–1935*. Havana: Editorial Política, 1985.

James, C. L. R. *The Black Jacobins, Toussaint L'Ouverture and the San Domingo Revolution*. 2nd rev. ed. New York: Vintage Books, 1963.

Jiménez Leal, Orlando, and Manual Zayas, eds. *El Caso de PM: Cine poder, y censura*. Madrid: Editorial Colibrí, 2012.

Jiménez Román, Miriam, and Juan Flores, eds. *The Afro-Latin@ Reader: History and Culture in the United States*. Durham, N.C.: Duke University Press, 2010.

Jones, Leroi. "Cuba Libre." *Evergreen Review* 4, no. 15 (November–December 1960): 139–59.

Knight, Franklin W. *Slave Society in Cuba during the Nineteenth Century*. Madison: University of Wisconsin Press, 1970.

Lasso, Marixa. *Myths of Harmony: Race and Republicanism during the Age of Revolution, Colombia, 1795–1831*. Pittsburgh: University of Pittsburgh Press, 2007.

Lewis, Oscar, Ruth M. Lewis, and Susan M. Rigdon. *Four Men: Living the Revolution: An Oral History of Contemporary Cuba*. Urbana: University of Illinois Press, 1977.

———. *Four Women: Living the Revolution: An Oral History of Contemporary Cuba*. Urbana: University of Illinois Press, 1977.

"Ley de abolición de la esclavitud." 1880. In *Documentos para la historia de Cuba*, edited by Hortensia Pichardo, 1:414. Havana: Editorial de Ciencias Sociales, 1977.

Lipman, Jana K. *Guantánamo: A Working-Class History between Empire and Revolution*. Berkeley: University of California Press, 2009.

Lipsitz, George. *How Racism Takes Place*. Philadelphia: Temple University Press, 2011.

López, Antonio. *Unbecoming Blackness: The Diaspora Cultures of Afro-Cuban America*. New York: New York University Press, 2012.

Lord, Susan. "Acts of Affection: Cinema, Citizenship, and Race in the Work of Sara Gómez." In *Gender and Sexuality in 1968*, edited by Lessie Jo Frazier and Deborah Cohen, 173–92. New York: Palgrave Macmillan, 2009.

Luis, William. "The Politics of Memory and Miguel Barnet's *The Autobiography of a Run Away Slave*." *Modern Language Notes* 104, no. 2 (March 1989): 475–91.

Martí, José. "Con todos y para el bien de todos, Discurso en el Liceo Cubano, Tampa, 26 de noviembre de 1891." In *Obras completas*, 1:697–706. Havana: Editorial Lex, 1946.

———. *La cuestión racial*. In *Obras completas*, 1:484–96. Havana: Editorial Lex, 1946.

Martiatu Terry, Inés María. "Una Isla para Sara Gómez." Unpublished transcript of an address given at Fiesta del Caribe, Havana, 2007.

Martínez Fuentes, Antonio. "Siglo XXI: Antropologia, 'razas' y racismo." *Catauro: Revista Cubano de antropología* 4, no. 6 (July–December 2002): 36–51.

Montalván, Olga. *De Conrado a Manuel*. Havana: Ediciones Unión, 1994.

Montejo Arrechea, Carmen V. *Sociedades negras en Cuba, 1878–1960*. Havana: Editorial de Ciencias Sociales, 2004.

Moore, Carlos. *Castro, the Blacks, and Africa*. Los Angeles: Center for Afro-American Studies, University of California, Los Angeles, 1988.

——. *Pichón: A Memoir: Race and Revolution in Castro's Cuba*. Chicago: Lawrence Hill Books, 2008.

Moore, Robin. *Nationalizing Blackness: Afrocubanismo and the Artistic Revolution in Havana, 1920–1940*. Pittsburgh: University of Pittsburgh Press, 1997.

Morales Domínguez, Esteban. *Desafíos de la problemática racial en Cuba*. Havana: Fundación Fernando Ortiz, 2007.

——. "Un modelo para el análisis de la problemática racial cubano contemporanea." *Catauro: Revista Cubano de antropología* 4, no. 6 (2002): 52–93.

Morrison, Karen Y. "Civilization and Citizenship through the Eyes of Afro-Cuban Intellectuals during the First Constitutional Era, 1902–1940." *Cuban Studies* 30 (1999): 76–99.

——. *Cuba's Racial Crucible: The Sexual Economy of Social Identities, 1750–2000*. Bloomington: Indiana University Press, 2015.

Murray, David R. *Odious Commerce: Britain, Spain, and the Abolition of the Cuban Slave Trade*. Cambridge: Cambridge University Press, 1980.

Nathan, Robert C. "The Blood of Our Heroes: Race, Memory, and Iconography in Cuba, 1902–1962." Ph.D. diss., University of North Carolina at Chapel Hill, 2012.

Nuestra Razón: Manifiesto Programa del Movimiento 26 de Julio. Havana: Movimiento 26 de Julio, 1956.

O'Kelley, James J. *The Mambi-Land or Adventures of a Herald Consultant in Cuba*. Philadelphia: J. B. Lippincott, 1874.

Ortiz, Fernando. "Cuba, Martí, and the Race Problem." *Phylon* 3, no. 3 (1942): 253–76.

——. *Cuban Counterpoint: Tobacco and Sugar*. Translated by Harriet de Onís. Durham, N.C.: Duke University Press, 1995. Originally published in 1940.

——. *Los cabildos y la fiesta afro-cubanos del Día de los Reyes*. Havana: Editorial de Ciencias Sociales, 1992.

——. *Los negros esclavos*. 1916. Reprint, Havana: Editorial de Ciencias Sociales, 1975.

Pappademos, Melina. *Black Political Activism and the Cuban Republic*. Chapel Hill: University of North Carolina Press, 2012.

Paquette, Robert L. *Sugar Is Made with Blood: The Conspiracy of La Escalera and the Conflict between Empires over Slavery in Cuba*. Middletown, Conn.: Wesleyan University Press, 1990.

Peña, Lázaro. *Discurso pronunciado por el Sec. General de la CTC-R, Lázaro Peña, en la Universidad de La Habana el día 26 de enero, 1965*. Havana: Imprenta Revolucionaria, 1965.

——. *¡La unidad es Victoria! Informe de Lázaro Peña*. Havana: Comisión de Propaganda del Comité Ejecutivo de la CTC, 1942.

——. *¡Unidos por la defensa de nuestras conquistas y por el mejoramiento colectivo!* Havana: Editorial CENIT, 1944.

Peñalver, Reynaldo. "Under the Streetlamp: A Journalist's Story." In *Afro-Cuban Voices: On Race and Identity in Contemporary Cuba*, edited by Pedro Pérez Sarduy and Jean Stubbs, 41–48. Gainesville: University of Florida Press, 2000.

Pérez, Lisandro. "Cubans in the United States." *Annals of the American Academy of Political and Social Science* 487, no. 1 (September 1986): 126–37.

Pérez, Louis A., Jr. *Cuba: Between Reform and Revolution*. Oxford: Oxford University Press, 1995.

———. *On Becoming Cuban: Identity, Nationality and Culture*. Chapel Hill: University of North Carolina Press, 1999.

———. "Politics, Peasants, and People of Color: The 1912 'Race War' in Cuba Reconsidered." *Hispanic American Historical Review* 66, no. 3 (1986): 509–39.

———. *To Die in Cuba: Suicide and Society*. Chapel Hill: University of North Carolina Press, 2005.

———. *The War of 1898: The United States and Cuba in History and Historiography*. Chapel Hill: University of North Carolina Press, 1998.

Pérez Sarduy, Pedro, and Jean Stubbs, eds. *AfroCuba: An Anthology of Cuban Writing on Race, Politics, and Culture*. Melbourne: Ocean Press, 1993.

Pérez-Stable, Marifeli. *The Cuban Revolution: Origins, Course, and Legacy*. New York: Oxford University Press, 1993.

———. *The Cuban Revolution: Origins, Course, and Legacy*. 2nd ed. New York: Oxford University Press, 1999.

———. *The Cuban Revolution: Origins, Course, and Legacy*. 3rd ed. New York: Oxford University Press, 2012.

Pinto Albiol, Ángel Cesar. *El Pensamiento filosófico de José Martí y la Revolución Cubana*. Havana, 1946.

Playa Girón: Derrota del imperialismo. Vol. 4. Havana: Ediciones R, 1962.

Plummer, Brenda Gayle. "Castro in Harlem: A Cold War Watershed." In *Rethinking the Cold War*, edited by Allen Hunter, 133–55. Philadelphia: Temple University Press, 1998.

Portuondo Linares, Serafín. *Los independientes de color: Historia del Partido Independiente de Color*. Havana: Ministerio de Educación, 1950.

Portuondo Zúñiga, Olga. *Entre esclavos y libres de Cuba colonial*. Santiago de Cuba: Editorial Oriente, 2003.

Putnam, Lara. *Radical Moves: Caribbean Migrants and the Politics of Race in the Jazz Age*. Chapel Hill: University of North Carolina Press, 2013.

Quiroga, José. *Cuban Palimpsests*. Minneapolis: University of Minnesota Press, 2005.

Reitan, Ruth. *The Rise and Decline of an Alliance: Cuba and African American Leaders in the 1960s*. East Lansing: Michigan State University Press, 1999.

Riera Hernández, Mario. *Ejército Libertador de Cuba, 1895–1898: Antecedentes históricos, fotos y biografías de mayores generales y generales de división y brigadas, anexos informativos*. Miami, 1985.

Ring, Harry. *How Cuba Uprooted Race Discrimination*. New York: Merit Publishers, 1961.

Roberts, Randy. *Joe Louis: Hard Times Man*. New Haven: Yale University Press, 2010.

Roca, Blas. *Los Fundamentales del socialismo en Cuba*. Havana: Ediciones Populares, 1961.

Rodriguez, Besenia. "'De la Esclavitud Yanqui a la Libertad Cubana': U.S. Black Radicals, the Cuban Revolution, and the Formation of a Tricontinental Ideology." *Radical History Review*, no. 92 (2005): 62–87.

Rodríguez López, Yusimí. "La Revolución hizó a los negros personas." In *Afrocubanas: Historia, pensamiento, y prácticas culturales*, edited by Daisy Rubiera Castillo and Inés María Martiatu Terry, 200–204. Havana: Editorial de Ciencias Sociales, 2011.

Rose, Chanelle Nyree. "Neither Southern nor Northern: Miami, Florida and the Black Freedom Struggle in America's Tourist Paradise, 1896–1968." Ph.D. diss., University of Miami, 2008.

Rubiera Castillo, Daisy, and Georgina Herrera. *Golpeando la memoria: Testimonio de una poeta cubana afrodescendiente*. Havana: Ediciones Unión, 2005.

Rubiera Castillo, Daisy, and Inés María Martiatu Terry, eds. *Afrocubanas: Historia, pensamiento, y prácticas culturales*. Havana: Editorial de Ciencias Sociales, 2011.

Sanders, Mark A. *A Black Soldier's Story: The Narrative of Ricardo Batrell and the Cuban War of Independence*. Minneapolis: University of Minnesota Press, 2010.

Sanmartín, Paula. *Black Women as Custodians of History: Unsung Rebel (M)Others in African American and Afro-Cuban Women's Writing*. Amherst, N.Y.: Cambria Press, 2014.

Sartorius, David. *Ever Faithful: Race, Loyalty, and the Ends of Empire in Spanish Cuba*. Durham, N.C.: Duke University Press, 2013.

Sawyer, Mark Q. *Racial Politics in Post-Revolutionary Cuba*. Cambridge: Cambridge University Press, 2006.

Schwartz, Rosalie. "Cuba's Roaring Twenties: Race Consciousness and the Column 'Ideales de una Raza.'" In *Between Race and Empire: African Americans and Cubans before the Cuban Revolution*, edited by Lisa Brock and Digna Castañeda Fuertes, 104–19. Philadelphia: Temple University Press, 1998.

Scott, Rebecca J. *Degrees of Freedom: Louisiana and Cuba after Slavery*. Cambridge, Mass.: Harvard University Press, 2008.

——. *Slave Emancipation in Cuba: The Transition to Free Labor, 1860–1899*. 2nd ed. Pittsburgh: University of Pittsburgh Press, 2000.

Seigel, Micol. "Beyond Compare: Historical Method after the Transnational Turn." *Radical History Review*, no. 91 (2005): 62–90.

——. *Uneven Encounters: Making Race and Nation in Brazil and the United States*. Durham, N.C.: Duke University Press, 2009.

Serra, Rafael. *Para blancos y negros: Ensayos políticos, sociales, y económicos*. Havana: Imprenta El Score, 1907.

Serra Robledo, Matilde, Matilde Serra, Ana María Rojas Lucero, Sara Legón Padilla, Nilda Sosa Delgado, Antonia Díaz Núñez, Gilberto García Batista, and Horacio Díaz Pendá. *El pueblo dice: Vivencias de la campaña de alfabetización de Cuba*. Havana: Cuidad de la Habana, 1999.

Serviat, Pedro. *El problema negro en Cuba y su solución definitiva*. Havana: Editorial Politica, 1986.

Shell-Wise, Melanie. *Coming to Miami: A Social History*. Gainesville: University Press of Florida, 2009.

Smart, Ian Isidore. *Nicolás Guillén: Popular Poet of the Caribbean*. Columbia: University of Missouri Press, 1990.

Someillan, Yamile Regalado. "The Cartooned Revolution: Images and the Revolutionary Citizen in Cuba, 1959–1963." Ph.D. diss., University of Maryland, College Park, 2009.

Thomas, Hugh. *Cuba: The Pursuit of Freedom*. New York: Harper and Row, 1971.

Torres, Andrés, and José Emiliano Velázquez, eds. *The Puerto Rican Movement: Voices from the Diaspora*. Philadelphia: Temple University Press, 1998.

Torres, María de los Angeles. *The Lost Apple: Operation Pedro Pan, Cuban Children in the U.S., and the Promise of a Better Future*. Boston: Beacon Press, 2003.

Tyson, Timothy B. *Radio Free Dixie: Robert F. Williams and the Roots of Black Power*. Chapel Hill: University of North Carolina Press, 1999.

Unidad Revolucionario. *Letter to American Students*. Miami: Schneer Printing Corp., 1963.

Urrutia, Gustavo E. *Puntos de vista del nuevo Negro; conferencia del arquitecto Gustavo E. Urrutia; inaugural del ciclo de conferencias de carácter social, científico y educacional el día 8 de julio de 1937*. Havana: Imprenta El Score, 1938.

——. "Racial Prejudice in Cuba: How It Compares with That of the North Americans." In *Negro Anthology*, edited by Nancy Cunard, 473–78. London, 1934.

Vasconcelos, José. *The Cosmic Race: A Bilingual Edition*. Translated by Didier T. Jaén. Baltimore: Johns Hopkins University Press, 1997.

Whalen, Carmen Teresa, and Víctor Vázquez-Hernández, eds. *The Puerto Rican Diaspora: Historical Perspectives*. Philadelphia: Temple University Press, 2008.

Young, Cynthia A. *Soul Power: Culture, Radicalism, and the Making of a U.S. Third World Left*. Durham, N.C.: Duke University Press, 2006.

Index

exchanges, 4; population of, 14; in rhetoric of 1895 war, 10–11; threat of U.S. authorities to, 11

Afro-descended, use of term, 28

Afrodescendiente, use of term, 28, 245

Agency, of Afro-Cubans, 5, 142

Agrarian Reform, 97–98, 123

Aguirre, Severo, 85, 86

Aid societies, Afro-Cuban, 13. *See also* Societies, Afro-Cuban

Alfabeticemos, 212

Allapattah, 150, 269 (n. 88)

Almeida, Juan, 39, 58, 65, 137, 139, 168, 193; invited to join UN delegation, 177; personal connection with Louis, 168; portrayed as black, 61

Álvarez Ramirez, Sandra, 244, 247

Amsterdam News, 157, 167

"Angelitos Negros" (Benítez Sisters), 63

Angulo, Ana Elsa, 109

Anticolonial movements, 77, 227

Anticommunism, 91, 124, 136, 139–40

Antidiscrimination: and constitution, 17, 86, 102; nonconfrontational approach to, 20

Antidiscrimination campaign, 3; Afro-Cuban response to, 6; beginning of, 30, 51; consensus on success of, 190, 194; controversy around, 62; end of, 199; focus on employment opportunities in, 52, 53, 54–55; goals of, 96; justification of, 65, 226–27; and limitation of potential for change, 62; linked to ideas of Cuban nationalism, 62; linked to legacies of Martí and Maceo, 62; linked to revolution, 63; pressure for, 42; proclaimed a success, 155, 183, 195–96, 198, 211; reinforcement of stereotypes in, 56, 70; response to announcement of, 53–54; results of, 3, 4

Antiracism: claimed as M 26-7 territory, 109; coexistence of with racism, 20, 70, 249 (n. 5); linked to

workers' rights, 109; and reproduction of ideologies and stereotypes, 4

Antonio Maceo Society, 99–100, 155

Aponte, José Antonio, 119

Appearance, 193, 239, 246–47. *See also* Beauty

Archival material, access to, 21–22

Arguelles, María, 103

Arithmetic textbook, 213

Armada, Santiago, 66, 187

Arma Nueva, 205

Armas, Chago, 66, 70, 187

Army, Cuban, 214

Art, limits placed on, 235

Article 20, 86

Artists, black: Benítez Sisters, 63; in popular press, 37, 39; spreading of ideas about race by, 63. *See also* Directors, Afro-Cuban; Gómez, Sara

Assimilation, 76

Athletes: Cuban Amateur Athletic Union (UAAC), 44; invited to promote Cuba, 158; in popular press, 37, 39. *See also* Louis, Joe

Baraka, Amiri, 170

Barnet, Miguel, 222

Batista, Fulgencio, 1; Afro-Cubans perceived as supporters of, 39–40, 51; alliance of with communists, 86; clubs' links to, 96–97, 98; legalization of Communist Party by, 85; outlawing of PSP by, 92; overthrow of, 92; portrayals of, 39; working-class support for, 85

Bay of Pigs, 224–26

Beaches, 14, 92, 93. *See also* Recreation

Beauty, 35. *See also* Appearance

Benedí, Lázaro, 48, 49

Benítez, Adigio, 57–60, 107

Benítez, Conrado, 24, 232; Castro on, 207; demonstrations celebrating, 205–6; demonstrations to protest murder of, 204–5; depictions of origins of, 221; as martyr, 207;

Emancipation, gradual, 8
Employment: Afro-Cubans' exclusion from, 14–15, 85; discrimination in, 19; focus on in antidiscrimination campaign, 52, 53, 54–55; lack of opportunities for black veterans, 14, 15; outline for reform in, 104; in tourism, discrimination in, 19, 240
En la otra isla, 236–38
Entralgo, Elías, 56
Equality: activists as defenders of, 73; African Americans used to validate claims of, 159; claims of, 173, 178, 179, 183, 211; claims of, challenges to, 162–64; closure of conversations about, 174–75, 191; pledges of, contradictions in, 238; promised in 1895 revolution, 9
Espín, Vilma, 192
Estenoz, Evaristo, 79, 80, 91, 116, 119
Eurocentrism, challenges to, 83
Exile community, 151–52, 265 (n. 6), 266 (n. 14); acknowledgment of racism by, 139; Afro-Cuban exiles, 118, 125, 141–50, 152, 265–66 (n. 12), 268–69 (n. 70) (*see also* Betancourt, Juan René); attitudes of toward African Americans, 140; calls of for restoration of democracy, 136; demographics of, 135; desire of for whiteness, 148; dismissal of racial problems in Cuba by, 135; exchanges of with African Americans, 21; focus on anticommunism by, 124, 136, 139–40; images of, 145–46; influence of on national discourses of race, 229; labeled racist, 124, 134; linked to U.S. racist organizations, 127; motivations of for leaving, 122–23, 125–26, 129, 134, 135; Movement for the Restoration of Democracy, 135–36; nostalgia of for Cuba, 138; organizations of, 147; persistence of racism in, 124; on relocation of UN delegation, 174, 195;

remittances from, 240; response of to antidiscrimination campaign, 138; silence of on race, 135–36, 147; tensions with African Americans, 268 (n. 66); treatment of Afro-Cuban exiles by, 4, 146, 147–48; use of anticommunist rhetoric by, 124; use of Martí's legacy by, 136–37; U.S. government's support for, 140

Fagen, Richard R., 125, 266 (n. 14)
Fanon, Frantz, 249 (n. 5)
FBI (Federal Bureau of Investigation), 165
Federación de Mujeres Cubanas (FMC, Federation of Cuban Women), 191, 192, 260 (n. 66), 263 (n. 118)
Federación General de Trabajadores de Oriente (FGTO, General Federation of Oriente Workers), 107, 108, 109, 263 (n. 106)
Federación Nacional de Sociedades Negras (National Federation of Black Societies), 100
Federación Nacional Obrera Azucarera (FNOA, National Federation of Sugar Workers), 85, 87
Federal Bureau of Investigation (FBI), 165
Federation of Black Cuban Societies in Exile, 147
Federation of Cuban Women (Federación de Mujeres Cubanas, FMC), 191, 192, 260 (n. 66), 263 (n. 118)
Fernández Aguílera, Lorenzo, 43, 44
Fernández Padilla, Oscar, 64
Fernández Robaina, Tomás, 111, 247, 264 (n. 141)
Ferrer, Ada, 10
Ferrer, Darsi, 242
FGTO (Federación General de Trabajadores de Oriente, General Federation of Oriente Workers), 107, 108, 109, 263 (n. 106)

138–39; Castro on, 30; class-based analysis of, 85, 86–87; closure of discussion about, 156, 194–95, 200, 219; coexistence with antiracism, 20, 70, 249 (n. 5); as counterrevolutionary, 122, 129, 131–34, 132; Cuban pledges to fight abroad, 194; documentation of persistence of, 19–20; emphasis on psychology of, 56; faced by Afro-Cuban exiles, 118; government's claim of victory over, 213; government's inability to eradicate, 72; growing inability to discuss, 194; limits on challenges to, 82; located in U.S., 155; nonconfrontational approach to, 20; persistence of, 3, 19, 124, 133, 227–28; return of racism thesis, 19–20, 241; as social problem, 55, 63–64, 104. *See also* Discrimination; Equality; Return of racism

Racism, state, 21

Rap, 251 (n. 51)

Raperos, 241, 247

Recreation, 14, 19, 81, 92–96, 133, 162–64. *See also* Societies, Afro-Cuban

Recreational societies, Afro-Cuban, 13. *See also* Societies, Afro-Cuban

Reform camps, 236–38

Religion: African-derived religions, 78, 114; Catholic Church, 142, 143; use of religious metaphors, 207–8

Remittances, 240

Renaming, 191

Resettlement Re-Cap, 145–46

Return of racism thesis, 19–20, 241

Revolución: articles about race in, 46–47; cartoons in, 70; coverage of announcement of antidiscrimination campaign in, 53; coverage of Castro's speech on antidiscrimination campaign in, 30–31; messages about blackness in, 65–70; "¡Negros No . . . Ciudadanos!," 1–2, 3; portrayal of Afro-Cubans in, 49; on

race relations in Oriente, 50; on relocation of UN delegation, 180

Revolution: Afro-Cubans as makers of, 114; linked to race, 22

Revolution (1868), 6, 7, 8, 10

Revolution (1895), 9, 10, 11

Revolution (1959): Afro-Cuban criticism of, 204, 282 (n. 26); Afro-Cuban leaders' support of, 194; Afro-Cubans' agency to participate in, 5–6; antidiscrimination campaign linked to, 63; Castro's depiction of, 231; condemned as racist, 242; decline of spaces for critiquing, 235; focal points of, 32; images celebrating Afro-Cubans' participation in, 64; legacy of as antiracist government, 31; linked to global racial struggles, 209; linked to wars for independence, 42, 57; obligations to, 220; raceless sentiments of, 3 (*see also* Antidiscrimination campaign); reaction of Las Yaguans to, 48; relationship of to Afro-Cubans, 49; relationship of to blackness, 2, 3; uncertainty about, 41–42

Revolutionaries, black, 64–65, 203, 238–39

Revolutionary Democratic Front (Frente Revolucionario Democratica, FRD), 147

Revolutionary Unity (Unidad Revolucionario, UR), 126, 136

Revolution *con pachanga,* 112, 263 (n. 120)

Rey Araque, Manuel, 55

Reyita, 246

Reynolds, Montgomery, 168

Rhodes, Teddy, 165

Risquet, Jorge, 63, 132

Rivas, Suárez, 85

Rivera, Aymee, 244

Roa, Rául, 161, 175, 274 (n. 76)

Roberts, R., 270 (n. 11)

Envisioning Cuba

Devyn Spence Benson, *Antiracism in Cuba: The Unfinished Revolution* (2016).

Michelle Chase, *Revolution within the Revolution: Women and Gender Politics in Cuba, 1952–1962* (2015).

Aisha K. Finch, *Rethinking Slave Rebellion in Cuba: La Escalera and the Insurgencies of 1841–1844* (2015).

Christina D. Abreu, *Rhythms of Race: Cuban Musicians and the Making of Latino New York City and Miami, 1940–1960* (2015).

Anita Casavantes Bradford, *The Revolution Is for the Children: The Politics of Childhood in Havana and Miami, 1959–1962* (2014).

Tiffany A. Sippial, *Prostitution, Modernity, and the Making of the Cuban Republic, 1840–1920* (2013).

Kathleen López, *Chinese Cubans: A Transnational History* (2013).

Lillian Guerra, *Visions of Power in Cuba: Revolution, Redemption, and Resistance, 1959–1971* (2012).

Carrie Hamilton, *Sexual Revolutions in Cuba: Passion, Politics, and Memory* (2012).

Sherry Johnson, *Climate and Catastrophe in Cuba and the Atlantic World during the Age of Revolution* (2011).

Melina Pappademos, *Black Political Activism and the Cuban Republic* (2011).

Frank Andre Guridy, *Forging Diaspora: Afro-Cubans and African Americans in a World of Empire and Jim Crow* (2010).

Ann Marie Stock, *On Location in Cuba: Street Filmmaking during Times of Transition* (2009).

Alejandro de la Fuente, *Havana and the Atlantic in the Sixteenth Century* (2008).

Reinaldo Funes Monzote, *From Rainforest to Cane Field in Cuba: An Environmental History since 1492* (2008).

Matt D. Childs, *The 1812 Aponte Rebellion in Cuba and the Struggle against Atlantic Slavery* (2006).

Eduardo González, *Cuba and the Tempest: Literature and Cinema in the Time of Diaspora* (2006).

John Lawrence Tone, *War and Genocide in Cuba, 1895–1898* (2006).

Samuel Farber, *The Origins of the Cuban Revolution Reconsidered* (2006).

Lillian Guerra, *The Myth of José Martí: Conflicting Nationalisms in Early Twentieth-Century Cuba* (2005).

Rodrigo Lazo, *Writing to Cuba: Filibustering and Cuban Exiles in the United States* (2005).

Alejandra Bronfman, *Measures of Equality: Social Science, Citizenship, and Race in Cuba, 1902–1940* (2004).

Edna M. Rodríguez-Mangual, *Lydia Cabrera and the Construction of an Afro-Cuban Cultural Identity* (2004).

Gabino La Rosa Corzo, *Runaway Slave Settlements in Cuba: Resistance and Repression* (2003).

Piero Gleijeses, *Conflicting Missions: Havana, Washington, and Africa, 1959–1976* (2002).

Robert Whitney, *State and Revolution in Cuba: Mass Mobilization and Political Change, 1920–1940* (2001).

Alejandro de la Fuente, *A Nation for All: Race, Inequality, and Politics in Twentieth-Century Cuba* (2001).